Torn Country
An Oral History of the Israeli War of Independence

An Oral
History
of the Israeli War
# of Independence

LYNNE REID BANKS

FRANKLIN WATTS
New York/London/Toronto/Sydney/1982

Library of Congress Cataloging in Publication Data

Main entry under title:

Torn country.

  Includes index.
  1. Israel-Arab War, 1948-1949--Personal
narratives, Israeli. I. Banks, Lynne Reid.
DS126.97.T67   956′.042   81-21999
ISBN 0-531-09855-9   AACR2

Maps courtesy of Vantage Art, Inc.

FOR "BOAZ"
*without whose like
there would have been no victory.
Without him,
there would have been no book.*

Contents

Foreword

A month before the war started, I was sent by the Haganah to organize illegal immigrants in Europe. I took a parachutists' course and was sent to Czechoslovakia—which was a great ally of ours at the time although it was already in the Communist bloc—to train others to be parachutists and to fly Czech planes back to Israel. We were buying weapons from the Czechs because there was a British and American embargo on arms sales to us.

It was the first time I'd ever left Israel. What I saw of the Jews in Europe—the survivors of the holocaust, even though the camps had been liberated two years before—was a terrible shock. It changed me from being a *sabra,* strong, happy and optimistic, to being a man who realized he belonged to a wounded nation. It took me out of my narcissism, the self-centered point of view of an Israeli youth.

From among the survivors, I gathered people to take the course in Czechoslovakia. They came mainly from the Jewish youth movements, groups that had been organized long before I came. First we taught them to dance and sing—Israeli music—and later the psychologists told me that it was the best thing we could have done. Then we taught them to fight, to do judo and so on. That really gave them self-confidence by teaching them to protect themselves, giving them the new spirit of Israel—of hope. I still meet them today, those people—they remember the songs, and they say they still ache from the judo exercises I taught them!

I recently made a documentary film about that period in Europe after World War II. During the pogroms in Poland and Hungary in 1946, they were still killing Jews, long after the Nazis. It took me some time to realize that every Jew I met, in Hungary, in Czechoslovakia, was a wounded man.

Some of the reactions, after the release from the camps, were incredible. Men and women who had clung to the laws and prohibitions of their religion seemed to throw every restraint aside. For instance, they would make love almost publicly. They didn't seem to care that they were doing something that opposed the traditional values of Jewish families. People who had lost their wives or husbands just joined other people and had children with them, sometimes without marriage—a wave of reaction to death. Jews were opposing death however they could.

And a year later, everything seemed to go back to the old ways. Jews went to Italy, to Milan, especially to buy wigs—the religious people—because by then they felt the need to go back to the old ways of life. But at the time I was in Europe I felt very painfully the difference between me and them. I felt that for the first time I was seeing real Jews. I felt like Joseph, looking for his brothers.

CHAIM GURI
Poet and film maker

Acknowledgment

My special thanks to Netanel Lorch, whose personal help and criticism, together with his splendid books on the War—*The Edge of the Sword* and *One Long War*—were invaluable; "Anni" of the Foreign Press Office in Jerusalem, who helped me above and beyond the call of duty; and Tamar Sachs and Avital Mossinsohn, whose practical help was invaluable. I should also like to thank most gratefully Sylvia Cooklin and "Topsy" Levan, not only for their transcribing and typing but for their committed and encouraging interest in the project.

Introduction

.

More than thirty years have passed since the first Arab-Israeli war of 1947–49, Israel's War of Independence, the Arabs' War of Catastrophe.

Many books have been written about this war, by scholars, politicians, soldiers, historians, diplomats, and journalists. This one is not so much a history of the war as a series of recollections and assessments by participants. My function has been to collect interviews and arrange them, to give as clear a picture of events as possible through the memories and in the words of a wide variety of people who remember them—sometimes as if they happened yesterday, more often with perspective: events that shaped Jewish history.

These are not only warriors' tales of battles, stratagems, and spoils. I have tried to cast my net wide, to draw in wives, children, and those whose contribution was far from the front line. This has inevitably meant that I have not achieved anything like a comprehensive picture. Though I interviewed some sixty people, I could have gone on indefinitely and still not scratched the surface of potential interviewees, in Israel alone. Those I did approach responded with great kindness and generosity, and I am indebted to every one of them, even those whom, because of a superabundance of material, I had to omit. I also apologize to the many who played important roles in the war whom I failed to reach.

The interviews were, with a few exceptions, conducted in English, which accounts for the simplicity and directness of much of the language. I have tried to use a light hand in editing and arranging the transcripts of my tape-recorded conversations to give a clear, flowing interpretation of the interviews. I ought to add that I cannot be held accountable for any of the views expressed, nor for the strict historical or chronological accuracy of any of the versions of events given—memories can play tricks after thirty-two years.

The majority of interviewees were Israeli Jews living in Israel. By definition this restricts the breadth and perspective of the book; but as a known sympathizer with Israel, it was, inevitably, impossible for me to achieve objectivity or balance. Most of those who fought on the Arab side in the war are now in Arab countries, which would be difficult, or even impossible, for me to visit. The few interviews I managed to get with Arabs in Israel, together with the recollections of Sir John Glubb, do not really suffice to give the other side of the picture. But although my brief was to show the Jewish side of the war, a task for which my prior knowledge, contacts, and sympathies best fitted me, this is not, I think, a jingoistic account. The honesty and thoughtfulness of many of those who contributed to it see to that.

LYNNE REID BANKS
London, 1981

Part 1
The Undeclared War –
November 1947-
May 1948

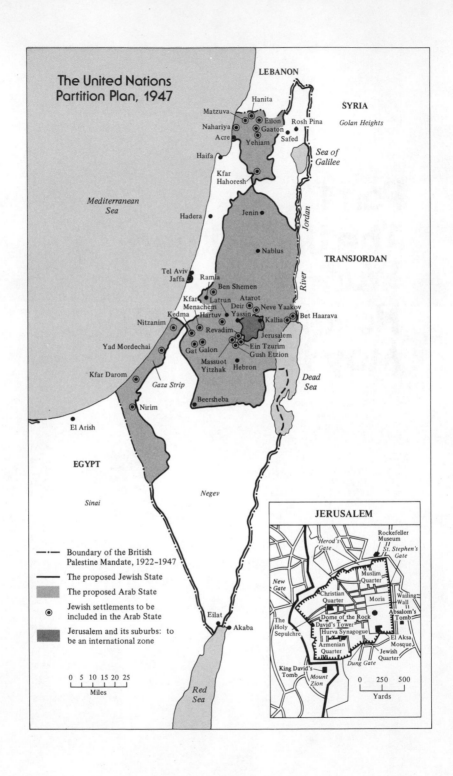

The United Nations Partition Plan, 1947

LEBANON

SYRIA

Hanita
Matzuva
Eilon   Rosh Pina   Golan Heights
Nahariya   Gaaton
Acre   Yehiam   Safed
Haifa

Sea of Galilee

Kfar Hahoresh

Mediterranean Sea

Hadera   Jenin

Nablus

TRANSJORDAN

Tel Aviv
Jaffa   Ramla
Ben Shemen
Kfar   Latrun   Atarot
Menachem   Deir   Neve Yaakov
Kedma   Hartuv   Yassin
Nitzanim   Kallia   Bet Haarava
Revadim   Jerusalem
Yad Mordechai   Ein Tzurim
Gat Galon   Gush Etzion
Massuot   Hebron
Kfar Darom   Yitzhak   Dead Sea

Gaza Strip
Nirim   Beersheba

El Arish

EGYPT

Negev

Sinai

Jordan River

—·—·— Boundary of the British
Palestine Mandate, 1922–1947

——— The proposed Jewish State

The proposed Arab State

⊙ Jewish settlements to be
included in the Arab State

Jerusalem and its suburbs: to
be an international zone

Eilat
Akaba

0 5 10 15 20 25
Miles

Red Sea

JERUSALEM

Rockefeller Museum
Herod's Gate   St. Stephen's Gate
New Gate   Muslim Quarter
Christian Quarter   Moria   Wailing Wall
David's Tower   Absalom's Tomb
The Holy Sepulchre   Dome of the Rock
Hurva Synagogue   El Aksa Mosque
Armenian Quarter   Jewish Quarter
King David's Tomb   Dung Gate
Mount Zion

0   250   500
Yards

The War of Independence, in common with many wars, was not an abrupt eruption of violence. It was the culmination of many years of tension and strife between Jews and Arabs. The violence that led up to this epic struggle—the first time since the Roman era that a Jewish army had taken the field in defense of a Jewish country—was not, however, confined to the Middle East. Apart from the long, awesome history of Jewish persecution, reaching back to biblical times, this war had its modern roots in savage pogroms in Eastern Europe in the nineteenth and early twentieth centuries, in the upheavals surrounding World War I and the Russian Revolution, and, of course, climactically, in the scarcely imaginable, and still unhealed, trauma of the Nazi holocaust.

At that time the Zionist movement, whose purpose was to return the Jews of the Diaspora to Palestine, had been active for more than forty years—the first wave of Jewish immigrants to return to Zion during the modern era even predated the founding of this movement by Theodore Herzl in 1897. The Yishuv, or Jewish community, in "the Land of Israel" (then a backwater province of the Turkish Empire) had been growing in spasms since the 1870s and could have become a majority of the population during the Nazi era had not the British held the mandate of Palestine, granted to them by the League of Nations in the wake of World War I.

The struggles of the British to reconcile conflicting promises—to the Jews (in the Balfour Declaration), to implement a homeland for them there, and to the Arabs (in various semi-official negotiations), to unite and decolonialize them—resulted in an increasingly chaotic situation. The British tried to control the mounting violence by bringing in more and more troops and resorting to more and more Draconian methods. Though they succeeded in stemming the flood of Jewish refugees, thus indirectly condemning untold numbers to their deaths, they failed to placate the Arabs or subdue, in Palestine, what they euphemistically termed the "disturbances," which were to lead, in the last weeks of 1947, to the outbreak of open hostilities.

This civil strife had been going on for many years. Arab resentment at the increasing number of Jewish immigrants in the twenties and thirties—Jews whose evident intention was to form a sovereign state in the midst of the Muslim world—coincided with the parallel development of their own nationalism. This resulted in spasmodic outbreaks of rioting and rebellion, notably in 1929, 1936, and 1939. World War II merely overshadowed this ongoing struggle, which was resumed full force at its end.

At this point the situation was exacerbated by the desperate efforts of the Yishuv to gather in about 100,000 European Jews, the survivors of Hitler's death camps. The British authorities feared that the inevitable Arab opposition to such a renewed influx would have a detrimental effect on British interests and prestige; but the ruthless measures taken to implement the British government policy of keeping Jewish numbers down encouraged extremism among Jewish dissidents. Terrorism, which had died down to some extent during the world war, flared up again.

There were two dissident organizations, or "armies": the Irgun Zvai Leumi, also known by its Hebrew acronym of Etzel, led by Menachem Begin, which had been active against the British before the world war; and the more extreme, but much smaller, Stern Gang, or Lehi, which waged a terrorist struggle also against Arabs and even some Jews regarded as collaborators.

The activities of both these groups were, in the main, opposed by the established Jewish leadership headed by David

Ben-Gurion, and also by a majority of the Yishuv. But they caused great problems for the British, who at the same time had their hands full trying to control increased outbreaks of violence caused by local Arabs and others from surrounding territories.

Meanwhile, the United Nations, then barely two years old, was trying to find a solution to the problem of a territory to which two embattled peoples laid valid claim. On November 29, 1947, a vote was taken in the General Assembly on the proposition that Palestine—that small portion of Israel that had not already been ceded by Britain to her Arab ally Transjordan—be partitioned into two sovereign states, Arab and Jewish, with Jerusalem as an international enclave in the Arab area.

The count was close, but the partition plan received the necessary two-thirds majority. What followed was predictable and highly charged drama. Jews all over the world—particularly those in Palestine—rejoiced: After nearly two thousand years of exile in the countries of others, they were to have their own state again. All six Arab delegates to the United Nations walked out of the chamber; outraged, their governments rejected the plan and threatened war if it was implemented. The British, for their part, agreed to wind up their mandate and withdraw but refused to support "any solution which did not have the approval of both Arabs and Jews"—in other words, their Middle East policy was in ruins, their will to keep order broken.

The role played by the British, both in the preliminaries leading to the partition vote and in the following months as they prepared to withdraw, was significant, and a number of contributors to this book have views and recollections about it. The first recollection harks back to 1946, which is outside my brief but nevertheless important in that it illustrates the determination of the British, from the end of the world war until their eventual withdrawal in 1948, to control civil strife not by any serious attempt to solve the problem but by disarming the population. Each side complained that this policy operated unfairly, militating in favor of the other. In retrospect, however, it is clear that the policy favored the Arabs at the expense of the Jews, who at that time were on the defensive against attacks by bands of Arab marauders: Settlements were threatened, individuals murdered, roads cut, and the British did little about it. The Jews therefore believed they must look to their own defenses and stockpiled whatever weapons they could find. Avital Mossinsohn, later to be a government spokesman and director of the Jerusalem Theater, then a boy of nine, tells of the "Black Sabbath" raid on his kibbutz (Yagur) in June 1946:

☐   The "big search" came just after the King David Hotel had been blown up. The soldiers went from house to house in our kibbutz. Our *gan* [kibbutz kindergarten] was on the second story of one building. I remember we were outside, and we took some sweets from the soldiers, but at the same time we knew that they were against us, so we ran upstairs and hung out of the windows jeering at them, calling them *"Calaniot"* [a reference to their red berets] and singing a song about "Fat old Bevin has a baby in his belly..." [Ernest Bevin, Britain's foreign minister, was much reviled by the Jews at that time].

The arms were there all right—it turned out to be the Haganah's main cache—hidden under the floor of the dining hall and under the dung in the cow yard, as well as under the new kosher kitchen the kibbutz had built for the old people. There was a rumor that an ex-kibbutznik had been seen leading the British to the right spots, but I never knew if that was true.... My father was arrested and interned for several months—my uncle too, but he was beaten up as well, hit on the head and kicked so badly he was in the hospital for several weeks.

The British also had been blockading the country to prevent the importation of weapons. In those early days, Arabs too were heavily punished for carrying arms. According to Anwar Nusseibah, a prominent Jerusalem Arab who at that time was secretary of the Arab National Committee, "a man could be sentenced to death for possession of a revolver. There was one famous case of a man called Sa'adi, in the north, who was hanged for a few rounds of ammunition." At the same time, the British government saw nothing inconsistent in continuing regular arms supplies to Jordan and Egypt.

In addition to dealing with arms seizures, the British had to decide—without, apparently, much guidance from Whitehall—to whom, and how, to hand over strategic strongpoints, as they commenced the monumental operation of withdrawing 100,000 troops and 2,000 police, with all their equipment, from their beleaguered enclaves within the country. Inevitably, this caused a great deal of ill-feeling all around. It has always been the Jewish view that the way the British handled the whole situation at the mandate's end was blatantly prejudicial to Israeli interests, reflecting an official and/or personal anti-Semitism emanating from the British Foreign Office and echoed, with advantages, by soldiers and officials on the spot. Netanel Lorch, one of the main contributors to this book, in his own volume about the War of Independence, *The Edge of the Sword*, blames the British for being "neutral in theory but generally pro-Arab in fact."

Recently, however, there has been a reassessment by other historians. One of them, Professor Gabriel Cohen, has built from his prolonged researches a less damning and more pragmatic theory about the British policy of withdrawal. Its details affect the view one must take of events more subjectively described later in this book by those who participated in and suffered from them:

☐   You know that generally speaking we felt that the British didn't behave fairly during the process of their evacuation. Some even believed there was a plot, that their intention was deliberately to create chaos in order to destroy the Jews, and so forth. This of course was nonsense.

There were two questions: First, were the British really going to pull out? Most people thought not, or that if they did, they'd be back within three weeks. This is nonsense too. The British Labour government of the day was probably one of the best governments of the U.K. in this century. Four or five central figures in Atlee's cabinet had powers of decision incomparable with other cabinets. On all but one item, until 1948, this cabinet proved highly effective. The exception was Palestine.

On this they never managed to formulate and execute policy, dragging it from committee to committee, from commission to commission. But once they made up their minds to evacuate—in September '47—*it was irreversible.* I dare say that from that date until May '48, theirs was the *only* consistent policy—the policy of evacuation. The Americans were not consistent—they had second thoughts on partition. The U.N. was not consistent—they started begging the British to stay. The Arabs were totally confused, and even we had second thoughts about statehood. But despite the great strategic importance to the British of Palestine, once they'd made up their minds they were entirely consistent.

When the last high commissioner of Palestine, Sir Alan Cunningham, returned to England, *nobody*—not the Colonial Office, not the Foreign Office, not the army—asked him his opinion of the situation or his evaluation. He was sent home with a driver and a pension. If the government had been seeking ways to come back to Palestine, wouldn't Cunningham's advice have been sought? But it wasn't. So that does away with the Machiavellian-plot theory.

Second myth: that the British deliberately, or by sheer chance, left most of the strongpoints in Arab hands. Even this is not exact. There was a strategy of evacuation, consisting of four or five principles. One was to try to keep law and order as far as possible, *as long as the British government was still responsible for it*—which meant until the evacuation could get under way. Now, trying to keep order while a civil war is developing is quite a job. Not that they expected it to develop into a full civil war in December '47, but when it did, maintaining law and order meant, basically, preventing the development of full-scale battles and preventing *either side* from achieving a decisive victory.

If the Jews had appeared to get the upper hand, the

5, 8, 9,
79-180,
203, 241-2,
274, 289

lreaded the intervention of Arab armies while they
l in charge. Here they would confront contradicting
ons—the commitment contained in the Balfour
:ion on one hand and military treaties with Egypt,
d Jordan on the other. But neither did they want the
o conquer any Jewish village or town because then
uld have gotten hell from the United States and in
I. So whenever a village was threatened with
occupation by the Arabs, the British would come to its help.
Usually we didn't need it.

In short, their policy was not to let the Arabs or the
Jews occupy each other's areas as long as they were
responsible.

This changed in April when the evacuation got started.
People forget that to evacuate one hundred thousand
soldiers and their depots and equipment in a short time, in
the midst of a civil war, was an operation in itself. A very
delicate one. If we and the Arabs were a bit frightened of the
British army, it's clear now that the British army was
frightened too in April and May, because, through the
process of evacuation, they were sending brigade after
brigade out. There had to come a point where they were not
sure they would be able to defend themselves during the last
stages.

I will return to Professor Cohen's assessment later. But what
of the views of people who had to cope with British behavior and
policy at the time? Of course, there was a great deal of bitterness,
and it was not confined to Jews. Ironically Anwar Nusseibah,
former Jordanian defense minister expresses anti-British feelings
as strong as any felt by a Jew at that period:

☐   The whole situation was chaotic. One felt that the British at
the time were either fed up and saw no reason—since the
mandate was coming to an end—to overexpose themselves
to the danger of two mad peoples fighting each other, or else
they had more or less lost interest, taking fewer and fewer

effective steps to maintain law and order within the country, so people had to organize themselves for self-protection.

I blame the British for many sins, and I think the policy they pursued in Palestine was one of the cardinal sins so far as my people were concerned, because it resulted in the disruption of my society and the expulsion of my people, and in the tragedy which we have suffered since. It was all done in defiance of clear commitments which the British had given us and which we had expected them to respect. Prior to the war they had a good reputation generally as people who kept their word, and the Arabs believed that, so what happened in Palestine was a great disappointment. But there it is.

Chaim Herzog, the Israeli general whose broadcasts at the time of the Six-Day War were to make his name world famous, was one of many Jews who had served in the British armed forces during the world war and then returned to Palestine. His view of the British had a double focus: His war service and his childhood in Ireland prior to his parents' immigration to Palestine had predisposed him to understand them; at the same time he saw the British through Israeli eyes, as inimical. His duties as liaison officer between the Jewish Agency (the shadow leadership till the British departure) and the British authorities brought him into close contact with them. He recalls:

☐   When I came back from serving in Western Europe as a lieutenant colonel in charge of a large area in Germany, I found myself on the other side of the fence—a very unpleasant feeling. One day you're the chairman of the mess in Germany, the next day you're not admitted to an officers' mess because you're a "native." I felt very bad indeed about the behavior of the British here, but there was nothing one could do. There were good ones and bad ones as far as I was concerned, but there's no doubt about it, there was a great deal of hostility. It was very unpleasant at times, though one tried to maintain a decent standard of behavior and language because one had a purpose, to get things going. In many ways I had an understanding of what motivated them, and when we began to talk I could really influence them in a way. But of course I felt very badly about their policy— obviously one of frustration—nothing thought out. Nobody had a good word to say for British policy.

This last is rather too sweeping. There were those who had and still retain warm feelings for the British, in spite of everything. One of these is Chaim Laskov, a successful commander in the world war who, in 1949, was to be made chief of staff by David Ben-Gurion.

☐ During the second world war, thirty-five thousand volunteers out of a community of half a million Jews [in Palestine] went to fight the Germans. We wanted to fight, and to this day I'm grateful to the British for giving me this opportunity. The only country that gave us this chance was Britain, which formed the Jewish Brigade Force during the war. It also gave us experience.

I think, barring individual excesses, that the British, both here and in Europe, were fair. It was because of their fairness that we were able to do a lot of what we did. We have to be grateful to them for giving us a chance to study military operations and somehow, by hook or by crook, bring a quarter of a million Jews [actually around 100,000] from the DP camps of Europe to Palestine. Those people had to be moved from Germany, Austria, and Hungary through British-controlled territory to the ports of Italy and France, and then loaded on ships under British surveillance. Of course, some others were stopped, also by the British. But somehow they were sufficiently human and correct to enable us to get them through.

The British people were in sympathy with us. It was the Foreign Office and the Colonial Office which sent orders to make the arms searches and so on. Of course, they were wrong about the Arabs. The Arabs were anti-British all the way; it was a fallacious approach to think that if the British hanged a couple of Jews, the Arabs would become pro-British. They were not pro-British in 1939, nor during the war, and are anti-Western until today.

The view that the British actually aided and abetted the organizers of Bricha (the secret organization that labored to bring the Jewish DPs of Europe to Palestine) is a highly contentious one. Most accounts of the exploits of Bricha point in the opposite direction, indicating that those British who helped, even to the extent of turning a blind eye, were the exceptions. The "sympathy of the British people" is also questionable, especially after two years of concerted terrorist activity by Etzel and Lehi, which included the retaliatory hanging of two British sergeants. But Chaim Laskov nevertheless represents a school of thought, particularly among ex-British army Jews, which excused the British excesses on the spot on the grounds that things would have been a great deal worse under any other occupying power. Netanel Lorch, who had harsh things to say about certain specific actions that affected him as an Israeli soldier, still gives them some good marks:

☐   I remember that in the sector next to mine [in Jerusalem] a
     search conducted by the British resulted in four people being
     detained. The evidence is that they were then released near
     the Damascus Gate where they were massacred by the
     Arabs. So that was one rather unsympathetic episode.
         On the other hand, the reason why girls were so vitally
     important to us was because the British, if there was one
     thing you could say for them, were gentlemen; they would
     search men but not girls for arms. I remember we divided the
     girls by categories—those who could carry small arms under
     their skirts, and those who... well, there was one rather
     plump girl about whom it was said that she could have
     smuggled a field gun, if we had had one.
         Carrying arms was still illegal and I think as late as
     February '48 people were being detained. There were still

courts-martial for people—mainly Jews—and I think there was a very deep sense of unfairness that Arabs could carry arms as much as they wished and nothing happened, while Jews were still being penalized.*

Others retained a sneaking admiration for the British for their gallantry during the world war, remembering the sound of Big Ben and its significance. Still others recall incidents of arms confiscated and then quietly handed back later; and during the siege of Jerusalem, some British soldiers, on an ad hoc basis, often took pity on hungry Jews and shared their rations or brought food for them from the Old City.

Alexander Zur, an ex-British army man who was to use his knowledge of English in negotiations with the British in Jaffa, draws distinctions between the different branches of the British services in Palestine.

☐   You see, I was pro-British, I always was. I liked the British. I fought alongside them for six years. Although when we [Jews] served, we also had trouble. Not only anti-Semitism. The main cause was their preventing us from participating in the fighting, because they saw the possibility of our fighting later against *them*. We would form the core of the Israeli army. We had experience.... The Haganah at that time was not a regular army; it couldn't be; it was an underground army. We were all brought up in the Haganah. To create a regular force from the Haganah and turn it into an army, you had to have the experience of a proper army. For instance, in my brigade, the Tel Aviv Brigade, all the battalion commanders were ex-British army officers.

I wouldn't have changed places with the British at that time, though. They were in a terrible spot. In any case, you have to distinguish between the soldiers, the police, and the

*It is only fair to stress that at an earlier stage Arabs were being executed by the British for carrying arms; they considered it most unjust that Jews never were.

civil servants. That's three entirely different psychologies
and personnel. As far as the soldiers were concerned, they
were told to do things and they did them. There's no doubt
about it, they didn't like us, and in many cases they fought
against us. And we had to fight back. When you met them on
equal terms and talked, there was no trouble.

The police were always against us, they hated us like
poison. In one case I remember there was a factory run by
Jews near Mikve Israel [south of Jaffa, where Zur lived],
and on one occasion the British police stormed the place,
took away all the Haganah's arms, disarmed all our fellows
who worked there in the factory and defended the place,
called the Arabs from Jaffa, and handed over all the workers
and members of the Haganah to the mob. They were all
killed.

They hated us because we never cooperated. And also
because of what I call the "Lawrence of Arabia" attitude,
which prevailed at that time.

The civil service was even worse. They thought of
handing over the Jews to the Arabs of Israel when they
moved out—and the result would have been the complete
annihilation of the Jews. That was the plan I am sure, there's
no doubt of it.

Loved or loathed—and it was chiefly the latter—the British,
in the immediate aftermath of the pro-partition vote at the United
Nations, found themselves unable or unwilling to keep the two
sides of the civil war apart. Concentrating on their own safe
withdrawal, they played a diminishing role in the mounting
violence, which began the day after the vote was taken. Only a
brief hour of rejoicing was allowed the Jews, but they made the
most of it. Mrs. Judith Shaltiel, the widow of the man who was to
command the official Jewish forces, the Haganah, in the battle of
Jerusalem, remembers...

☐   ...crouching on all fours on the floor with friends in our
home in Tel Aviv.... We were the only ones with a radio.

We all knelt there with our ears to it. And when it was clear
that partition had gone through, we went out in the street
and danced the whole night and were very happy. In the
morning, the war started.

A young girl who was to become one of Israel's most
distinguished writers, Shulamith Hareven, recalls a similar
experience in Jerusalem, so soon to come under prolonged and
traumatic siege:

☐   I rushed out into the street, like everybody else. I wasn't in
    pajamas as far as I can remember, but lots of people were.
    The funny part was that the British were driving around in
    jeeps, and they took some of us kids on board and in general
    seemed to join in, though they hardly knew what it was all
    about. So we drove around town in British jeeps that night,
    and the next day, it all started.

Another woman, Netiva Ben Yehuda, a demolition officer in
the Palmach who was soon to play a heroic role in Israel's battle
for survival, adds this memory:

☐   After two months on the Syrian border I was sent to take
    another demolition course, which finished exactly on 29th
    November. We'd had the course in the Negev, to avoid the
    British, and we had an end-of-course party and then came
    back through the *moshavot* [cooperative agricultural vil-
    lages]—and then, in Rehovot, we saw flags and people
    dancing and we didn't know what it was all about.
        We saw a taxi—a big beautiful one—and we reckoned
    there was somebody important in it so we blocked the road
    and stopped it. A few of our very tough-looking people went
    along, and found Golda [Meir, later prime minister of Israel;
    at that time a member of Ben-Gurion's executive committee]
    in the taxi. They asked her, "Why's everybody shouting at
    you?" And she said, "What, don't you know? Last night the

United Nations declared we have a state." So we had no leave. We went straight back to our units.

The whole country was in the process of mobilization to face the threat that had already erupted into violent attacks in the north and south as well as the central sector. The irregular nature of these attacks should be stressed: It was not until the mandate ended and the state was declared in the middle of the following May that there was any *official* military involvement by the Arab countries. But there is no doubt that those first six months of "unofficial war" were the worst for the Jews. A typical comment comes from Shimon Avidan, a kibbutznik and Haganah commander who was to distinguish himself in the coming struggle:

☐   The first months of the war were by far the hardest. There were times, between December '47 and March '48, when I was not sure we would stay alive another week. The Arabs were much better organized; they got active help from the British forces. Our people were concentrated in a small territory along the coast, and the Jewish settlements were like islands in an Arab sea. The Haganah units which fought in those first months were really the ones who decided the outcome and bore the brunt—those, and the settlements, some of which had no more than forty-five, fifty people, all aware of a strong moral obligation to stand firm.

Likewise Yitzhak Rabin, later to be prime minister but at that time the young commander of one of the crack Palmach (commando) units, the Har El Brigade:

☐   There is no doubt that at the beginning everything looked, to put it mildly, not too bright, especially from the beginning of December '47 until March or April. During this period we were almost totally on the defensive. The British were involved, and the whole picture was of isolated Jewish settlements that had to fight for their existence. But an even worse aspect was the *type* of struggle—of the war to keep these various dispersed parts of the Jewish community linked together. I would say that this period should be called the War on the Communication Lines.

At this early stage, the Jews were up against three main elements. In the north, groups of Syrian and other irregulars calling themselves the Arab Liberation Army, under their freebooting leader Fawzi el-Kawukji, were making incursions across the eastern borders, which grew bolder as the British stood by, doing little or nothing to repel them. In the south, the so-called Muslim Brotherhood, a fanatical religious sect that had declared a holy war some years before upon the Jewish intruders, were mounting raids from Egypt on the settlements of the northern Negev desert. But the chief danger was posed by the Arabs of Palestine itself. Encouraged by the mufti of Jerusalem (who had spent much of the world war in Germany aiding the Nazis) and led by a relative of his, Abdel Kader Husseini, the local Arabs endeavored to blockade Jewish Jerusalem and thus starve the city into submission.

What sort of force was available to meet these threats? First, the word *force* must be pluralized, for there were four forces on the Jewish side, each, to begin with, having its own officers, its own headquarters, its own separate—and disparate—ethos, methods, strengths, and weaknesses. Briefly, then, these four were: the Haganah (Defense), the Palmach (Shock Troops), the Etzel (National Military Organization), and the Lehi (Freedom Fighters of Israel). The first two were sanctioned by the leadership under Ben-Gurion; the latter two were dissident or terrorist organizations.

The Haganah, founded in the 1920s as an underground defense force, consisted of two main branches, the Khish, or field units, fighting men under the age of twenty-five, and the Khim, basically garrison troops over the age of twenty-five and women auxiliaries. Many of both branches had had training and experience (though few, as will be seen, of battle) in the British army and some in other European armies; those who had been in the world war had received spasmodic training, necessarily clandestine and often interrupted by British searches, with a motley assortment of weapons over a period of years.

The Palmach, the elite striking arm of the Haganah, maintained its own separate command and regarded itself as a group apart from, and above, the "ordinary" Khish, or field troops. Its origins and ethos are well described by a woman who prefers to be known as "Tsippi." (It may be noted that the Israeli "girl fighters," although not nearly so numerous as is often imagined, were all with the Palmach.)

☐   Our army—the one I was a member of, the Palmach—was ready on the 29th November 1947. It was an army which carried itself, meaning we were working in our kibbutzim half the time and getting our training and carrying out actions the other half. We hardly cost the Jewish Agency anything. A few weapons, a little money for special courses, but hardly anything. On the other hand we were a real trained army. Those who had finished training were on reserves in the kibbutz or the city . . . but they had been for at least a year before that in service.

There was no other army in Israel, including the Haganah, including everybody, who lived with their fellow soldiers for a year in tents in the kibbutz and got an organized training; and this is a very important fact which has to be understood before speaking about the War of Independence. You must also understand that to leave home and go to live in a kibbutz, not as a kibbutznik in its best sense but in tents, with very little clothing, and work, and train, and all that, while you are very young, you have to have some ideals. You have to love it, to love your friends and to believe in all of it. It took a certain sort of person— someone who loved the earth, agriculture, nature; and someone who loved others. In a word, not a materialist. All that was a precondition. This already separated people. Because certain people by their nature could not join the Palmach; it was against their characters. They would not have been accepted—they would not have made it. What sort? Egotists. Spoiled people. People who demanded a lot of comfort. They would have been very unhappy.

There were some very patriotic youngsters who at the same time did not like the open-air life and did not see the point of settlement. They were not our people. They *wanted* to fight, and we didn't. We wanted to protect. We wanted to bring immigrant Jews in. We wanted to stop anyone harming us, but if possible not to fight. It was an army that was *prepared*—it had the technical and moral preparations. . . . If we had to fight, we'd fight, but that was one big difference between us and others.

A man who made a different decision—of which he is just as proud today as "Tsippi" is of hers—was Ezra Yachin, who as a boy joined the Lehi, or Stern Gang. He recalls:

☐   As a child I read stories about the Maccabees, about Samson, about heroic Jews. At the same time I looked at Jews living here and their behavior was completely different. We were murdered by Arabs. The British forbade our people to come here, and they supported the Arabs in killing us as well. I didn't understand. Why was it important to fight at the time of the Maccabees, and not now? So I decided I was going to stand.

It is interesting how one came to it. I got excited when I read about one of our boys getting wounded. I asked myself, have I the right to suffer if someone else bleeds? And I answered yes, on condition that I will endanger myself as he does.

I thought it would be simple for me to decide that I wanted to join the underground, but it was not that simple. I was not an adventurer. But I found I did not belong to myself. I belonged to our people, and at the same time I belonged to my parents. Even if they just suspected that I had joined these people who endangered their lives day and night, it would be real torture for them. One saw no end to it at that time. It was very difficult, but I realized the other

boys also had parents . . . . So after the decision I told my
father what I was going to do, and I felt a great relief, and
also a wonderful feeling of freedom. From the moment I
decided to join Lehi, I felt that I personally was free from
foreign rule.

At the end of '44, when I left school, I joined the post
office as a messenger boy, delivering telegrams, because
there I could discover secrets from telegrams sent by the
British government. Later I pasted up posters for the
underground on walls. It was very dangerous. Boys who did
it were often arrested—one of my brothers was sentenced to
a month's imprisonment, and when the month was up,
instead of being freed, he was sent to a detention camp in
Africa, and there he stayed till two years after the state was
declared. The British used to imprison our boys, let them go
again, and the next time there was an underground attack
they would collect them all up again. Once a policeman shot
at me but he missed. That was when I was delivering
pamphlets.

I was fighting to liberate the state. We made great
efforts for it. At the same time we had to realize that many
Jews here didn't like what we were doing. In a way I
understood it. There was much fear about fighting the
British Empire. We were such a small group of Jews in this
country—little more than half a million, many of those not
of age or condition to fight. And the British had all the
power of a great and triumphant empire. They'd just beaten
Hitler. And those who didn't have very, very deep faith
felt afraid of the results of our actions. "My God," they said,
"you want to anger the British? They'll slaughter all of us.
How can we fight them?" So because of that fear, the
established leadership was against us, and also for political
reasons, because we were not of their party.

It was actually not a struggle between ideas but between
emotional feelings. There were those of us who believed we
had to do it however difficult or even painful it was. Because
it was an obligation to fight to be free, not to give in—to

stand. And there were the others who felt it was impossible, that it was safer to stay small, to lie low so they wouldn't see us. . . .

People like me are different. It is as if we saw someone dear to us in danger. Such a person gets a tremendous power to save the loved one's life. That's how I feel and felt then— that we had a chance to survive, and that chance was by *withstanding*. Until now, our cause has not been properly explained.

We initiated the fight. We really wanted that war, strange as it sounds. Peace is not the most important thing. Giving in, giving things up, like land, for the sake of "peace" is like someone who commits suicide to avoid being murdered. At that time we had to break the peace in order to get free. We were called extreme, but we are condemned to an extreme destiny. We have to choose between Europe in the early forties — the Holocaust—or the Israel of the Six-Day War. There is no middle way.

Yet a third view is given by Chaim Laskov, who was one of "Ben-Gurion's men," as members of Khish were sometimes rather sarcastically called by those in the Palmach. He viewed the coming struggle from the viewpoint of a professional soldier.

□   In 1947 people from the underground organization looked upon the coming conflict in terms of the previous troubles we had had in '36, '39—in other words, gang warfare. In gang warfare, the individual weapon counts—raid, counter-raid, and so on. In my view, what was going to develop was something entirely different: confrontation with regular military forces.

And suddenly one man, nonmilitary in his bearing, behavior, dress, everything, said that his reckoning was the same. That was Ben-Gurion. Despite all his efforts to come to some sort of an agreement with our neighbors, he thought we would have to get ready for a full-scale war with the armies of Lebanon, Syria, Jordan, Iraq, and Egypt.

I was very worried, because people from the Palmach, Haganah, Lehi, and Etzel were misunderstanding the point, underestimating what we were going to face. So when Ben-Gurion said, "Listen, here's what we need: we need aircraft, tanks, artillery"—then I knew he was thinking in terms of organized conflict. He was the one who introduced the whole idea.

It was clear that if the Arab states attacked, they would have the initiative. If the other chap starts off with the initiative, it takes a bloody battle to grab it from him. I was wondering how this was going to be done with our armies, which were all geared to premeditated hit raids. Now it would be a case of full encounters, with the best man winning. The best man is the best-trained man with the best equipment.

As yet, no war had been declared. The British were still theoretically in control. No Arab government had officially committed its forces. The Jewish shadow government under Ben-Gurion did not acknowledge that open war had begun. But the country was embattled.

☐   They didn't even admit it was a war. We were fighting like mad in battles night after night; we were dying like flies— and nobody would even dignify our efforts by saying, "Right, we're at war with the Arabs." It was called "events," or, by the British with their penchant for euphemism, "disturbances" or "unrest." I know what we called it. One big *balagan*.

So says a private soldier in the Palmach, newly arrived from Britain, whom I shall call Boaz; he will be heard from again. And *balagan*, the Hebrew word for chaos or muddle, was heard frequently in those days. Netiva Ben Yehuda peppers her accounts with it:

☐   For me, the worst fighting was till April. Why? Because we didn't have anything—there was such a terrible *balagan*—

and the politics! The Etzel and the Lehi nearly ruined us. They kept on killing the British and the British did more and more against us. They used to find guns on us and smash them on the road—you could feel it on your body. I remember once— You know what a Bren gun is? The heaviest on the field for the infantry. And in all Galilee we had no more than a dozen. They "caught" six of them, in the main street of Tiberias, and they put them on the paved road, side by side, and they ran over them, this way and then that way—and we cried! We didn't let them see us crying, but we couldn't help it.

And then people were getting killed, and the *balagan* got right out of this world. There was no registration of the dead. No one announced it to the parents. Parents might be informed by chance on the street. And there were no plans. We had to show our muscle but not to fight back. So we would, so to say, run among the Arabs waving a Sten gun in the air.

The worst was the uncertainty. We were so young. Yigal Allon, who was head of the Palmach all over the country, was twenty-nine. We were nineteen. A captain might be twenty. Our commander Mula Cohen, who commanded the whole of the eastern Galilee and had the lives of hundreds of soldiers and thousands of settlers in his hands, was twenty-four. Now we were faced with problems day by day which we had never experienced. And nobody prepared us. There was a sort of puritanism about the Second Aliya.* They never talked about blood and killing. Nobody told us anything, but they expected my generation to fulfill our role.

*The second wave of immigrants who reached the country in the early twentieth century.

"Events" of the Undeclared War, Sector by Sector

JERUSALEM

Then as now, Jerusalem was divided into the Old City to the east and the new, western sector, which also extended to the south, known as Jewish Jerusalem. The Old City, encircled by the mighty walls built on the orders of Suleiman the Magnificent, contained four ethnic quarters—Armenian, Christian (Arab), Muslim, and Jewish—as it had for centuries before the first houses were built outside its walls by Moses Montefiori in 1867.

Jerusalem stands inland among the Judean hills and at that time could be reached from the main Jewish population center of Tel Aviv on the coast by only one route. This led across the plain past kibbutzim such as Hulda and Na'an, past the famous monastery of Latrun—where the British had built one of their numerous strategic forts, which was named after their designer, a man called Teggart—and thence into the narrow wadi through the foothills known as Bab el Wad.

Along the edges of this defile were a number of strategically vital Arab villages and outposts. As soon as the real fighting started, at the beginning of December '47, the local Arabs, under Abdel Kader Husseini, developed a rough but effective system of temporary recruitment to mount attacks on Jewish transport, that is, anything that moved on that road but especially trucks carrying supplies to Jerusalem. Yitzhak Rabin, whose Har El commandos had been given the responsibility for keeping the road open, explains:

☐   In the beginning we hadn't any means to fight effectively. We had to save the transportation capacity mainly to ship food to Jerusalem. The defenders and weapons had to be mixed up with the products—in the flour and the other stuff. I think we suffered most of the casualties during this period in the convoys.

Israel Diskin, a lawyer now in his seventies, was on one of the first convoys to suffer the sort of assault that was to become the unvarying hazard of every vehicle attempting the ascent to Jerusalem.

☐   On 18th December I was sent from Jerusalem to Tel Aviv by Va'ad Leumi [national executive of the Jewish leadership] to Argaz, a factory making truck bodies, with a letter to the company ordering the preparation of armored trucks. The purpose was to prevent the interruption of communications between Tel Aviv and Jerusalem; these armored trucks would serve as protection for people traveling between Jerusalem and Tel Aviv under fire from Arab assailants.

When I presented the letter to Argaz, the answer was, no trucks —they didn't yet have the iron sheets to cover the chassis. I remained in Tel Aviv for that Saturday with my brother, but I was anxious to get home to Jerusalem. On Sunday there were no buses, nor on Monday. On Tuesday morning there were six buses, but not armed, ordinary buses, vintage 1936; in each bus twenty-five persons, including two under-eighteen girls each hiding a locally made Sten. They were under age so that they couldn't be sentenced to death if caught by the British.*

We were the first convoy from Tel Aviv through Rehovot and Kibbutz Na'an. At the kibbutz we met a convoy dashing toward Tel Aviv from Jerusalem, informing us that they'd been attacked and had several wounded.

At the first roadblock a Scottish sergeant entered the

*The British never sentenced a woman to death.

first bus, where I was, to search for arms. But he didn't search; he just pretended, shouting, "Okay! Go on!"

I suggested to the driver—on my own responsibility since no one was in charge—that we go back to Rehovot or Tel Aviv, because I was afraid that if we entered Bab el Wad, we would be annihilated. The young girls told me, "Get out, if you're afraid!" I said, "We're a convoy of a hundred and fifty civilians with a few girls to guard us. We'll be wiped out."

In the end I agreed to go with the rest but suggested keeping a distance of a hundred to a hundred and fifty yards between the buses, so that if our bus was attacked, the rest would be able to retreat. I went from bus to bus, ordering this distance to be kept. They all agreed, and we recommenced our journey.

On entering Bab el Wad, I raised my eyes and repeated the words of the psalm, "I will lift up mine eyes unto the hills, from whence cometh my help." Before completing my appeal, I heard shooting from both sides. The driver, Jacob Fedorenki, accelerated sharply. I looked back and saw that the other buses were keeping the distance I'd suggested. The shooting was going on terribly. We all sat on the floor of the bus, with heavy firing keeping up from both sides. We already had two lightly wounded—one girl in the leg and a man in his back.

Thanks to an earlier suggestion of mine that the windows should be opened, there was no shattering of glass. Nobody made a sound. Suddenly Jacob informed us that a front tire had been punctured—the Arabs always fired at the tires. I asked if the gas tank was bullet-proofed. He said no. I ordered the doors open so that we could escape quickly if the tank exploded. Jacob drove on with the doors open.

The girls, meanwhile, were shooting back at our attackers. Jacob told us that the other tire had gone and he couldn't continue. The firing had continued solidly, but now suddenly it stopped.

I noticed we were surrounded by British soldiers. A

captain came in, asking if we had any wounded. I answered that we had two, lightly. Then I thanked him for saving us and asked, "Who are you?" I remember he was smoking a pipe. He answered, "We are the convoy of His Excellency the High Commissioner Sir Alan Cunningham."

I expressed to him, on behalf of the whole convoy, our thanks for saving us. We proceeded to Jerusalem. Our bus had to be abandoned but we squeezed into the other buses. Several days after this, the armored buses began to make the journey, but despite the armor, several people were killed on the next convoy.

"Tsippi," one of the guards, has a different perspective:

☐   I was on some of the convoys.... My job was to hide the weapons from the English. On the road to Jerusalem they were still involved right up almost to the day they left. They would stop us, and search.... We used to carry the guns under our coats and always we carried a few cases of beer. We used to bribe them with the beer and usually it would help. I remember one time when they insisted on searching one of the trucks, and one girl in it had a lot of weapons; so we said she had typhus and she lay there, looking at death's door. We told the soldiers, "Of course you can go in, if you don't mind taking the risk—" They took one look, and ran.

One time, as we got off the truck, it happened that one piece of the gun I was hiding fell on the floor. I stepped on it and I didn't move because if I'd moved the soldiers would have seen it. In the end a very young Englishman dropped his coat at my feet and said, "Okay, pick up my coat —" He helped me. It was luck.

When we'd got through the British lines, on we'd go; then we had to take out our guns again. The road was narrow, and we were lucky if there was no blockade, no car that broke down on the way, blocking the path. These were the main problems: the shooting from the hills, the block-ades, our own trucks getting damaged and blocking the road. Then there were all kinds of tricks the Arabs tried on us, like putting a mine into the body of a dead dog or things like that which we might not notice.

This went on till Abu Ghosh, where the Arabs were friendly. The worst I remember there was someone throwing a rotten tomato! The Arabs of Abu Ghosh didn't shoot at us. I don't know why... I had a few guesses. First of all, they had this flirtation with Geula Cohen and Lehi—they had saved Geula Cohen when she escaped from the British prison. She was the Lehi's radio broadcaster. The sheikh of Abu Ghosh, or one of his sons, hid her. They were very involved with Jews altogether. Kiryat Anavim was right across the road, of course; maybe those friendly Arabs made a better reckoning of our strength, or maybe they were afraid that if they fought us, we might spoil their beautiful village.

Of course it was all very frightening. Only a stupid person is not afraid. They were shooting at us, we were shooting back with Stens.... But I think, luckily, we never understood the full meaning of life and death. We were so young. We were very active and we had a good time, being together. The friendship helped us. I once asked a psychologist: How come that in other wars there were breakdowns, but in that war, which was the longest, there were very few? He said that, first, there was no time for breakdowns, and that the comradeship, the idealism, people with the same "common denominator" being together, kept us psychologically in good condition.

On the success of convoys in getting through depended the survival of the Jews of Jerusalem. Their ordeal began in December and continued till June. Sometimes the siege became hermetic when the road was cut completely. At other times it was broken; supplies got through; the tension eased. But throughout, the population of Jerusalem had to contend with the harshest and most nerve-racking conditions—in addition to food and water shortages, which were, on occasion, very severe, and intermittent sniping and shelling, a feeling of uncertainty and isolation prevailed. Chaim Herzog remembers:

☐   The siege was terrifying, a great provider of stories. We were burying our dead in gardens under heavy artillery fire from the Arab Legion*—thousands of shells landing, bullets flying; someone would be walking in the street and he'd suddenly drop dead from a stray bullet. There was no water†, just the reservoirs or cisterns, so each family had to live on one pail of water a day, however hot it got. We collected a sort of green weed and cooked it, and that was what we ate, plus three slices of bread a day. People were literally hungry, and there were children who'd never seen fruit.

   That lasted from December '47 and became very serious in January and February. It was broken two or three times and did not end till 10th June.

Meron Benvinisti, the son of an old Sephardic family who later became deputy mayor of Jerusalem and had a special interest in its post-'67 Arab population, recalls:

☐   I was only a boy when the whole thing started. What strikes me now is how normal life was. Perhaps it's always like that. People think back on hostilities and terrors, but only when everything is over. . . . At the time, people wake up and go to work, unless shelling or something else stops them. For children, many more ordinary than dramatic things are going on, and that's why I have few outstanding memories.

   I remember my mother being cross with me. Twice. Once when I was going upstairs and stumbled over our one-bucket-a-day of water. The water was distributed by trucks or tankers; you had to go out and line up for it; and every drop you didn't drink was used three times—first for

---

*Actually, the Arab Legion was not involved until early April.
† The Arabs blew up the pumping station at Latrun in June.

washing, then for laundry, and finally for the lavatory; so
none was wasted. My spilling that bucketful was a tragedy.

   The other time was when I went out and found a house
that had belonged to a British official in a security zone. I
don't know how it happened that for so long nobody had
dared to go in there—the British had been gone for some
weeks. Anyway, I went in, and found a whole kitchen full of
food. We needed it—it was during the worst period—so I
went and fetched my elder brother, who brought a sack and
we took it. While we were still out, the shelling started.
When we got back my mother was so angry. She said,
"Never mind food—I want you safe."

The chief fear of the Jewish population at that time was that
the Arab Legion under Sir John Glubb would intervene. Glubb's
views on the Legion's task and role have not altered with the
years. He claims that the Legion was not engaged at all until
after the British left in May '48 and that all the trouble in Jerusalem was caused by just one thing: the Jews' refusal to accept the
decision of the United Nations that it was to be an international
city. He stoutly denies that King Abdullah of Jordan had any
designs on Jerusalem for his capital.

☐   Never heard of such a thing. The whole basis of everything
     which we agreed to and which the British government told
     us to enforce was that Jerusalem would be an international
     city. It never occurred to Abdullah or anyone else in Jordan
     that Jerusalem would be an Arab city or have anything to do
     with Jordan. Of course, they didn't want it to be a Jewish
     city!

        Although Israel had accepted partition, they intended
     to occupy Jerusalem; they had a sort of mental reservation
     on the partition plan. This made a [peaceful] solution
     impossible.

He goes on to say that the Jews in Jerusalem faced nothing worse
than "a few men with rusty rifles" and dismisses the siege with the

following account of a shopping expedition he made in Jerusalem
(from Amman) about two months before the mandate ended.

☐   It was quite unpleasant. You were likely to get shot around
     every corner, either by an Arab or a Jew. I remember seeing
     one or two of what we called "Catch-'em-Alive-O's." Half a
     dozen old men with rifles— Half the time they'd say, "Have
     you got any ammunition? I haven't got any!" and somebody
     else would say, "Well, I believe there's a chap in Ramallah
     who's got some, if you run up there you might get twenty
     rounds"—I mean, that was the basis of the thing. This is not
     an army.

As to food supplies, Glubb avers that the city was never
completely cut off. "Their convoys used to get sniped coming up
to Jerusalem," he mentions, "but there was no shortage of food
that I could see."
It would appear from this that King Abdullah's chief officer
did not realize how close the local Arabs had come to success in
their attempt to starve the city into surrender. Dov Joseph, a
Canadian whom Ben-Gurion appointed as military governor of
the city, describes in his book *The Faithful City* the stringent
system of food and water conservation he had to institute and
enforce and the very stern measures he had to take to keep the city
fed and functioning. Often he, like the beleaguered man in the
street, suffered psychologically from the suspicion that the Jews
of Jerusalem had been all but forgotten by their leaders and well-
fed fellow Jews in Tel Aviv and the rest of the Jewish sector. The
true heroism of the city at that time was its citizens' determination
to hold out with no end to their ordeal in sight.
To begin the story of this ordeal at the point at which the
United Nations declared in favor of partition, we must enter the
Old City. Life there is described by a woman who still lives in its
recently rebuilt Jewish quarter. Rivca Weingarten was one of
three daughters of the rabbi who led the Jewish community in the
Old City. Her family had occupied the same house for two
hundred years.

☐   The relations between Jew and non-Jew in the Old City in
the past were very fine. We all lived in the same quarter;
children grew up together, speaking two languages and
familiar with each other's cultures and traditions. It is
important to differentiate between those who were neighbors and the "politicals."

I remember on November 30th, the day after partition,
I intended to go to work as usual. I was surprised not to see
anybody in the streets of the Old City. I called for a girl
friend of mine, and we started walking through to the Jaffa
Gate. We didn't see a soul; all the shops were closed; and I
soon realized there must be a strike.

As we came out of the Jaffa Gate, we saw a crowd of
about three hundred Arabs holding sticks and stones. I
knew all too well what it meant, remembering the riots in the
past. I told my girl friend, who was a new immigrant, to walk
beside me and not do anything else. But I knew this might be
my last hour. As we went forward, three Arab boys came
toward us, but at that moment an Arab called out: "Leave
her alone! She's the daughter of the *mukhtar*,* she is from
among us!"

We continued toward Mamilla Road, safe, thank God.
But this very same group later broke out up Princess Mary
Avenue, bent on shooting, burning, and looting; when they
were pushed back by the Haganah near the Jaffa Road, they
went on the rampage in the Commercial Center instead.

I was working at the time in a building in the vicinity,
and all the other workers and myself stood for hours in the
windows, watching the riot—burning buildings, looting,
people being killed and injured—and only after some hours
the British came to try to save those who remained.

Leo Wissman, a master furniture maker whose business was
located in the Commercial Center, recalls the crowd coming
down Mamilla Road:

Mukhtar: a civilian leader, usually chief of an Arab community, but in
mixed communities the term also applied to Jews.

☐   The English police and military did not stop them. They set
    fire to everything, destroyed the workshops.... I saw
    personally how the Arabs came up the street, while two or
    three English armored cars backed away. But just as they got
    to the shop three doors from mine, some shots were fired—
    by the Etzel, not the Haganah—which made the Arabs go
    back.

Meir Pa'il, who is now a historian and politician on the Left but
then was a special operations commander of the Haganah, was
also there, in a military capacity:

☐   Some of my people—about ten—using grenades and pistols,
    succeeded in stopping Arab looting of the Commercial
    Center in the Mamilla vicinity. Nobody knows it till now—
    It was what we call a dirty job. When you see three or four
    thousand Arabs looting, with twelve or fifteen people to
    defend, what should you do? You throw some grenades here
    and there and threaten them, and they begin to run away.
    There were no kids there, just adults looting, and neither the
    British police nor the ordinary Haganah troops could stop
    them. I would have done the same to a looting Jewish mob.

Immediately after this, the pattern of action and reaction was
intensified. Netanel Lorch, historian and recent secretary-general
of the Knesset, recalls:

☐   Right after partition, Arabs went on the rampage and the
    British police—this was quite important in terms of the way
    the Arabs read the signals—stood by. Incidentally, one of
    them, when a shop owner complained that his place was
    being burned and looted, advised him to "go to Begin." The
    fact is that the British forces, which could have stamped it
    out at that point with a bit of determination and show of
    force, did nothing, and there was a great deal of emotion
    about it. Haganah, following a doctrine which in retrospect
    may seem naïve, said, "Well, we have to keep a low profile if

we don't want the fire to spread." So when masses of unarmed Jews marched down Jaffa Street to avenge the Commercial Center, twenty or so of us stood across the street
with our backs to the Arabs and our faces to thousands of
angry Jews. The first casualty of the war was my glasses,
which were broken in the scuffle . . . . We weren't armed,
only with sticks or truncheons or something. Incidentally,
there was also an internal political aspect to this, because the
Etzel had decided to take revenge in order to show that
Jewish property was not to be lightly attacked. There were
hardly any casualties there, by the way—I don't know why.
Needless to say, the general philosophy of preventing the fire
from being spread didn't work out in the end. It spread
rapidly, and in the end it engulfed most of the country.

After that first day of rioting, the Old City and the New were
cut off from one another. The British, anxious to avoid trouble,
would have been glad to see all the inhabitants of the Jewish
quarter within the massive walls evacuated to the New City.
However, they reluctantly sent in convoys that were supposed to
carry only essential supplies and medical staff to the cut-off Old
City community. Rivca Weingarten, who had unwarily ventured
out to go to work, had to resort to stratagems to return home.

☐   I had a personal problem. I had left the Old City to go to my
     office and in the afternoon the Haganah transferred all the
     Jewish employees to New Jerusalem, including me. I rang
     up my father to tell him what had happened, asking him to
     arrange for me to come home, but he told me it was
     impossible, because shooting and bombing inside the quar-
     ter had already started; he said no one knew what was going
     to happen and I should stay where I was.
        But my roots are too deep in the Old City. Under no
     circumstances was I ready to stay in the New City. I went to
     the Magen David Adom [the Jewish equivalent of the Red
     Cross]. I'm ashamed of my feelings that day: Knowing that
     ambulances were still allowed to go in to fetch out dead and

injured or women in labor, I waited there, hoping something would happen in the Old City that required an ambulance. After three days something did, and I rode on the ambulance and got back to my home, where I stayed until the end.

The Jewish authorities outside the walls were determined to keep the Jewish foothold in the Old City. Knowing the pious and unbelligerent nature of the citizens of the quarter, many of whom were old, they smuggled in administrators and soldiers, the one to organize and direct, the other to defend, the community. They also did their best to prevent the inevitable exodus to the New City. This description is given by Malca Tarragan, another woman who has since returned to her old quarter:

☐ Many years ago in the Old City there were groups of students living in cooperatives and going each day to study at the university. They also worked with Jews in the Old City and with the children. I worked with this group. Then, just before the War of Independence, when I was a student of biology living in the New City and a member of Haganah, a group of Old City students came to me. They asked: "What do you do in the New City?" I told them I was a kind of policeman. And they said, "Come with us, and be one of a group of teachers in the Old City."

This was the idea of Yitzhak Ben Zvi, who was the head of the Jewish Agency at that time.* He asked teachers to come and live in the Old City. The problem was that the Jewish quarter was cut off from the New City by a lot of shops, inside and outside the walls, run by Christians and Arabs; if Jews wanted to enter our little quarter, they had to come in by way of the Jaffa Gate, passing through this Arab area. After the declaration of partition in November, Jews living in the Old City were afraid to go in or out. We were as isolated as Jerusalem itself was isolated from the Jewish areas on the coast.

*He was later Israel's second president.

The Old City was divided into four sectors, Jewish, Christian, Armenian, and Muslim—but there was no such clear division before 1948. Many Jews lived then in the Muslim quarter, to be near the site of the Temple.* After the Six-Day War you could see that many houses in the Muslim sector had little holes in their doorposts where the *mezuzahs*† that had once been nailed there had been pulled off. Afterward the Arabs filled the holes with cement to hide all traces of Jewish occupancy; now the two quarters are kept quite separate—Arabs there, Jews here—no mingling.

But during the troubled time before the state, there were many attacks by Arabs against Jews; many Jews were killed—this is going right back to 1929.

A wall was built between the Jewish and the Arab quarters, which eventually acted as a blockade.

Now you must understand something of the daily life we led at that time. From the first—right back when I came, in December 1947—working life had come to a stop, because most people who lived here worked outside, in the New City, and now they couldn't get out, so they were idle. No one could get out except on a convoy, escorted by the British, three times a week. Even so, only the old could leave. The Haganah didn't let the young people out, except by special permission, because if there were no young people in the Jewish quarter, there would be no excuse to fight to keep it. Morale dropped very low.

After three months, the government started to plan for the war that was coming and tried to improve the situation in the Old City. They brought in good surgeons, dentists, doctors, and also an administrator, Avraham Halperin. It was like a little municipality, and Halperin was the "mayor." He entered in disguise, as a male nurse.

He then began to do many, many good things here. He reorganized the life of the quarter. He knew the Old City like

---

*The Second Temple was destroyed by the Romans in A.D. 70, leaving only one remaining wall, now regarded by religious Jews as their holy of holies.
    †*Mezuzah*: prayer container which practicing Jews affix to their doorposts.

I know my finger. In these narrow streets, you can pass from house to house without using the street—across the roofs and underground. He knew these ways. He brought with him a man from Solel Boneh [the national building firm] and a budget to reorganize the life of the quarter and create jobs. Men were paid to build fortifications within the quarter. Passages were made so that people could move about it without being exposed to fire. He made shop-keepers open their businesses. He put others to work on civil defense. He paid people to flatten one area for a miniature airstrip. Girls and women made clothes; there was a laundry for the soldiers' uniforms; the children had sports and activities after school. He even paid the old men to pray in the synagogue. Everyone had a task. It was a flourishing time for the Old City.

But Halperin made a mistake. He centralized every-thing into his own hands. And that upset a certain man who, until that time, had been the "big man" of the quarter, Rabbi Mordechai Weingarten.

Weingarten was the *mukhtar* when I arrived. It was his privilege to distribute the food in the quarter, from the central kitchen, and he saw Halperin as a rival. Halperin consulted him, but he didn't give him any real authority or prestige. Now comes a very delicate question. Weingarten's house was guarded by British soldiers and they used to drink tea with him. One day, half an hour after they came out, a British officer came and told Halperin he was not allowed to live in the Old City any more. How did they know he was not a male nurse?

We all liked him very much and we were frightened what would happen to him. They didn't harm him; they just banished him. He left the Old City, but after a while he came back again on one of the British convoys; but when the local British commander saw him, he said, "I know you, you were banned—never come back here again." After that, we didn't see him. We were all afraid, and we decided to continue in the way he had shown us.

He was replaced by Moshe Rousnak. This man feels

bad until today because he was not the right person. He will
keep a pain in his heart until he dies. He knows the mistakes
that were made and he suffers all the time. I don't suffer in
that way, because I did all that I could do—my best—but I
was just a little cog in the wheel.

Rivca Weingarten, daughter of Rabbi Weingarten, claims
that her father (now dead) was not strictly a *mukhtar* but
president of the Jewish community, the essential difference being
that a *mukhtar* would have been appointed and paid by the
British whereas a president was elected by the inhabitants and did
his work on a voluntary basis. She vividly recalls being shut into a
dark room with other children in 1929 while mobs roamed the
streets chanting, "Slaughter the Jews!" More riots in 1936
reduced the population of the Jewish quarter and made life there
"very, very miserable." She states that the only people who
remained were well-off people who stayed for religious and
ideological reasons and the very poor "who could not afford to go
and live elsewhere."

☐   When the U.N. declared the partition of Eretz Israel, the
Jewish quarter was the first to feel the result. On 30th
November 1947 the Arabs declared a three-days' strike in
the Jewish quarter and set siege to it. This meant that those
who left the Jewish quarter on the 29th could not return
home, whether they were men who had gone to work,
children to school, or housewives who went shopping.
Families were torn apart; nobody, of course, knew how long
the siege would continue.
    At this stage there were a little more than 7,000 Jewish
inhabitants in the quarter. By the time the British left there
remained only seventeen hundred Jews here, including old
men, women, and children. This was due to the policy of the
British that whoever wanted to come back into the Jewish
quarter was not allowed to. They used the excuse that the
tiny quarter was surrounded by Arabs and that it was
dangerous to come in—actually impossible. But, they said,
those who wanted to join their families *outside* could leave.

There were families who held out a week, two months, three, four, but the exodus was inexorable. Life became more miserable every day, for several reasons. The dwindling number of inhabitants were not prepared for war. We had no cellars of food and other things which are usually prepared to face a war. And we never thought— I mean, we very timidly believed that whatever happened in the country, nobody would harm a small Jewish community in the Jewish quarter of the Old City. But, of course, the reality was completely different.

We had no army, but very, very few members of all three voluntary organizations, the Haganah, the Etzel, and the Lehi. They could not compare to the armies that surrounded us, all the Arab armies, and we lived, first of all, in fear, and second, we never knew when it would all end.

At first we still had food coming in to us with the British convoys, newspapers, letters from outside, but in time this contact became less and less. There was fighting all along— bombs were thrown, shooting took place and so on, but the real fighting started on 15th May.

Not surprisingly, Sir John Glubb takes a rather one-sided view of the causes of the battles that went on behind the Old City walls well before the intervention of the Arab Legion:

☐   The Jews of the Old City were completely Arabicized. They lived absolutely cheek-by-jowl, hand-in-glove with all their neighbors. They had not the least desire to have any trouble with any of them. But unfortunately for them, just before the fighting began, contingents of the Haganah were pushed over the wall and into the Jewish quarter. If that hadn't happened, there wouldn't have been a shot fired in the Old City, because, as I say, the Jews had lived there for two thousand years and were as Arabicized as the Jews of England are English. But this contingent of the Haganah who got in started opening fire. There'd been no quarrel between neighbors until then.

This view, it must be said, accords with that of Rivca Weingarten, who stressed to me the distinction between the neighborhood Arabs, with whom the Old City Jews had always lived at peace, and "politicals"—on both sides. Of course there is another view—that of the fighters, of both sexes, who regarded the Old City as a most important objective in the coming struggle. As one of the most ancient and holiest Jewish sites in the country, it could not be yielded up. These people viewed with thinly veiled contempt the pacifistic attitude of the "Old Yishuv" residents, who would not join the struggle and actually impeded it.

One of the milder of these was a woman who now leads a small left-wing political party called the Civil Rights movement, Shulamith Aloni, and is a maverick figure in the current Knesset (Israeli Parliament). At the time she was a teacher. Her outlook was predicated upon one of the most effective influences felt then, and indeed, now, by Jews (even secular ones) with regard to their land: the Bible.

□   I was in the Old City of Jerusalem from December '47, which was when the siege started, and later on, in May, I went down to Tel Aviv to receive the children who'd been evacuated from Jaffa, to build a school for them, and then rejoin the Palmach and take my part in the war.

My job was to receive new immigrants. I knew a little Yiddish and the Polish and other languages which I know now is from this time when I had to work with them, to prepare them for the army and to send them, after two or three weeks of training, straight to the war.

Now people tell stories, heroic stories. It *was* a heroic time, but we weren't really aware how heroic it was. I remember in the Old City during the siege, people like myself tried to carry on a normal life, though there was no water, and many other hardships. We did it, not because of idealism, but because it was a very natural part of our duty and was taken for granted. I say "we"—I mean people who were brought up in the youth movement, people who, from the age of fourteen, had already been in the Haganah.

It was spring, and looking out over the Valley of Gehenom while I taught the children about Jeremiah the Prophet was like coming back to the Bible with its stories of courage.... The exciting thing was the link with the past, the tie to history, to our sources. But not the way it is today in this country, with religious coercion and the notion that being Jewish is a matter of rituals. The great thing at that time was that you belonged to a place, to a country, to its views and its light. You could see the trees and the mountains and the cemetery there, and the old times came true; we felt it was a kind of a revival, going back into history—and history coming forward to here and now. And from here and now, to the future. And that's why the prophets and their morality had so much influence over us.

A woman who felt the contrast in the two outlooks very strongly was Rika Meidav. Her story appears, highly colored, in two novelized accounts of the war, *O Jerusalem!* by Larry Collins and Dominique Lapierre and *Genesis '48* by Dan Kurzman. Her fiancé was killed in the final battle for the Old City in May; she later married his brother and now lives in Haifa.

☐   My job was to be a soldier, but I had a special responsibility to look after the children of the quarter. I got in with the last convoy before the British left—it was very difficult to get a permit. Morale was very low; the people had no food, no arms, almost none—we had one big machine gun, which had to be moved from one position to another to show the Arabs we had arms, when in fact we had almost nothing at all. We were told we could expect "something substantial" in the way of help, but actually nothing very substantial arrived, just a few more Haganah people, so we began to make all the arrangements for defending the quarter while the fighting was going on.

The children played a very important part. We had to protect them; and yet we had to use them. It was a moral problem. You see, they were very agile, and small and quick, and they knew the Old City inside out. We didn't have enough manpower, so the children used to receive all kinds of arms and grenades, and they used to run from one position to another. A number of them died that way.

The local women, who lived there, very simple people, helped very much. They used to cook for the soldiers. Even when the shelling was very heavy they would manage to prepare something hot, even though there was nothing much to prepare. I specially remember a Yemenite woman; you know the Yemenites—they can make a meal out of a few herbs, somehow—and she used to risk her life to collect bits of food and make meals.... Until today, when I visit Jerusalem on Jerusalem Day I meet these people. We haven't lost contact because there was a special feeling that we all belonged to each other. It remains a true feeling. The people were so sincere, their contribution came from their hearts and it was important.... Even after it was all over, the government never thought of telling those people that they had done something that mattered, but they had.

It's a very difficult thing to make war where there are civilians. First of all, many of them were old or too young to be useful, so they had to be gathered together and cared for, and kept from running in the streets or getting hysterical.... Then some of the religious people did not want to help. They didn't understand the point of it all; they were not much use. They were ready to surrender the Old City the next day. We had them against us, too.

To leave the Old City for the moment, the problem of internecine conflict between secular, nationalist Jews and traditionalist religious ones existed in the New City too. Netanel Lorch, the historian, was assigned to one of the most reactionary ultra-Orthodox quarters, Mea Shearim, in that period when the British were still much in evidence.

☐   I was put in charge of the Hungarian Houses in Mea Shearim. I had some fifteen boys and girls in my platoon.

There was a British police station across the road and an Arab shop about twenty yards from where we were—it was a ticklish situation.

One day somebody came up—no one I knew—and he turned out to be the leader of the Naturei Karta [an ultra-Orthodox sect]. It took me some time to understand that what he was trying to convey to me, in Yiddish, was that if we didn't get rid of the girls he was going to tell on us to the British, because it was immoral and against Jewish law for boys and girls to be together in the same room. As there were about twenty of us crowded into a very small room, nothing immoral could possibly have happened, but I went along to the Kolell committee—a group of men who make sure that people who live in these collectively owned houses live up to the rules of Halacha [Jewish Orthodox law].

I told them, "Look, I have enough trouble trying to protect you against the British and the Arabs. I want you to get this man off my back, because if you don't, I'll take my youngsters and leave. I don't live here, you live here—it's your problem." There followed a fantastic theological discussion as to whether the man who'd lent his apartment to us had the right to do it; some said he did and some said he didn't.... Under other circumstances it would have been farcical. In the end, they decided to put a guard outside my headquarters to ensure that I didn't have to talk to that man again. So I had my own guard against the British and Arabs and another against the Naturei Karta.

This theme of internal schisms was to haunt the Jews nearly as fatally as it did the Arabs throughout the war, in various forms. But, inevitably, tragedy and setbacks were great unifiers. Divisions were obliterated temporarily, for example, in a great wave of mourning for the deaths of thirty-five university students who, in January, went to the assistance of a group of four besieged Jewish agricultural settlements known as Gush (Bloc) Etzion, just south of Jerusalem. Creeping by night through the hills, they were ambushed by local Arabs and annihilated to the last man. Dan

Bitan, then a schoolboy and now director of the Department for Gifted Children in Israel, remembers...

☐ ... sitting in our school and hearing the news of the deaths of the thirty-five young Palmachniks who went to help Gush Etzion. Thirty-five deaths! It was a catastrophe to us—the largest number, I believe, that had fallen at one time till then. Before, when one or two men died in one engagement it was enough to shock everyone. For the thirty-five, it was a day of national mourning. We could hardly grasp the immensity of it.

These "immense" casualty figures were to pale into insignificance all too soon. But in these early days of the fighting, many events assumed proportions that would be dwarfed by later cataclysms. "Boaz," the Palmach private, recalls a significant moment in his early training that also does something to explain how the disparate elements of the Jewish forces could be, at least in part, united.

☐ My first action was an easy one. They sent us, more or less for practice, to take a camp which the British had left in Arab hands. They hadn't really dug in yet and we simply chased them away. There was still a bit of light left in the sky when we'd finished.... As we stood there, in the most motley assortment of clothes, some of us even in dusty white shirts that we'd been wearing for Shabbat, we saw other groups coming toward the camp over the low hills around it. "Look!" we kept shouting. "Here comes another lot!" They kept coming, crowds of them, more and more, and suddenly somebody yelled out: "It's an army! We're a real army!"
  You must remember that a lot of them had been acting as underground couriers, dodging the British, keeping their heads down, and others had come from the DP camps on Cyprus or even straight from Europe.... Now suddenly we felt we weren't on the defensive any more, as we'd always been—we were out in the open with guns in our hands, a fighting force.

We all felt a sense of elation, but of course it wasn't our way to say it. We'd already begun turning away from all the histrionic ranting and raving the old-time Zionists had fed us on. So suddenly, in the midst of this elation, somebody stood up and cried in dramatic tones: "And here we are, brothers! A real Jewish army for the first time in two thousand years, the dream of our forefathers coming true, a fulfillment of the Zionist ideal!" We all broke into a roar of laughter, though in our hearts we knew it was true.

On February 1 the offices of the *Palestine Post* (now the *Jerusalem Post*) were blown up, the first of a series of sabotage actions against the Jews of Jerusalem. Chaim Herzog remembers:

☐ I can distinctly recall rushing down to the area [of the *Palestine Post*] and seeing the destruction and havoc, and above all, the fact that the *Post* appeared the next day. That was the way things happened then; you just didn't allow adversity to get you down. It was in smaller format, but all the printing presses in town got together and helped them get the paper out. David Courteney, an Englishman who had settled here, had a regular column, which that morning began with the statement that words are stronger than bombs.

A few weeks later I was going to Tel Aviv with my wife. Travel was only by convoy to Tel Aviv (which was another world, where there was no shooting, plenty of food and so on). As we walked past Ben Yehuda Street at 6 A.M. to get the bus I saw trucks driving down it. We were sitting on the armored bus in the bus station when we heard this devastating detonation. A number of British deserters, working for the Arabs, had driven those trucks we had seen, loaded with explosives, parked them in Ben Yehuda Street, and run. There were fifty people killed there, and all the buildings in the street were practically destroyed.

Shulamith Hareven also has cause to remember these "events":

☐   I was already a "medic"—a teen-age member of the
     Haganah medical service. I didn't have to be sent for. The
     town was very small then—you heard an explosion and you
     just ran. We all had a kit.... For two years or so after the
     war I kept the habit of carrying a personal bandage or two
     with me wherever I went. And those were the first real
     wounded that I had to take care of. Of course I'd seen
     injured people before, as a child in Warsaw—no doubt that
     was a terrible shock for me, but I had no sense of shock now.
     We were all working like demons and no one had time to
     think. And that was how it went on really, starting in a big
     way in February and ending the August after that. It was like
     one long twilight.

As Herzog asserts, there was plenty for the medics to do.
Shortly after the Ben Yehuda Street explosion, the Jewish
Agency was bombed:

☐   I worked in the Jewish Agency building and was there at the
     time. This time the vehicle was an American consular car,
     which had been stolen, driven into the courtyard of the
     agency, and left. Fortunately a guard had driven it around to
     the side a bit, or I wouldn't be here now.
          Actually, I was saved by the fact that I'd gone to the
     men's room, which was at the back of the building, and just
     as I came out the explosion occurred. The entire area was
     enveloped in a white fog: It was the plaster coming off and
     fragmenting. Then some terrifying figures came groping
     through the fog with bright red spots of blood all over them.
     I began to help them. Then I suddenly thought, my wife is in
     the building. I rushed through into the front and recognized
     a skirt in the rubble—it was my wife. Another man helped
     me take her down to an ambulance, and there inside it was a
     decapitated body. I covered my wife up so she shouldn't see
     it and we took her to the hospital.

An immediate sequel to this story gives an interesting
glimpse at the attempts going on at the time by the United Nations

to play its part in the implementation of its resolution on partition. The British were not being very cooperative, as Chaim Herzog hints:

☐   At that time I was also the representative of the Jewish Agency to the advance unit of the U.N., which was supposed to set up the Jewish and Arab states, and I had arranged a lunch that day between Colonel Roscher Lundt, the U.N. military expert, and Reuven Shiloah, from our side. Shiloah was wounded in the blast; in fact, he was scarred for life on his face. But I'd fixed the meeting, so I left my wife in the hospital and rushed back, with my shirt still bloodstained, and went to the U.N. delegation headquarters, which was at that time in a small cellar opposite the King David Hotel, because the British wouldn't give them proper quarters. I knew this lunch was important; we were working on the U.N. group to convince them that we *could* establish a state—something they were beginning to doubt due to the fuss the Arabs were making.

I took Lundt to Shiloah's house. Mrs. Shiloah had prepared something—we were under siege at that time and there was very little food. I assumed that Shiloah would still be in the hospital, but suddenly he appeared, looking like the Invisible Man, his face covered entirely in bandages with just holes for his eyes, nose, and mouth. We then had this strange lunch—I remember Shiloah sucking through a straw—and we talked about everything. Then I took Lundt to the remains of the Jewish Agency to show him what had happened, and when we got there, the workers were already rebuilding the wall that had been blown down. This was about three o'clock, and they were already rebuilding....

So he walked around in silence, very moved by the whole experience, and then he looked at me with tears in his eyes—this Norwegian colonel—and said, "People like this can never be beaten."

An oft-told story bears repeating here, because it has great

relevance to the contradictions and conflicts of the accounts
about the fight for Jerusalem that follow.

Sir John Glubb, then known as Glubb Pasha (an Arab title),
had been in Transjordan for some eighteen years but not as a
serving British officer. He had resigned from the British army
when invited by King (then Emir) Abdullah to serve him by
recruiting and training a Bedouin army, which he had done with
notable dedication and success. When the prime minister of
Jordan was sent by Abdullah to confer with the British foreign
secretary, Ernest Bevin, Glubb Pasha accompanied him as
military adviser and interpreter. The situation was put to Bevin
like this:

☐   The Jews, we told him, are very highly organized—they've
     got a shadow government, weapons, an army—whereas the
     Arab population of Palestine has no organization at all;
     they've done nothing about it. Now they're alarmed, and
     they're appealing to Jordan to come and help them. The
     telephone wires are red hot with their appeals. What would
     be the attitude of the British government, we asked, if we
     were to assist these Arabs in the areas allotted to them? And
     Mr. Bevin said, "Our policy is to accept the partition plan.
     As between you and the Arabs in those areas, that rests
     entirely with you. But for heaven's sake, don't go near the
     areas allotted to the Jews." And that was our arrangement—
     to assist the Arabs in the areas allotted to them. And the
     Jordanian government thought it had solved the crisis.

To this day Sir John insists that his Arab Legion scrupu-
lously avoided exceeding the brief outlined above. Yet it is
undeniable that even prior to May 15 it did intervene in certain
actions. One of these was the battle for Ma'ale Ha Hamisha and
Nebi Samwil, mentioned later by Yitzhak Rabin. The other was
the final assault on the long-besieged Jewish settlements of the
Etzion Bloc, which occurred on May 14 and which will be
described in its place.

It is intriguing, incidentally, to note the view of this

professional soldier on the comparative state of preparedness of the Arabs (the local ones at least, and he later makes a similarly deprecating appraisal concerning the regular Arab armies) and the Jews.

By way of contrast with this opinion, historian Netanel Lorch describes the situation one month after the meeting in London of Bevin and Glubb:

☐   In my book I describe it as "the Ides of March." It was the lowest point we reached, in military and political terms, not to speak of morale. Jerusalem was cut off from the coast, the Etzion Bloc was cut off from Jerusalem and so was the Dead Sea potash works. Then western Galilee was cut off. Even the road beween Haifa and Tel Aviv, one of our main communication routes, was under attack at certain points, specifically in the Carmel area.

    The Haganah was basically an organization of the New Yishuv.* Particularly in Jerusalem, there was a great element of the "old" Jews, who, to be honest, were not on the whole attracted by the Haganah; and there were certain Oriental communities whose participation was also minimal. So among those who were active, the casualty rate was frightening.

    Politically, that was when the United States decided that the moment had come to disavow partition and come up with some fairly meaningless trusteeship plan. It was the New Zealand representative at the U.N. General Assembly who voiced our feelings when he said, "What the world needs now is not resolutions, but resolution."

Inevitably, there was a lighter side to these traumas. Regardless of what the Arabs may have believed about Jewish preparedness, the Jews, in fact, were acutely conscious that they

---

*The New Yishuv was that section of the Jewish community that had immigrated to Palestine in the early twentieth century; they were mainly secular socialists.

were short of everything—not only food and weapons but auxiliary supplies—and Haganah personnel were ordered to collect whatever they could long before the British left by whatever techniques seemed likely to be most effective. Dr. Pinchas Blumenthal, a Haganah officer who later became the first director of the English department of Israel's Television Schools Program, remembers one almost farcical incident:

☐   Once I disguised myself as an idiot Arab telephone worker and went into a six-story building occupied by the British and began collecting all their telephones, which the Haganah needed. Every time some Englishman would shout, "Hey, you, what are you doing?" I would respond with imbecile grimaces and mumbles of "No Inglisi."

On the third floor I suddenly came face to face with a man I recognized who was also busy collecting telephones. We stood at opposite ends of a corridor with drawn pistols and I said to him, "I know you—you're my milkman." He said yes, and he was also a member of Etzel, and all the phones in the building were going to his organization.

I said, "Look here, we've got two options. We can divide the building—top three floors for you, bottom three for me, or the other way around, I don't care—or we can shoot it out right here." And he thought about it and said, "You're lucky you met me, an intelligent man." So we settled it and I went on with my collections.

One floor was occupied by an Austrian Jew who was working for the British. He was in possession of the thing I wanted most, an electronic telephone exchange and the special container for transporting it. I just marched in and started dismantling this thing. He made a great fuss, saying, "That's my property!" I said, "I've no time to play around. I'm taking it, and if you care to give me your name and address you might get it back after the war." "Oh, well," he said, "if it's a matter of force—" I told him it was, and I took it.

The crucial importance of such items as communication

equipment, uniforms, and so on is often forgotten in the more dramatic stories concerning the conservation of food or the massing of arms. I make no apology for breaking away from the Jerusalem saga at this point to inject the account given by Teddy Kollek, who was later to be the first mayor of Jerusalem after it was reunited (officially at least) by the Six-Day War. At that time he was in the United States.

☐   We had a delegation of Haganah in the United States, and our primary function, in the beginning, was to try to counteract the exaggerated and silly propaganda of the so-called Bergson Group,* which was doing much more harm than good to our cause. They'd recruited a few loudmouths like Ben Hecht, a few senators, some public-relations people — they'd even opened an "embassy" in Washington in a large, expensive house and raised a lot of money, not in order to do anything real but to make a noise. They sent one illegal immigrant ship and made sure to publicize it, even though they knew that publicity meant the people would be caught by the British blockade. That illustrates the difference at that time between the Revisionist ideology and tactics and those of the Labor groups. *We* tried to tell the facts as they were.

   After November, we started getting hold of war matériel—not so much arms as auxiliary matériel, of which vast quantities had just become available as war surplus: anything from canteens to shoes, uniforms, machinery, and especially communications equipment. At the same time we were still in the business of buying ships for illegal immigration and sending them to Europe to pick up people, and only gradually we got into the purchase of arms, components, explosives.... Later we started with light aircraft, taking off their wings and packing them and sending them out as prefabricated houses or agricultural machinery.

   And then we thought we should actually go in for

---

*A group of Palestinian and non-Palestinian young men active in the United States from 1939–48 in connection with Zionist causes.

collecting arms. Many people had brought home souvenirs
from the war, small machine guns, pistols, and so on. Jewish
ex-servicemen gave up these souvenirs gladly—hundreds
and hundreds of small arms, which we shipped under one
cover or another. A lot of other surplus we also got free
because there were a lot of highly motivated Jewish scrap
merchants around. The planes we had to pay for, and the
warehousing, collecting, packing, and shipping.

You couldn't purchase arms openly in the States, as our
agents could in Mexico. As it was we had the FBI treading
on our tails all the time, particularly with regard to
recruiting personnel, for example "Mickey" Marcus. He'd
been to West Point, he'd been in the Military Government in
Germany.... He was not very involved in Israeli affairs, but
he had friends who were, and who knew what we were
looking for—some leadership talent, someone to train our
boys in more organized warfare techniques.... We met him.
He took a bit of persuading, but in the end, he came over.

We were followed about by the FBI: We couldn't make
calls from our hotels, only from phone booths. We were
"investigated" to the point where several of our people had
to leave the U.S. We set up a whole security system to enable
us to carry on. The people who purchased the planes slept at
a different hotel every night.... It was really "hot pursuit."

To return to Jerusalem. What Yitzhak Rabin dubbed the
war on communication lines was in full swing, the main priority
being to maintain the link between Jerusalem and the coast. This
could not be done efficiently except by capturing the villages and
strongpoints that overlooked the wadi road and provided ideal
strategical emplacements from which to disrupt traffic. The
operation, code-named Nachshon (after the biblical character
who was the first to enter the Red Sea when its waters parted
during the exodus), was the first "open" military operation
undertaken by the Haganah, and responsibility for it was
assigned to Rabin and his Har El commandos.

☐   The convoy system broke down in the middle of March.

Then we had to face a new phase of the war, when a big force was concentrated for the first time for the first offensive operation—to break the siege on the road to Jerusalem.

At that period, the attacks on us were made by a relatively small nucleus of Palestinian groups. Whenever they attacked, they mobilized men of the villages for one, two, or three days of fighting. Then most of the villagers used to go back to their normal work. The only way to secure the road was to prevent the existence of villages adjacent to it. They were not villages in the real sense. They were, in practice, bases for the attacks on the convoys.

One of the first villages—and it was a real village, not a mere "base"—to be captured, after a fierce battle, was Kastel. Now a well-known writer, then a very young private, Yoram Kaniuk describes it as a "huge village. Today you can only see one house on the top, as you go into Jerusalem . . . a strongpoint, from which our convoys were being devastated." It had changed hands several times, with heavy loss of life on both sides, before it finally fell to the Jews at the beginning of the second week in the month of April.

☐   We had a big fight, and we won. After the battle, the Palmach had to leave to fight somewhere else, so some soldiers were brought from Jerusalem to hold the village in case of another counterattack; but a small group of us— about five men—were left to guard this new lot so that they wouldn't run away.

They were just rabble—raw newcomers. Although I'd only been in the army a few months, I was already a veteran. Really, we'd had so many battles, almost every night, we'd become old-timers . . . . So we were guarding them when the Arabs counterattacked.

These Jerusalem boys started running away, and we were left, four or five of us up there, and we started shooting wildly, without aim. In order to get us out, HQ sent some thirty-five guys up to help us. Some of the best fighters of the Palmach, most of them officers. By this time we were surrounded on our hilltop, just shooting in all directions, and without knowing it, we killed a very important Arab leader, Abdel Kader Husseini, a relative of the mufti.

The death of Abdel Kader Husseini was an important turning point in the struggle, for it seriously affected the morale of the local irregulars who, until then, had been fighting in fierce, if spasmodic and uncoordinated, opposition to Jewish attempts to fulfill the objectives of Operation Nachshon. Accounts of his death vary wildly and may be cited as a typical example of how accounts of important events contradict each other.

Netanel Lorch writes in *The Edge of the Sword* that Kader was approaching a central strongpoint, thinking it empty, when he was gunned down by a Jewish machine gunner. An Arabist (an Israeli) to whom I showed the following account by Kaniuk pooh-poohed it, saying, "Kader wasn't killed by us at all. One of his own men shot him during the battle; it was some long-standing feud." Professor Howard Sachar, an American Middle East expert, avers that all these accounts are "palpably false," that Kader was "shot in the act of surrender, much to Ben-Gurion's embarrassment."

Here is Kaniuk's version, which I give in detail because he claims to have witnessed the event:

We looked down and we saw a man in a *kefiya* [red Arab headscarf] with bandoliers across his chest, walking about with his men and shooting, so we shot at them. None of us knew exactly who shot him, but we saw him fall. Later one of the commanders had me on the radio as the man who killed him; it was a turning point in the war—when the news got around among the local Palestinians that he was dead, they lost heart and a lot of them left—from Katamon, for instance. It's not really important whose bullet killed him. I wish it were not mine.

Then these thirty-five Palmach officers reached us and one of them gave an order that became famous. He said that the privates should retreat and officers would cover them.

And so we ran, and the officers were nearly all killed up
there, in order to let the five of us go.

In the immediate aftermath of the struggle for Kastel, a
nearby village called Deir Yassin came under attack. This
incident has had such repercussions and has caused such
controversy that the best course seems to be to give two accounts.
The first account, which is the fullest and gives the background, is
that of Meir Pa'il, soldier, historian, and politician.

☐   I took part as an observer in the Deir Yassin operation of the
Irgun and Stern group. I wrote the official report of that
action.

   We [the Haganah] knew about it. So I took one of my
people with a camera and I took a tommy gun and I joined
the attackers. I saw the whole attack. I even saw the
massacre. I tried to prevent it.

   Why did the Etzel and the Sternists decide to attack this
village? They saw things were beginning to develop. Kastel
was taken by the Fourth Battalion of the Palmach. Some
Arab villages were occupied on the other side, not far from
Hulda, and the Nachshon operation to clear the heights
around Bab el Wad had begun around the 5th or 6th of
April.

   They wanted to do something in Jerusalem. The
initiative came from the Stern group. They approached
Irgun, and they joined forces, but the maximum they could
assemble was a hundred and thirty people. They thought
about what to do and decided to raid Deir Yassin, which no
one asked them to do anyway.

   When they came to the commander of the Haganah in
Jerusalem, David Shaltiel, they asked him for some auth-
orization or permission. He said, "Why should you go to
Deir Yassin? We have no troubles with them. If you want to
help us, all right, why don't you raid Ein Karem? It's very
important for us, because Arabs from Ein Karem are raiding
our people in Kastel." And they responded that it was too

difficult for them to do. Then he asked, "Why not raid a much smaller and closer Arab village, not far from Metza, called Colonia? They are shooting our transport on the road." They said that, too, was too difficult. They insisted on going to Deir Yassin.

David Shaltiel really had no choice at that point. He saw he couldn't stop them. So he said to them, "Okay, you have permission, *but* you should know that we've had no trouble with these Arabs till now. Our idea is that when the British go, we will seize the village, let the Arabs stay there, and then build an airfield. If you must raid the village, I insist that you stay on and hold it; because if you just raid and evacuate, the Arabs will have a moral justification to open hostilities against us."

On Friday, April 9th, the attack began, and I joined them. What was my idea? I didn't know of course that there would be a massacre, but I wanted to get some estimate of these irregulars' combat capabilities. Because we knew that sooner or later we'd either have to fight against them or incorporate them into the Israel Defense Forces. So I decided it was worthwhile to go along and observe them, and then report to the Haganah on their units and what they could do, fighting in the field. They performed very badly. Altogether apart from the massacre, my report on their military capabilities was very negative.

They tried to attack the village. They didn't succeed. Even though the villagers were not prepared. First, they came late. Instead of attacking by night, they came by day. They just managed to occupy the eastern half of the village; they couldn't occupy the higher, western side. Some Arabs, around ten or twelve, shot at them, using only rifles, no automatic weapons, and pinned them down on the eastern side.

Then they sent someone to the Shneller* camp. They

---

*An orphanage taken over and used by the Haganah, chiefly as a training center.

woke up a Palmach company commander named Yakki*
and asked for support, for help. So Yakki came with a
platoon and occupied the rest of the village in a few minutes,
without a single casualty, in a professional manner. When I
saw Yakki, I said to him, "Yakki, you know we have a saying
in Yiddish, *Varf sich avek*—get away from here. Don't get
mixed up with this Irgun and Stern group. Go home and go
to sleep." Because he and his company, that same night, had
already mounted a raid on Ein Karem, they were very tired.
So they withdrew.

And when the Palmachniks had gone away, the Stern
group and the Irgun began what I'd call an uncontrolled
looting and massacre performance. Just...groups went
from house to house, and looted, and shot people. Mostly
women, kids, and older men, because most of the younger
ones had escaped. They even took about twenty-five grown
males and put them on a truck and made a small parade
through some quarters of Jerusalem and back, and put them
in a line in some kind of quarry, and shot them. I saw it and
the man who was with me photographed it.

I tried to find the commanders to say, "Why should you
do it?" But they wouldn't listen—either because they
couldn't control it, or they let their people do it, claiming,
you know, that the Arabs deserved it.

It was midafternoon before some people arrived from
Givat Shaul—just Jews, citizens, who were ashamed. They
began to shout and cry, and then the massacre was stopped.

Then they took the villagers who were left, two
hundred, two hundred and fifty, and put them on trucks and
drove them through Jerusalem, and put them on the Bab el
Damesek [the road north from the Damascus Gate]—this
was Friday evening—mostly old people, women, and children. And then on Saturday evening I went and wrote my
report and sent it to Israel Galili with the film. And that

---

*This and most other names mentioned are the first or nicknames of the
fighters. Even between officers and men, only first names were ever used.

report is still in the files. I didn't keep a copy in my pocket.... In this report, I told the whole story and delivered my opinion of their combat abilities, which was very negative.

On Friday evening, the Stern/Irgun group informed Shaltiel that they intended to evacuate the village on Sunday morning, the 11th. They boasted: "We are assault troops. It is not our function to act as a garrison. We are leaving."

Shaltiel reminded them that they had promised that if they went ahead with the raid they would hold the village. "I have no other company to do it. You made the raid, so you are causing us quite a lot of damage." They wouldn't listen.

On the morning they left, David Shaltiel sent around a hundred young people from the *Gadna*—cadets aged seventeen—to hold the village. And they discovered the bodies. The attacking force had done nothing to conceal them. It was terrible. It was these young people who counted the bodies—about two hundred and fifty, mostly old people, women, and kids. They died by shooting or by grenades which were thrown into the building *after* the village had been conquered. So the victims had not been fighting. Which meant, two hundred and fifty killed, two hundred and fifty taken out, and two hundred and fifty just fled— mainly men.

To stand against such a damning indictment as Pa'il's it is only fair to give at length an account of another eyewitness—a member of the Lehi force that attacked the village. Ezra Yachin, then a committed young terrorist, now a mild-mannered art-gallery owner who is as convinced as ever that all his actions in those days were ideologically sound and politically justified, tells his story:

☐ It was spring, 1948, and we were at war with the Arabs in Jerusalem. This was not a conventional war between armies as we know it today, but a battle between civilians. Day by day many people whom we knew personally were either hurt or killed by the Arabs—wherever Jews and Arabs lived in neighboring areas. The Arabs used their own homes as bases, coming out to control the roads and using their rooftops from which to shoot at any Jewish target: perhaps a man on his way to work, a woman going to market, or a child on his way to school or out at play.

Hiding behind walls was no way for us to defend ourselves. We had to attack, which meant sabotaging Arab houses. When we began to do that, Arabs evacuated Romema, Lifta, and Sheikh Bader; the Jews from the north of Jerusalem left their homes too.

We knew that we would have to capture Arab villages, as a way of breaking the siege of Jerusalem. The Haganah took Kastel only after many fierce and bitter battles. After that, a group of Lehi men were called to a meeting and told of the plan to conquer the village called Deir Yassin.

One of our Lehi commanders informed us that manpower and arms were seriously limited and that our underground methods of hit-and-run warfare were totally inadequate for capturing positions of importance. That is why our organization contacted the Irgun and the Haganah and discussed with them the issue of Deir Yassin. The Irgun agreed to cooperate with us and to take every precaution against hurting women and children.

We were very worried about how this could be managed. A loudspeaker warning system was suggested, though we believed that this would jeopardize our chances of success by removing the element of surprise.

We met again that evening for final instructions and the distribution of weapons. The Lehi had a workshop for manufacturing explosives, enough for both ourselves and the Irgun. But the shortage of submachine guns and rifles could not be overcome. At about that time, the Irgun started producing their own submachine guns, although the lack of ammunition meant that its mechanism had to be altered to fire only one shot at a time, but we were not told about that. Of course, this put limits on the efficacy of the action. We were not told, either, that the guns were untested and that the alteration meant that many of them were not even functioning. There was no time to check, and the fact is, they were not checked at all. I personally got a new American rifle—a carbine—one of two that reached Jerusalem.

The attack would come from three directions: the Irgun from the south, another, with both Irgun and Lehi fighters, from the north, while a smaller group would approach by the unasphalted "main" road. This latter group would come behind an armored car equipped with the loudspeaker. I was with that group.

Our HQ was based at Givat Shaul. We were to move off from there at about 2 A.M., expecting to have to clear road-blocks and fill in trenches en route, which we knew would take time. The tension kept us wide awake. Shortly after leaving Givat Shaul for Deir Yassin, our path was blocked by a trench that had been dug by the Arabs. We had to use our hands and helmets for the job of refilling it with sand, earth, and stones. We smoothed it over and went on but had the same time-consuming job to do again some sixty or seventy meters farther on. Dawn was just breaking when we approached the village, so we left the third trench unfilled, hoping that the loudspeaker would be heard from the spot where we found ourselves.

The shooting started up from the direction of the group heading in from the south. One of our comrades, who was born in Iraq and knew Arabic, used the loudspeaker to annouce to the Arabs that we did not want to fight them or hurt them in any way and that they should come out of their houses.

Now, I can't say if the villagers really heard his words, but the noise woke them and they opened fire on us. Some of our boys and girls were hit immediately; one boy was killed outright.

We took refuge behind some stone walls, but our leader, Dror, objected strongly to this, insisting we had come to take the place, not to defend ourselves. "Who's ready to join me and get into the village, despite the shooting?" he asked. Two Etzel fighters and others from Lehi, including myself, joined Dror and moved on. None of us had the slightest experience of open warfare, but common sense informed me that it must be almost the exact opposite to underground methods by which you hide while attacking and then run away. In this new form of attack, you must run forward into the fray.

Dror repeatedly saved my life, telling me, "Listen, that's no way to fight. Crouch down beside a wall until you discover where the snipers are ... but I'll look after that for now." We exchanged weapons because he was a very good sniper—I gave him my carbine and he gave me his Sten. His bravery was exemplary. It worried me, though, because he drew Arab fire toward himself while shooting at two snipers. Dror urged me to move up into a winding alley, and on doing so I came face to face with an Arab armed with a rifle. Instantly he started to release the bolt.

The measure of those fearful seconds! Who would shoot first? Who would survive? It was I who pulled the trigger first ... but it didn't work. My foe turned to leap over an old wall, and as he did so he shot at me. I felt a pain in my right thigh and I thought I must be hit. Once, in a skirmish with the British, a bullet had penetrated my left thigh but I had been unaware of it for a while. This time I examined my leg. It was in quite good shape, and only a slight scar remains now.

Dror had clambered up onto a rooftop from where he was able to spot my assailant who was dressed in the uniform of an Iraqi officer—and shot him. At that, another Arab appeared and started to pull away the dead man's rifle, only to run off when he saw me approach. Thus a much-needed rifle came into my hands.

We pressed on, clearing out a group of houses in the center of the village, trying constantly to get in touch with the boys who remained in the rear, fully realizing that if we didn't move forward we would be surrounded. We resolved this by placing two Etzel comrades inside a house to observe whether the Arabs would try to surround us.

Now there were only three of us, and we wanted to maintain control of the road. We waited under great stress to see how things would develop. Why didn't the others come?... We heard Hebrew voices nearby.... Two Etzel boys with the news that we might have to cease fighting, as ammunition was running low. Our frustration was complete. What, withdraw, just as Dror, Giora, and I had gained control of the village center? We sent the Etzel boys back to HQ, hoping that the news of our success would change their decision. It did, and we were instructed to stay where we were until the others joined us. Fortunately, we also found some cases of ammunition in the abandoned houses which enabled us to keep fighting until eventually the village fell to us.

Even so, the battle was far from over. Many of the villagers had run up into the hilly areas where they took up strategic positions and shot at us for many hours—right through till midnight, or even later till the following morning. But at about midnight a few of us were recalled to HQ, where a good few unarmed Lehi fighters were waiting to take over our weapons and relieve us. There were about a hundred of them in all—we hadn't enough arms for them.

When we were relieved, I and my group went back to Givat Shaul to tend the wounded and get some rest. There I met and spoke to some comrades who had fought in different sections of the village and learned about the fierce struggles for each house. To take a house, you had either to throw a grenade or shoot your way into it. If you were foolish enough to attempt to open doors, you got shot down—sometimes by men dressed up as women, shooting out at you in a second of surprise. I also heard about the *mukhtar's* house —a difficult place to capture. The firing went on interminably until at last the Palmach came to assist with machine guns and then the house fell to us. It's true their arrival helped us and undoubtedly saved some lives;

but that's not to say we couldn't have captured the village without their help.

It's hard to remember exactly how long we stayed in Deir Yassin and when the evacuation orders were received. The British were getting ready to bombard the village, because they knew the Lehi and Etzel fighters were there— we heard their plan from our intelligence.

We asked the Haganah to take over control, on the premise that the British would not bomb *them*, but surprisingly they had received orders to obstruct our evacuation and to shoot at us if we tried to leave the village. But the Haganah boys refused to do it.

Most of the male villagers had gone into the hills, so we gathered together those taken prisoner, mostly women and children with a few men among them. They were put into trucks and deported to the Arab side of Jerusalem, near the Jaffa Gate [*sic,* actually the Damascus Gate]. We had no suitable arrangements for holding prisoners. Later on, we heard that it was not at all an easy situation to control. When the trucks arrived in the city, many of the Jews in the Mahaneh Yehuda district wanted to get at the prisoners, and our boys had a tough time protecting them.

In the battle for Deir Yassin, almost all the fighters, mostly Lehi people, suffered wounds. One of them was killed, and so were three Irgun members.

Our feeling was that we would be acclaimed for our action. The bitterness that existed between the disparate organizations was bound to fade following the Palmach's great assistance to us. We were united now—in the same boat.

More painful than all our struggles against the British had been the knowledge that many Jews, chiefly the Zionist establishment, opposed us for political reasons. We felt sure that having thrown ourselves into the battle on behalf of our people, they would now support us and accept us.

And actually when we evacuated Deir Yassin, the whole population hailed us. When our trucks reached

Romema and other districts, our people saw us and realized where we were coming from.

But shortly after—the next day—we read the papers and listened to the radio describing us as cruel people. The British criticized us similarly and supported the Arabs all the way. Our own political leaders apologized for us and even campaigned against us—a harsh campaign, showing us up as the most awful types of people. Before the action to take the village they had decided it was most important to the Jews to capture Deir Yassin. Strategic plans had been drawn up by them, involving the creation of a small air base near the village. All the more reason, then, for us to be shocked and agonized by their campaign of vilification against us.

I must say here that we were most affected by the deaths of the women and children in the village. We had not initiated that awful war, one that endangered the existence of the Jews in this land. The Arabs continuously announced their intention to destroy us. Their newspapers and broadcasts were full of it. And remember, it was less than three years since the Holocaust. And here were the Arabs saying they were going to carry on with what Germany started.

Our very lives were at stake. I told you I worked in the post office. The Arabs who worked there with me were friendly enough until war broke out, and then they suddenly changed. I couldn't believe I was looking at the same human beings. They would look at us and make the gesture that suggests the ritual slaughter of animals for human consumption, saying "You wanted a state..."

I remember being horribly shocked when an Arab came in to work smiling broadly right after a Jewish woman, her child, and her baby in its carriage had been killed by a grenade. These Arabs worked alongside us and yet they were happy to show their feelings of pride in such killings. They threatened to take our homes and kill us and take our sisters and wives for themselves. These threats the Arabs then shamelessly reversed, turning them into foul accusations against the Jews, saying we did to them all that they had imagined doing to us.

As to the propaganda that our enemies have made of the action, till today, I can say with conviction that if it were not Deir Yassin, they would find something else, like Kibya,* done by the Jews. The same sort of thing happened when the Palmach seized enemy territory in areas where the Arabs did not run off before the arrival of their conquerors. The Palmach also killed women and children, but Deir Yassin has become *the* name used in propaganda because it was the first shock—the first time we had made a real conquest. A reason for reviling the Jews can always be found by those determined to look for one.

So far as I know there was no random killing of civilians after the village fell to us, and all the other atrocity stories are lies.

It should be pointed out here that even Meir Pa'il, whose account is so much at variance with Yachin's as far as the massacre was concerned, refutes the tales of rape and butchery that have appeared in such books as *O Jerusalem!* and that regularly recur in Arab propaganda. "It was a hot-blooded not a cold-blooded massacre," he said, "but there was no rape or mutilation." (It is worth noting that notwithstanding all the blood-curdling threats beforehand and the subsequent highly colored stories, there is no single authenticated case of rape on either side in this war.)

Meir Pa'il's response to the rest of the Revisionist denials, past and present, is as follows:

☐ Now for what the Irgun said happened. The idea was to bring up a loudspeaker to tell the people to flee, but first of all it didn't reach the village. Not that that is important, because if you are beginning to shoot, no one hears a loudspeaker. Then they claimed they met heavy opposition, but there was very little—it was an easy job, as proved by the

---

*Kibya is an Arab border village that suffered a retaliatory attack by Israeli commandos in 1953. Some sixty-seven villagers died when their homes were blown up.

fact that in broad daylight twenty-five Palmachniks occupied the stronger, western side of the village without even
one soldier wounded.

Then they said they took a lot of casualties, which
inflamed them. Nonsense. They had four dead only, and
some wounded, not many. [The Irgun says "forty casualties
out of a hundred men, four fatal."]

I wrote to Galili, "If you ask me for my explanation for
these people's behavior, why they did this whole bloody
massacre, I think this is the outcome of twenty years of
Revisionist education." They killed British, they killed
Arabs, they put bombs in Arab markets—it is part of the
Revisionist pattern. They put two bombs in the Jaffa Gate
and one in the Damascus Gate—in the market. In the
beginning. It was their style. I think our best stance with
regard to Deir Yassin morally is to claim that it is not *our*
pattern to do these kinds of things; it is the Irgun's and the
Lehi's pattern. They were dissidents, they didn't obey
orders—it was their style, and they were the minority.

On the propaganda side, an interesting sidelight is given by
an ex-Lehi member, Mattityahu Shmuelevitch. Although he did
not take part in these events, being confined to a British detention
camp for terrorist activities at the time, he has spent the last few
years refuting accusations against the Likud* as part of his job as
director of the Prime Minister's office.

☐   What made Deir Yassin "Deir Yassin," I would say, was
     what we call "the war among Jews." The Jewish Agency,
     before the following elections, for political reasons wanted
     to blacken the name of the Irgun and condemn their way of
     killing women and children at Deir Yassin. So this spread
     through the world as the truth, starting with the Jewish
     Agency. Later, the Israeli government—not the present

*The Likud is the present ruling party of Israel, the political descendants of
the Revisionists.

Likud administration but the previous Labor Parliament—
had to issue a booklet telling exactly what happened. There
were witnesses, people from Deir Yassin telling the truth
about what happened—immediately afterwards in Jordan.
You can find it in libraries, in documents, witnesses who say
exactly what happened.

It was not the reason for the flight of the Arabs. What
caused that was the Kawukji issued a call to them to leave
their homes to clear the way for Kawukji's men to kill the
Jews, and that in two weeks they could come back to their
homes, and to Jewish homes. And it's a very funny thing
that both the prime minister then—Ben-Gurion—and the
prime minister now—Begin—issued calls to the Arabs not
to leave, that nobody was going to harm them if they didn't
fight. Those are the historical facts, and it's very easy to
certify them.

The question Matti Shmuelevitch raises, about whether the
Deir Yassin incident caused the flight of many Arabs, is an
important one, for Menachem Begin, in his book *The Revolt,*
disagrees with the director of his office. He writes:

> Throughout the Arab world and the world at large, a wave
> of lying propaganda was let loose about "Jewish
> atrocities"... designed to besmirch our name. In the result it
> helped us. Panic overwhelmed the Arabs of Eretz Israel.
> Arabs began to flee in terror, even before they clashed with
> Jewish forces. Not what happened in Deir Yassin, but what
> was invented about Deir Yassin, helped to carve the way to
> our decisive victories on the battlefield. The legend... helped
> us in particular in the saving of Tiberias and the conquest
> of Haifa.

Meir Pa'il contradicts:

☐   It's said that this atrocity caused a large number of Arabs to
     flee. It's not so. I made some research within a radius of ten

miles around Deir Yassin. If this theory is right, why didn't
the people of Abu Ghosh take fright and fly? Take Ein
Karem. They should have "learned their lesson" and fled.
We had to fight harshly against them later. And Malka, Beit
Iksa, Colonia, Nebi Samwil, Sheikh Jerach; we had a lot of
trouble with them.

　　So even in the close vicinity, it wasn't so simple. The
story that because of Deir Yassin Arabs were beginning to
run—excuse me! That is a story maintained and stressed by
Arab propaganda on one side and Mr. Begin's propaganda
on the other. His assertion that this horror story was useful
in clearing out the Arabs is garbage. Real garbage.

More will be said about the refugee problem later. But one
thing Deir Yassin undoubtedly did do was to give the local Arabs
a rallying cry. It was first used a few days later when a convoy of
doctors, nurses, and patients heading for the Hadassah hospital
on Mount Scopus was ambushed.

　　Chaim Herzog, in his role as liaison officer between the
Jewish authorities and the British, was, as he puts it, "ineffective,
unfortunately," in trying to save the Hadassah convoy.

☐　Between seventy and eighty people were massacred in full
　　view of Jerusalem. The British forces were two hundred
　　yards away from them and they wouldn't move. I was there
　　all the time, urging and begging them to do something. They
　　kept saying that they would deal with it, and it would be all
　　right....Of course, we didn't exactly realize what was
　　happening; we knew the medical staff were holed up in these
　　vehicles but we didn't know they were gradually being killed.
　　You could see from the rooftops the smoke and so on, and
　　the British were quite nearby—they allowed this massacre to
　　take place. Afterward we had a great deal to say. We accused
　　them of every vile purpose. But it didn't help very much. I
　　told them it was sheer murder—by this time the relationship
　　was bitter, terribly bitter.

Netanel Lorch witnessed the incident too:

☐   One of my most shocking experiences was standing up on the Schneller tower, an observation post, watching from a distance of twelve or thirteen hundred yards how the Hadassah convoy was going up in flames, and this feeling of impotence. With good field glasses you could see very precisely what was happening, and there was absolutely nothing you could do about it. We didn't even have a machine gun with that range. It was deeply demoralizing.

This was the first, but not the last, occasion on which attacking Arabs used "Deir Yassin!" as their battle cry.

Meanwhile, Operation Nachshon was continuing. Two brief accounts by those who were there give a strong "feel" of the fighting. Menachem Roussak,* a member of Kibbutz Na'an, who was a Har El commander under Rabin:

☐   We were posted on both sides of the road in the hills. We had no artillery at all at that time; only after the first cease-fire did we get our first guns. The Jordanians were shelling us with cannon, and from the air the British were helping them direct their aim—their artillery officers were British, too.

During a heavy barrage, we suddenly had to abandon one of the hills. It was at the back of us, on the Jerusalem side, and it seemed that the Arabs would cut us off from Jerusalem and we would be isolated. We had a choice, either to say "All is lost" or to stand and fight.

Everything depended on us. If we retreated, Jerusalem would be cut off and heavily besieged. We were responsible for the safety of 100,000 people. These were difficult moments—to decide, and then to explain to our people who didn't know the situation. We explained to them that if they

*Not to be confused with Moshe Rousnak, Halperin's replacement in the Old City.

could hold out a bit longer.... And, in fact, after two days the Arabs were pushed back and all the strongpoints were again in our hands.

Here is what Uri Avneri, then a private soldier and now editor of the satirical weekly *Ha'olam Hazeh* and a left-wing member of the 9th Knesset, remembers:

☐   My first major fighting was in the Nachshon operation. It was the job of my brigade, Givati, to open the road from the coastal plain, past Hulda and Na'an, and meet Har El, which was doing the same going west.

All our battles among the Arab villages along the route were fought at night. We dared not engage the enemy by day at the beginning, because we had no artillery or anything like it—it was all close combat, meaning that you were generally only a matter of a few dozen yards from the enemy and in eye contact with your own side.

This kind of fighting puts a premium on the small unit, even on the individual soldier, and it suited the Palmach ideology. The man is important, not the mass. A section — eight or nine people—was important. I remember how proud I was when I became a section leader in the middle of the war. Today a section leader is nothing—a joke. Anyone below a lieutenant colonel is nobody. There's a different kind of class structure now, because of it. Much worse, if you believe in an ideology, in equality, in humanism.

Anyway, we opened the way to Jerusalem for a few days. I was on the last big convoy that passed unmolested before the road was cut again around Passover, '48.

Ben-Gurion was also on that convoy; according to Rabin, "he wanted to be there" (in Jerusalem). Rabin, however, did not.

☐   Unfortunately, we were not given enough time. I had managed to bring three big convoys of supplies into Jerusalem, and then I was ordered to move into the city with my brigade and to abandon the maintenance of the free road. I believed then that it was wrong to decide about it, because we were in the process of clearing the area adjacent to the road on both sides, north and south.

But the information was that the British might accelerate their timetable of withdrawal, especially from Jerusalem. In those days the key strategic positions in Jerusalem were held by the British, and any evacuation, without the presence of effective forces there, could not be accepted by the Jewish community because they might be taken over by the Arab forces. No doubt this could have resulted in the whole situation in Jerusalem changing to our detriment.

His unease at leaving Operation Nachshon incomplete was justified. As soon as the Har El Brigade withdrew, the Arabs retook a number of the strategic high points and reestablished the blockade. Jerusalem was cut off again on April 20. The Har El Brigade, having been prematurely withdrawn from their road-clearing operation, was now given the task of securing Jerusalem. Yitzhak Rabin:

☐   This operation had the code name "Yevusi." A special headquarters commanded by Yitzhak Sadeh* was formed under which my brigade had to serve. Har El had to carry out most of the offensive operations and I was asked to present a plan of how to take Jerusalem. I offered a plan after wasting four or five days, believing that the British would evacuate, but they did not.

The idea was to have a pincer operation from north to south; first to capture the northern part of Jerusalem, to link with the Hadassah hospital and the university on Mount Scopus; then to continue to Augusta Victoria and to Malkia to the road that leads to Jerusalem from Jericho. We had to

---

*Sadeh was one of the original founders of the Palmach, a much-loved commander known affectionately as "The Old Man." He died shortly after the war.

capture the St. Simone monastery in Katamon to have a link with the Jewish quarters such as Ramat Rachel, and to close the northern and southern pincers.

This plan was submitted and approved by Yitzhak Sadeh and Ben-Gurion. Before that, we started with the preliminary action which was intended to capture Nebi Samwil and Beit Chanina and to create a link to Neve Yaacov, which was in our hands even though isolated from Jerusalem. This operation didn't succeed, because there was a delay in the attack of the Fourth Battalion. The Arab Legion, stationed at the radar station between Ma'ale Ha Hamisha and Nebi Samwil, took part in the action. That came as a surprise to us because they were supposed to be under British orders. We lost forty-four killed and many more wounded. No doubt it affected the capability of the Fourth Battalion for a while.

Then we turned back to the real operation. The Fifth Battalion captured Sheikh Jerach and a link was created to the Hadassah hospital and Mount Scopus positions. But the British put an immediate ultimatum to the Jewish Agency that we had to evacuate—our presence would endanger their line of withdrawal.

"Boaz" was a member of the Fifth Battalion—one of the few of that heavily decimated contingent who came through the war safely. He tells the full story of the Sheikh Jerach action and its sequel.

☐   You know the business with the Hadassah convoy, when the Arabs killed the doctors and nurses in an ambush. Well, those men had been based in a district to the north of the Old City called Sheikh Jerach, which was in any case an area we needed, so we were ordered to take it over.

This time it wasn't enough for me to carry my full pack and rifle; they said I could be the sapper's assistant and carry the dynamite—fifteen kilos of it in a sack on my shoulders. Fortunately his English was good so he was able to tell me exactly when I was allowed to pick it up for him.

However, beforehand we had a party. It must have been Pesach [Passover] because I remember some local rabbi came and conducted a Seder [Passover service] of sorts— quite a feast we had—sardines, jam, a morsel of bully beef, and some sweet lemonade, all in meager quantities. At the end there was a drop of wine in which to drink to the coming battle.

We waited, as usual, till dusk, then got onto the trucks which drove us to the outskirts of Jewish Jerusalem. Then we got started. We had to be dead quiet because we had to pass by a big British camp. They must have got wind of us somehow because they were combing the whole area with huge searchlights. Every time we saw one coming we froze— they couldn't see us unless we moved. The fifteen kilos of dynamite on my back made it easier to keep my head down; it also made me sweat, and during the stops the cold turned my sweat to ice. Freezing when the searchlights hit us became no mere figure of speech.

When we'd passed the camp we had to cross a main road, along which a British armored car was patrolling. Every time it went by, a little group of us would dash across. Dash I couldn't, but I *shlepped* across somehow, and soon we were in Sheikh Jerach.

It was occupied by some Iraqi troops and the local irregulars. They had their base in an unfinished building, which the Nashashibi family was having built for themselves on the hillside—it was just a huge concrete shell, with unglazed window holes, but it had a door which we had to blow in, so my moment as sapper's mate had come. We had to approach it ahead of the others. The sapper hissed, "Come on, quick!" and dashed forward. Easy for him, all he had to carry was a revolver. I lurched after him with the dynamite. We came under fire from the defenders of the place, who started shooting into the cornfield where we'd all been crouched.

We got up to the door and I dumped my load and, with rifle and pack suddenly light as a feather, tripped across to where the rest of the boys had moved, leaving the sapper to blow open the villa doors. At that, quite a few of the defenders leaped out of window holes and made off, but a few were left inside—as we burst in, we could see them running up the bare concrete stairs from floor to floor above us. We potted at them with rifles and lobbed a couple of our ultimate weapon—two-inch mortar shells—onto the roof. That was enough for them. They came down and surrendered to us and were hustled off somewhere; I don't remember exactly what happened to them.

Then there was a lull in the fighting; we'd captured this huge building and some others nearby. Most of them seemed to be palatial villas, presumably summer residences belonging to the Arab nobility from places like Damascus and Baghdad. They were empty of course. We did the usual, blew open the doors of any houses we thought might be sheltering snipers, and then gathered in the Nashashibi building for a nap.

We were roused by the arrival of a British officer, a captain I think, who came to tell us we had to get out at once. Our commander, naturally, refused. The captain said he'd be back in the evening. Meanwhile our commander got in touch with our HQ, and I believe it went right to the top, right to Ben-Gurion, who ordered us to hang on to Sheikh Jerach and not to budge.

When the captain came back he wasn't as friendly as before, especially when he heard that we weren't going to move. This time he brought an ultimatum—we were to get out by that evening or they'd drive us out.

So at nightfall we took up our positions. The first thing that hit us was their searchlights—one particularly powerful one was mounted on the YMCA tower—and then we heard the sounds of heavy armor coming toward us. You wouldn't believe what they threw at us—you'd have thought they were facing a full panzer division. There must have been a whole regiment, complete with three tanks, Bren-gun carriers, troop carriers, armored cars—the lot. They even brought up a field kitchen.

They surrounded the villa with this lot, and shouted at us to surrender.

I was up on the third floor with two of my friends. One of them was a boy called Yitzhak. He was one of those who always stood by me in the lines during night attacks to translate the orders—we'd been together from the beginning. We were crouched in a dark corner of a balcony, keeping out of the searchlight beam.

When nobody came out, the British opened up with the most fantastic barrage. Cannons, mortar, machine guns —it sounded as if they were trying to raze the whole building to the ground. It seems absurd now, when you think we were only armed with rifles and Stens. They kept the whole place lit up with searchlights so that they could shoot at anything they spotted moving through the window holes. Fortunately the walls were about a foot thick.

What I didn't realize was that as soon as this bombardment began, our officer ordered a withdrawal and got most of the men out through the back, through some holes in the fence, and somehow, with the help of somebody who knew the city, back to our lines. The only ones left were people like me who hadn't been on the ground floor when it all broke loose.

So there we were, the three of us, crouched in this dark corner, while shells and hand grenades burst all around us. And then Yitzhak began to panic. It seemed impossible that we wouldn't be killed. He wanted to make a run for it, to get downstairs, and urged me to come with him. I hung on to him and told him not to move, but he broke away and dashed for the stairway. Of course, in one second he was caught in cross fire and I saw him drop.

Just at that moment, the British commander must have realized that something was missing from the battle. There was no return fire. So he called a halt to the barrage. The searchlights went out. An incredible darkness and silence fell.

The moment the lights went off I ran to where I'd seen Yitzhak fall. I could see he was badly hit; he was unconscious. I shouted down the stairs, *"Khovesh! Khovesh!"*—I knew that much Hebrew, it meant a male nurse. There was no answer—I suppose they were halfway back to the Jewish city by then. So I ran down the stairs and to my amazement, instead of the whole hundred or so of our group, I found just a handful of them, poking their heads out from under the staircase where they'd been sheltering. I thought at first all the rest must have been killed.

There was still a corporal in charge, and he told me, "Go on, quick—you're the only one who speaks English— go out and tell them we surrender!" By this time the soldiers outside were battering against the doors, which had been barricaded from inside, and yelling at us, in broad Scots accents and language that hardly bears repeating, to come on out.

It turned out that they were an Argyle regiment which had sworn revenge against the Jews for an Etzel attack on some mess or other in which two of their officers had been killed. I believe they would have taken their revenge on us— the underground was all one to them—if their officers hadn't restrained them.

Of course, I didn't realize then that there was any restraint in the offing. The ferocious threats they were bellowing through the door gave no indication of it. Our corporal gave me a shove, and I tottered toward the door and yelled above the din, "We want to surrender!" The comic thing, if there was one, was that, due to habit and some confusion of mind at the time, when the door fell in and I walked out I had one hand over my head and the other was still grasping my rifle.

Half a dozen of them pounced on me, grabbed my rifle out of my hand and pushed me with my face against the wall. They seemed to be in quite a state of agitation. Apparently they mistook us for Etzel, for whom they harbored feelings of terror as well as vengeance. They all had fixed bayonets, if you don't mind, and while a couple of them prodded me in the rear, the others were yelling "Come out, you bastards!" to the others.

I tried to tell them about Yitzhak, but they just prodded me a bit harder. I really thought I was in for it. I thought we all were. The British commander told me to tell the others to line up, but in my singular mental state at the time such Hebrew as I had deserted me. I shouted out something or other, which was apparently so weird that even in extremis the others couldn't keep from laughing.

Another jab from a bayonet, combined with humiliation, drove fear from my mind for the moment and replaced it with anger. I turned around and shouted to the officer, "Can't you see what your men are doing?" He ordered them to step back three paces. The jabbing stopped, which was nice.

The captain who had brought the ultimatum had been doing his sums and now asked, "Where are all the others?" I said I supposed the villa must be full of dead and wounded. I told him about Yitzhak on the third floor. He said, "All right, you show these men where he is."

So I went with two men back into the building. I was given a torch. As we went upstairs I could see that among all the debris of the battle were a number of unexploded hand grenades, evidently thrown in at us by inexperienced or nervous chaps who forgot to pull the pins out. One was right on the stairs where we'd have to bring Yitzhak down, so I bent to pick it up....

Of course they went quite mad then. One of them fairly screamed out: "This fucking bastard could blow us all up!" They still thought I was from Etzel, desperate to do or die to get a shot of a few British.... They grabbed hold of me and shouted down for someone else to come up and guard the grenades against my kamikaze intentions.

We went on up and I found Yitzhak. He was making a sound in his throat which I'd already become familiar with from seeing other men dying. I shouted downstairs for a stretcher, and they brought one. I still didn't know what had happened to the others. The only other casualty we had was one man who'd been a bit slow coming out before and had collected a bayonet wound in the thigh.

Yitzhak was put in an ambulance and taken to the Hadassah hospital. Now we were all lined up and the soldiers searched us. They were in quite a state of nerves themselves, but not too much to prevent them from helping themselves to any wallets, watches, or pens they happened to find. They even took my diary that I'd been keeping ever since I reached the country. They made us keep our heads turned away, not wanting to be recognized, in case we "terrorists" decided to get our revenge later.

By this time the field kitchen was dishing out tea to our gallant adversaries to cheer them after their harrowing ordeal by fire. Needless to say there was none for us.

I was still official interpreter. An officer came and said to me, "Tell them we'll drop them at Romema"—or some unknown place. When I passed this on, one of our men who knew the city said, "Don't let them take us there, that's right in the middle of an Arab quarter." So our officer suggested they take us to Hadassah hospital, which they did. They loaded us on their troop carriers and trundled us up to Mount Scopus. By this time we were half hysterical with relief, and we could even make jokes about the fact that they posted one soldier at each corner of each truck with their rifles leveled at us in case of some desperate act on our part—little did they know we were far too exhausted to so much as thumb our noses at them.

We arrived at Hadassah. It was almost unbelievable— so beautifully clean and light—lovely girls in snowy white overalls wafting about, and clean smells—another world. We dragged ourselves in there looking like god knows what, filthy, exhausted, and desperately hungry and thirsty.

As we came in I got my first look at the British commander in a good light. He was immaculately got up, with a little swagger stick tucked under his arm and a huge red handlebar mustache. My surroundings made me bold. I went up to him and said, "What about all our things that your men took?"

He gave me a disdainful look and barked a sardonic

laugh. "Have you never heard of the spoils of war?" he asked, and walked off.

Yitzhak died that night.

The irony of the whole operation was that it all went for nothing in the end. When the British eventually pulled out, they handed it back to our people, who promptly entrusted it to the Irgun. They, of course, failed to dig in properly, and at the first determined push from the Legion they ran like rabbits, so that was one of the vital districts that we had to do without until '67.

Gabriel Cohen elaborates his theory about British withdrawal strategy by contrasting their behavior over Sheikh Jerach, in the north of Jerusalem, with Katamon, in the south, where the Jews carried out a contemporary operation.

☐ We were thrown out of Sheikh Jerach by the British; but they promised us they would give it back when they left Jerusalem. Now why were they so insistent on Sheikh Jerach? Because it was on their withdrawal route. But they kept their promise. When they left Jerusalem on May 14th, they gave Sheikh Jerach back to the Haganah. The fact that *they* handed it over to the Etzel, who let it fall to the Arab Legion, was not the fault of the British.

But the main thing is, at the very same time we also occupied Katamon. Katamon was not less important than Sheikh Jerach, from the point of view of the Arabs. It raised hell in the Arab world. All the consulates were there and they were cabling to Cairo, to Damascus: "The Jews are occupying Katamon—do something!" A lot of pressure was brought to bear from all the Arab capitals on London to do something about it. *But in Katamon they didn't interfere.* They left us to fight it out with the Arabs. Why? Because this was *not* on their route of withdrawal. They couldn't interfere everywhere. Sheikh Jerach was crucial for them, Katamon was not. That's proof of how the principle of priority of withdrawal routes had the upper hand.

To conclude, for the time being , the saga of Jerusalem, here is Shulamith Hareven's recollection of the siege and her part in the capture of Katamon:

☐   One of the prevailing memories of the whole siege was the smell. The city smelled like anything. There was a shortage of water, so all the lavatories smelled, of lavatory and of Lysol, which kept being poured into them; and the smells of cordite and shells and blood and bandages—all mixed with an unbelievable smell of flowers because it was a marvelous spring; there were flowers all over the place and nobody to pick them. This combination of the smell of flowers and the smells of war was typical of the city and the time.

   A few days after the battle of Katamon there was a new smell—the smell of corpses. Not many. A few people had been caught in the cross fire—the rest had fled. They lay in the streets and the little gardens, and there was no means to identify them or to bury them because there was no one to do it. So for the sake of hygiene we got the order to burn them. Tuvia, another medic, would put a blanket over them and pour a bit of gasoline and I would set the match....That was the night we couldn't sleep, however tired we were.

   But perhaps my most memorable experience in Katamon was a happy one. It happened about three days after we'd taken it, and all the streets were empty...it was a ghost quarter. The hospitals were running out of everything by then. There were not enough bandages left, never mind anything else; we had already torn up a lot of sheets....I was working with Tuvia, and we had several times passed a locked door; I'd noticed a sign on it which said "The Knights of Malta." I supposed it was some holy place belonging to this order. And then, suddenly, I remembered learning at school that these knights were also called "The Hospitalers," so I said, "Let's break the door and see what's inside." So we did. And we found a complete houseful of bandages and drugs and medical equipment.

   So I telephoned to the district doctor that we had found

a small hospital, and that he should come right away with a car to take the stuff. He said, right, he'd come in his little mini-car, and we said no, bring a truck. He couldn't believe it. He came and we showed him, and he stood there and burst out crying.

THE NORTH

While Jerusalem was struggling under siege and a dangerous proportion of the Jews' very limited resources of manpower and weaponry was being concentrated on clearing the supply route from the coast, other equally crucial and menacing battles were being fought both in the north and the south of the country.

Perhaps the most serious threat to the Jews' territorial integrity, before the actual invasion by regular Arab forces, was posed in the north by Fawzi el-Kawukji's "motley body of volunteers from various Arab countries," as Netanel Lorch described them, who, even before the U.N. partition vote, had been making sorties against Jewish settlements in Galilee, which were isolated from the main Jewish area. Sir John Glubb's considered view, as a professional soldier, of these members of the self-styled Arab Liberation Army is belittling:

☐   They were private groups of bandits led by Kawukji. They were completely disorganized. Just a large gang. . . . I daresay they'd be alarming to Jewish settlers, but they never did a single thing. They never captured anything or defeated anybody. They spent half their time scrounging off Arab villagers. A totally disorganized collection of roughs.

A not much more laudatory, though rather more alarming, view of them was taken by one of the Arabs whom they had ostensibly come to aid. Seif Addin Zu'bi, an important Arab landowner, who was later mayor of Nazareth for ten years and one of the first Arab members of the Israeli Knesset, from the outset took a pessimistic view of Arab prospects:

☐   From the day partition was declared, I knew it was not going to work out. The division into Jewish and Arab states was illogical—it was not split into two areas but into bits and pieces. Struggle was inherent in this incoherent division.

But partition of any kind would not have been a workable solution at that time because the two people were so intermingled. And it was clear that the Jews had a policy of putting settlements close to Arab centers. In Haifa, for example, the Jews settled in the Hadar Hacarmel—above the Arab quarter. Contiguous with Jaffa was Tel Aviv and so on. In all these Jewish settlements, the Haganah had trained men, ready for war, while in the respective Arab villages or towns there existed disorder and anarchy.

The Jewish plan was clear. They were preparing. They had British officers like Wingate* to help them get ready for war. They also sent their boys to fight in the second world war. They already foresaw the War of Independence that would take place later on. So there was a disparity between Jewish order and Arab anarchy. I knew from the beginning that the Arabs could not win, could not overcome the Jews. It was a very grave situation and I suffered pangs of apprehension from my conviction of the outcome. From the time of the Bloudan conference [1937], in which the Arabs decided to put King Abdullah at the head of the attacking Arab forces, I knew there was no hope of success. I knew Abdullah didn't want to fight—he wanted peace, but on his own terms. The Arab leaders did not have the capacity to evaluate properly the capabilities of the Jews.

But there was no action I could take. Anyone who

---

*Orde Wingate, a non-Jewish Briton who allied himself with the Haganah and helped train them in commando tactics in the thirties. He was, however, dead by the time serious preparations for war with the Arabs were in progress. Seif Addin Zu'bi is evidently referring to long-term Jewish planning, going back to the thirties.

raised his voice in dissent against the Arab Liberation Army, which took control of this part of Palestine at that time, would have been shot on the spot. Many were killed, and not only those who said wrong things; those who gave sound advice—not to take an aggressive course—were killed to silence them.

The Arab Liberation Army contained some elements of riffraff—even some who were freed from prison to fight the Jews. They took over the town of Nazareth and commanded everybody to behave according to their own laws, or rather their misdeeds, and nobody could oppose them. Many preferred to keep out of the way, to dissociate themselves from what was going on. Young men were taken by force to serve. It was a reign of terror.

A man who, in his childhood, actually experienced the brunt of an attack by Kawukji's band was Elon Salmon, later the editor of the *Jewish Observer* in London.

☐   As a boy as I lived in Kibbutz Mishmar Ha'emek in Jezreel. Near us were three Arab villages, Abu Shusha and Upper and Lower Rubaya. Their inhabitants were quite friendly with us—they used to bring their corn for the kibbutz to grind, and they often attended our little clinic. We'd send tractors to help out with their crops and so on—we had good relations. I remember walking through the villages on nature rambles and exchanging grins with the village children.

But early in 1948 all these tokens of good neighborliness stopped, and by mid-March we noticed that a lot of them seemed to be pulling out, taking their belongings. There'd been no harassment, certainly not from our kibbutz; they just left as soon as things got tense. Mishmar Ha'emek started to suffer from snipers lurking in the hills, but that was merely a nuisance compared to our troubles when Fawzi el-Kawukji, at the head of his Arab Liberation Army, took up positions in the two Rubayas and Abu Shusha and trained his artillery on our homes.

I'll never forget the night of the first attack. It came on April 4th, just as we were sitting down to supper in our children's house.* The father of one of my friends came to tell us to go across to another, stronger building when we'd had our meal. Some of the children went at once, but it was my favorite pudding and I saw no need to abandon it, so I, four other children and our teacher stayed behind.

I was just tucking into my pudding when the first shell exploded. I'd never in my life heard any noise as loud as that, and as I lay where I'd dived, under a bed in the dormitory, I remember thinking the whole kibbutz was being blasted to dust. The bombardment intensified every minute; although we were used to the sounds made by small arms and could distinguish between the rifles, pistols, Sten guns, and the two machine guns which constituted our kibbutz armory, the sound of cannon was new and terrifying to us. It was dark, and the explosions drowned out the voice of our teacher who was trying to calm us.

A lull in the shelling came at last, and with it some of the kibbutz men who led us through a scene of devastation to where the other children were. I well remember the shock of seeing, through the darkness, the familiar scene now disfigured by bomb craters, smashed houses, and broken trees . . . .

The firing continued at intervals all night. We began to hear rumors of casualties, this one injured, someone else killed . . . . This might have demoralized us if some of the teen-agers had not come along to get us organized into groups, telling us we might be needed to help in the defense of our kibbutz. At that, all fear left us, and our morale soared. The next evening reinforcements arrived from a neighboring kibbutz, and two days later we children were evacuated by British armored cars to Kibbutz Mizra, some distance away. The British had arranged a truce with Kawukji to allow this.

*Children are raised communally in kibbutzim and live in their own houses apart from their parents.

Only much later I learned how nearly our kibbutz had been captured. Mishmar Ha'emek, heavily outnumbered and outgunned, was saved, not so much by the courage of its defenders as by the incredible incompetence of Kawukji and his much vaunted Arab Liberation Army. If he had had the wit and the will to press his attack that April day, our kibbutz would have fallen. The fact that it hadn't did not prevent him from issuing a triumphant communiqué to the effect that Mishmar Ha'emek was in his hands and that all the Jews in it had been killed.

A similar attack by Kawukji on Ramat Yochanan was also driven off by Palmach and Khish companies, and these Jewish forces went on to take some Arab areas in the region.

Before allowing one of the most distinguished generals of that and subsequent wars, Avraham Yoffe, to describe the process by which these battalions were mobilized, here is the story of one early engagement—a guerrilla operation—that was carried out before the Jewish forces had been organized into a coherent military force.

At that time women were still actively engaged in fighting units; though not numerically on a par with men, their individual participation was at least equal. I say "at least" because, then as now, women had to prove themselves by acts of courage and even strength exceeding that expected by men of men. Netiva Ben Yehuda was one of these women; she had been trained as a demolition officer and had been engaged in spasmodic actions for several months even before the partition resolution in November. Following the action she describes below, in which she was compelled to shoot some sixteen Arab soldiers in a face-to-face engagement, she became one of the most "wanted" individuals by the Arab forces, who dubbed her "the blond devil." Accounts of her story have said that she was pulled out of the battle lines to protect her from the possibility of Arab vengeance, but, as will be seen, it was not that simple.

☐   The first time I was in battle— The plan was stupid! You have to remember that we were young and inexperienced, and not supported by the high command, only by the HQ of Palmach—they gave us a lot of support, and [Yigal] Allon supported us, but he was not around. Everything was decided on the spot. So we did some very foolish things.

Every plan we suggested, they told us, "No, you have to mine a bus. Show them that at least we are reacting to their attempts to stop our communications on the road."

It was decided that near Nebi Yusha will be the first retaliation. We were to mine the bus that went every day at the same time from the Huleh valley west to Malkia. Only *Najada* would be on the bus. They were the Arab version of Haganah.

I was responsible for the plan, and my commander okayed it and we sent it to the high command and the answer came back, "If you do it this way, the bus will rise up in the air and drop back on the spot. Maybe the Arabs will be killed but this is not what we want. We want the bus to go down from the road, down the mountainside to Lake Huleh, so people can see what we could do if they go on attacking us on the roads."

The road was steep and winding and was supported at a certain point by stones on a bend. We chose this place, which was very good for an ambush. We had to put the charge on the inside of the bend so the bus would be blown outward and over the steep edge.

I couldn't take the wire across the road, so I had to be on the same side as the charge. I and one man were there alone, and we hid under a bush, behind a rock, for hours, while the rest of the group stayed above on the far side. The road was very busy, Arabs going by on donkeys, all kinds of British traffic.

Now the stupid thing was that the explosive was a new kind, made here in Israel. We didn't know anything about it—how it would stand up to rain, for instance. And we found it wouldn't, because when the bus came at last and I tried to detonate the charge, it wouldn't work.

The contingency plan was that if the mine didn't blow,

the force that was on the far side of the road would start shooting, and when the bus got to where the driver had his back turned, the Bren gun would start shooting, and the bus would stop.

Another stupid thing was, we forgot to take into account that if the bus stopped at that angle, the doors would open on my side. Now all hell broke out. All the force was shooting and the people in the bus were shooting and I was shooting because those who managed to get out of the bus were coming straight at me.

There was a wall above the road and a wall below it, supporting it. As men jumped out of the bus they dropped to a different level—to my level—and then they were out of the fire field of the force. I couldn't move because I would have been hit by my own force. And the Arabs were dropping down and then running straight at me. I had to keep shooting them. They kept coming because they were above and didn't see what happened to the men who'd jumped ahead of them. I had to kill all of them in order not to be killed first. The Sten gun had jammed at the first bullet, so I thought, it's better if only one of us is killed, so I said to my guard, "Take the Sten and go back, cross the road far away from the shooting and rejoin the others." I used his rifle.

When things were a little bit quiet I remembered I had to collect the wire. That was a whole story. When we planned it all, we didn't have a long enough wire; we had to take all the electric wires that were in Ramot Naftali. And Ramot Naftali was encircled. We couldn't leave them long without electricity. I'm not only talking about wire for irons and lamps, I'm talking about communications, the surgery—every bit of wire we found, we took, and every few yards we twisted the ends together. Very bad in the rain. So we couldn't leave without taking that wire with us. So I picked it all up—maybe two hundred yards of it, all the way back to the mine.

And then I saw— There was one person we had to make sure was killed. He was an Arab who was in charge of

demolition for the whole Galilee. And as I came near the
mine, near the bus, I saw a man, running on the curb of black
stones at the edge—running *on* it. And I thought, you
stupid, why are you running there, so exposed? And my
second thought was, *he* is the demolition officer. Because
nobody else would run on the curb, no one else would think,
where would another demolition expert put the mine?
Where might there be booby traps?

So I shot him, and he threw his hands up, and fell
headfirst down, with a shout. And I collected the last of the
wire and went back to the place I'd been in and crossed the
road and joined the others. And as I crossed I saw that there
were four or five Arabs crouched between the bus and the
wall, where the force above couldn't see them. We had to
blow up the bus, and we shouted at them. We warned them
that we were going to kill them. We shot the gas tank of the
bus and threw a Molotov cocktail that we had had ready in
case the mine didn't go off, to blow the bus up. But it didn't
go over, and afterward the regional commanders told us off
for not doing the job properly.

Avraham Yoffe, now head of Israel's Nature Conservancy
and a member of the Knesset, at the time a formidable soldier,
tells in characteristically laconic style how these Jewish battalions, which so ably defended Jewish territory against incursions, were formed.

☐   Even before the U.N. vote, some of us who'd fought in the
     British army were called to meet Ben-Gurion. He'd taken
     over as head of the Haganah. At that time Israel was
     parceled into areas, and each of us got command of an area
     in which we had to raise our own battalion. Nobody told us
     how. Nobody told us a thing, just "Go to your assigned areas
     and raise a battalion!"

     My area was in the vicinity of Tiberias, in Lower
     Galilee. I'd had experience in the British army, I'd been in
     the Haganah before that, and they decided I'd make a

battalion commander. And the first member of my battalion was—me. So far nobody else was in my battalion, and I wasn't happy about the whole idea.

So I went to the officer in charge of manpower and I told him, "Look, I didn't say no to Ben-Gurion, but I'm saying it to you because I don't need it. And I've got problems with my knee." Not housemaid's knee as in Jerome K. Jerome, but something wrong with it. "I want to get out," I said. So *he* said, "You won't need to walk. You'll be a battalion commander, you'll get a pickup and you will *ride*." So my hopes of getting out of it came to nothing.

A few days went by and suddenly every Israeli was dancing for joy because of the partition decision in the U.N. I thought, for them there's rejoicing. For me, now it starts. I've got to start raising this battalion.

The Haganah was some help. They had an organization of sorts, but it was mostly on paper—names, location of arms, that kind of thing. I had to go around and tell people to start preparing for the war. I didn't have any transport after all, and no place to put people. I didn't have any uniforms. But I started to work. I started then, in November, and about three months later I had a skeleton infantry battalion. How did I do it? For example: Ein Gev was the other side of the Kinneret.* They didn't have enough people and were in a very bad situation, having to protect their kibbutz and its life and keep working their fields. We couldn't go by car, so we went across the lake in boats. And I made a deal with them. "Look, I'll give you seventy men; you'll give them your weapons, you'll feed them, and they'll protect you. Their company commander will see to it that you're safe."

So they got security. I got my weapons, my food—no clothing, that nobody had. And while they were there, they started to train themselves as an infantry company.

And I did the same in other places. One company was in

*Sea of Galilee.

Tiberias and one in the Jordan valley and one in Kfar Tabor. All those villages in Lower Galilee had a company, and I gave them officers. They were already trained before, by the Haganah, as section leaders, sergeants, officers. And in the meantime I started a school for commanders for my people, and a technical school for machine gunners, artillery crews, and so on, again on the same lines. I would give it to a village which was in a bad position, threatened by surrounding Arabs. I gave them the people, and they had to feed them. They protected the village and at the same time gave them training.

One day Haganah in Tel Aviv sent someone to me who, I recall, was quite interesting. It was Colonel [David] Marcus.* They sent him to see the different activities going on in all the regions. For two or three days I took him around—I even showed him my school—a colonel of the American army! He looked at the boys and their training and equipment, their food and lodging, all that sort of thing. I think he felt sorry for them, actually, but at the same time saw what was going to be. I remember he said to me, after seeing how little we had, "Look here, my friend Avraham. How would you like, when you go into action one of these days, to have artillery on your right, artillery at the back, a battalion of tanks on both sides, and air support overhead?" He was thinking, perhaps, of what our army would be in ten years or less, but at that time he was joking, and I told him, "Oh well, I wouldn't mind." And then I went on with my job, doing things which were a far cry from *his* idea of an army.

While I was building my battalion I had to keep all our roads secure and open. Communication—that was the most important thing. We achieved this by clashing with the local Arabs—we were in the midst of Arabs at that time, and if we wanted to move about we had to show some force, to show what we could do. We had a mobile unit, a few men in a pickup with a machine gun and some rifles, which were

*"Mickey" Marcus, the American officer recruited by Teddy Kollek's unit.

actually a "gift" from the British army at that time. And we used this as my "mobile force." We used to go anywhere and everywhere in the Beisan valley where there was trouble.

We had many shooting clashes with them. Sometimes we'd go at night and actually attack the Arabs in their camps if they gave us trouble. There was one village called Khakuk about three miles from Ginnosar and to get through you had to pass a Bedouin camp. And they were, shall we say, not friendly. So we usually went with our "mobile force" at night. Sometimes they shot at us. So we'd come again at night and attack, and kill and get killed. I remember the first victim of the war in my battalion was in this sector—I sent the boys to fight somebody and they returned with one on their shoulders.

Mount Tabor is surrounded by villages. There was a group of terrorists in one of the villages and we attacked them at night. We didn't do much—blew up one house, perhaps one or two were killed, but that stopped it. *We* suffered casualties from ambushes. Farmers would go to their fields and the Arabs would ambush and kill them, and after that we'd go after them.

Just before Pesach, '48, they decided the time had come to make bigger units: brigades. The brigade commander came to me. He was a friend from another kibbutz. "Look, Avraham," he said, "you've raised a battalion—you know how to do it. You give this battalion to your second in command and go and start another one." I wasn't at all pleased. I mean, I'd been working hard, and just as I started to see the fruit of my work I was taken away! But the point was that the new battalion I had to raise was around my own kibbutz where I'd left my wife and baby daughter. I knew all the people around there, who'd known me before. I could dictate to them how many people I needed, what percentage of the male population had to be given for the battalion. I felt more secure and knowledgeable than before.

It was with this battalion I fought all the wars—the Thirteenth, which was called after my nickname, "Gid'on,"

because it was near Ein Harod Spring, where Gideon was a
hero. I liked the name because of the associations with the
Bible and the area.... I started this battalion around
Pesach. And by the time the British left, on May 15th, and
the state was declared, and the real war started, I was in
command of my new battalion and in good spirits.

The British withdrawal, however, was by no means complete
in the north at the time of some of the biggest battles, which took
place there in February, March, and April. Gabriel Cohen
elaborates on his theory of the British withdrawal strategy, as it
affected the north:

☐   When they left the towns, Safed, Tiberias, Haifa—or were
     planning to leave—it was most convenient for them that
     whoever, Arabs or Jews, was the stonger at that point would
     get the upper hand as quickly as possible. Because they
     didn't want a real war to break out while they were still there.
          Compare what happened in Tiberias to what happened
     in Safed. In Tiberias you had Jews and Arabs, in Safed you
     had Jews and Arabs. But in Tiberias, potentially the Jews
     had the upper hand. There were more of them and they were
     armed. In Safed, the Arabs had potentially the upper
     hand—they were twelve thousand, we were only two
     thousand and all the villages around were Arab. Everything
     was in their favor.
          So now comes the key to understanding the British and
     also, perhaps, to why we won the war and the Arabs lost it.
     When the British were planning to leave Tiberias and the
     fighting started, they offered the Arabs evacuation and gave
     them transport. And the Arabs accepted. Now, when they
     left Safed, it's true they gave the Arabs the two police
     stations, the key strongpoints, and they offered the *Jews* a
     free, guarded evacuation. *But the Jews refused.* And we
     managed to turn the tables in Safed. I mean, they gave in,
     and we fought. When the British commander in Safed

invited Jewish notables and offered them a chance to get out, it took real courage to say "No, we are not going."

He adds that without doubt certain British officers in the middle or lower echelons, if they had had a free hand, might well have helped the Arabs by handing over certain strategic positions to them. He explains this by saying that after three years in Palestine, they often came to see the Jews as the cause of their being there, to feel that "if I'm killed, I'll be killed by the Jews."

Yerucham Cohen, who was the intelligence officer chosen by Yigal Allon as his aide-de-camp, takes up the story of the situation in the north:

□　The whole upper Galilee and the Huleh valley were cut off because the Arabs held Tiberias, so actually the only way the Jews of Galilee could go south was in convoys with a very strong escort, once a week. A delegation met Yigal Allon and Ben-Gurion, commanders of the Haganah. Allon, who was born in Galilee, came to Ben-Gurion and said, "Look, I am the commander of the Galilee. I want to give up this position. Give me a brigade and I will start fighting." Under pressure from the people in Galilee, Ben-Gurion approved. Yigal took me as his intelligence officer.

　　The first step was to liberate Tiberias. The Palmach liberated the city in a night attack. The road was still blocked north of Ginnosau, which was Yigal's kibbutz. The plan was first to conquer Safed and thus eliminate any chance of its being the capital of a Palestinian state. To do that we had to bring up a Palmach battalion, the First, and for that we had to open the road between Tiberias and Rosh Pinna. This was done in a joint action, when the First Battalion—toward the end of April—came through the Jordan valley, through Tiberias north, and at the same time we started pressing on this area, which is between the Galilee and the Jordan River north of the Sea of Galilee. After all this area was cleared and the road opened, we decided to mount the attack on Safed and transfer all the forces there. They had to be

smuggled in, because the road to Safed was not in our hands.
So by night we used to advance through the hills. But the
Lebanese tried to dictate their strategy to us, and on May 1st
they attacked Kibbutz Ramat Naftali, which was named
after the code name of Orde Wingate.

All that day I flew over that area there, throwing
homemade bombs out of the plane on the attackers. The
door was removed and I was tied to the seat, and on each
circuit of the battlefield I had to throw out three homemade
bombs. We flew at about six hundred feet; each time I
identified the target area I would tell the pilot and then take
a box of matches and light the head of the bomb. After that
we knew we had twenty seconds. I would shout: "Now!" and
he would turn the plane so that I could slide the bomb off my
arms—and then I'd take the second and third bombs and do
the same. I don't know if they did much damage, really; but
anyway we could see and hear them blow up. The bomb was
simply a metal pipe full of explosives and there was a fuse
full of sulfur which I lit and then got rid of it quickly.

The defenders of Ramot Naftali were calling for help all
the time over the radio, and I went to Yigal Allon and I said,
"Look, the Lebanese are very close, they're already in the
yard, we must send help." But Yigal said, "I can't send any
relief because my forces are now around Safed." So the
message came, "We are evacuating the place." And Yigal
sent one back: "Anyone who evacuates and comes down to
the road will be shot by my men."

The end was that the kibbutz was not captured. The
Lebanese retreated, and don't ask me why because no one
actually knows. So ended the only real action of the
Lebanese, which was intended as the first step toward the
capture of Safed. They'd wanted to create a corridor, and
this kibbutz was right in the middle of it.

In the middle of the fighting, Lorna Wingate, Orde's
widow, arrived to visit Ramot Naftali. I said it was
impossible, but she insisted at least on flying over the
kibbutz in my plane. She wanted to throw down Wingate's

Bible to encourage the kibbutzniks to fight. She was a bit of
a crazy type, like her husband, but even today he is our
symbol of a commander.

On April 28 the British left the Rosh Pinna police fortress
and a neighboring army camp and the Haganah took them over.
But the fort at Nebi Yusha was left in the hands of the Arabs, and
the Palmach made an effort to retrieve it. Yerucham Cohen
continues:

☐   It was a night attack. The idea was that the unit would put
     dynamite charges against the wall of this Teggart fort, and
     through the hole the attackers would penetrate the building
     and conquer it. When they arrived at the wall, they found
     out that someone had forgotten to bring a small wooden
     thing like a bench, which was vital to the plan because the
     level of the ground was lower than the level of the floor
     inside, so we had to raise the charge, stand it on something.
     It was a very embarrassing situation.
         The defenders of the fort saw us and started throwing
     grenades. One of our forward scouts had been wounded,
     and he suggested we use him instead of the bench—he would
     crouch on all fours and we would put the dynamite on his
     back. Of course his friends refused to do it.
         Meanwhile the grenades were causing a lot of casualties
     to the attacking force. It was a famous tradition of the
     Palmach never to leave wounded comrades on the battle-
     field. So when the defenders of the fort were reinforced near
     daybreak and our men had to withdraw under heavy fire,
     they were impeded by the many they had to carry. The Arabs
     had positions on the other side of the wadi through which the
     retreat took place and, as daylight had come, were shooting,
     wounding, and killing more and more. At last it was impos-
     sible to carry the dead any more and twenty-eight were left
     on the field.
         Then all efforts were turned to Safed. The first attack
     on it was between the 4th and 5th May, and it failed, because

we failed to capture the main position in the town, which is the citadel in the heart of the city. Allon and I were in Rosh Pinna and we had to walk back; on the same day we planned the next battle, which was on May 9th, and after severe battles—really fierce, fighting tooth and nail—I got the news from the commander of the attack that all targets had been achieved; that means, the police station on Mount Canaan, the police station in town, the citadel, and two other positions on the border between the Arab and Jewish sectors.

At first light I took a plane and flew over the area, and I actually saw—and this was before our troops had entered the Arab part of Safed—an enormous crowd of people gathered near Miron, and following with my eyes the line of people along the roads, I saw that the line ended about one kilometer away from Safed. Which meant that the last people to run away from the town were already a kilometer away. Our information later was that the first to run away were the so-called volunteers from Syria and other military forces. The Arab citizens of Safed, realizing they had been abandoned, also left the town and fled across the Lebanese border.

El'ad Peled, now senior deputy mayor of Jerusalem and a retired major general of the Israeli Defense Forces (IDF), recalls his principal role in the battle of Safed:

☐   Before the British left I was assigned to the units reinforcing Safed, a fairly small Jewish community of some 1600 surrounded by 16,000 Arabs, including some of the closer villages. A very large and strong Arab population. The Jewish quarter was tiny, and it had some bad memories of the riots in '29, '36 and '38 in which whole families were massacred.

We were based on Mount Canaan; our cover story was that we were a camp of sports instructors, though the British knew well enough what we really were. We had supposedly very good information as to when the British were going to leave their police fortresses in the Galilee; we would know about it and be able to take over—the EDT [estimated departure time] was around May 10 if I remember correctly.

One night in mid-April I stood on Mount Canaan and watched the firing going on in Safed against the Jewish quarter. A terrible night.... The Arabs had all the topographical advantage and were shelling the Jews without mercy. In the morning I got information from some outposts that some military cars, Bren carriers, and a lot of troops were taking up positions around our base. I went out and had a look. They were British, so I thought they were having a practice maneuver for their eventual withdrawal a month hence.

Around two o'clock I was standing out on the balcony when I suddenly saw a military convoy heading for Rosh Pinna with white flags fluttering. My first reaction was amazement—what could it mean? And then suddenly it struck me. *This* must be the evacuation! And then minutes later, heavy fire opened on the Jewish quarter.

They had gone a month early!

My first action was to post sections around us to protect our base, and everyone was put on battle alert. The firing from Safed became heavier hourly. Over the radio I heard our commander in the town call for reinforcements from Ayelet Hashachar. He was told there were problems— we were short of everything; but then a message was sent saying, "One house after another is being destroyed by the Arabs; there will soon be no need for reinforcements because we will all be killed."

He was told that a unit of Khish would be sent by night, but the answer was, "We don't want Khish, we want the Palmach." I was asked by my commander in Kibbutz Ayelet Hashachar if I could spare some men. I said I couldn't *spare* anyone, but if it was an order, I'd have to. Two hours later, the order came. I was to take a selected group and try to infiltrate into the Jewish quarter to help organize its defense. Replacements for me would be sent from Rosh Pinna.

The problem was that the quarter was surrounded by

Arab inhabitants. The only possibility was to go to Ein
Zeitim, a kibbutz, and from there to creep through the wadi
and up the hill and infiltrate their lines more or less where
the cemetery is today.

I sent the replacements to take over my men's positions
and I called all my Palmachniks together. It was night. I had
a kind of a parade at which I had to pick the thirty-five men
who were coming with me. I called for volunteers, but when
they all stepped forward, then I had to decide. Some of these
men still don't speak to me, because I didn't choose them. I
took the best weapons we had, and from the reinforcement
units reliable tommy guns and explosives.... Everybody
carried very heavy loads.

It was now about 4 A.M. and I told them we would have
to run if we wanted to arrive alive because it would soon be
light. So we started to jog. And while we were climbing the
hill, the sun rose. We were shocked, because we had our
backs to the Arab village of En Zeitun, but by a miracle they
must have been sleeping very well. And we reached the
forward position of the Jewish quarter at about five o'clock
in the morning.

We were all young kids at that time, nineteen, twenty—
I was just over twenty. And we were exhausted. I quickly got
word that the morale of the Jews of the town was very low.
They were in a state of despair, expecting, perhaps, the same
fate as those who had died in earlier times in the town.* At
first I didn't know what to do, but then I got a bright idea. I
got my boys to stand up and sing, and we marched into the
Jewish quarter singing the song of the Palmach.

The townspeople hadn't slept all night because of the
bombardment and afterward I found out that their morale
took a sharp upward turn when they heard us singing, and
everybody said, "Now the Palmach's come, we are saved."
This became a sort of legend of the war, and it was said that
Safed was saved by two things: deeds—and a miracle. The

*Safed has a long history of anti-Jewish riots.

"deeds" were the prayers that were said; the miracle was the arrival of the Palmach.

Still the people were deeply tired and depressed, and when we arrived—young, too young perhaps, fresh, *stupid*—well, we made our first station in the courtyard of the synagogue of Ha'ari Hakadosh. On a Saturday. In that extremely Orthodox community. And what did they do? They came to us, they lit fires, they cooked for us, they made us coffee—there was nothing they wouldn't do for us. And we were happy, because in the last month on Mount Canaan, we'd had almost nothing to eat, whereas in Safed they had plenty.*

It seems strange to me now, after taking part in much larger scale battles in later wars—I commanded a division in the Six-Day War and here I only had some two or three hundred fighters altogether. Anyway I was made commander in chief of all the Haganah forces, and then the head of the Etzel there, Shmuel Pearl, came to me and subordinated the Irgun to my command—the first time it had happened in Israel, till then.

I decided that the first priority was to raise morale. Our arrival and our self-confidence had a wonderful effect at first; but after a few days things settled back again to being hard and trying. I claim I was the first to proclaim Jewish independence in a way, because I issued a proclamation announcing Jewish military occupation in the town under my command, and I appointed a sort of miniature municipality, with officers for sewage and supplies and food—a proper council. I appointed a chief civil adviser, and then mobilized everyone who could work to build fortifications. Another famous story is that a very Orthodox rabbi issued a declaration that it is a privilege and a duty to do this work on Shabbat and holy days. After we had the Seder everybody went out to continue the work.

---

*Netanel Lorch, in *The Edge of the Sword,* says, on the contrary, that Safed was starving and that soldiers acted as porters, carrying supplies to the town on their backs.

So we established a little independent Jewish state there in Safed. We even had stamps, which are quite valuable now, I believe. And all the time, day and night, we were in a permanent fight. Attack and counterattack, and my men suffered casualties—it was quite a rough period. This continued till May 5th when the Thirteenth Battalion came to liberate Safed. That first attack failed. But then they tried again on May 10th. And that time I was wounded.

When the second attack was launched, in the morning we realized that the Arabs had evacuated the city. It was a very strange quiet.... As the sun rose, we realized there were no Arab inhabitants left in the city. But there was one building from which fire was still coming, the police station within the town. We took the building after a heavy fight, but when I arrived I realized that there were some Arab soldiers left on the roof, shooting, and they wounded some of my boys.

I wondered what could be done to get them off there. There was a kind of iron trapdoor leading onto the roof, with the ladder up to it, so I decided to use dynamite to blow the iron door out and then we would use a handmade flamethrower to storm the roof. We set the charge; but I didn't think about the fact that it would also blow the hinges off the top of the ladder. My plan was that the man with the flamethrower would go up first, and I would follow with a machine gun. But when the first man climbed up the ladder, it fell, and the flamethrower started a fire on the second floor of this building, cutting us off from the stairs.

We dashed to the windows to jump out, but the windows were all barred. Then, halfway down the stairs I saw a fire extinguisher, and I thought I would just jump over the fire and get it. What I didn't realize was that I was soaked with the highly flammable chemicals which had filled the flamethrower—as I jumped through the fire, it caught me and in an instant my clothes were blazing.

I started to run. I screamed. Two of my friends pulled my legs out from under me, rolled me on the ground in some blankets, and stifled the fire. Then they wanted to take me on a stretcher to the hospital, but I said no—I was the commander of the city and no one was going to see me on a stretcher! I would walk. So with two soldiers supporting me I walked to the hospital.

The medical team was rather a "scratch" one, very amateurish—the "anesthetists" were a pediatrician and a dentist. They gave me so much chloroform that I passed out for twenty-four hours.

Four days later, on May 14th, the Haganah evacuated all the hospitals in the north because they anticipated the invasion of the Lebanese and the Syrians. I was sent to a hospital in Petach Tikva, which I'd chosen to be near my parents.

Meanwhile, some friends of mine had taken a bundle of burned clothing to my parents with the announcement "These are your son's ." My parents became crazy, but my mother decided that I wasn't dead and that she was going to find me. She went around to every hospital in the Tel Aviv area until she found me. When she saw me, she took off my sheet first of all to see if I still had legs.

The northern-front commands, realizing the imminence of invasion by Arab armies from Syria and Lebanon, were intent upon securing as much territory as possible before zero hour on May 15th. Yerucham Cohen:

☐   The battalion which had fought in Safed had been severely mauled, and we were short of people, but we decided the next step must be the capture of the main route the Lebanese must take into the heart of Galilee. For this we took the First Battalion, and again, they had to infiltrate through the mountains, walking all night—that was already May 13th. They arrived too late to attack that night, and had to hide in the mountains, the whole battalion, for an entire day in order to attack early the following morning.

On May 14th, taking my usual early flight along the Syrian-Lebanese border, I noticed the sun winking on metal on the road leading south toward our border. I flew lower and discovered a very long military convoy on its way to Israel. That was about eight in the morning. I immediately alerted Yigal [Allon] because we'd thought they would come through Metulla. Yigal alerted all the kibbutzim, and all the men who could bear arms were sent to the border. One battalion was hiding in the mountains. We couldn't fetch it down because it would take a day. The other was around Safed. Still, we did what we could.

We knew what their strategy was. The Syrians actually came to the border, turned east, went up to Kuneitra and turned south, straight through the Jordan valley, and they attacked Zemach and the kibbutzim, including Degania. On the 14th at around seven o'clock, the last moment we could fly, I saw the convoy leaving Kuneitra, going south. The pilot managed to land almost in the dark; I went to HQ and told Yigal, who immediately informed the military commander of the Jordan valley that he should expect the Syrians the next morning. Which is what happened.

Netiva Ben Yehuda, the demolition officer, recalls the role she played in the war in the north in that period:

☐   On the 15th May the Arab nations around us declared they were going to invade the country, so we were given orders to blow up all the bridges that connected us with the Arab countries. Our part was to blow up the Litani—the famous bridge they still blow up every now and then today. An enormous one. And a second one on the Hatsbani and the third one on the Atsaf—there are these three rivers crossed by three roads. The Litani is in Lebanon, the other two in Syria.

Three companies had to go on the same night and blow the three bridges. So we prepared everything ready to go up. Each bridge would take a ton and a half of explosives, which means, a hundred and fifty people, each carrying twenty kilos on his back, and the Litani is twenty-five kilometers inside Lebanon, the Hatsbani ten kilometers. It happened that at the same time there was a struggle going on for Nebi Yusha, and so one of our companies was ordered to go up and take Nebi Yusha, finally. That was one company less, so how were we going to blow up three bridges?

So we decided to do the operation on two consecutive nights. All the officers were sent up to Metulla, where we were to start from. I was assigned to prepare the materials; I was not going on the operation, because after you prepare the gelignite you have such a fearful headache you can't fight. The gelignite had been lying for years underground, hidden from the British, and it all had to be kneaded, like dough. All day I kneaded and kneaded this stuff, and another officer had to go on the operation.

A company of Khish was to go to a halfway point and capture a mountain to keep a way open for the retreat after the blowing of the bridge. After half an hour they came back—couldn't find the mountain! So I went up with my group and we conquered the mountain and then we stood and watched the bridge being blown up from afar. Oh, it was so beautiful, that 15th May—it was like fireworks for the new state, even though we didn't know yet that the state had been proclaimed.

So they came back from the bridge to where I was, and we walked the ten kilometers to Metulla; after such a day and such a night I couldn't go to the second bridge, but despite my headache—and you can't imagine such a pain, you couldn't get it from anything else unless you swallowed pure nitroglycerine—I kneaded all day, and by evening everything was ready. But the other officer said that he had a splitting headache and couldn't go to the operation, so I had to.

We started very early at night, walking northeast toward the second bridge. We understood it was empty terrain, walking up, and down, and up again, across the rocks and the mountains in a straight line till we found the bridge. But we found out that all the Arabs, who had been "brushed" out of the Upper Galilee by what we called

"Operation Broom"—to clear the Arabs out to make room for the fighting—had run into this mountain and were encamped there in sort of shantytowns like Rio de Janeiro, with dogs and rifles....We had to creep like snakes—maybe we went twenty kilometers instead of ten, to avoid them.

And then we arrived at the place where the bridge was, and because the night before we'd managed to blow one bridge, on this night about ten armored cars and heaven knows what were all ready for us.

The land near the bridge was flat, a ploughed field. You can imagine, on such terrain—it was like a stage—the slightest light showed the enemy exactly where we were. We all lay down flat in the furrows. Fire came at us from all sides. And we all had these packs of gelignite—if a bullet had hit one pack it would have set us off one by one like dominoes. We couldn't even fight, with those packs. We lay there and waited for the commander to decide what to do—I thought maybe we could use the explosives to demolish their armored cars and so on. There we lay, a hundred sappers side by side, most of us resting our heads on the packs.

It was the first time we'd ever worn proper helmets, and they were U.S. Navy ones. You know in the navy they're not worried about bullets, they're worried about shrapnel, and the helmets are not designed for use by infantry. When you leveled your rifle, the butt pushed the helmet around so the "face window" was turned to the side and you couldn't see. Also, a bullet could pierce it. And my runner, lying between me and the rest of the sappers, got hit in the back of his head and went crazy. If the bullet had struck him two inches lower it would have sent his pack and the rest of us sky high.

Some of us got up and tried to load the piat* we had, but in the dark and under fire we couldn't manage it.

It took three hours to disengage from the enemy. Three

*A piat is a portable armor-piercing weapon, like a bazooka.

hours! One minute can seem like a year under fire. At last we started to crawl back. We had four killed and another four injured. The way back was the most terrible thing that ever happened to me. First of all we had to run with the stretchers. To run with a stretcher, even taking turns, as well as all the rest of what we had to carry, was a nightmare—when they want to punish you in the army they make you do that. We had to avoid the Arabs' encampments. The rocks on the ground were as black as night; we kept stumbling and falling. There were four carrying each stretcher: When one stretcher-bearer fell, the other three would fall too. My runner, the one with the head wound, kept screaming. Several of our wounded died from the effects of the falls with their stretchers. We were still carrying the ton and a half of gelignite. Everybody who was capable had to take over the packs, rifles, and so on of others who were exhausted. Sometimes today when I carry heavy shopping up the stairs to my flat, I marvel how I did it. When we got back to Metulla as dawn broke, I was carrying three rifles, a machine gun, and two packs of gelignite.

I had not slept at all for over forty-eight hours, but almost the moment we got back we were ordered into a jeep to go to Nebi Yusha and help our company there. When we arrived we found them in a huge empty fort which the British had used and which the Arabs had taken over. This was what had given us all the trouble to capture—we hadn't been able to penetrate it, and a month before twenty-eight men had been killed there in an attempt to take it—their bodies had never been found.

The fort had fallen into our hands just before my group arrived. The Arabs had made the inside of it indescribably filthy—they had fouled the floor so that you could scarcely walk there. We were so exhausted we were almost fainting, our tongues were swollen and stuck to the roofs of our mouths. We took some old metal filing cabinets the British had left and tipped them on their faces onto the floor, fell onto the backs of them and, I would say, passed out.

We were awakened by a terrible noise. The shock was unimaginable. We were being shelled. They had managed to hit the hinges of one of the heavy metal shutters. The shutter fell in on two of our people, lying asleep on the filing cabinets. I jumped up and saw them lying there with their two heads smashed.

That broke us. We ran about shouting, crying, bumping into each other, half mad, hysterical. We jostled and almost tumbled over each other running down the steps and out into the village. We took shelter in a house there. The bombardment stopped. But we couldn't sleep any more. I and a few others decided we would go to look for the bodies of the twenty-eight Palmachniks who had been killed the month before. We had experience of looking for bodies. We looked for the vultures.... And we soon found the dead men. I will never forget it. They had been eaten to skeletons by the birds and by animals. We could only identify two of them. One held his glasses case in his hand, with his name in it. The other had some identifying mark on his undershirt.

After that I was very ill for some weeks. The others all went to some front or other, but I was left behind. Only during the first truce I was able to rejoin them.

I remember what happened after that, but not so clearly. Everything until May 17th is branded on my memory, but that was my last real battle, at Nebi Yusha.

Avraham Yoffe, the "builder of battalions" in the north, recalls an important action he was responsible for at the time, which was part of Operation Matateh (Broom), aimed at clearing the Arabs out of strategic areas.

☐   I got an order from the Haganah to clean the area of the Beisan valley of Arabs—not of all Arabs, but the armed ones from across the border. The great problem was that in the middle of all our kibbutzim was an Arab town, Beisan, of about 5,000 people, built around a road junction—a whole system of roads passed through it. You couldn't get control of the roads without taking this town.

We had plenty of informers—spies, you might call them—who let us know exactly what we were up against. We knew who lived where, how many rifles and machine guns they had, the names of the leaders—a lot. So we knew we were outnumbered. I had at that time the Thirteenth Battalion, a very good battalion, but of its four companies only one was properly armed. Eighty men against 5,000 villagers, many of them under arms! The plan was this. Beisan was surrounded by kibbutzim. So first of all I gave orders to each kibbutz to man a roadblock on a road leading to Beisan—Ma'oz on the east, Nir David on the west, and many others. I had two reasons. First, I got extra soldiers, and second, they brought arms from their kibbutzim, which at that time didn't belong to the army. They had their own private arms.

There was a command point not far from Beisan, an old place which, in ancient times, was called Skitopolis. The villagers occupied this strongpoint, so I had to do something about it. At night we attacked it. The defenders' surprise was so great that they fled down the hill, leaving the place to us.

In the morning I took over an Arab Legion camp which was near the place and I connected up the telephone lines. I had with me an Israeli from one of our spy units, and he talked to the military commander of the village in Arabic: "You're surrounded. There is no hope for you. Your reinforcements have been driven away. Why shed blood? You should surrender. Collect all weapons and put them in the police station, and nothing will happen to you."

The Arab laughed. "We have a lot of arms, a lot of soldiers. We're very strong. We're not doing this." So I said, "At eight o'clock we're going to start shelling you. The bloodshed is upon your head if you don't surrender by then."

But I didn't have any artillery. I had two mortars with eight shells. So I put six-inch water pipes all around the area to look like guns. And at eight o'clock I started to shell. Actually I was bluffing. After four of my eight shells, the white flags came out.

So we got onto them by telephone. But the commander

was not there any more. I guessed he had run away, but I was sure he would be caught by my roadblocks. And so he was.

I entered the village on foot. A citizen from the town came toward me. We met on the Roman bridge, and we went in and took over. The man who led the citizens, a Christian, who gave me the surrender, was a good friend of mine, with whose family I'd lived in the village in the past when I was working around that area.

Years later, it occurred to me that there was a parallel between the way I took this village and the way Joshua took Jericho in the Bible. Did he take it by force? No. By noise. Like me.

The Arab villagers stayed where they were for the time being, but about two hundred Arab Legionnaires fled. Some of them were caught by my roadblocks. And their arms were a bone of contention afterward, because the kibbutzim wanted to keep them, and I said the arms were mine. And I got them. Which made me the richest battalion commander in Israel, for arms and for transport too. Before, I'd had one pickup. And from this time I had eighty trucks and pickups and private cars. One car belonged to this Christian fellow, my friend. The driver brought me the keys. He said, "Don't break the window, take the keys and keep the car."

I came to the villagers, and I said, "Look, you're going to be with us now. I will see to it that you get all the food you need"—because they were short of things like oil, flour, salt, kerosene. "I'll bring you all these things, but stay, and be quiet." But still, after a day or two I sensed an uneasy feeling going around. We'd done nothing to harass them. I thought at the time we were going to be friendly. But it was around this time that the Arab populations of Haifa and Tiberias fled. And the leaders of the village came and told me they wanted to leave and go to Transjordan. That was about five kilometers. I was flabbergasted. I was shocked—to see a whole community getting up, without harassment, taking with them what they could by hand, because I didn't give

them any transport. I said to them, "If you want to go, each
family has to give me a rifle. Because I know that you have
rifles." So they came, and they handed me their rifles; and in
less than two days the town was empty of Muslims.

My friend, whose name was Adam, came to me and
said,"What about us?" I said, "You can stay, you're not a
Muslim." He said, "But my people want to move to
Nazareth"—because Nazareth at that time was under the
forces of Kawukji, it wasn't in our hands. So I said, "Okay, I
will see that you get transport." And I arranged trucks for
them, told them to pile all their things onto them, and I
would take them to Nazareth. And then the village was
empty.

The vexed question of whether or not it was the policy of
Israeli commanders to "get rid of the Arabs" all over the country
is partially answered in this story told by Yehuda Bauer, now
professor of Holocaust Studies at the Hebrew University, then a
junior officer in Khish:

☐   I know for certain that it was not a matter of policy. It was
the decision of a local commander. Once I was driving a
command car with three others in the center of Galilee and
suddenly we saw a long miserable "convoy" of Arab
villagers on the road, with a Jewish officer. We stopped the
car and asked him, "What the hell's going on here?" He said,
"I'm driving them off." We asked him who gave him orders
to do it. He said, "My battalion commander." So I said,
"Who's he?" and he gave me the name.

We stopped the "convoy" and told him to go back to
the village, and that Jewish officer drew his gun on us. So we
drew our guns on him and told him that he would face a
court-martial if he went any further. I told him that I was
there on behalf of Moshe Carmel—which was true enough,
though not for that purpose—and that although I had no
rank, I would go immediately to Carmel and tell him what
was going on. We were all yelling at each other....

So the villagers went back. They were only just beyond

the village, you can see it there today if you go. And we went
down to Nazareth, which was Carmel's HQ. It was all very
informal in those days—no problem to get access to the
commander. He was furious. He grabbed the telephone and
phoned this officer and yelled at him at the top of his voice
to stop this nonsense. So I know from personal experience
that there was no policy. But at the same time I must say that
had we not appeared on the scene, or had we come six hours
later, those villagers would have become refugees.

Thus some villages were evacuated and others not,
purely at random. It depended on the moral fiber of the
commander. In Galilee most commanders were all right—
that's why most of the Galilee Arabs stayed. But elsewhere
you had some who came from countries where there was a
terrible attitude of hatred for the Arabs—the feeling that
these people wanted to murder us. "We will get them out.
They can feel lucky that we don't kill them, just drive them
off." That kind of attitude.

All the above operations in the north came under the code
name of Operation Yiftach (named after Jephtah, the biblical
judge whose home was in Gilead). Yiftach was part of a larger
operation code-named Plan Dalet (D). This was an old plan. One
of its authors Yigal Yadin, world-famous archaelogist, general
and deputy prime minister in the 9th Knesset, recalls:

☐   I prepared the nucleus of Plan Dalet in 1944 when I was
     head of planning in the underground, and I worked on it
     further in the summer of '47 when the chief of staff [Yaacov
     Dori] fell ill. The plan was to take control of the key points
     in the country and on the roads before the British left.
     Because if these positions were not in our hands when the
     Arabs attacked, as we expected, it would make defense
     impossible for us.

     The key points were the Teggart forts, police stations,
     the main Arab villages, and the main roads, which we had to
     control by May 15th or we would be in trouble. For a long

time we had collected files on each of these targets and distributed them to the commanders who had to complete the ones included in their districts by reconnaissance. By May 15th most of these targets were in our hands, so we could face the situation with much more confidence, although still very, very worried. The balance of power was not in our favor, handicapped as we were by the lack of tanks and heavy artillery.

Part of Plan Dalet involved the capture of centers of mixed population, including the cities of Safed, Tiberias, and Haifa. Jaffa was not included as it had been assigned to the Arab sector, being, despite its proximity to Tel Aviv, almost entirely Arab.

HAIFA

The battle of Haifa came toward the end of April. The British commander, General Stockwell, announced to Jewish and Arab leaders that his forces were about to withdraw from their positions in the town itself in order to concentrate on the port, which was one of their main evacuation points.

The Jews had both numerical and tactical superiority in Haifa. They had settled in the Hadar Hacarmel, higher up the hills, whereas the Arabs inhabited the lower part of the town near the docks. Although there had been a good deal of harassment in the form of sniping, Haifa was one of the few mixed areas where some possibility of a compromise between Arabs and Jews existed. As in the Old City of Jerusalem, the two communities had lived together for many years; their commercial enterprises were to some extent interdependent.

Yoseph Varshitz, now one of the directors of the Givat Haviva seminary for Arab-Jewish studies, illustrates with his story the lost hope of stemming the flow of Arab refugees, which was already assuming flood proportions:

☐   Just before the war actually began I was sent to Haifa to
    work on a committee established by Golda Meir, the
    Committee for Arab Problems. It was composed of repre-
    sentatives of groups who were interested in Arab problems
    or had connections with Arabs. My task was to go down to
    the old town and buy Arab newspapers. Once I made a
    flying visit to the office of the Arab newspaper *Falastin*
    because I had a friend there—a Communist. It was in a
    neutral area so we could meet and talk about the problems,
    and then he said, "Oh, sorry, I have to go on guard." They
    had guards just as we had.
        About half the Arab population was still in Haifa at
    that time. Government officials, oil company officials, and
    so on went away—there was nothing for them to do; a lot of
    work had stopped in many places, and people who still had
    work sent their women and children away to Lebanon,
    Syria, and other places, because there was constant shoot-
    ing.
        A part of the Arab local committee was against fighting
    in Haifa because of the unfavorable tactical situation—Jews
    were up the hill and Arabs down below. But the mufti and
    his people did not want peace in Haifa, so fired from time to
    time—the Jews fired back—and so it went on. There was no
    unity of opinion among the Arabs; some responsible
    leaders, who may have been in favor of fighting the Jews in
    other places, were opposed to it in Haifa.
        So when the British said they were leaving, the Jews—
    not yet an official army—swept down and occupied the
    downtown Arab area. When this happened, General Stock-
    well, the British commander, tried to have an organized and
    legal capitulation of the Arab population to the Haganah.
    Most of the Arab leaders had left, and the few who remained
    tried to negotiate with the Haganah, who said everybody
    could stay but they had to give up their arms and also their
    people under arms—there were all sorts of fighters there at
    the time, from Syria, Jordan, Lebanon, and so forth, and
    the Haganah said these people had to be handed over.

The Arab leaders who had stayed contacted their high command and after some deliberation they said they were very sorry, and appreciated the proposal, but would have to go away and could not agree to the capitulation. The British general was astonished. He said the terms were very generous. The mayor of Haifa wept. Despite the fighting, people were used to one another. They had had a lot of business relations and they got on together. Perhaps the Arabs could imagine Haifa without the Jews, but the Jews couldn't imagine Haifa without the Arabs.

Even if the Arab leaders had wanted to stay, there were two obstacles. First, they would have been the only Arabs in the whole country to capitulate and live under Jewish rule, and this would have been a very heavy decision to make at a time when the whole Arab world was saying "we will never agree to live under a Jewish yoke." It would have been very difficult for the Arabs of Haifa to make themselves the only exception.

The second obstacle was that the whole atmosphere just then was not exactly friendly. There was quite a lot of shooting, and, as in any war, there was a little looting. So although the Haganah was telling people not to go away, I can understand why they did it.

The Communists were also telling them to stay. I remember one Arab standing near the monument to King Feisal, distributing leaflets which I had printed on a Jewish printing press. The leaflet said, "Don't go away. Reaction and Imperialism want you to leave. Stay, and let us build our independent state together with the Jews who are building their independent state."

Until the 15th May one felt there was always a slight possibility of avoiding all-out war. If Arabs and Jews in Haifa could live together perhaps others could too, and then the Arab armies might not have invaded—a small possibility, but, perhaps, if enough Arabs had stayed, there might have been a change of atmosphere. This was exactly the reason why their leaders from outside wanted them to leave.

It is possible that the Arab whom Yoseph Varshitz saw
handing out leaflets by the memorial was Tewfik Toubi, notable
in the Arab community of Haifa and a member of the Knesset.

☐   I supported the U.N. resolution of November '47 to form
     two states, as a way out of foreign rule and of the animosity
     and national strife that was the lot of the entire Palestinian
     population, Jewish and Arab, at the time. With that aim I
     supported partiton. I did it by political activity, by working
     within the Communist party among the population, partic-
     ularly in Haifa, where I lived.
          I called upon the people to stay in their homes. I
     distributed leaflets at that time, advising people not to leave.
     Some did heed, and some still today remember my call and
     the calls of our comrades not to run away. But at the same
     time, British forces in Haifa were putting trucks and vehicles
     at the disposal of the Arab population, encouraging them to
     leave.
          Then there were the atrocities that took place, before
     the fall of Haifa, in neighboring areas such as Bal el Shikh
     (now Tel Chanan) where there was a massacre. A real
     massacre. It is in the Haganah literature of the war, written
     of course from their point of view—as a reprisal, an attempt,
     so to speak, to quieten the source of fire. But it was a
     massacre—entering the village, killing men, women, and
     children. And it was not the only case, apart from Deir
     Yassin. And this had repercussions among the Arabs.
          Thus the Zionist leaders, together with the British and
     the Arab reactionaries, cooperated, sometimes without
     deliberate intent and sometimes agreeing among themselves
     upon what should be prevented: the formation of an Arab
     Palestinian state. The secret meetings between Golda Meir
     and King Abdullah were part of this—the annexation by
     Abdullah of part of what should have been an Arab state,
     the taking over of the rest by the Jews—all depriving the
     disorganized Arab Palestinians of any chance of forming an
     independent state of their own.

For my part, I watched my relatives, my friends, my own brothers leaving; but I worked on the conviction that we should not leave our homeland. I said to myself, it is better.... Of course, in Haifa we had some choice; we functioned under fear, not force—in other places they were driven out. But if they had stood up... as it happened in certain villages in Galilee when the population refused to budge. Our comrades worked among them, encouraging them not to go. People in those villages today will tell you that thanks to the Communists, they stayed two, three, four nights in the mountains without leaving the area, and then insisted on returning to their villages.

Of course there was a risk. But the tragedy of leaving their homeland was a bigger tragedy, a bigger risk than remaining, standing up and defending their rights. And I feel very satisfied. I not only stayed, myself, but served the interests of my people by asking them to stay, and afterwards, despite all the difficulties, it proved to be the right decision.

Ben Zion Inbar, one of the commanders of the Haifa area, describes the strategy for taking the town:

☐   Haifa was a town in which Arabs and Jews lived together; but there were definite Arab quarters and Jewish quarters. The Arabs were mainly downtown, and the Jews up in Hadar Hacarmel. From the beginning, from the U.N. declaration, fighting had been going on between the two sides. By the beginning of April, there was already a clear division between Jewish and Arab quarters; the town was closed from the seashore road because in that area only Arabs lived, and also to the east. Until April 20th the British army was still in command of several posts, which gave them control of all sectors. The only place through which we could enter and leave the town was through Beit Hataassia [the Industry Building]; the road there led to the suburb towns between Haifa and Acre, to the Galilee and all points north.

On the 21st, without warning,* the British evacuated all their posts. Our intelligence informed us at 4 A.M. that the British soldiers had pulled out. So we took over their posts and realized that we had to start liberating the town, especially the communication routes. We decided to start at once, on the night of the 21st to 22nd April, to attack the lower town. But first we sent a platoon under Yitzhak Soroka to take over the road which led out of the town over the Wadi Rushmaya. He was subsequently trapped there, in the midst of the Arab forces, and my battalion began to make arrangements to clear the area and rescue him.

On that night we started off from a number of points in Hadar to attack the town; and by early morning we had liberated all the town except the wadi. To relieve it, we sent a company from Neve Shanan, down toward the Arab quarters, to release Soroka's platoon. We gave them what help we could under fire, but they had a hard time there. The Neve Shanan company had to fight from house to house and only reached its target by noon the following day.

On that morning, the 22nd, when we took the main road between the Hadar and the lower town, we heard that the Arabs shouted to their community to gather near the port. When we heard it, we manned the biggest mortar which our forces had at that time—a three-inch mortar— and when all the Arabs gathered in this area we started firing on them. When the shells started falling on them, they rushed down to the boats and set off by sea for Acre. During the day they asked for terms of surrender. There were negotiations until evening, when they told us that they had had orders from their high command not to surrender— they were going to leave the town. Before the war we had had good relations with them, so the Jewish leaders asked them not to leave, but it was useless, because the mufti had

*Other sources claim the British did give warning.

promised them that after ten days all the Arab countries would invade and the inhabitants would get back not only their own houses but the Jews' as well, not to mention all the women and other "spoils." Therefore, they refused to surrender and left, all but about 2,500 who remained out of 60,000.

So we took over the lower part of the town. The British didn't interfere because, they said, they were not in charge of the country any more but only wanted to stay in a few outposts to guard their withdrawal. So we agreed to make joint patrols with the British and allowed the Arabs to leave, after giving up their arms on their way out. We took a lot of arms from them, but the British took these arms under their control and only handed them back to us when they finally left on May 15th.

Yitzhak Soroka, mentioned in that account, subsequently a professor at Technion University who still lives in Haifa, tells the epic story of the twenty-four hours his platoon spent trapped in Wadi Rushmaya:

☐   At that time I was already enlisted, though not officially of course, but we studied and trained in order to assume full-time duties in the Haganah. I was a platoon commander in a battalion which was mostly made up of Technion students. And as far as I can remember, we were stationed at what was then called the Telsch Hotel, now the Megiddo. A day or two before all this thing happened, we were planning what at the time was called the "Scissor Plan," which was intended to relieve some of the pressure which the Arabs were putting on Haifa. At that time they were shooting alongside Herzl Street; in fact, it was quite dangerous even to cross the street.

There was a plan which essentially called for two or three or four units to go down from Hadar to the lower part of the city, and by destroying strongpoints and positions, to relieve the pressure. In accordance with this plan, I went to

the top of Shuk [Market] Talpiot, which at that time was
just on the edge of the Jewish part of Haifa. I climbed onto a
roof to look at the area I was expected to operate in, in the
coming few days. And while I was there, looking downtown,
I was called back to my commanding officer who said,
"Forget about everything else, we are now going to take
Haifa, because the British are leaving." So in fact they
changed the plan completely.

Then I was advised that my unit was to start right away
by taking over the Najada Building, which controlled the
Rushmaya Bridge. The Arabs had cut communications
between Haifa and the settlements north of it by shooting at
this bridge. This was very short notice indeed, because when
I was given this order it was midmorning and we were
supposed to start the operation at midday. I went right away
to Beit Hataasia again, a building which overlooked the
Wadi Rushmaya, at that time in the Jewish part of the
Hadar, and my second in command went back to our HQ
and assembled our platoon, which was brought down to
Beit Hataasia in Hadar.

We made a hasty plan. It called for us to drive two of
what then passed for armored cars—you can see the remains
of some of them today as you drive up to Jerusalem—to the
far side of the bridge over the wadi—that is, the Arab side,
where the Najada Building was located. The idea was to take
them by surprise and to take over the building. This part
went rather well; we went down and managed to take the
building within a couple of minutes, because we really did
have the advantage of surprise. There were only a few Arabs
in there at the time. Another group of ours was supposed to
take over a second building, a little farther down, but they
didn't succeed and were evacuated shortly afterward, so we
were left isolated in this building we'd taken.

Soon enough we found that actually we were trapped,
and we couldn't, for instance, stay on the roof, which was
exposed to fire from higher buildings. The whole building
was exposed because those around it had been destroyed,

and for the next few hours we were subject to rather heavy fire and in fact the Arabs were able to get close enough to the building to throw in hand grenades, quite a few of them in fact, and it's rather unpleasant, to put it mildly, to have hand grenades exploding in a building while you are in it. One came in, bouncing down some steps toward where our wounded lay, and without thinking I picked it up and threw it out. It exploded right in the window.

For the next few hours we were in a very tight situation. We had three killed, maybe ten or fifteen wounded. We ran short of ammunition. We had no food with us, only a little water. As the situation deteriorated, considering the fact that the lower building wasn't occupied, our commanders decided to try to bring us back, but all efforts to failed, and I think three of the "armored cars" which were sent down to bring us out were set on fire and barely managed to retreat. However, they did manage to throw us a bag of bread, I remember, which we somehow got inside. One man went out to recover the bag, which had been thrown down to us from the bridge, without realizing that the entrance to our building was pinpointed by Arab machine gunners. He was killed instantly. But afterward we managed to fasten several iron bars together into a pole with which we were able to drag in the bag. Not that anyone felt like eating.

At this time the nature of the battles was a little different. In most cases they were only short encounters, so you would take your fifty or a hundred rounds of ammunition and it was usually enough. But my people weren't used to engaging in fighting that lasted a few hours, in this case all day. Very soon we ran short. This was very serious.

Anyway, when our forces saw that it was useless to try to bring us out they gave up, because we advised them that it was no use. We had a very good connection by walkie-talkie to our people, which was very important to us, for morale and otherwise—we were able to keep in touch with everything that was going on in Haifa. They advised us that at midnight they would start to take Haifa, moving down from the Hadar. One group would come down from Neve Shanan and try to make contact with us.

When night fell, the Arab attacks slackened off. Perhaps we were getting used to the situation, and actually we marked time, waiting for the general attack on Haifa to take place. It started some time during the night, and simultaneously a company moved down from Neve Shanan, trying to reach us. Unfortunately, it took them quite a few hours, and the first to reach us did so only at about ten the following morning, that is, almost twenty-four hours after we'd entered the house.

By about 2 P.M. they'd managed to clear the neighborhood and about four or five o'clock we were brought back into Haifa. And that was the eve of Pesach, 1948. So we were allowed to go home and attend our family Seders.

JAFFA

As already noted, Jaffa was not included in the Jewish sector in the partition plan; it was to be an Arab enclave. Plan Dalet, as devised by Yigal Yadin and others, had not envisaged its capture along with Tiberias, Haifa, and Safed. But as hostilities between the two sides increased, it became obvious that it could not simply be left alone. Taken together with the Arab villages that lay east of the town, linking it effectively with the Arab townships of Lydda and Ramle and with the hill villages of what is now known as the West Bank, it constituted the edge of a wedge into the heavily populated Jewish sector that could interfere with communication routes and cause trouble in other ways. In addition, Jaffa was a danger spot in itself, for there had been considerable shooting on the "border" between it and Tel Aviv.

Alexander Zur, at that time a member of Khim, the "home guard" sector of the Haganah, gives a personal slant to the situation existing around Jaffa at the time:

☐   I lived in Holon. A few months before the shooting started in November '47, I was put in charge of the whole area south of Jaffa, in other words, Mikve Israel, Holon, Bat Yam, to the sea. We were the force which was organized to defend the south of Jaffa. Between us and the Egyptians there was nothing. Nothing at all. The Jaffa-Ramle road was kept open by the British. But they didn't defend Jaffa until later on when they saw the Arabs were losing; they moved in and said, "We are staying until 14th May."

     Their commander came to see me. He came to the gates of Mikve Israel, and asked for me; I invited him to come to our headquarters. He said "I have two orders to carry out. One is to keep the road open, the other that you should not move into Jaffa until May 14th." I agreed completely. Then he invited me to his HQ inside Jaffa and took me with a military escort. I went under an Israeli flag, and this was two or three weeks before the fall of Jaffa.

     So the position was that we encircled Jaffa from the south, the Tel Aviv force from the north, and the British in the middle. The British put up tanks to threaten us on the hill between Holon and Jaffa; they threatened to open fire on Holon if we moved. And that was the position until Operation Hametz (Leaven) at Passover, after which Jaffa was more or less finished.

The objective of Hametz was to isolate Jaffa and open a road to the airport at Lydda (which had been assigned to the Jews). In this operation the Jewish forces first brought artillery into play, though when it is spoken about today, ironic quotation marks are set around the word *artillery.* Ephraim Shorer, one of Israel's first artillery officers, who later rose to the rank of colonel and was to lose his only son in the Yom Kippur War, describes how "artillery" came into the Israeli army:

☐   In the British army I was an artillery man. The Haganah, Etzel, Lehi, had no artillery men at all. All they had was so-called infantry. Artillery people were experts in modern warfare. So, long before the first piece of artillery arrived in

this country, we'd already started to gather those who had
been artillery men in the British and Russian armies from
the refugees who arrived in Israel through Cyprus. Fighting
with big guns was such a different thing from fighting with a
rifle.

The first guns arrived in Israel three months before the
British left. It was all very hush-hush. They weren't real field
guns—they were anti-aircraft light guns from Switzerland.
They weren't really what we wanted, but that's all we had.
These thin-barreled things were really meant to fire at low-
flying aircraft and we tried to use them for field work.

The first artillery battle was the battle of Jaffa—strange
as it may seem. Jaffa was still Arab. The first to invade Jaffa
were the Etzel people—it was before the official establishment of the Israel Defense Forces so the Haganah fought
separately. The Etzel concentrated all their forces and
attacked Jaffa and got bogged down, because there weren't
enough of them and there was a British regiment there,
helping in the defense of Arab Jaffa. So they only captured
part of it, the part close to Tel Aviv.

The Haganah was called in for an encirclement of Jaffa
from the south, where Holon and Mikve Israel are. That
was the Givati Brigade in its early stages. Afterward they
were the people who stopped the Egyptians from advancing
on Tel Aviv.

I was sent there with my two guns. We actually loaded
them on trucks because they were light enough—no problem there. We covered them up, to hide them from the
British, and brought them to Mikve Israel at night. We
positioned them so they could be aimed by the last light of
that day. The target was a hill called Tel Arish, manned by
Iraqi volunteers. There were already volunteers there,
mainly from Iraq but also from Syria.

Well, that battle failed. We took the hill but it was
recaptured by the Iraqis in the morning. We suffered heavy
casualties—not the artillery so much because we were
behind, but the infantry got it.

In the morning a British delegation came to Mikve Israel in two armored cars. They wanted to talk to the officer conducting the Israeli offensives. That was Shimon Avidan, who was the brigade commander of Givati. He could speak English and so could I, so I joined him. This young British officer said, "We want you to stop firing, otherwise we'll call in the RAF." And sure enough, about half an hour later five RAF Spitfires buzzed over our positions, machine-gunned a little, and disappeared. Then they came back again to show they meant business.

Next, the British said, "Look, we are going to put our armored cars all along the road to the south, with their guns aimed at you from both sides. We don't want you to interfere with what is going to happen."

And what happened was—the evacuation of Jaffa. That is a scene I will never forget. All of a sudden, trucks and horse-drawn carts and people on foot on one side. And if you looked at the other side—to the sea—boats, all moving toward the south, toward Gaza.

Thus the British, with a full regiment of armored cars protected the evacuation of the Arabs of Jaffa—most of them—against us. And Jaffa surrendered. There were still a few thousand Arabs who remained in Jaffa, and they surrendered to the Haganah. Not to Etzel, by the way!

Shmuel Toledano, then a young intelligence officer who later became adviser to the government on Arab affairs, and a Labour member of the Knesset, has painful memories of Jaffa's capture which continue to affect his political outlook.

☐ We knew that we had to capture Jaffa and the surrounding Arab villages as quickly as we could, because we feared that soon the Arab armies would invade, and having the enemy within the country would have been very serious for us. So we were ordered to get maximum information about Jaffa so that we could capture the town, the sooner the better.

I had quite a few intelligence networks. I think the best

one was the well-known "prostitute network." We had
about five or six Arab prostitutes in Jaffa who really gave us
the best information then. It wasn't military secrets; we
wanted to know all about the Iraqi forces then in Jaffa—
about three hundred of them. Now it's astonishing and
nobody would believe it, but this Iraqi platoon was based in
Jaffa, shooting at Tel Aviv. They were sent in before the
invasion, uniformed, armed soldiers serving in the Iraqi
army.

Nobody could capture Jaffa before the British left. So
we got the information. We had a sergeant in the British
police force who worked with us—I can tell it now, it's not a
secret any more. He told us exactly when they were going to
evacuate Jaffa.

I was with the troops who entered Jaffa. It was an
extraordinary thing. For a Jew to enter Jaffa till then had
been extremely dangerous—it was an all-Arab town, 70,000
inhabitants. But when we entered Jaffa and conquered it in
April 1948 we found an almost empty town containing only
about 4,000 Arabs. For me, it was something like a dream. I
couldn't believe that we were masters of Jaffa.

The Arab population left Jaffa for two reasons. First,
because the Etzel had been shelling Jaffa for three weeks
before the Haganah entered, making the Arabs very much
afraid; some already began to leave as a result of that
shelling by Etzel. Then, there were rumors, based on the
Etzel's reputation—many Arabs were under the impression
that the minute the Jews entered the town, the inhabitants
would all be slaughtered. So the departure of the Iraqis was
a signal for the exodus of the inhabitants.

The Iraqis slowly but surely realized that they couldn't
hold Jaffa. Rather than be taken prisoner they decided to
leave the inhabitants to their fate, and they withdrew via
Ramle, which was then still under Arab control.

Although the shelling by Etzel softened up the town for
the Haganah, and they had also made minor incursions and
captured small areas before the Haganah entered, it was our

main force which captured and held Jaffa. We entered in a column of armored cars from Mikve Israel. The Etzel were well trained for individual fighting, while the Palmach was trained for war; we were also more heavily armed. The Etzel, as individuals, were courageous and willing—but they were not trained as the Haganah was.

So we entered Jaffa. I had mixed feelings. On the one hand, I felt satisfaction at capturing a town, being masters of a town which had done so much harm to the Jews over the years. But on the other hand, when I entered the houses and saw the coffee cups still—you know—on the kitchen tables, abandoned when the people just ran away, it was a shock to me. I just couldn't bear to see the tragedy and I felt it in every building as we entered them one after another. I saw how families had left, not knowing where to go. Some went by boat to Gaza, others fled by land— But one saw the families were ruined. It wasn't like the feeling one has during a war, on the battlefield, not when you see the houses, the life of the family broken into, ruined— That feeling for me was terrible.

And it affected my views on life. Not only Jaffa. Later I interrogated prisoners of war. Maybe it was then that I came to the conclusion that there must be another way. Since then I've tried to find it. In my previous job in the Knesset [adviser to the government on Arab affairs] I did my best to find some common language. We have to live together. Wars are no answer.

A further comment on the vexed question of the importance of the dissidents' contribution in the capture of Jaffa—Begin, in *The Revolt,* claims almost exclusive credit for the Irgun forces— comes from Alexander Zur:

☐   The Etzel attacked Jaffa from Rehov Herzl [in Tel Aviv]. That's all. They went to the sea, being shot by British soldiers—they were merely meddling. They never did any- thing properly. They were not a military force, the Etzel.

They were troubleshooters. They fought against the British, shelling and bombing.... But when you need regular soldiers.... They didn't have the ammunition, they didn't have the commanders. Our people were all regular soldiers. I was a major in the British army. In spite of the fact that they didn't let us fight so much, we learned as much as we could. The Etzel were insignificant, even at Jaffa. They made a lot of noise, but the whole thing collapsed. Mind you, psychologically they had some effect [on the Arab population] because they'd been shooting into the town. And I'm not saying they were not brave fellows. Many of them were killed. But mainly in vain.

THE SOUTH

The general picture in the south was of isolated Jewish settlements under attack—sometimes sporadic, sometimes fierce and sustained—by local Arabs and units of the Muslim Brotherhood. The first attacks came early, right after the declaration of partition in November, falling on settlements in the northern Negev such as Kfar Darom (a religious kibbutz), Nevatim, Negba, Nirim, and, as already mentioned, the four settlements of the Etzion Bloc farther to the northeast just below Jerusalem.

Kuba Villan, a member of Kibbutz Negba, who was to direct one of the epic defenses of the whole war, remembers how it all started:

☐   After the U.N. voted for partition, among the first victims of the Israeli-Arab struggle were people from Kibbutz Negba. It was the end of November. Our neighbors, Kibbutz Gat, called on the phone to tell us that they were without a truck. In those days you couldn't manage without a truck—we had to have some means of communication. You can't realize— It was so easy to cut telephone wires, and we had no doctors, no nurses, no supplies—nothing. In Negba we had two trucks, so we lent one to Kibbutz Gat. We sent the other one as well, to bring back the driver. On their way home they were attacked by Arabs and three members of the kibbutz were killed.

One day there was a convoy, which wanted to go to Kibbutz Gat, passing through Negba. We had to deal with the British officer who was in this neighborhood, based at the police station. I went to him because I could speak English. An armored car of ours brought me to the very verge of the road and from there I jumped into the police station and talked to the British officer, but when it was time to go he didn't want to give us an escort. The road was full of Arab trucks and I feared for my life. Our boys were standing with machine guns, covering me, and suddenly an Arab policeman said to me, "You and I are going to help each other." So we went out together, arm in arm. The Arabs did not shoot because of him. And our boys did not shoot because of me. And so at a certain point we shook hands and said we might see each other in better times . . . . He ran to his position and I to mine, and even today I believe that this is the way to solve our problems.

At that time we knew we must prepare ourselves for war. That meant to buy weapons. Today you pay taxes and the government provides artillery and airplanes, but in those days it was up to every group to take the initiative. There was nobody to push you. You had to decide on your priorities. Maybe you needed weapons more than you needed shoes.

In the days of the mandate there were many British camps in our neighborhood and some of us earned money working as hired laborers in those camps. We were able to make deals with some of the soldiers and buy a lot of weapons. In comparison with some other places, Negba was considered to have quite an armory! But the problem was logistical.

When you have several sorts of weapons, you have to have several sorts of ammunition, a problem which doesn't

exist in a regular army. For example, we had some
American Brownings but no ammunition for them. We had
to sell cows in order to buy some ammunition *from the
Arabs!*

Then we started digging in. We knew we could expect to
be attacked sooner or later. The British had built a lot of
forts, which were used as police stations all over the country.
We had one a mile away from us called Iraq Suweidan.
When the British left, they handed this over to the Muslim
Brotherhood. That was at the beginning of March. So that
in March the roads were cut; we couldn't move south, and
Jews below us in the Negev couldn't come north. If you
stand on the roof of the fort, you can see exactly how things
stood.... We had no artillery, only two-inch mortars. The
distance was seventeen hundred meters, right out of our
range. That fort caused us a lot of trouble. The army tried
seven times to capture it, and only succeeded, much later, at
the eighth attempt.

The attack, back in January, on Kfar Etzion has already
been mentioned in connection with the legendary "Thirty-five"
who were wiped out when they went to its defense. The ordeal of
these four isolated settlements went on for months. Many
attempts were made to relieve and reinforce the defenders. Yigal
Yadin remembers his role in one such attempt:

☐   One of my worst moments was in March-April when the
settlements of the Etzion Bloc were besieged and without
food. I had to make one of the most difficult decisions of the
war. All our transport, primitively armored by our own
hands, had to be used to bring supplies to Jerusalem. With
each convoy we had to fight a new battle. During a lull
when Jerusalem was better supplied, I had to make the
terrible decision to send *all* these trucks—about two hundred—south to Gush Etzion with supplies.

The whole thing was based on surprise. Quick unloading and quick return. Everything went all right on the way,
but they took a little too much time to unload and on the

way back they were waylaid at a place called Nebi Daniel. Some of the men were killed and the whole lot had to surrender and were taken prisoner. That was a terrible moment because as a result we had no capacity, for a long time, to send convoys to Jerusalem.

Chaim Herzog recalls one of his successes in negotiating with the British:

☐   When the Israeli units were trying to break through into the Etzion Bloc to save the settlers and were ambushed and cornered at Nebi Daniel and were going to be wiped out, I had a major part in negotiating their release and safe passage to Jerusalem with the British authorities.

May came. The British pullout was nearing completion. In many parts of the country battles were raging for supremacy of control over roads and strategic strongpoints. It was still not clear what British intentions for the future were, nor even precisely when they would evacuate the last points. But what was no longer in doubt was that the Jews had to expect a massed (if not coordinated) assault upon their new state, if and when they declared it, by the regular armies of the Arab states surrounding it.

Just before the final British withdrawal and the commencement of the "real" war, the Jews suffered one of their most traumatic defeats—the fall of the Etzion Bloc. In the course of this, an event occurred which is spoken of by Jews today much as the Arabs speak of Deir Yassin. It was the massacre of Kfar Etzion, not by the Arab Legionnaires but by local irregulars fighting with them, who gunned down the Jewish settlers in the act of surrender.

Yaacov Edelstein, now a journalist on the religious newspaper *Hatsofeh,* then a member of Kibbutz Kfar Etzion, tells his story:

☐   The battle of Gush Etzion, which included four settlements on the way from Jerusalem to Hebron, lasted for six

months, during which we were under siege. There were
almost unending battles; many were killed; but I want to
speak mainly of what happened on the last day.

The last attack on Gush Etzion started on May 12th,
when a large Arab force surrounded mainly Kfar Etzion, my
kibbutz, which was the biggest of the four and the center of
the bloc. This force included Arab irregular bands and
Legion soldiers, who fought together. The Legion was
commanded by British officers.

By midday on the 13th the irregulars, together with an
armored column of the Legion, managed to get into Kfar
Etzion. There were by then about a hundred and fifty people
in our kibbutz, including twenty women. Our commander
sent an emissary to the Arabs to begin negotiating a cease-
fire, but they shot him.

When the Arabs entered the kibbutz it was obvious that
we had no chance. Our commander had to decide whether to
have a Masada type of battle, till the last soldier was killed,
or to try to save those who were still alive by surrendering
our fighting men.

The commander managed to pass a message to some of
our positions; the people gathered in the center of the
settlement, where they were surrounded by Legionnaires
who told them to raise their hands. They did so, and some of
the Legion soldiers photographed them, and then shots
started coming from all directions. Many of the forty people
standing crowded together were killed immediately; those
who were not killed in the first volley started to run away,
among them myself and some friends who had not been
wounded.

But actually there was nowhere to run to, as we were
completely surrounded—wherever one ran, one was bound
to be caught. But we ran instinctively. On our way we met
some Arabs who shot at us, killing several more. Only four
of us remained, running toward a little wood which we
called Song of Songs because it had been a meeting place for
lovers in happier times. There we hid among the trees and
rocks.

We heard the sounds of shooting from the kibbutz and realized that our *chaverim* [comrades] who had remained in their positions earlier had begun to fight when they saw that it was useless to surrender. The Arabs would not accept a surrender and were bent on killing all of us.

Suddenly an elderly Arab appeared in front of us. He appeared to be wearing a Jewish prayer shawl and held phylactery bags* [*sic*]. He saw us hiding and said, "Don't be afraid; you are under my protection." It is an Arab tradition that if prisoners are taken under someone's protection they are not to be harmed, though it's not always strictly observed. He only found two of us, myself and my friend Isaac Ben Sira; the other two stayed hidden.

We went with him. On our way we were stopped by a group of irregulars who put us up against a wall and wanted to shoot us, but the old Arab stood between them and us and said, "You've already killed everyone in the village. Leave these alive." The Arabs wanted to kill him as well, but while they were arguing about it some Legion officers appeared and ordered the irregulars to take us to Rabat [Amman] and to show us to King Abdullah as the first Jewish prisoners. That saved us. From afar, we looked back to see the two who had been hiding with us being caught and shot. We were taken to Legion headquarters, which was opposite the Russian monastery.

There we were met by a crowd of Arabs who wanted to attack us; they would have torn us to pieces but for the Legionnaires, who had no choice but to fire into the crowd to clear a way for us and for themselves.

From there we were taken, through Jericho, to Amman and then to a prison camp near the Iraqi border where we stayed for about a year.

Meanwhile, the other three settlements of the Etzion Bloc began to conduct negotiations through the Red Cross for a surrender, but the irregulars continued to fight against

*These are the appurtenances of Jewish orthodoxy. It seems highly unlikely that an Arab would be wearing them.

them—they did not want to hear of surrender; but the
Legion was prepared to listen, and on May 14th the whole
bloc fell. The three remaining settlements surrendered and
all their members were taken prisoner. Some of the married
women and the children had been evacuated with the help of
the British when the fighting had begun, months before.
During the siege about two hundred and fifty people died
out of the four hundred settlers and many were wounded. It
could be compared to the siege of Masada.

It was clearly impossible to discuss a surrender with the
irregulars because they did not have the necessary organization to receive prisoners and conduct negotiations. Only the
Legion, under British officers, had such an organization.
Therefore, the irregulars killed all that were left in Kfar
Etzion, including twenty women, who defended themselves
to the last, and all the wounded in our hospital and those in
the bunkers in the settlement. Altogether, on that last day, a
hundred and fifty people were killed in Kfar Etzion, leaving
only four survivors; one of them was a girl called Alisa
Feuchtwanger, a telephone operator. The Arabs tried to
rape her; she was saved by a high-ranking Legion officer
who brought her to Hebron.

I want to point out that when the gangs broke into our
kibbutz and started to fire into the crowd, they cried out
"Deir Yassin!"

The day after this tragedy, the British mandate formally
ended. The last British units withdrew, the last high commissioner
sailed away; that afternoon, in a stuffy hall in Tel Aviv, Ben-
Gurion declared the State of Israel. And the Arab armies moved
to the attack. Shulamith Hareven:

☐ On that night we heard a rumor that we might be bombed
from the air, which had never happened. They took all the
girl medics of Jerusalem and put us into one flat, as if to
make sure that if a bomb found us, there would be no girl
medics left! There were lots of pieces of nonsense like that.
Plenty. Jerusalem was utterly, utterly unprepared.

Sir John Glubb's view on the preparedness of his side:

☐   In every war, everyone is scared and thinks the other fellow
      has all sorts of things. I don't know what the Israelis had,
      except when we got the business end of them. But I can tell
      you exactly and with perfect truth what we had.

      Of course, before the mandate ended, we were supplied
      by the British army. They provided ammunition, rations,
      vehicles, and did all the administrative side, which also
      required one or two British officers. In '48 I think I had two
      in Legion HQ. Three of our four regiments were com-
      manded by British officers. We only got our artillery two
      months before the end of the mandate. That meant we had
      to have several British officers to organize the artillery,
      because no Arab officers knew anything about it at the time.

      Before the mandate ended, I agreed with the com-
      mander in Cairo to load a ship with ammunition. He loaded
      one up according to our list. It steamed out of Suez and
      down the Gulf, where it was overtaken by Egyptian launches
      and the Egyptians pinched the lot.

      The result was that when the war began we had two or
      three batteries of field artillery. We didn't make our own
      mortars, as the Jews did. We had a certain amount of 303,
      that's rifle ammunition, and that was all. And that ship of
      ours was just about sent out before the U.N. passed a
      resolution in which all member nations undertook not to
      supply weapons to either side. And the British stuck to that,
      absolutely. Not so much as one bullet! Not only that, but
      every regular British officer with the Arab Legion was
      withdrawn.

      The great advantage the Jews had was in having lots of
      money. Every Jewish colony had concrete trenches and
      dugouts and barbed wire and minefields and everything. We
      never had a farthing. Anyone who claims otherwise is just
      distorting history.

The Palestinian Arabs were, for their part, in disarray, as
Anwar Nusseibah makes clear:

☐   As the mandate fell apart, we had to set up our own courts, defense forces, financial section—everything. And just before the end of the mandate I tried to get hold of the other committees in other cities and towns to try to coordinate with them some sort of regional or countrywide organization, but I didn't succeed very well. People thought at the time that the madness could not go on, that there would be some sort of effective intervention. Not by the British, but on an international level, or by the Arab armies, that somehow order would be restored and that things would go back to normal, but it didn't—it got worse and worse.

On the Israeli side it's very clear that they were very, very well prepared for what happened. It was all planned, all controlled. Although they claimed at the time that they were surprised and outnumbered, it's not true. They had more forces in the field, according to statistics that came out afterward, than all the Arab armies combined.* They were also in a stronger position, even as far as arms were concerned. Men, discipline, training—in every way.

We approached the war in a very weakened state. Also there had been a lot of internal strife within the Arab ranks, between the so-called hard-liners and the moderates, and when 1948 came upon us, people were still concerned with feuds within the Arab community. There was a different situation on the Jewish side.

Netanel Lorch, ironically enough, took a similar view, from the Jewish side:

☐   The Jerusalem high command did not have a clear military doctrine at that time. The assumption was that there were still people who had faith in the United Nations; we had accepted the internationalization of Jerusalem and we now know that there was a real expectation of international aid for Jerusalem. Military operations were planned only when it was absolutely necessary.

*This became the case only toward the end of the war.

Netiva Ben Yehuda:

☐ We started the war in platoons. The first fight using a company was around April. It was weeks after that that we went to war in brigades. Every few weeks we had to adjust ourselves to a new way of fighting. The training was lousy. They sent men to training exercises with five bullets each. The arms situation—I can't describe! Of course they couldn't bring in, officially, even a bullet as long as the British were here. We never had enough bullets. Every time we went into battle, in February and March, we were told: "Save your bullets! Shilling a bullet! Remember, we don't have bullets!" Do you know how many people were killed because of that? When we used automatic submachine guns we were ordered to shoot only one round at a time. And when we conquered the enemy positions we'd find a mountain of cartridge cases. They didn't even aim; they just scattered bullets in all directions.

Pinchas Blumenthal tells his story of the desperate situation as the British pulled out of Jerusalem:

☐ You have no idea what kind of tricks one had to use . . . making noises so that they shouldn't guess we had no weapons. We had none of our own. One tried to get weapons if there was danger. If I was informed that an Arab attack might come, I would go to my friends in Kiryat Shmuel to borrow weapons just for one night. Two pistols!

The British were leaving, but no one knew precisely when. I was in charge of this part of town. On the 14th I went out and saw a British officer giving orders to set up a machine-gun nest on the roof opposite our house and another below. This was awkward, because at zero hour, when the British left, I had to run down and take over as many houses as I could, but if there were going to be machine guns, what could I do?

So I went over to him and introduced myself. I said, "I'm an officer of the Haganah. What are you doing?" He said, "Oh, just setting up a machine gun, it's not so bad." I got quite friendly with him and invited him over to my house at eight o'clock when he finished for a drink.

I went to the Jewish Agency and asked for five bottles of whisky and some Player's cigarettes. Then I went to a very interesting part of town, on the border between Katamon, which was Arab, and Rehavia, which was Jewish. There were Christians there living with Arab girls, or, say, Swedish or Norwegian gentlemen living with Jewish women—all kinds of prostitutes, whom I made a point of getting to know. There were glorious possibilities of all kinds of affairs.... So I said to a certain prostitute, "I've been very nice to you, and seen to it that nobody molested you. Now, will you please invite me tonight and also a British gentleman." I gave her the whisky and cigarettes.

She was perfectly cooperative. I told her one more thing. "Do me a favor. When you pour the drink, pretend that you've filled my glass every time you fill his."

Well, we all came and had a party. After half an hour my second in command fell asleep, but I kept on till three in the morning. The British officer grew more and more unsteady on his feet. In the end, he said, "That was the first decent party I've had in this bloody country. Glorious evening! Whenever I can do anything for you—any present you want—" Well, I knew what I wanted, so I said, "When you know when you'll be leaving, just ask anyone around town for me—I'll come right away—and you just mention the time."

Next morning at 7 A.M. there was general mobilization for the Jews up to the age of sixty-five—anyone who could walk on two legs. I waited. Nothing happened, and at 9:45 word came through high command that the British would not leave that day. So all our people were being sent home. And at that moment someone came asking for me. I ran to where the British officer was and he said, "My friend, I know what I promised you, but I'm afraid I can't; because this morning we had our briefing and I had to give my word of honor that I wouldn't disclose our time of departure to anyone. So I can't—I'm sorry. But," he added, "a good soldier such as you, if you look up there at the roof and see how busy the soldiers are up there, packing their things, I'm sure you'll assume that in about fifty minutes the last of them will have left."

Good enough. I grabbed some men with rifles, and ten minutes after the British had gone I had taken over the David Building and the machine guns.

On that very day of 15th May I was on the seventh floor of a building in Jabotinsky Street under attack by Arabs. They came at us, and I had altogether eleven rifles. Italian rifles. You know about Italian rifles? The point about them is, they don't work. And I had just sixty-two bullets. I told my men, I made it quite clear: "Don't try to shoot them at a distance. Wait till they get within thirty yards." They had machine guns and I was afraid we would run out of ammunition. The Arabs were shooting at us, making one hole after another in the walls, and I was running from room to room saying, "Don't shoot, DON'T SHOOT! If anyone shoots, I'll hit him!" And one man shot out of nervousness. And I hit him.

Ben Zion Meitiv, member of Kibbutz Nirim, where a massed attack by the Egyptian army was anticipated hourly, recalls:

☐ We had, between all of us, a hundred rounds of ammunition. And our firearms! We had such a mixture. We had some old Italian rifles—we used to say, put a straw in the muzzle of an Italian rifle and you've got a broom. But there's an old Yiddish saying, "If God wills, even a broom will shoot."

With each side claiming in all seriousness to be outnumbered, short of money, starved for arms, plagued with inner dissent, and, in the case of the Jews of Jerusalem, undernourished and exhausted as well, the wonder is that the official war, when it broke out on May 15th, was fought so fiercely, so destructively, and with such heavy losses on both sides.

Part 2
The Official War

Phase 1:
The First Four Weeks

☐ There was one funny thing which many people don't realize, which was that when the state was declared on 15th May, in Jerusalem nobody knew, because we'd no electricity at that time, and having only the old-fashioned type of radio, nobody heard about it till the next day.

Even when I did hear, I must say it didn't mean very much. We all said, "Oh, those people in Tel Aviv, those politicians—!" It wasn't such a big moment. It was just part of our ordinary life in Jerusalem then, which was altogether very unordinary. What we were really concerned about was the Etzion Bloc, which had fallen the day before—we heard about *that,* of course . . . . I was actually supposed to go there as a medic just before it fell. A friend of mine was ahead of me in the line; she went instead and was taken prisoner.

Thus Shulamith Hareven remembers what others have described as the greatest moment for the Jewish people since the fall of the Temple. Many others, like her, who for months had been engaged in repelling Arab attacks, struggling to keep lines of

communication clear, and in sundry other ways fighting for an
Israel not yet officially in existence, also failed to react to its
"birth," being too preoccupied with preparing for invasion by the
regular armies of Egypt, Iraq, Syria, Jordan, and Lebanon.

This preoccupation, and the apprehension that caused it, are
expressed by "Boaz," the Palmach private:

☐   What we were facing— I sensed it at the time, but I didn't
     fully realize it until it was over. They attacked from all sides;
     we had the feeling that we were frail corks, being used to stop
     up hundreds of holes in a leaky dam, that a flood of our
     enemies might be expected at any time to overwhelm and
     drown us. There were never enough of us, and so many had
     already been killed— As fast as we stopped one leak, we
     would be withdrawn and rushed somewhere else to plug
     another. Except for the local irregulars and Kawukji's men,
     who had all the primitive ferocity of a barbarian horde, we
     were facing something that we ourselves were not: regular,
     trained, properly equipped national armies, attacking us
     simultaneously on four or five fronts with the declared
     intention of destroying us.

The view of the invasion taken by Palestinian Arabs was, not
unexpectedly, rather different. Anwar Nusseibah:

☐   The Arab armies, you know, never really attacked. You
     smile, but it is true. It was more in the nature of a
     demonstration than a war. In other words, the Arab
     countries were under pressure of Arab public opinion at the
     time to do something, because even before the end of the
     mandate the Israelis had occupied many of the areas allotted
     to the Arabs under partition, had expelled many Arabs from
     their homes and so on, and the Arab heads of state were
     under tremendous pressure to do something about it, to stop
     what was in the nature almost of genocide of the Arabs,
     although Israelis presented a different picture. Their picture
     was that *they* were threatened with genocide, all these Arab

armies surrounding them coming in and so on. Azzam Pasha, secretary of the Arab League at the time, said very, very clearly, "We are merely going in after the British withdrawal in order to restore peace and order, that is all." I don't believe the Arab armies came in to grab territory.... That is a misinterpretation of Arab aims.

In actual fact it seems clear that the Arabs' main trouble was that they all had different, and often clashing, objectives, none of which was centered upon helping their Palestinian brethren. True, the avowed aim of all Arab governments was to foil the Zionists and drive them out; but barely subsidiary goals were to enlarge their own territories and power and/or prevent rival Arab rulers from doing the same at their expense.

It had not been until the Jewish forces claimed such notable successes as the capture of Tiberias, Safed, Haifa, and Jaffa, shortly before the mandate ended, that the Arab high commands were belatedly galvanized into efforts to coordinate and prepare for all-out war; at that stage their hopes were pinned not upon their own military supremacy so much as on the major world powers to intervene on their side and compel the Jews to submit to their demands.

There *was* a master plan, of which Iraq seems to have been the prime mover, in which the Syrian and Lebanese forces were to pin down the Israelis in the north and the Egyptians were to create diversions in the south while the Iraqis themselves would, with the aid of the Jordanian Arab Legion, strike through the center, with Haifa as the ultimate target of all five armies. Haifa was to fall to the Arabs on May 21st, a mere six days after the departure of the British.

This plan fell asunder because of a divergence of priorities. Abdullah was more interested in Jerusalem and was not prepared to risk his elite Legion—upon whom he relied for the defense of his realm—on what he deemed to be lesser targets. In fact, Abdullah had even initiated secret meetings with Jewish leaders (notably Golda Meir) in an effort to persuade the Jews to refrain from declaring their state, but his terms were, from the Israeli point of view, absurd—he wanted to annex the whole of Palestine in exchange for "trying to dissuade" other Arab nations from going to war.

Abdullah's demur forced a radical last-minute change to the master plan, which resulted in the launching of the Arab attack in a state of disunity. In addition, the political leaders were at odds with the military, who knew all too well that they had neither the equipment nor the manpower for anything more prolongd than a swift knockout blow. Were this to fail—and recent Jewish successes had indicated that it well might—the Arab commanders were by no means sanguine, but as usual the politicians had overextended themselves: Their people had been led to expect a quick and decisive triumph and there was no way to extricate themselves from military involvement.

Nevertheless, Haganah commanders soberly considered that the advantage lay with the Arabs. The Jewish troops had been fighting for months and were very tired, whereas the Arab regular soldiers were fresh, if not eager. The Arabs could boast of heavy armament, tanks, and planes, of which the Jews had very few as yet, though now that the British had gone there was the potential for bringing them in—Jewish missions to armament factories in Czechoslovakia, for instance, had had notable successes and much war matériel was in Italy and elsewhere awaiting shipment.

Here is how Chaim Laskov assesses the situation:

☐   We were surrounded. The enemy's main target would be Haifa, the second, Tel Aviv. Jordan, Syria, and Iraq had to go for Afula and from Afula to Haifa; Egypt would go for Tel Aviv. The major danger was that the country would be cut in two at Tulkarm-Netanya, only eight miles. How were we to grab the initiative? You can't will it into your hands, you've got to fight for it.

Until May 15th, the individual weapon was still what counted—the side with more rifles caused more casualties. Our casualties were soaring up. That phase, of the individual weapon system, failed, and we paid heavily for it. But from May 15th we were employing bigger weapons. We had artillery, only 65-mm., which is just as effective as a Mills hand grenade *when* it explodes, and many of the rounds didn't, but we could move it around. We had armored cars. Then we got something more than light planes—some Spitfires and 109s arrived. The first plane was assembled from two Egyptian Spits that had crashed.

Now one thing favored us. After Gush Etzion fell into the hands of the Arab Legion, King Abdullah decided that he might as well stake his claim to be the commander in chief of the United Arab forces. This was granted to him because, among the Arab leaders, he was the only one who had had some sort of victory over the Jews. And he changed the entire scheme. He shifted the Arab Legion to Jerusalem, which caused the Iraqis to shift toward Jenin on the way to Netanya. The Syrians, therefore, and the Lebanese, stayed in northern and eastern Galilee.

And now this man, Ben-Gurion, against all advice, directs an attack at Jenin, directs an attack at Latrun, directs an attack at Ashdod—all out—with what little we had.

THE NORTH

The most dangerous situation here lay in the Jordan valley (just south of the Sea of Galilee) where old established settlements such as the two Deganias and Zemach suddenly found themselves in the front line against the Syrians. But farther north the Lebanese were making what turned out to be their one real push of the war.

Yerucham Cohen, Allon's information officer, recalls that after the Yiftach Brigade's First Battalion had attacked the invading Lebanese at Malkiya with some success, despite a lack of the heavy arms to match those of their opponents,

☐ ...the situation was very poor, and Yigal [Allon] decided

that I should try to go by car to Tel Aviv, which had already
been bombed by the Egyptians' Spitfires. I drove through
Tiberias, but I had to go through the Jordan valley to get to
Tel Aviv. At Porush, which is just above Degania, I stopped,
and for two hours I actually watched the battle the
kibbutzniks fought against the Syrians. I was supposed to
hurry on but I couldn't—I was shocked to see it all
happening before my eyes, like a movie at a cinema.

Eventually I went on, and that time I saw [Yigal] Yadin
and Shimon Avidan and asked for reinforcements.

Yigal Yadin recalls these as among the worst moments of the
war for him and sums up the opening phase of the "real" war like
this:

☐   The Egyptian army was actually progressing toward Tel
     Aviv. The Syrian army was descending toward the Sea of
     Galilee, attacking Degania, the first kibbutz. Jerusalem was
     being heavily bombarded by the Arab Legion, who were
     trying to conquer it. We were in a hopeless situation—not
     having the arms to respond and not having enough reserves
     because we put most of them right on the frontier to absorb
     the first shock.

     Some leaders from Degania, well-known Zionist fig-
     ures, came to Ben-Gurion in Tel Aviv and said, "In a few
     hours the Syrians will capture Degania." Ben-Gurion said,
     "I'm sorry, I have nothing to help you. If you like, go to
     Yadin. Maybe he has something." They came to me, elderly
     people, very respected. They were crying. I said, "I'm sorry.
     The only advice I can give you is, prepare Molotov cocktail
     bottles and throw them at the tanks." They said, "What do
     you mean?" I said, "It's the only way. It's proved itself. I can
     do something else for you. I can send [Moshe] Dayan to
     command." He was less well known then, but they knew
     him—he was born there. "I'll put all the forces in the north
     under his command." And they went home, and one wrote
     in his diary later on, "We came brokenhearted from this
     meeting."

The result was that when the first Syrian tank came into Degania they threw a bottle onto it and it was stopped. But the turning point there was quite a different one.

The day before I spoke to them, there had been a boat with supplies in the Mediterranean. There were some 65-mm. guns there from the 1870 Franco-German war. They were given orders not to approach because the British, right to the last, were still blockading us. Miraculously, two British frigates passed this boat but let it go.

The morning the British left, the boat landed and unloaded four of these guns. Ben-Gurion wanted them sent to Jerusalem. I wanted them sent to Degania. I said, "I'm a Jerusalemite. I know they will hold the Jordanians for a little longer, even without guns." I think it was the longest debate we had. I remember banging my fist on the table and breaking the glass top.

In the end we compromised—the guns would be sent to the north for one day and then immediately to Jerusalem.* They had no sights. They were put on a mountain just above Tiberias. When the Syrian tanks began to approach, these guns suddenly began to shoot. They were taken completely by surprise. They knew we had no guns, and although the shells fell into the lake and too far to the right, a terrific row immediately broke out among the Syrian commanders; they withdrew, and that saved the day.

Ephraim Shorer, the artillery officer, was active in this engagement after other battles:

☐ After Jaffa, we returned to base, grubby and unshaven. Our unit was not yet organized. I'd been promised time to organize a proper, well-trained artillery unit, but this happened—the Jaffa business—only a few days after the guns arrived. And just as I got back to our unit, I was called

---

*There is some doubt about this. Some experts say that *two* guns were sent to the north and two to Jerusalem. Subsequently, the Degania guns were sent to Jenin.

again to HQ who said, "The Arab Legion is attacking
Gesher in the Jordan valley, and there is an ultimatum by
Abdullah. You're to take those two guns and go there
immediately to strengthen the defense of Gesher." So, still
unshaven, I took my unit up there.

We positioned ourselves, thinking we could win the war
with those two little guns. Luckily there was no battle! But
after that I stayed in the north. I was to participate in a
number of battles in that region—early battles, including the
one in Safed. But before that I was suddenly called back.
With great glee I was told: "Artillery pieces—real artillery
guns have arrived, and you are to take them into your unit."

Now these anti-aircraft pieces, by the way, were new,
but the guns that arrived now— Well, perhaps you've seen
films about the Southwest passage, Afghanistan, and all
that, in which the guns were dismantled, loaded onto mule
trains, and taken up mountains. Very small guns. I have
never seen such small guns in my life. Ancient French things
dating back to the last century, small caliber, 65-mm. I
nearly cried when I saw them. Of course, I'd had in mind
something from the second world war, something I'd had
some dealings with before. I just looked at these things—I
didn't know how to start. I mean, guns are not something
you fire "maybe." You've got to have a good bore and good
ammunition and very accurate instruments, otherwise you
never hit your target.

So I said, "Look, if I'm to command this unit, will you
look through all those volunteers arriving in Israel now?"
(This was just after the British left, in May.) "Maybe there's
a Frenchman who knows these guns." And by luck, they
found a Russian Jew who'd been an artillery officer in the
French army, and he knew them. He became our instructor,
and I said to HQ, "This time you've got to give me time. I
have to prepare the unit properly. These are proper guns—
we have to learn to know them." They didn't even have
sights. They told me, "The instruments are coming on the

next boat." But then, they'd told me to expect twenty of these guns, and all I got was four.

So we started with one battery, four guns. We had plenty of problems because guns are supposed to come with books that are called range tables, which give you the elevation, the range, and so on—putting it very simply, because there are other factors, like how much charge you give it. So we had to prepare our own range tables.

We went to Herzliya and put a gun on the beach, using surveyors' instruments with a three-kilometer base. We fired into the sea at different elevations, took readings, and interpreted the range. This was all very primitive, yet it worked. I was given two weeks to train my unit. My deputy and I sat at home—we lived in Tel Aviv at the time—evening after evening, trying to make those range tables into something.

All of a sudden a dispatch rider came to tell me to come at once to HQ. When we got there, we were told: "Orders from Ben-Gurion. You are to take this unit immediately to the Jordan valley because the Syrians have invaded and have already taken Kibbutz Massada and Sha'ar Hagolan and Zemach. They're attacking Degania already and if you don't hurry there'll be a catastrophe." I said, "How can we? We're not trained, we haven't got sights yet or anything— Give us handguns and we will go and fight—" But no. "Orders from Ben-Gurion."

This was our first real artillery battle with the "new" guns. Luckily, we won. Our guns had a range we hadn't got with anything else. Our mortars had only had a range of two to two and a half kilometers—these had seven kilometers. We gave the Syrians a surprise, and they withdrew.

Things were progressing more favorably along the coast. As the mandate ended, the Carmeli Brigade (named for its commander, Moshe Carmel) captured the Arab town of Acre, north of Haifa, and western Galilee was soon in Jewish hands.

THE SOUTH

Despite the successes in the north, matters were very serious elsewhere. Dov Joseph, the military governor of Jerusalem, wrote in *The Faithful City* that Ben-Gurion had the responsibility for putting out "a thousand fires" at once with strictly limited resources. The Legion, already in control of Latrun and thus of the supply route to Jerusalem, was shelling the city. In the south, the Egyptians were moving in: Kibbutz Nirim was under siege. Kfar Darom had already been severely hit. Egyptian units of the Muslim Brotherhood had spread east across the Negev to link up with the Arab Legion south of Jerusalem.

Ben Zion Meitiv:

☐   It was Saturday, 13th May. As information officer for the area, I got information from an Arab who announced that the police post near our kibbutz [Nirim], which had been held by the British, had been taken over by Bedouin policemen. He said the corporal and the sergeant had quarreled about the radio and had each gone off to get more members of his tribe. So the post was empty. I took some soldiers and captured the place, and stayed there.

After a few days I got information that there were some units of the Egyptian army approaching the Palestine border. At 8 A.M. on Friday one of my agents came to tell me that the Egyptians were going to attack Nirim and were already taking up positions. So at ten o'clock I got on my horse and rode around to all my Bedu friends and told them, "Tomorrow there'll be a battle. For your own sake, since the fight between us and the Egyptians is nothing to do with you, you should move away." Later on, years later, I met some of these old neighbors again. They had never forgotten that I'd come to warn them.

Then I returned to the police post, which was where my agents used to bring me my information. That's where I stayed, and I watched the battles for my kibbutz from outside.

Ours was almost the first kibbutz to resist. And the Egyptians had enormous superiority of weapons: tanks, armored cars, artillery—against thirty-five boys and girls. Papers found on their commanding officer when we captured him later, explaining how it was that he failed to capture Nirim, described some electrified towers which came out of the ground, opened fire, and went down again! Pure imagination, of course. But they threw such a heavy bombardment of shells at the kibbutz that they thought we were all dead. There was very little left standing. They couldn't imagine that we would resist, nor could they guess that we had, between all of us, a hundred rounds of ammunition.

So when thirty rifles opened fire, the Egyptians were astonished—they'd been sure they were going to walk in with no resistance. They ran away and they didn't come back—but they held the kibbutz under fire for some four weeks.

I was outside, as I mentioned, at the police post. I tried to approach but I couldn't get in. The eastern side was open, but the kibbutz was besieged from the north, south, and west. They were just about able to take out the wounded at night, but it was days before I managed to get in because of the shelling.

It was in a fearful state. My home was completely destroyed, everything from my past, all the souvenirs from my childhood—gone. I don't think I can explain or express what I felt.

But still, I didn't doubt it would all be rebuilt. We were so optimistic, I didn't have a moment's doubt that we would triumph in the end. Perhaps you'd call me naïve. We were sure that when the British left, tens of ships loaded with arms, just outside our territorial waters, would come in and

that then we'd have all the arms and ammunition that we
needed. The whole world would help us, we were sure—it
was waiting! Nobody would let us go under.

The situation in the Negev is described by Yehuda Amichai,
now one of Israel's foremost poets:

☐   I was in the Seventh Battalion of the Palmach. We fought in
all the battles of the Negev, from early spring '48 to early
spring '49.
        First we acted as a kind of guerrilla force because the
Negev was all cut off; there was only a tiny little passage
through the Egyptian lines. We actually had only Stens;
later on we got a few German and Czech rifles. Some of the
rifles, which had been made by Skoda in Czechoslovakia for
the German army, still had swastikas on them. It was a very
ironic thing, but of course you don't really react much to
such things at such a time. Anyhow, this battalion, which
was the youngest in the Palmach, was only created early in
'48; we had our staff commanders, but our rank and file were
mostly eighteen-year-olds from high school with just a few
old-timers like myself who'd been in the British army. We
took shape into some kind of battalion; I think we were
about three hundred men—maybe two hundred of them
knew how to shoot—and a hundred and fifty girls. There
was no morale problem. Everyone was eager. They'd mostly
come from youth movements, Hashomair Hatsa'ir* and
Hatsofim, the Scouts. They were all used to living together,
boys and girls.
        We reached the desert after a very strange journey—it
was hard to get down there. The night before we'd had to
pass through the enemy lines, just smuggle ourselves
through. We were stopped at Iraq Suweidan, the fort near
Negba. We were coming as reinforcements to the Negev
and it was important that no one should find out we were

*The left-wing pioneer movement.

there. So we stopped off at Beit Tuvia, which was the last *moshav* [cooperative farm settlement] before the Negev, in sight of a belt of enemy land, with kibbutzim, of course, inside the belt.

They put us into the houses of the *moshav,* vacated by the women and children who'd been evacuated some weeks before. I, with the ten men of my squad, were to sleep in the kindergarten. Later I wrote a poem about it—young soldiers, not so far from kindergarten themselves, sleeping surrounded by all these teddy bears and toys.

And then the next night we just crept through the lines to a kibbutz called Ruhama in the eastern Negev, very much exposed. We went into a wadi and dug ourselves in—no tents—we were just sleeping on the earth, and the girls cooked us very bad meals .... It was a strange time.

Colonel Marcus, who helped a lot to build up the Israeli army, came down and asked Yigal Allon (who was then the commander of the south), "What about the reinforcements you were promised?" So Allon pointed at us, and Marcus said, "These children? I thought they were a troop of youth scouts!"

And then when the shooting started, the battalion was split up into tiny groups and we all went out to take part in little skirmishes—only at night. During the day, without tents, we just had to sleep in the wadi in our dugouts. While we were there we were fairly safe at that time because the Egyptians hadn't got that far, but at night we had to initiate these little guerrilla actions; the main idea was to clear the inside of the Negev of the enemy and to give the Egyptians the impression that there was a big force there. So we'd shoot at a gun post, capture a small hill and hold it for some hours, shooting from it, and so on.

We had to be back by sunrise because we had no air force to protect us. I remember when we'd come back to our wadi, the girls would be there, lined up—because they didn't come out with our fighting units; I think this is one of those strange legends of the war, to keep the Americans happy,

that a lot of girls took part in combat—on the whole I only
knew two or three girls who actually fought. Mostly they
just waited and cooked bad meals. But in the morning they
were all lining up at the entrance to the wadi, looking to see
who was coming back and who wasn't.... After these
actions night after night, in which we usually suffered some
casualties, we'd drag ourselves back, very tired, and sometimes the girls would start weeping. It was a real partisan
war.

The Egyptians, meanwhile, were still making headway in the
direction of Tel Aviv. Kibbutz Yad Mordechai fell after a heroic
resistance, but Kibbutz Negba still stood in the way of the
invaders. Kuba Villan, who was to command the defense of that
kibbutz, tells how the settlement's ordeal began:

□   Negba (which means "toward the Negev") is in a very vital
     strategic position. The fort of Iraq Suweidan overlooks an
     important road intersection, which runs from Tel Aviv to
     Gaza and the Negev in one direction and from Ashkelon
     toward Hebron in the other; that was only a dirt road then.
     So the Egyptian and Arab armies decided that within seven
     days they'd meet in Tel Aviv. Why should they bother with
     the Negev? They could ignore all the Jewish settlements
     there. Once they'd conquered Tel Aviv, they'd have con-
     quered everything.
         But if they moved north, bypassing Negba, their lines
     of communication would be endangered. They did some
     aerial reconnaissance and saw that Negba was a large
     concentration, because the groups that used to go to the
     Negev were always gathering here at night. Later, we found
     the enemy's maps and military orders which said that the
     "Zionist fortress, Negba," had to be conquered.
         So immediately after they invaded Israel they decided
     to conquer Negba. But they did nothing for about four days.
     We were lucky—the delay enabled us to entrench ourselves
     in fourteen positions. If they'd attacked at once, we might
     not have been ready.

At first they just sent a few tanks and reconnoitered the place. There was a bit of shooting here and there, which just sharpened us up for the real onslaught.

Then came the first air attack, and in it our commander, Yitzhak Dubnow, was killed. You know, when you believe in someone, believe that he is your pillar, and then suddenly he's dead, you think the whole world is crashing.... Dubnow was among the officers who'd established the Palmach; he was a very great authority and a moral leader. The effect on morale was devastating.

Kuba Villan's wife. Rachel, gives her views of these events:

☐　We had a meeting in the kibbutz. We'd decided to stay with the men, but someone came and told us we had to be evacuated—all women with young children and some others as well, so that for every child there would be someone. The truck came for us at night and we all left. Kuba wasn't in the kibbutz then; he was up north taking a course. We were taken to Herzliya and put into an empty school. Naturally it was very uncomfortable—there was nowhere to wash clothes, no proper beds; we slept on mattresses on the floors of the classrooms. Later they tried to billet us in people's houses in the area, but not everyone was willing to take us in; they made excuses, for example: "My husband needs his sleep, I can't have children here," and so on.

After a few days, news came that Dubnow, our commander and our white hope, had been killed in the first bombardment. Only three of us were told at first. None of us knew how to break it to the others—we felt, I think, in our hearts, that without Dubnow our kibbutz might be lost. The burden of such news was terrible to carry; we were afraid of the effect on morale when everyone knew. In the end the army sent someone to make the announcement, so we didn't have to do it. Everyone wept, but there was so much to do we couldn't fall into despair.

Then we heard they'd called on Kuba to take command. He came to see us on his way south. We had to say a quick good-bye. I knew what he was going to. Who knew when or if I would next see him?

Kuba Villan:

☐ Shimon Avidan, the local area commander, was asked by the members of Negba to send for me. He called me out of the course and I was taken to the war room, where he told me that Negba had to fight to the last bullet. I started arguing with him. What did he mean, the last bullet? He showed me the situation on one of the war maps, how the Egyptians were advancing. The Israelis had to try to stop them at Gedera, and we had to fight to block their way.

So it was in Negba that one of the most extraordinary things happened that I know about through my readings of history. If you look at our war cemetery, you will see there, in the names of the fallen on the headstones and on the walls, the symbols of cooperation, of an ingathering of exiles, of mutual support. In that cemetery are buried people from France, Poland, Chile, Argentina, England—from sixteen countries altogether. Our own members were the backbone of the resistance, but we were helped by groups from neighboring kibbutzim, members of Kibbutz Artzi [the left-wing kibbutz movement]—young people, the oldest was only thirty-four.... We proved what can happen when farmers turn themselves into soldiers, though I had to convince them, when I first came, that you can't run two businesses at once—you have to make war or milk cows. Anyhow our cows were killed. But we were defending our homes. It's very difficult to explain to a Sudanese soldier why he should die. It was easy to explain to our people why they should stand. They had the feeling that they were adding to Jewish history—maybe two sentences, or a word, or just a comma—something. They had the feeling that, for the first time, they were masters of their fate. They had to decide their own future—no one else.

Rachel Villan:

☐	Letters came quite often, and sometimes the men would be got out of the siege, by night, and come for a rest. The extraordinary thing was that they all managed to shave every day, even in the trenches, to keep up the general morale, and the women left behind in the kibbutz always saw that they got hot food. They'd cook at night when the shelling died down and somehow heat up the food to serve it by day. Apart from their clean-shaven faces, the men, when we saw them, always looked exhausted, and their clothes were filthy and ragged.

Shimon Avidan, one of the most distinguished commanders of the war, who now lives in retirement in his kibbutz in Galilee, is still able to enter subjectively into his feelings about the ordeal he and his men were facing in the south:

☐	One of the hardest things for me is to be put in a position when I can't help, when I am "played" like a chess piece by events beyond my control. In a war there are days which are without end; minutes which are like a year; and there are other times when minutes and days end too quickly.

One of the hardest days was when the Egyptians broke through our lines near Beit Tuvia. This was one of our battle techniques—to accept the attack of the enemy, form defense positions, and to pin down their operational reserves. And there at night we took a hill called Hill 69; they opened an attack with artillery and tanks and slowly but surely our foxholes were filled up with sand. We were still short of all kinds of materials—we had no spades even, and we used all kinds of makeshifts to dig with. The commander was killed, and the second commander was killed, and another commander ran away, and panic seized those who were left. They fled, and the Egyptians mowed them down like flies from pursuing tanks. Then the men in the next strongpoint started to retreat. I, together with some other people from the staff of the brigade, stopped them in the middle of a field—in open terrain—we pushed them down and used our fists and yelled at them, and so slowly we had enough force to concentrate groups which advanced against the Egyptians and stopped them.

On the same day, the Arab Legion attacked one settlement called Gezer on the old highway from Ramle to Jerusalem, and I got desperate calls—no more ammunition, many people killed—and all I could do was to lie to them, say we were sending reinforcements. Soon it would be dark, the enemy didn't fight at night—"Hold out!"

At six o'clock the Legion entered the settlement. There were twenty-four people left, and they took them all prisoner, boys and girls. That was a long, long day.

The abrupt switch in Avidan's account from the southern to the central sector illustrates the technical dilemma, not only of those who were in command of war operations but of those who, many years later, try to organize accounts of them. The war fronts have to be dealt with separately and yet they were interconnected and interdependent. Soldiers telling their war stories "jump" from one phase of the war to another without explanation or transition; from one front to another in the same way. What was going on in one battle area directly influenced the conduct of the war somewhere else.

In parenthesis here I would emphasize that the Israelis were still essentially amateurs—in the true sense—at nearly everything they were then engaged in doing, from state building to soldiering. Before following General Avidan's lead and proceeding to the central front, here is a story told to me by Israel Galili, then head of command of the Haganah, which admirably illustrates the dichotomies existing within the country on this account:

☐   When Mickey Stone [Colonel David Marcus] came to Tel Aviv after his tour of the southern command and was invited for the first time to take part in the meeting of the security committee under the chairmanship of Ben-Gurion, he began his speech by saying, "First of all, you will have to decide if you are at war—if a war is going on, or not." This was in March. For three months we had been in a war situation, so his listeners were astonished, and one of them dared to give vent to his astonishment. So Mickey retorted, "I'm sorry, you are not at war. How can it be, if you are, that the Palmach boys in the Negev are catching cold because of lack of sweaters and shoes, whereas in Allenby Street and Nachalat Binyamin Street [in Tel Aviv] the shopwindows are full of clothing and you don't try—or maybe you haven't the power—to commandeer those goods? You haven't mastered even minimal logistics." Well, of course, even for Mickey Stone it took time before he understood that we were an army in the making, without authority to compel people or requisition supplies, without resources of state.

It is important to realize that this situation—the groping toward "professionalism" through the early chaos and confusion—continued even after the declaration of the state and the emergence of what had been underground forces into an official, but still disparate, army. This will be seen in reports of sector commanders, which were given to Ben-Gurion and Galili after these first four weeks of fighting.

JERUSALEM AND THE CENTRAL FRONT

There remains to this day a good deal of dissension about exactly what Jordan's aims in this war were. Netanel Lorch, John and David Kimche, and other Jewish historians insist that Abdullah wished to make Jerusalem, with its Muslim holy sites, his capital, and that his soldiers' actions in attempting to isolate and starve out its Jewish sector were only a means to the end of capturing the whole city eventually. Sir John Glubb, on the other hand, as has been seen, denies any such intention on the part of Abdullah, at least as reflected in the orders he received. He recalls:

☐   The day the mandate ended we crossed over to assist the Arabs of Judea and Samaria. I knew there had been some secret meetings between King Abdullah and Golda Meir but at the time he didn't confide his political activities to me. And I didn't want him to, because of course one's position was always open to all sorts of intrigues and accusations and charges and so on. So I very carefully and strictly adhered to the letter of my duties as commander of the Jordan army. I know that the king was most anxious not to fight; his solution was to accept partition but to assist the Arabs of Judea and Samaria, which was contiguous to Jordan. Galilee was cut off, next door to Lebanon. Gaza was next door to Egypt. We had no access to those, not being allowed to cross any area allotted to Israel, so all we could do was help the people from north of Jerusalem up to Nablus.

Our orders were that Jerusalem was international, so we couldn't go up there; we made an earth track up a spur of rock running up to Bethel. The approach to Jerusalem is more complicated actually, full of gorges and so on; we couldn't go that way because we'd been told on no account to enter the international area around the city. So when we got to the top of the hill there, we found the Israelis pouring troops up the road from Tel Aviv into Jerusalem.

We'd been told not to go into Jerusalem. So for five days we sat, north of the city, watching the Israelis occupying the whole place. If the Israelis had succeeded in completely occupying Jerusalem, they'd have driven down to Jericho. Meanwhile, we were on the hills from Ramallah to Nablus. Once the Israelis had got down into the Jordan valley, they'd have surrounded us. We'd all have been in the bag.

It was common knowledge at that time that the Jews intended to take over the whole West Bank. If we'd stayed on the hills—where we'd every right to be, the inhabitants having invited us—they'd have bagged us. Of course we were spread out. I sent one battalion up north to Jenin and Nablus, and then, in order to prevent the whole Israeli army from taking Jerusalem, we put a battalion at Latrun, to close the road.

The Teggart fortress at Latrun—that vital spot, the key to Jerusalem—had actually lain empty for forty-eight hours at the time Glubb sent in his forces. On May 14, Kawukji, who had been occupying it, pulled his men out without prior notice and without informing his so-called allies. Had the Israelis capitalized on this godsent opportunity to secure Latrun for themselves, much bloodshed would have been avoided. As it was, the chance was lost. The Legion arrived to fill the breach and dug in, not only in the stronghold itself but in several flanking positions. No fewer than four subsequent efforts by the Israelis to dislodge them failed, at a disastrous cost in lives and morale.

The position of the Jews in Jerusalem was perilous. Their outposts to the south—Gush Etzion—had fallen even before the final British withdrawal. It had been decided to abandon the potash works at the northern tip of the Dead Sea, together with its attendant settlement. Two other settlements—Atarot and Neve Yaacov, flanking the road to Ramallah—had been evacuated, exposing Jerusalem from the north.

The hopes of the seventeen hundred Jews left in the Old City fluctuated. Rivca Weingarten:

☐ When the British left Eretz Israel on May 15th, the real fighting started. There had been fighting all along—bombs were thrown and shooting took place and so on—but after May 15th it got more serious. I must stress the fact that we were a tiny quarter, with a tiny population and a very, very small number of real fighters. When the Arabs attacked us in the beginning, we had no weapons or ammunition, we had not enough medical equipment and not enough people who could stand up against the many soldiers who surrounded us and the tens of thousands of Arabs who lived around the Jewish quarter. So even if something quite minor happened—say, the bomb that was thrown at this house, our house here, which was on the boundary of the quarter, or something similar on the other boundaries, a house blown up, a fire breaking out—what could we do? I mean, we couldn't go anywhere except deeper into the quarter.

And so it happened throughout the fortnight that we fought, that whatever happened we could only move deeper and deeper into the Jewish quarter, until at the last all the Jews were gathered together at the Yochanan Ben Zakai synagogue, one of the four Sephardic synagogues in the Jewish quarter. It is partly underground; the street is much higher than the synagogue floor. And the Arabs—whether regular soldiers or not—walked past in the street pointing their rifles into the synagogue where the people were gathered, warning them that if they didn't surrender the place would be blown up.

Malca Tarragan was not so sure that these withdrawals were inevitable:

☐   The first day of the war—the evening of the day Ben-Gurion declared the state—I was in the communal kitchen when a little boy called everyone to come there. He told us the British army had left the Old City. Immediately all the Haganah and Etzel and Lehi people took over the British positions. And that first Shabbat we spent in the Armenian Church, very high, from which we could see out over the whole of the Old City.

That evening the Jewish Agency asked us over the radio to leave the church because it was a holy place. We didn't want to, but they repeated their order until we did leave. And the moment after we left, the Arabs took the Armenian Church over.

The next day, Sunday, I was ordered to fill sandbags. I was in Habad Street. That's still much higher than the Street of the Jews. At 10 A.M. a woman was wounded. And she told me, "Never again will I go into Habad Street!" From that day, we lost the Old City. Because we moved downward, little by little, day by day, losing the advantage of the high ground, until we reached the synagogue, where we stayed until the surrender.

On May 19, after waiting five days, Glubb felt compelled to commit his troops...

☐   ...to prevent their encirclement if the Israeli army built up strength and drove down to Jericho. There was absolutely no alternative. We had to go into Jerusalem to survive at all. But, of course, the theory that Jerusalem was an international city had been destroyed in advance by the Israelis, who not only occupied the entire area of the city [except the Old City] but also the Hadassah hospital area, the university, and everything. If they had agreed to carry out the internationalization plan, as we were trying to do, there wouldn't have been any need for them to protect anybody from anything—the city would have remained at peace.

The Legion moved in, took Sheikh Jerach from the ill-prepared Irgun unit, and from this and other eminences belabored Jewish Jerusalem with mortars and shells in an effort to force a surrender. There is some discrepancy, here again, between Jewish accounts of the Legion's armory and Glubb's:

☐   I've seen reports by Jewish writers of our entry into Jerusalem. One said that "The Arab Legion advanced in massive strength preceded by lines of *tanks*. Heavy artillery opened fire, lighter artillery accompanied with a bombardment, infantry poured in..." et cetera. The entry into Jerusalem was carried out by four old armored cars, which the British army had given to disposal, and a company of infantry. No artillery was used. Not only that, but every regular British officer with the Arab Legion was withdrawn by the British government.
      Our artillery was limited to firing four rounds a day. This myth about the tremendous bombardment of Jerusalem— I got a letter from a Jew the other day, saying, "You are the only Christian who has bombarded and massacred in the Holy City." *We hadn't any ammunition!* That's on the

lowest level. I always adhered strictly to only shooting at
military targets. But the Israelis had large numbers of their
own homemade mortars and ammunition, and they could
bomb the Old City from the New City.

Photographs of the bombardment, as well as eyewitness
reports by those who suffered under it—not to mention "ear-
witness" reports of hearing British officers roaring commands
and abuse at their Arab subordinates in several close engagements—make the above rather hard to credit, but Glubb's air of
complete sincerity makes disbelieving seem discourteous.

No one denies, however, that a concerted and determined
attack was launched by the Legion on the Old City on May 16.
For two days the demoralized inhabitants of the Jewish quarter
radioed increasingly desperate appeals for help, indicating that
they were momentarily expecting to succumb. David Shaltiel, the
commander of the Haganah in Jerusalem, decided, for what
Netanel Lorch calls "humanitarian, not military, reasons," to try
to take the Old City in order to save them.

Lorch explains the background to this controversial figure:

☐   David Shaltiel was appointed by Ben-Gurion to a large
    extent because of his diplomatic ability, which he did have.
    In the Haganah he was always busy with acquisition of
    arms, which was a matter of smuggling and negotiating, and
    so on, or with intelligence. He had never been a field
    commander. Ben-Gurion appointed him because he still felt
    at that time that Jerusalem was basically a political problem,
    and that probably accounted for a good deal of the waste.
    You can't operate in military terms on a humanitarian basis.
    You have an objective and you try to achieve it. You don't
    send in forces after a force which is lost. That's a very basic
    rule of warfare, which was not kept in this case.

One of the officers most fundamentally concerned in
Shaltiel's plan was Uzi Narkiss, who was to lead the successful

attack on the Old City in the Six-Day War nineteen years later. In 1948 he was deputy commander of a Palmach battalion.

☐   The plan was that the Etzel people, who were very noisy but did not have more than between one and two hundred soldiers in Jerusalem, had to capture the Shechem [Damascus] Gate and the Rockefeller Museum and to penetrate the Old City from there. The Lehi—only a few dozen—had to take the New Gate and get in through that. The Haganah main force under Shaltiel—I think two battalions—had to penetrate the Jaffa Gate and to raise the Israeli flag on the Tower of David. And the Palmach was assigned, in a diversionary operation, to capture Mount Zion in order to help all the others.

Nobody but Shaltiel himself relished this plan. Yitzhak Rabin, whose crack Palmach shock troops were to be sidetracked on the "camouflage" operation, was furious.

☐   I told him what I thought in frank terms. I said, "Your plan is idiotic. It can't work. But Jerusalem is more important than either of us, so I will try to carry it out."

Narkiss says that the battalion commander, Yoseph Tabenkin, "did not think the Mount Zion operation was important enough. So he told me, as his second in command, that he was going to Tel Aviv to arrange some things concerning the battalion and I had to take command of this operation."

Netanel Lorch:

☐   It was right after the massacre in Kfar Etzion. There was a real fear that if the Jewish quarter fell there would be a massacre there. So our two platoons of people who were supposed to be distributed in different units were taken as fighting units, and we, as squad leaders, were told to penetrate into the Jewish quarter through the Jaffa Gate.

Simultaneously, the Palmach undertook to penetrate through the Zion Gate.

They undertook it with reluctance. Uzi Narkiss:

☐ I brought our battalion to Yemin Moshe, a district just across the valley from the Jaffa Gate. Out of the thousand who'd come to Jerusalem with the battalion at the beginning of April, there remained about two hundred and fifty. Most of the rest had been killed or injured, and a few had deserted; so in all there were a hundred and twenty-five soldiers for the Mount Zion attack on May 17th.

I talked to David Shaltiel and reminded him of our agreement, which we'd reached when he had arrived [to take command] at the end of March and he had told me to capture Kastel. I had said, "Okay, we will do it"—we were very good at attacking, we were *plugot makhatz,* shock troops. But we were not experts in holding. We needed to be relieved.

So now Shaltiel said, "Okay, we will relieve you after you take Mount Zion." He asked me if I had an Israeli flag to hoist on the tower on Mount Zion. I said no. I was not accustomed to such a thing, nor did I think it was important. This was a lesson we learned—when we entered Jerusalem in the Six-Day War, every command had flags. Still, I thought he sounded a bit critical of me and I took it personally.

Anyway, with or without flags, Mount Zion was captured, which put one platoon out of action. So there were about a hundred men up there and we had to defend the place. All day I was waiting for Shaltiel to keep his promise to relieve us, but it wasn't done.

Meanwhile, the situation in the Old City was very difficult. Shaltiel called me again and asked me to try to break through the Zion Gate to break the siege on the Jewish quarter. You must always know, before beginning any military operation, what your objective is, and on this occasion the mission, as I understood it, was just the breakthrough. As to what we would have to do then, no details were given.

(In this connection, Netanel Lorch remarks that it wasn't clear what would have happened if they *had* been able to link up with the Jewish quarter. "Would the Jews have been evacuated? Would we have held on to the impossible perimeter of the quarter? Or tried to capture the whole of the Old City? There were no clear-cut answers to that. It was left open.") Narkiss continues:

☐   So I told Shaltiel, "Okay, we will do another operation. We'll break through the Zion Gate and get into the Jewish quarter. But once more, the same condition: Someone has to come and relieve us here first, because until now, no one has come." He said, "I know, but I'm sending a company to replace you."

Netanel Lorch:

☐   The whole thing was pretty much of a mess and we lost some very precious hours. The briefing took rather long. I must say that when you stand today at the Jaffa Gate and look down and try to re-create the plan, even under the best of circumstances it would probably have been suicide.
    The idea was, since the Jaffa Gate was totally closed off—they had established a concrete wall—we would penetrate through the little grate in the Citadel. A very distinguished archeologist gave us some detailed explanations, which in different circumstances I would have found fascinating. In these circumstances we felt they were just a waste of time, and we wasted some additional time because nobody had prepared the flag that would be hoisted on David's Citadel, and more time still was lost because our driver was not familiar with that area. This was the same Commercial Center which had been looted in November and to which no Jews had had access for six months.

So he took a wrong turning and more time was lost. In any case, rather than getting there at ten or eleven o'clock at night we got there at five or six in the morning, and when the day began, our so-called armored trucks, homemade "sandwich trucks" [armored with steel plates lined with concrete], made their way in toward our target.

We'd been told that the Arabs in the Old City were panicking, fleeing, that they had only light arms and no machine guns—and all of a sudden some very concentrated machine-gun fire opened up on us. We were like sitting ducks. One of our commanders with a good sense of humor said, "If intelligence tells us that they have no machine guns, then they can't possibly have any, and if we think they have, it's probably ten Arabs with rifles being given the order to fire, fire, fire, fire, fire. We just *think* it's a machine gun, because intelligence is never wrong."

We were about a hundred and twenty people—four platoons: two of our training corps, one of Moriah, a Haganah field battalion, and one Irgun. In Jerusalem, on a lower level, cooperation between Irgun and Haganah was perfect. There was a strong feeling of solidarity untouched by the squabbles in Tel Aviv about ideologies and doctrines, et cetera.

Narkiss recalls that night:

☐   When you look at Mount Zion from Yemin Moshe, it looks very tiny, but once you are on it, it's a large area. So one platoon had to defend this whole place. Another had to break through the Zion Gate, and another had to support it. The breakthrough force did not number more than eighteen soldiers plus the commander, who was "Dadu," David Elazar, who afterward became chief of staff.

The soldiers were tired—very, very tired. I remember that never in the Palmach had we asked for volunteers. That time I did—my people were so exhausted I had to ask for volunteers to do the breakthrough. Anyway, they did it.

Dadu with his eighteen men reached the Jews in the Old City.

Netanel Lorch:

☐ During the night we wasted, the Palmach had captured Mount Zion. The following night, when we finally started, having lost any possibility of surprise because during the whole day we had been there and the Arabs knew precisely what was coming, thc Palmach was able to penetrate through to Zion Gate to link up with the Jewish quarter for a couple of hours. Meanwhile, I was with a group which tried to penetrate through to the Jaffa Gate, which was a total failure.

In retrospect, I might say that it served as a sort of diversion exercise for the Palmach, enabling it to penetrate through the Zion Gate without a single casualty. This is rather typical of warfare—the successful operation has no casualties while the failure ends up with a good many. If only it had been planned that way, we could have saved ourselves a lot of blood. I think there were some twelve killed out of a hundred and twenty.

There was one fellow who was killed the first night, trying to jump from one of the trucks into an abandoned shop in the old Commercial Center. I had no way to evacuate him. Though my people were being trained as NCOs, they were still pretty raw recruits. I decided that for their morale it would be terrible for them to know they were spending that night with a dead comrade, so I pretended he was only wounded. To keep that up for a whole night was quite an effort.

In any case the attack failed. We never even got to the little platform by the grate, outside the Citadel. The idea was to leave the leading car, continue on foot to the iron grate, and blow it up with a bungalow torpedo charge, then rush in and occupy the Citadel. Instead, all hell broke loose. They'd had a whole day to prepare for us. They were waiting with machine guns, hand grenades—it's enough to drop a hand grenade from the Old City wall to make it impossible to get near it.

If there'd been better coordination, or any at all, between the Palmach and the Jerusalem command, they might have got together during the previous day and said, "All right, this one has lost surprise. Let's keep it as a diversionary attack. Let's pretend we're attacking, but not attack seriously, and let's concentrate our real energies on the Zion Gate." But the command structure was not very clear: who was giving orders to whom. The Jerusalem commander [Shaltiel] would not accept orders from the Palmach commander [Rabin] and vice versa, and there was a lack of coordination at the higher level.

We made up for it to a certain extent on the lower level. I remember that a friend of mine, who happened to be the operations officer in the Palmach Battalion, came to us in the Tannous Building and said, "Look, we're going to attack tonight near Zion Gate. Let's at least coordinate our fire so we won't kill each other." In the higher echelons, the very acrimonious relations which had existed earlier had given way to hardly any contact at all. In a military situation, someone has to be the boss.

Meanwhile, on Mount Zion, Uzi Narkiss was waiting for his relief.

☐   They finally arrived—eighty men with a commander at their head. But it was not a company. They were people who had been collected by Shaltiel's forces from all over Jerusalem. Old people. He said he had no others. Maybe. So I asked the commander, "Are you ready to replace us in maintaining, and holding, the corridor from the Zion Gate to the Jewish quarter, a hundred and twenty meters?" He said, "No. I've never met these men under my command. It's not an organic company. They're people from all over the place. I've never set eyes on them before. They don't even know each other.

They're not strong enough." I understood what he felt. "Are you sure?" I asked him. And he said, "Yes."

So I told him, "All right, we'll go into the Old City, and you'll reinforce the few troops who are with the besieged Jews." He wasn't particularly happy, but he entered with his force.

One of these "old people" was Leo Wissman, the furniture maker from Mamilla Road, then aged forty-three. After "watching the last of the British march away," he had spent time digging trenches around the district of Nebi Samwil, donating blood, buying some of the new stamps, and in general living life as normally as possible under abnormal circumstances, until he was approached by a Haganah commander who told him, "Last night the Old City was conquered, and we need people there—not to fight, but to bring relief supplies, to help." Wissman recalls:

□   I was very attached to the place, so I said, "If it's only a question of being there to hold it, not to fight—" Because to fight you need training. Even though I had been in the Haganah since 1932 and had done a little shooting, I had never thrown a live hand grenade.

So I went along. On the way I met a friend of mine and told him the news: "The Old City's been taken!" He didn't believe it. "But we've been told," I said. In reality, the Old City hadn't fallen, only Mount Zion. The fact was that if we had known the truth, I don't know how many of us who were ready to go there would have agreed to do it.

As we were getting ready to go in, we got the first new rifles to come into Jerusalem. They were not cleaned of their oil, even—straight from the factory—we had to clean them. When we took hold of them, we looked—we looked like real soldiers.

But when we got to Mount Zion, which *had* been captured the night before, I got the most impressive sight of my life. At about eleven o'clock the guns began firing from all directions. The commander came to us and said, "We are

going into the Old City after two thousand years." I can't
explain the feelings I had—I, a Zionist from my youngest
days! But until then we had not known that we were going
into the Old City as fighters.

Our task at first was to take in supplies to the men who
were in there—sanitary materials, ammunition, and other
things. After the Zion Gate had been broken into, we had to
go five or six times, from Mount Zion into the Old City,
carrying supplies.

At five o'clock in the morning I asked the commander,
"Are we to remain in the Old City or are we going back?"
And he said, "You're staying in." So we stayed in the Old
City, which was all very fine, only what happened? At six in
the morning the Arabs came to shoot up the house where we
had put all the supplies.

And later still, at noon, the Arab Legion arrived and cut
us off again from the Zion Gate, from the New City. The
plan had been to send another group of Palmach to break in
through the Jaffa Gate. But that attack was not successful. It
was very difficult. The car that was brought to the Jaffa Gate
to blow it up was bombed by the Arabs.

And here begins a very, very hard story. Who was
responsible that the Palmach, who conquered and opened
the way through the Zion Gate to the Old City, left the place,
without taking into account that the other way, through the
Jaffa Gate, had not been opened? The old question— Who
was in charge of this group, of that group, who had the
responsibility, who had the duty—? There was no coordination.

Uzi Narkiss:

☐   At about four o'clock on the morning of May 18th I decided
to withdraw from the Old City. Why? First of all we had
information that the Arab Legion was entering Jerusalem
from the north. The other reason was that I had been
promised that after we had broken through the Zion Gate,

we would be relieved. This bunch of middle-aged people couldn't be called a company. It wasn't feasible to assign them to replace us. And that's it. We withdrew.

Just south of the city, in a kibbutz called Ramat Rachel, a most dangerous concatenation of forces was threatening the perimeter of Jerusalem. The irregular Egyptian units known as the Muslim Brotherhood had made their way east across the top of the Negev, via Beersheba and Hebron, and linked up with the Legion. In this one spot, therefore, the forces of Egypt and Jordan cooperated, with telling effect, showing in microcosm what might have happened had there been more comprehensive coordination between Arab armies.

Their joint attack began on May 21, three days after the abortive attempt by the Jews to relieve the Old City. After two days of heavy bombardment, an infantry assault by the Arabs took Ramat Rachel. The Arabs celebrated their success by an orgy of looting in which they were surprised by a counterattack by a Khish unit, which, however, handed over the kibbutz to a Khim (home guard) garrison. They were chased out again by local Arab villagers the next day. Yet another assault by the Jews recovered the kibbutz, or what remained of it—it was now severely battered; but this did not lessen its strategic importance, and on the afternoon of May 24 the Legion mounted a determined attack involving armored cars and half-tracks. This restored the kibbutz to Arab hands.

The story of the final Jewish counterattack is told by two soldiers who participated, a commander and a private. The commander was Menachem Roussak:

☐   At Ramat Rachel there were Egyptian soldiers, and, it seems, some Saudis too, as well as others. The settlement passed from hand to hand. It was defended by its kibbutz members and also, in the last stages, by some people from the Etzioni Brigade and by Palmachniks of Har El.

   One day our forces were in the main building, while the Arabs occupied the rest of the kibbutz—a critical situation.

The Arabs were firing at the main building with cannon from Bethlehem, in addition to their forces inside the settlement. The whole building was being attacked by shells and bullets from all sides. The kibbutz was in an important strategic position: If we could not hold Ramat Rachel, we could not hold Arnona or Talpiot.

So Yitzhak Ben Zvi came to my headquarters and said he wanted to talk to our people in Ramat Rachel. It was impossible to get there—too dangerous—it was under heavy fire, and we could not endanger him. So we went with him to an outbuilding where we had our communications center, and he spoke on the radio to the commander in the kibbutz, Yehoshafat Arkadi, who later became head of information. The Arkadi and Ben Zvi families were friends. I stood near Ben Zvi and heard him say, "Fati—" (Fati was Arkadi's nickname)"—all Jerusalem is depending on you. Hold on!" We all realized then that it must be really vital if the head of the National Executive gave such an order.

Of course he received the answer, "We will hold out." And luckily that same night a unit of Palmach came and we were able to capture all of Ramat Rachel and also the Jordanian post nearby, where there were Jordanians and Egyptians fighting together. From the moment Ben Zvi came to my headquarters to ask those few tens of people to hold out for the sake of the whole of Jerusalem, we knew we couldn't fail. To tell the truth, even I, who was responsible there as regimental commander, didn't know the situation was so critical.

"Boaz," who took part in that vital assault by the Har El contingent, relates:

☐   We went along in buses to the outskirts of Jerusalem, where we got off and went into a couple of buildings—empty Jewish buildings that had been evacuated due to the massive shelling around Ramat Rachel. We usually started out on an action in the late afternoon, to be ready for night fighting.

This time we arrived about dusk and then had to rest and eat something—I don't know what the cause of the delay was— the whole thing was such a *balagan* at that time, such a complete muddle. We stayed there till early in the morning, when we were called, and scouts led us through rubble and undergrowth toward Ramat Rachel.

We found a good hiding place there, where we stayed, no one knew why, getting more and more worried because the sky was getting light—we were used to fighting in the dark.

Finally we were lined up in readiness and told to pick up our things—metal ammunition boxes of bullets for the Spandau, a light machine gun, and a few shells for the two-inch mortar. That was our "artillery." We started moving across a field toward the kibbutz. The Arabs, who were occupying the tallest building in it, must have seen us, because they began firing at us as we came. Not far from me I saw my friend Latsi hit in the leg. How we got across I don't know, but by running almost on all fours we got to the wall.

There we gathered in groups, platoons, I suppose you'd say; then we had to make a dash for it across the clearing— irregularly and from different spots. We ran like mad to the kibbutz dining hall, which was the only building left in the hands of the Haganah. One of our chaps, running just in front of me, caught a bullet right in his back pocket, where luckily he had a flashlight. When we made it to the dining hall he actually laughed as he pulled the bashed-up light out and showed it to us.

The dining hall, now Haganah HQ, was a massive two-story building, built like a fortress. There were lots of sandbags around the windows because the Arabs had been pounding away at it from their high spot and from all around. The people who had been holding the place came down thankfully from their positions and handed over to us. We were posted at various strongpoints, and all day we fought to keep the Arabs out.

We had some wounded, whom we took down to the

basement of the building to be treated by a doctor we'd
brought with us and a young nurse, who were down there
working without pause the whole day.

The basement opened out on to a corridor which led to
the outer door, and somehow one of the Arabs managed to
kick or blow this door open and throw grenades into the
corridor. One of them landed near this nurse, and she got her
legs full of shrapnel. The doctor bandaged her up, and
although she couldn't walk, she went on crawling around
helping the wounded. Once, when I helped a wounded man
down, I saw her bandaging one of her *chaverim* from her
group in Haifa. He was in a bad way. She kept her face
turned from him so that he wouldn't notice she was crying.

They kept pounding at the building with 5-pounders,
and all day the window holes kept getting bigger. We got
very hungry. We were hungry already when we arrived
because of waiting all night without food, and now we had
hardly anything to eat or drink. Then somebody found some
cans of food and opened them, and we found ourselves
scooping jam and sardines out of cans with spoons—no
bread, of course—and there was a tank of oily water which
we drank by bashing our cups down to scatter the oil.
Needless to say, vomiting and diarrhea were soon added to
our discomforts.

We had to hold on till evening. Then we crept out in
darkness and surrounded the buildings the Arabs were in. I
remember throwing myself down behind a bit of cover and
discovering it was a dead bull—a lot of the kibbutz animals
were casualties. Under cover of darkness the Arabs were
also busy, bringing in more men and machine guns. We
threw grenades and got them out of some of the buildings
and obviously killed a few of them.

At the end they were all collected in this one, very tall
building. Then through our lines came "Moshe Piat." He
was quite a character. He had earned his nickname by
working with the one and only piat in the regiment. A piat
was a kind of bazooka. He held it to his shoulder and fired at

close range. The shell had a sharp nose; it penetrated into the
inside of the target where it wrought havoc. Moshe used to
stroll around the battlefield looking like a little bespectacled
bank clerk, carrying his piat as if it were a briefcase or a
lunchbox.

As we edged nearer to this last Arab stronghold, the
officer called to Moshe and along he came, smiling at us all
as if he'd come to sign autographs. He aimed at one of the
windows where there was a machine-gun post and scored a
direct hit, silencing it. The Arabs who were still left in there,
ran, so Ramat Rachel was finally ours.

Of the many conflicts and contradictions in accounts, none
is more important or intriguing than the question of whether the
military aims of the Arab Legion did or did not include the
capture of Jewish Jerusalem. That there was not much effort to
do so after May 24 is not in dispute; but on that day, according to
Jewish historians, there was a determined effort to penetrate the
New City from the Damascus Gate. Netanel Lorch adds these
personal reminiscences to the full account of this attack, which is
given in his book:

☐   From Tannous I was transferred to Notre Dame where I
     commanded the sector. At first it was twenty-four hours on,
     twenty-four hours off, but then there was nobody to relieve
     me and I was there continuously, roughly from 23rd May to
     10th June. We had hardly any sleep. I would say there were a
     lot of casualties, but the main problem was that we were
     perpetually hungry and I felt like a louse. I had about a
     hundred and twenty people at that time. I timed my rounds
     of positions so that maybe I could be in two positions while
     they were having their meal. Maybe I could have two meals
     rather than one without anybody noticing, because I was
     continuously hungry. A rather mundane fact....

     I don't know if the Arabs realized how close they came
     to starving and thirsting us into surrender. Dov Joseph's
     book tells how he, as military governor, evolved a ration

system that was quite fair; we [soldiers] got more than the civilian population, but we still didn't get by any means enough to eat—or to smoke. We had no cigarettes. When we got a handout of five cigarettes, we knew: Ah-ah, they want us to attack somewhere tonight! I remember one of my boys found in an abandoned Arab pharmacy some anti-asthma cigarettes and in desperation we started smoking those, but they were terrible—they make you cough.

The Legion made one attempt to penetrate into the New City. It was on May 24th—my birthday, and I got some hours off and missed the attack. My relief was on. They moved an armored car up to the New Gate, where young boys, sixteen or seventeen years old, stopped it with a Molotov cocktail. Then they brought up an ambulance, which was also stopped, and these vehicles made a road-block.

Subsequently, we had a two-hour cease-fire and I went down from Notre Dame and we found the bodies of Arab soldiers in the courtyard. Their idea had been to move up with armor along this very narrow road and pile the infantry into the courtyard of Notre Dame; so they were stopped in the nick of time. Once they realized this wouldn't work, they decided that they wouldn't try to capture Jerusalem outright but try to force us to surrender by making the siege hermetic at Latrun.

But we didn't know that they'd decided not to attack again. And they kept us on our toes. Every morning at 10 A.M. like clockwork they used to come up from the Damascus Gate, right there in the open, with 17-pounders, and shell Notre Dame. There was nothing we could do about it—we had three light machine guns there, which was a very considerable part of the Jerusalem arsenal at that time— until the "Burma Road" was opened. I remember very clearly when the first medium machine gun into Jerusalem came to Notre Dame.

I remember standing there waiting for ten o'clock, and sure enough, they turned up. Our people were given strict orders not to fire unless there was a direct attack against Notre Dame. It's pathetic to read Glubb's memoirs, moaning about their shortage of ammunition—his people were wasting it all over the place. You can still see the holes in the walls of Notre Dame—those thick walls were being broken down by artillery, for what purpose was unclear.

In any case, we waited there with our new, medium-range machine gun until they came up on their daily exercise, and then I ordered, "Fire!" And that was the last time they did it. For the first time we were able to fire down to Damascus Gate.

Sir John Glubb, notwithstanding the holes in the walls of Notre Dame, sticks (if I may put it that way) to his guns:

☐ There was never any question of our capturing the New City, whatever the circumstances. It was never suggested to me. We hadn't come to help the local Arabs to attack the Jews! We'd come to defend them, because we knew that Israel was a highly organized state, and also of course European in their level of education—they were turning out their own mortars, their own bombs, their own armored cars, and everything like this, whereas the Palestinian Arabs were an ignorant, Eastern, agricultural people, who couldn't do anything.

And afterward, when the U.N. was by way of standing between the two, on more than one occasion we used to get bombarded by mortars from the New City. We'd ring up the U.N. and say, "Hi, we're being bombarded, can you stop them?" And the U.N. would reply to me, "We can't stop them, I'm afraid! The best thing for you to do is send a few shells back, and then they'll stop."

We had orders from our government, "Whatever happens, always obey the United Nations." But as far as we could see, there wasn't much use doing that, because the Jews took no notice. I remember the Hadassah and the Hebrew University, which theoretically were included in the

U.N. area. The chief U.N. representative would go up there to have a look and be stopped by an Israeli sentry who said, "Get out." He'd say, "But I'm from the United Nations." The sentry said, "I couldn't care less: get out of here."

Despite the repulse of the Arab Legion at Notre Dame, the situation of Jerusalem was still desperate. Ben-Gurion passionately believed that unless the siege could be broken at Latrun the city would be strangled into submission through lack of supplies. Latrun was the throttling noose.

He therefore ordered—against the advice of Yadin and most of his other commanders—an all-out attack against the Legion at Latrun on May 24. Those who were called on to carry out this foredoomed assault, with raw troops, in daylight, begged a delay of twenty-four hours, which Ben-Gurion gave them, but then it had to be done.

This first battle for Latrun was one of the most traumatic of the war for the Jews. Netiva Ben Yehuda:

☐   War carries no insurance schemes. Things happen. You expect casualties, you even know that 10, 20 percent of them are probably due to mistakes and the *balagan* of a war. You can't control everything. But you can't keep quiet when you see high officers make such obvious mistakes as happened at Latrun.

Not one general wanted to implement Ben-Gurion's order. Not one. So he took one officer, who was such a nothing, he said, "Yes, yes, I am ready!" He didn't have soldiers, so he took immigrants fresh from Cyprus.... Is that a way to run a war? To prove what? That Ben-Gurion's "regular army" didn't fight by night? If it will save one life, why must you fight by day?... You know, there isn't a thing in the world worse than dying in vain during a war.

Chaim Herzog was one of the commanders of the operation:

☐   It was terribly hot. We attacked late. Many of our attacks were delayed; it was always disastrous when they were. In general this attack was a terrible mistake because Latrun *had been in our hands* and then we'd left it, because we'd had to rush the same battalion down to stop the Egyptians. We'd left this vital area empty—the Arabs as well as the Jews left it—for two and a half days, 15th to 18th May. Had we had some overall approach to strategy then, we'd definitely never have left Latrun empty.

The whole thing could have been done by a strategy of indirect approach. We should never have gone head on at Latrun, we should have gone around and cut them off. Then, to use unseasoned troops.... We'd asked for a week to train the brigade—most of the people were from the British detention camps in Cyprus—but they said we had to attack immediately because otherwise Jerusalem would fall.

I was the operations officer, and it was just too terrifying for words. Burning heat, they didn't have water bottles.... There's a little fly called *barkhash* which ate away at everybody, people were suffering terribly from skin diseases.... Crops hadn't been harvested, we had to push through high grain and weeds. The general staff had jeeps but the troops moved on foot, and they were just mown down by the Legionnaires who'd been waiting up there for three days. The retreat was not organized. It was every man trying to save himself, and there were many acts of bravery, getting wounded men out. That was one of the worst things I can recall.

Of course, the attacks relieved the pressure on Jerusalem. Glubb's forces were limited, so our attack did pull forces away from the city when the Legion had to reinforce Latrun. But it should have been done in a different way.

Uri Avneri:

□ It was a terrible battle to be in. A day battle—a hell of a difference. During the night we'd occupied the heights around Latrun from the south. My section was sent to guard the flank on one of the hills. When the battle started next day, the enemy didn't see us. We kept our heads down and watched as if from seats in a gallery. I had the unique experience of seeing a hundred people being killed before my eyes. It went on one or two hours. Our people were routed. They were killed as they fled like madmen, running through the unharvested field.

Shimon Avidan:

☐   The attack was made by people who had come from camps in Cyprus four or five days before. They had a training of two days. They didn't know their commanders. They had no common language. They didn't know the country—they'd never smelled the soil or seen the things that grew here. And they'd no sense of direction.

Sometime after the battle, we found a group of bodies—no longer bodies, bones—of wounded people who had run in the wrong direction because they didn't know where they were. They had been under the command of an ex-British army officer, who had received a direct order from Ben-Gurion, which should never have been given, because the minister of defense is not a commander in the field.

So I don't think his decision was the right one. It's true that the situation in Jerusalem was desperate; but all the same, the defeat of Latrun was a very hard blow to us and had a bad effect. And soon after, the Palmach opened up an alternative way, which we called the Burma Road, which made it possible to bypass Latrun and reestablish the link with Jerusalem.

"Tsippi," who had carried guns on the convoys:

☐   I was with my regiment in Hulda when the Givati Brigade tried to conquer Latrun. I and some friends of mine who were visiting me were terribly worried about the battle—I was doubly worried because I was a radio operator by then and I'd read all the messages.

So when the whole awful thing happened, and we knew the battle had failed, we took a jeep, put some cans of water in it, and drove out from Hulda as far as we could go in safety. I went because I could speak Yiddish. Our idea was to call to these boys who were retreating, or fleeing from the battle, and help them get back safe. Because these were people who'd come from Cyprus only a few days before. They didn't know anything—no Hebrew—nothing—and some of them were being killed because they ran in the wrong direction, right into the Arab guns. They were all mixed up. Some of them had never even got to Latrun at all, and now that the battle was over and lost, they'd lost all sense of direction. It was burning hot—a terrible *khamsin* [dry desert wind]—the sun was blinding them, and they didn't know where to go.

We called them in Yiddish and asked them to come and drink water, and then we pointed the direction. It was awful to see them.... Somebody who fights and gets killed, that's bad enough. The thought that they might get killed simply by running the wrong way was somehow worse.

I always ask myself if it wasn't a mistake to take them at all. They were survivors of the holocaust. And many of them were killed before they could enjoy the fact that they'd come home. No one knew who they were; no one knew if they had families. *We* had our families and our lives here to fight for, but they had nothing— They hardly knew what they were doing. It was awful—cruel—I don't know if we had the right to send them there straight away.... It still troubles me, when I think about it.

The first battle of Latrun and the final recapture by the Jews of Ramat Rachel happened on May 25. Three more desperate days elapsed before the climax of the struggle for the Old City was reached on May 28.

Rika Meidav speaks about what was going on inside:

☐   The people that really were sent by the Haganah fought
hard, very hard. I specially remember one—a young boy,
full of life and spirit, who used to laugh all the time and
really show the Arabs that we were still alive there. When we
had no more guns, we made grenades ourselves. You make
them by taking cans and putting in all kinds of stones and
little things, and some dynamite. . . . It made a lot of noise,
just to show them we were not finished.

Rivca Weingarten:

☐   While the inhabitants were gathered in the underground
synagogue, the fighters—the Haganah, Lehi, and Etzel—
and the few doctors and nurses we had, collected in the last
hospital remaining in the Jewish quarter, Misgav Ladach.
One doctor risked his life to take a Red Cross flag up on the
roof to remind the Arabs it was a hospital. But they paid no
attention, and blew it up.
    And that was the thing that broke us, because we had
nowhere to go and there was nothing to be done, and that
night we evacuated the injured and brought them to Batei
Machasi, which was the last gathering place.

Leo Wissman:

☐   The fighting was very hard, and we [the "old people"] were
able to help, chiefly by building fortifications and standing
guard by night to give the forty or so younger people who
had been fighting there a chance to sleep. In '67 I met one of
these younger men again, and he told my son, "You can
be proud of your father. He raised our morale." I could
stand for ten hours in the night, better than younger people
who were already deadly tired, and I remember toward the
end I would say: "Send me five minutes to sleep, or two
minutes, and I'll be back."
    On the Thursday night I made a tour of the old
synagogues, and I saw the old men and women, and the

children, in conditions I can't describe. So I realized that if
the next day the fighting was not stopped, none of us would
live through it. I firmly believed that the Arabs would kill us
all if they overran us. The only hope was to surrender to the
Legion.

So in this mood, when I came back from making my
rounds, I wrote a letter to my wife to explain that if we had
known where we were going to, and what we were going to—
Unless she realized that we had been misled, she would think
I had been irresponsible, leaving her like that with a baby. I
gave the letter to a young girl. But later I changed my mind
about it and took it back. I destroyed it. I don't like to
remember that letter, that I wrote it, even. It came from my
deepest heart when I thought I was going to die.

Even Rika Meidav saw the inevitability of surrender:

☐ It was obvious we had to surrender, because who could fight
under such conditions? You had to consider the civilians.
There were so few fighters, and no help from outside. The
decision was made by Moshe Rousnak and Rabbi Weingarten. I thought we could fight on a little longer. There were
some who thought we should, and others who said we must
consider the danger to the population. Then Weingarten, as
head of the community, took it upon himself to decide to
surrender.

Rivca Weingarten:

☐ I want to stress that it was a decision taken by the three
fighting organizations. I understand that they got agreement
from headquarters outside Jerusalem, and that they saw no
alternative but to give up.

Both Yitzhak Rabin, in his memoirs, and Menachem
Roussak, to me, expressed horror and astonishment at the
surrender. Roussak:

☐   I was ordered to reconnoiter to see if anything could be
done. So I went with another commander and we climbed to
the top of the belfry of the church that stands on Mount
Zion. Standing right up there next to the clock, I directed my
binoculars to the Old City, and I didn't believe what I saw.
        I saw Jews with white beards, women and children and
soldiers with white flags walking toward the Legion positions. They were surrendering, and no one knew they were
going to do it! I was horrified—there'd been no communication—we outside knew nothing. Despite all our efforts,
the Old City was yielding. For me, everything went black—it
was as if I had witnessed the destruction of the Temple. I
who had been in there myself at one time with the Palmach
and had been involved for many months saw the surrender,
and I seemed to see the ghetto surrendering to the Nazis.
        I could not look, and ran quickly to the field radio and
told headquarters that I'd seen the Jews of the Old City
offering surrender and that there was no more to be done. I
just can't forget it. It was a tragedy—to see the Arabs triumphant, and Jews with white flags carrying the Scrolls of the
Law.

Sir John Glubb describes his side of it as...

☐   ...a very unpleasant military operation, because there were
masses of tiny little houses, and you could only get from one
to another by knocking a hole in the wall and shooting your
way out. And so we progressed from house to house in the
most unpleasant manner. But the minute the shooting
ceased, I went into the Jewish quarter to talk to the Jews,
whom I found a very charming lot of old people, most of
them deeply religious—that's why they were living there. I
had considerable conversation with them, and I personally
organized our Legionnaires to help carry all their luggage
and that sort of thing.

Rivca Weingarten:

☐ Of the two rabbis who went to surrender to the Arabs, one was a Sephardi and one an Ashkenazi rabbi. When they contacted Abdullah El Tel, the Jordanian commander, he said he insisted on negotiating with the men responsible for the military forces as well as the head of the Jewish community. So the head of the Haganah, Elimelich Naveh, went with a few others to meet Abdullah El Tel, and the agreement was signed.

Now Tel came to Batei Machasi—of course it was in ruins—and he gave an order that the fighters should stand on one side of the compound and the residents on the other. He was amazed to find out that there were fewer than thirty soldiers, with no ammunition whatsoever. They put their rifles down—they did not have even one bullet left—and Tel looked at all the others: many of them old men who were mostly scholars of the Law. That same minute Tel changed his mind and said *all* men should be taken as prisoners of war, and also he shouted out, so loud that everyone heard it: "Had I known that this was the situation—that you had no fighters and nothing to fight with—I would not have wasted so much ammunition on you. I would have fought you with sticks and stones."

So this explains why men of fifty, sixty, seventy years old and these two rabbis aged over eighty were taken as prisoners of war, because Tel's idea was that when he came before King Abdullah he should not lose face through having too few prisoners.

Of course I wanted to stick to my father and my mother who was partly paralyzed by a stroke she had had when our house was bombed. But she cried bitterly and begged me to leave for the New City and my sisters, because I had just been married and she wanted our family to be carried on, in case something happened— So my parents went away as prisoners, and we were taken out.

To be honest, I must say that the Jordanian soldiers behaved wonderfully well. I will never forget what my eyes saw. We had to walk to the Zion Gate over rubble and ruins, and the first thing the soldiers did was to give us all cold water to drink. They gave out bananas to the children and cigarettes to the soldiers and I also saw them carry old men and women in their arms to help them reach Zion Gate.

Later, when my parents were returned to us—they were among the first batch of those prisoners to be released, through the Red Cross—they told how, as they were being led into captivity, there were mobs of Arabs—not their former neighbors but Arabs from villages taken by the Israeli army or those from other countries—which tried to attack them. And the Jordanian soldiers did their very best to keep the mobs away. They even declared a curfew in order to enable the prisoners of war to pass through the alleys safely and to reach the trucks and buses. The same story repeated itself when they got to Jericho—a mob of thousands surged toward them, wanting to kill the Jews, and the Legionnaires shot into the mob in order to protect our people.

Leo Wissman:

☐ In the afternoon we came into the hands of the Legion, and they really protected us against the local Arabs. That night we spent in prison near the Jaffa Gate, and the next morning we passed through the Via Dolorosa and then by trucks to our final prison.

There were about three hundred of us. The women and the badly injured were sent out to the New City. So on that Sunday morning, my wife first heard that I had been in the Old City.

We drove in trucks across the Mount of Olives toward Jericho. We could see the Old City burning . . . . I could not imagine how it must feel to the people who had lived in that place to see it all destroyed. And it wasn't the only place where it happened . . . .

The journey was very quiet till we passed through Jericho. Some of us were very frightened, but I was optimistic that I would live and come home sooner or later.

However, I had doubts when we passed through that town. The Arabs had found out that Jewish prisoners would pass through and there they were, lining the road on both sides, shouting, "Deir Yassin! Deir Yassin!" Both there and in Amman, where we stopped for gas, the Arabs came around us crying, "Deir Yassin!" and wanting to kill us. But the Legionnaires kept them off.

After that we came to desert, desert, desert. Then in the distance we thought we saw a gallows, but as we got nearer we saw it was a camp. The guards were Circassian or Bedu. A Legion sergeant asked us if the soldiers had stolen anything from us. Yes—our watches. So most of the men got their watches back. Mine hadn't been taken—I'd worn it around my ankle!

We spent nine months in that prison camp. It was hard for us. We got letters every five, six, seven weeks. Whoever got a letter would go away, while those who didn't would go another way, so as not to see the ones who did.

After about four weeks the first parcels came through the Red Cross—about thirty. We were all socialists, so the question came, how to divide thirty parcels among six hundred men—three hundred of us, and three hundred from Gush Etzion. Everyone got something, but if there was something personal in a parcel, the owner kept it. I found a hankerchief in my parcel, and as I took it out I noticed it wasn't clean—then I saw that the "dirt" was writing! "Today we got the first vegetables from Tel Aviv. We are all well."

Thus the Old City fell. It was one of the few real triumphs of the war for the Arabs. Though by most accounts the Legionnaires behaved well, irregular units who fought with them lost no time in looting and destroying everything they could lay hands on. The quarter remained in ruins until reconquered by Israel in 1967.

After the disastrous first attack by the Jews on Latrun, a new command structure was brought into being for the Jerusalem area, including the Jerusalem corridor. David Marcus was appointed supreme commander of the Jerusalem sector on May

28, the day the Old City surrendered. Two days later, a second assault on Latrun was mounted.

The prospects of success were improved by the fact that in the few days previously, two Arab strongpoints had been captured, which meant that the attackers' flanks would not be harried as before. An armored battalion was to spearhead the attack on the fortress, which was to be penetrated by sappers. A separate but coordinated attack was to be made from the east, via Sha'ar Hagai.

This supporting attack, by green troops, was turned back by enemy fire. The armored brigade, not realizing what had happened, went ahead—literally ahead—leaving its infantry, which it was intended to cover, far in the rear. The armored brigade made another tactical blunder when they got within assault range of their target. Finding that their sappers had been left behind, they used flamethrowers, which set light to the wooden parts of the fort near the gates (nobody got near enough to discover they were not locked). In a short time the whole area was brilliantly lit, enabling the Arab defenders, with yells of glee, to pinpoint their targets. "The enemy's night had turned into day," as one Arab Legion officer put it. Thus the second Israeli attempt to storm Latrun ended in another rout.

I want to leave the Jerusalem sector for a moment to glance at the fierce fighting that was continuing on the central, or Iraqi, front.

The Iraqis' main aim had been to reach Haifa and gain control of its port and oil refineries. Iraqi volunteers had already participated in battles as part of Kawukji's irregulars; but when the "real" war began, the regular Iraqi army sent an advance party of armor and infantry to the Jordan valley, where, as Netiva Ben Yehuda recounted, at the eleventh hour the bridges across the Jordan had been blown up.

Using pontoon bridges and a ford, two Iraqi units crossed the river and assaulted Kibbutz Gesher. The defenders of Gesher drove them back and succeeded in flooding the area, but they had to withstand a siege that lasted a week before an Israeli surprise

attack at Belvoir—a crusader fortress farther to the south—
together with a demand from Glubb for support around Jerusalem, influenced the Iraqis to withdraw to the east bank of the
Jordan.

When they realized that Kawukji had withdrawn from what
is known as the "Arab triangle" opposite Jenin, leaving a gap in
Arab lines, the Iraqis moved their center of operations there. In
this sector they were crucial in preventing the Israelis from taking
Jenin, which the Carmeli and Golani brigades attempted to do on
June 1.

Carmel, since his success in taking Acre, had been proceeding southeast without meeting much resistance, mopping up in
the hill villages of Gilboa, and eventually he stood poised on the
heights above the Arab town of Jenin, which lay, all but empty,
below them. Had they struck at once, they might have carried the
day; but a series of intelligence flaws and hesitations, combined
with heavy Iraqi opposition, brought about one of the most
serious lost opportunities of the entire war.

The following incident, which has earned a place in the more
detailed histories of the war, is told by Shlomo Baum, a
professional soldier who in the early fifties was to lead the
notorious Commando Company 101 in reprisal raids against
Arab villagers in Jordan.

☐   In Jenin I was a machine gunner and the deputy commander
      of the squad. I think that all that year of '48 I was in a state of
      craziness. Most of the time I just didn't feel any fear at all.

      Jenin wasn't a successful action. My battalion, the
      Thirteenth, was okay, but the Twenty-first and Twenty-
      second took a lot of casualties; they didn't fulfill the
      expectations of headquarters.

      We stopped on two hills before the city of Jenin and its
      Teggart fortress. We were quite short of ammunition. The
      orders were strict, to shoot only with careful aim so as not to
      waste bullets. And at night a truck bringing ammunition,
      plus hand grenades and two hundred kilos of explosives,
      was supposed to come.

The driver didn't exactly know the way from the main road to the hills we had captured, so he asked one of the soldiers which way to go. This soldier had a very, shall we say, strange sense of humor, and said, "You just drive straight." So the driver drove along the main road, and a few hundred meters from Jenin he ran into machine-gun fire from the strongholds of the Iraqis. At first the driver thought that some Jews were shooting at him by mistake, so he shouted, "Don't shoot! I'm from the Thirteenth Battalion!" But then he realized he was being shot at by the enemy.

He managed to jump out of the truck with the sergeant who was with him. It was pitch dark. There were Iraqis all around them. The Jews dived under the truck. The Iraqis came closer and closer to it. The driver, whom I knew, was a very courageous man and quite cold-blooded. He realized he was surrounded, so he thought about how to get away. There was no use trying to fight—he had one Lee Enfield rifle and ten bullets to deal with a whole platoon of Iraqis. So he just took off his shoes, and so did the sergeant; they crept out onto the road and made off so silently that nobody spotted them.

Meanwhile, the enemy soldiers came up to the truck and started to examine it. On the seat in front was a Molotov cocktail. And the bottle fell on the road and exploded, and one of the soldiers caught fire. So they thought that the truck was booby-trapped, and they fled.

When our driver and the other man reached headquarters they reported the loss of the truck to the battalion commander, Avraham Yoffe. Then it appeared that in the truck were twelve thousand cartridges—all for our two Vickers machine guns. In the morning the Iraqis made an assault on our positions, which were about 1500 meters from Jenin; we managed to push them back, but there was quite a shortage of cartridges.

After the attack we looked through binoculars and could see that the truck was untouched. It seemed the Iraqis were afraid to approach it, after their comrade was burned. So the commander asked for volunteers to go and fetch it; but the trouble was, it was under fire from the Teggart fort. So the driver and another man and I volunteered to go out in broad daylight and fetch in the truck.

We went out in a jeep. We had to drive for three hundred meters of unprotected road, through machine-gun fire, and we managed to come through that unscathed. We put the jeep into the ditch, and then we tried to start the engine of the truck. The starter was okay, but every one of us tried to start the truck, and none of us could do it. Afterward we found out that the distributor had been damaged by a bullet. And they were shooting at the truck like hell, and we knew that apart from the twelve thousand cartridges, there were about two hundred kilos of TNT in the back.

After we'd come to the conclusion that we'd never start the truck, came the problem of how to get out. We had a Bren gun. So two guys took a position in the ditch and started to reply to their machine-gun fire, while I got into the jeep. I made two false starts, going forward for about thirty meters and then going into reverse behind the truck, thinking that if I did it a third time at least they wouldn't start shooting until they were sure we were really going on along the road. I waited about five minutes between the first and second "feints"; then the others jumped on the jeep and we went like hell straightaway, arriving safely back at the battalion, although with flat tires and fifteen holes in the jeep. Later the truck was towed back with armored cars, with all the stuff in it safe and sound.

Meir Amit, now a Labor member of the Knesset, was also in the Thirteenth Battalion at Jenin:

☐   That was the worst thing that happened to us. First of all, we were unprepared. The Iraqis came from the north and the Carmeli Brigade was holding around Jenin. I'd been in a different brigade before, but had been told to go and join the

Thirteenth Battalion under Yoffe. He was very good. He
gave us leadership, he had a sense of humor, and he knew his
way around. But still, I was among strangers.

It was night when I got the order, and I went to a place
in the hills for briefing. In the late morning we were taken by
bus through the valley of Jezreel. I can't believe now how we
survived. Machine guns from Jenin were just bursting their
fire across— It was very stupid to move like that by day, but
everything happened so quickly, and somehow we got into
the town of Jenin. We went up the hills in the northern part
and captured one of the far hills, and then I got a bullet in my
leg.

It wasn't serious, but I couldn't walk. The battle had a
tragic end because the pressure from the Iraqis was very
heavy and the Carmeli Brigade that we were with had to
retreat, and we suffered a lot of casualties. I myself somehow
got down the hill, more or less crawling, and then was
evacuated. I was very thin at that time, and Avraham Joffe
joked that he couldn't understand how they managed to hit
me.

The defeat at Jenin made Ben-Gurion even more convinced
that radical changes were needed in the Israeli army if it was to
bring about the ultimate defeat of the enemy

The first essential was the unification of his forces, sections
of which were still, even at this late stage, operating more or less
autonomously. A few days previously, on May 28, the provisional
government of Israel had officially established the Israel Defense
Forces (or IDF, known colloquially by its Hebrew acronym as
Zahal). The Irgun, which until that time had been fighting its own
war under its own commanders, agreed to be incorporated into
this unified force all over the country except in Jerusalem, which,
being outside the Jewish area designated by the partition plan,
was not considered by them to be under the provisional
government's jurisdiction. Lehi did the same, though they were
later to go to extreme lengths to prove to the world that it *was* an
integral part of the Jewish state, a typical piece of Revisionist

doublethink. In fact, as will be seen, both dissident groups still clung to their own identities, whatever agreements to the contrary their leaders might have signed, a subjective viewpoint that was to bring about great traumas in the near future.

Shortly after the second attack on Latrun, three soldiers of Har El, heading for Tel Aviv on leave, made their way safely on foot to the coastal plain by a route that ran roughly parallel to the main, but blocked, highway. They reported that this route, with an effort, might be made passable to motor vehicles, enabling supplies for Jerusalem to bypass Latrun.

This bold scheme was put in hand, and hundreds of workers, many too old for military service, were mustered in two groups—one working from the Jerusalem and one from the Tel Aviv ends—to straighten and lay the road, working by night toward each other.

By this time the Egyptian advance positions had reached Hartuv, some seven kilometers south of Latrun, where of course the Arab Legionnaires still were, and it is one of the minor miracles of the war that the "Burma" road-building program went unmolested between the two to its successful completion.

With regard to the third attack on Latrun, which took place in the second week in June, it is often asked why this was necessary when an alternative route to Jerusalem, bypassing the fortress "noose," had already been made viable. The official answer is, in part, the necessity to pin down the Legion forces to prevent their discovering or interfering with the "Burma Road"; but chiefly it was mounted because by this time the United Nations had appointed a mediator, Count Folke Bernadotte, whose first objective was to establish a truce. Both Arabs and Jews, sensing the approach of a cease-fire, fought harder than ever to gain control before the fighting was brought to a temporary halt.

The third battle for Latrun was one of those incidents that occur in any war—had it been successful, it would have been hailed as a brilliant coup; because it failed, it was an endless cause of recrimination against the leadership that had insisted on it. This time the main drive was to come from the Jerusalem cor-

ridor, east of the stronghold. This meant attacking from the hills
behind it. Because of operational delays, the attack was not
launched until June 9, on the very brink of the first truce. The
assault is described by "Boaz" of the Har El Brigade, one of the
two Palmach units that participated.

☐   We collected on the Bab el Wad road, as near to Latrun as
     the transport could get without being seen by the Legion. It
     was early evening, almost dusk. I can't be sure, but I think it
     was Yigal Allon who addressed us in the waning light and
     told us that it was on Ben-Gurion's orders that we were here.
     He had insisted that, before the first cease-fire came on us,
     we free that part of the road that was overlooked by the
     Legion, who were firing at anything that moved there with
     mortar and cannon. We had nothing that could effectively
     silence them; the only answer was to dislodge them from the
     police station in Latrun.
         This had been tried before, with tragic results. But
     never on the scale evident all around us now. Our brigade,
     Har El, was to go first, with Givati following and the Third
     Brigade of the Palmach going in from the north. There was
     apprehension and a premonition of disaster in the air.
         We set off in full moonlight through wheat fields and up
     the slopes. Although we were told to be quiet, it seemed the
     Arabs knew or saw that we were coming, because as soon as
     we were in range we were hit with a barrage the like of which
     we had never met before. Besides the familiar crash of
     cannon and mortar, we were showered with anti-personnel
     shells that burst into metal fragments over our heads.
         We were used to fighting in the hills near Jerusalem;
     they were higher but craggier and strewn with boulders that
     gave protection. The hills here were lower and quite smooth,
     and we felt exposed without the friendly rocks for cover. We
     instinctively fell back, something we did not usually do
     without an order, but there were newcomers among us,
     some of whom had hardly seen battle before and some who
     had only just arrived in the country.

We shook ourselves and continued up again, moving more cautiously, almost on our stomachs, but still taking continuous casualties all the way. We had to take turns to run down again with wounded to the hollow, halfway down the hill, where the doctor we'd brought with us had somehow found a low-lying spot which gave a little shelter. He was working desperately, trying to do something for the ever-increasing number of boys lying wounded and dying around him. He was helped by an eighteen-year-old girl who managed a smile and a comforting word for the boys whose blood was soaking her sleeves. I wonder if she sensed that she, the only woman there, was a symbol of hope and sanity as she calmly showed us where to lay our wounded comrades before we returned, running and crawling, up the hill to join the ever-decreasing number of men.

We had lost contact with each other. We were just going forward blindly now, not even knowing exactly where the enemy was. We'd started as a regiment. By the time we were three-quarters of the way up, there were only about half of us still on our feet.

Then, as we neared the top, we saw the Arab forward posts. We got to our feet, formed a long line, and ran forward in the old style, not knowing by now who was leading us. We threw grenades into the heaps of stones and sandbags which were their positions, and the Arabs who were not hit ran back and down the other sides of the slopes toward Latrun.

Now all became relatively quiet. We lay down in the undergrowth and waited for a counterattack and also for something more to happen from our side. But we knew by now that we had a cock-up here, and indeed, as we learned later, the Third Brigade was still stumbling about somewhere when they should have been ready to reinforce us on another flank. Most of our officers had never fought before on these particular hills and didn't quite know where they were, and rumor was already rife that even this bloody hill, that had cost us so dear, had been taken by mistake and we should have been somewhere else.

All we could do now was to try not to fall asleep. We stared into the darkness and listened for movement from the other side—wherever that was. Someone suggested that we spread out more along the heights; and only a few minutes later, two men who had been sent to the outermost edge of our line came running back to report movement from below.

An officer ran along the hill and sensed immediately that the seeming inactivity on the other side was a trap. They had spread out too and were crawling quietly up the hill to surround and finish us off, what was left of us. The officer rushed along the top of the hill from group to group whispering one word: "Run!"

And now there was panic, as those who hadn't yet got the order asked their fleeing comrades, "What's going on?" We ran, trying to drag the wounded, and leaving them, a thing Palmachniks had never done before. Someone called, "Who here belongs to Amos?" Amos was the brave, modest, much loved leader of our *makhlaka*[army unit]. Four or five of us answered, "We do!" "He's lying back up there, he's badly wounded!"

We turned back and ran up the hill, rushing in all directions until someone called, "Over here—" We came together, to find Amos lying with a shell wound in his back. As we lifted him he whispered, "Leave me. I'm finished." But we took him, each man a limb, while I picked up the rifles and we stumbled back down the hill with Amos crying, "No! No! Enough!"

Then the officer who had given the order to retreat came running up toward us. When he saw Amos, who was bleeding heavily, he shouted, "Can't you see it's hopeless? Leave him and run!" One of the boys, a platoon leader, almost crying, said "No." But the officer pointed up the hill and in the early dawn light we could see scores of men running almost shoulder to shoulder, firing their submachine guns. It *was* hopeless—they were getting nearer— and the officer was now screaming at us to follow the others. The platoon leader, now in tears, put a grenade into Amos's hands—he was almost unconscious—and we ran.

The Arabs were stopped from chasing us beyond the hills by some other unit, which shelled them with some antiquated artillery. Or so I gathered, though by this time nothing was clear. It was fully light now and we dragged ourselves listlessly through the wheat fields toward the road where there were jeeps waiting. The rays of the rising sun touched the top of the wheat, and a flock of birds rose toward the light, singing in a new day. I could have wept. *This* was life, not what we had been doing all night. For these birds everything was as usual, but not for those left on the slopes. For those who'd come back, nothing would ever be the same again, not least because of the rumors that Allon and Yadin had known all the time that the attack could not succeed. They had pleaded with Ben-Gurion that they didn't know the terrain, that they had raw troops, that it was suicide. But he had insisted.

Ephraim Shorer tells of another deeply regrettable and demoralizing event that occurred just before the first cease-fire:

☐   Did you hear the story of David Marcus? He was a colonel in the United States Army and he had to come under cover, so we called him Mickey Stone.

He was supposed to organize, very early on in the war, a few so-called brigades into one division and become its commander. His deputy was to be Yigal Allon; operations officer, Rabin; artillery officer, myself.

After the two battles at Latrun failed, the "Burma Road" was opened, over which we passed to Abu Ghosh, where we set up headquarters. A number of brigades were formed into this new division, with a big battle plan to conquer Lod, Ramle, Latrun, and Ramallah. It was code-named Operation Lar Lar from the initials of these towns.

"Mickey Stone"—Marcus—couldn't speak Hebrew, so he spoke English with interpreters, including myself. The brigade stationed at Abu Ghosh was the Har El of the Palmach, which had already suffered very heavy casualties in the battles around Jerusalem. They were really run down as far as fighters were concerned. Then there was the Jerusalem Brigade with Shaltiel as its commander, and the Moriah Brigade, one of the best. Also included was the Yiftach Brigade from the North. There was the Seventh Brigade, which had failed at Latrun, and all these were to form the first division.

Operation Lar Lar was just being planned when the United Nations imposed the first cease-fire. And the night before it came in, Mickey was killed by accident.

We'd been to Jerusalem to meet with Shaltiel. Marcus was to assume command of the division. We were at Shaltiel's headquarters. Shaltiel was very much of a soldier, saluting and all that as if we were in some proper army instead of an army of Palmachniks.... and while we were there, we ate something that really poisoned our stomachs. We came back to our headquarters, and we were all ill.

The night before the first cease-fire, both the Jordanians and ourselves were very nervous. We thought that somebody would try at the last moment to "establish some facts." So the defenses were alerted and every little noise was treated as abnormal. We were told to be very careful because of the sentries all around.

But we all had diarrhea.

Mickey and I were in the same room. And he told me, "Look, I have to go." He was sleeping half-naked, though it was chilly, so when he was going out he took his white sheet, draped around him. It was early morning, around three o'clock. He went down from the monastery we were staying in in Abu Ghosh into the vineyards. He did what he had to do. And on the way back he was challenged by a sentry. He answered in English. He didn't know the password. And he was shot.

I heard the shots, woke up, and jumped out of bed. I ran outside. Everywhere the sentries were shooting and shouting: "It's the Legion! They're Englishmen!"—because of the Legion's British officers. We jumped over the low stone walls and found Mickey dying.

I was among the first few who reached him. He died

very soon after. The man who shot him wanted to shoot himself—he'd killed the supreme commander of the division.

A last, laconic story about Jerusalem from Netanel Lorch as the first truce approached:

☐ So I would say that, in the words of Remarque, "all was quiet on the western front," because the lines did not change. But there was one rather Münchhausen exercise we undertook at one point. The Legion had brought up a gun to the top of the Jaffa Gate, which they fired point-blank into our positions, and we had no field artillery to take care of that; so I was told to use an improvised weapon which had been homemade, developed by scientists in the Hebrew University. It was very precise. If I could go up to about two or three hundred yards of that field gun, and fire *directly into its barrel,* we could put it out of action.

So we walked into one of the buildings on Mamilla Road—it's still there, a building with lots of these iron, Arab-type shutters. We aimed this weapon through the slits in one of them. I had worked it out that it would take more than three seconds for the Arabs to register—after we had flung the shutter back—which window it was and home in on it. We had to open the shutter and fire in three seconds.

By this time we had some very well trained people. Four of us aimed very precisely, and then at the right moment the shutter was flung back. Two shells were fired and one of them actually penetrated the barrel of their field gun and blew it up. After the second shell we'd planned to get out of the way, quickly; but we pulled it off, and for it we got mentioned in dispatches.

On the night of the 8th to 9th June, we finally went over to the offensive. The idea was that we would swing around and try to establish a line which would run from Notre Dame to the Rockefeller Museum, but we were stopped about halfway. We took the Swedish school at that time.

Notre Dame is like a sort of Hebrew *chet* [three sides of

a box]—on one side it was bordered by the Old City and on two by no-man's land. So actually we had to take care of the three sides of the perimeter; the fourth faced the Jerusalem municipality, which was more or less secure. By this type of operation we would have been able to make Notre Dame part of a continuous line.

Something rather fantastic happened in one building, which was called "house with the gutters." In that building, our people were able to penetrate, and they occupied the lower two floors while the Arab Legion had taken refuge in the upper two, and for a couple of hours they were there in the same building. The Arabs threw down hand grenades from the upper floors, and our people were trapped underneath. The Legionnaires could not escape, but it was a sort of mutual trap. In the morning our people retreated, after blowing up the staircase; some of the Legionnaires escaped. And then the first truce came on us, and the fighting stopped.

Phase 2:
The First Truce

The first truce, which began on June 10, 1948, and lasted for one month, was to some extent a period of rest and recuperation for the exhausted troops on both sides, especially the Israelis, some of whom had been fighting more or less uninterruptedly for months.

"Boaz":

☐   The last days before the truce had been the worst. It seemed we only had defeats in the field to remember. There was the horror of Latrun still in our minds and the shame of leaving so many on the field—the breaking of a taboo with us. There was the defeat on Radar Hill. And the gradual realization, as statistics began to be known, that in little more than three and a half months of intense fighting, almost nightly forays, we had lost about one-third of our brigade; of the others, a large proportion had been wounded, some as many as three times, each time being sent back into battle. For the rest, the constant lack of sleep, shortage of food—and the food we did get was insufficient to replace the awful expenditure of physical and nervous energy—combined with the worry about parents and friends and the emotional wear and tear of comrades dying or just being "lost sight of" in all the confusion, had reduced us to a state of exhaustion.

So the truce came in the nick of time—many of us felt we couldn't face another battle. It was not just the fear, which we had learned to live with, but simply the thought of running up another hill, in ragged boots, with ill-assorted equipment, that was almost unbearable.

We were expecting the truce, because they kept telling us that we had to take this place or secure that place before the lines were determined by the U.N. Yet when it actually came, it seemed unbelievable—we felt that if we relaxed we would suddenly be told to get ready for another battle. But quiet had descended—no more crump, crump of shells on the hills around Bab el Wad. One looked around, dazed, taking some satisfaction in seeing at least some familiar faces still about, reckoning up what we had managed to achieve, despite all our inexperience and the tragic mistakes and losses.

We could scarcely believe it when we found ourselves on buses and trucks going through the now peaceful Bab el Wad and then emerging onto the fertile plain below.... For men who hadn't seen green fields for months, or even had enough water to drink, let alone fresh fruit and vegetables, it was a life-restoring sight to see the irrigation sprinklers on the lush fields of the kibbutzim and *moshavim,* lavishly watering the crops. Battle-worn as we were, we were like children on an outing. We clapped and cheered and sang songs, rejoicing in the thought of the rest and good food that were waiting for us. I myself—and many others, I found out later—had developed an ulcer in the past months. It had had ideal conditions—bad food and continual nervous tension. But not only we ulcerated "older men" (I was then twenty-two, compared to most of the others who were still in their teens) looked almost cadaverous. We were all a sorry sight as we drove into Sarafand—ill kempt, badly shaven, wearing a weird assortment of tattered, filthy clothes—the mere semblance of a uniform. But we were happy.

There was not much rest or joy among the commanders, however. A meeting was called by Ben-Gurion, at which there was an exchange of views about what had been achieved and what had gone wrong and what must now be done to prepare for the next round.

That meeting, in Ramat Gan, was convened by Israel Galili, head of Haganah command under Ben-Gurion. He took copious notes and can still quote the reports of the various commanders verbatim:

☐   The meeting of the front commanders took place two days after the first cease-fire came into force. There had been very hard fighting until June 11th, and that was expressed in the pronouncements of these people, who hadn't seen one another for many weeks and were very tired, tense, sad, and concerned about what was going to happen when the fighting started up again. They felt a heavy responsibility on their shoulders and great anxiety for the predicament we were in.

   They suffered most of all from the scarcity of elementary supplies. For instance, the commander of the Givati Brigade tried to give a picture of the situation in his brigade. He said, "Well, I understand fully that there are severe shortages. We haven't any big guns. We have no aircraft. But I cannot understand why we have no *socks*—why we have no *helmets*! In my brigade, troops were killed for lack of helmets. Why do my soldiers have to go to battle in pajamas because their uniforms are torn and there are no spares for them to change into?"

Another commander said, "How can my soldiers fight properly when they are suffering sharp concerns about their families?" It was a problem of material welfare, which at that time was not organized. Or, "How can my people be in service for months without leave? And when they get a rare opportunity to visit home, they meet an environment where the rule is 'business as usual': People are entertaining themselves— Thirty miles or even less from the front they find a scene of tranquillity and plenty, at least on the face of it." The discrepancy between conditions at the front and in the rear—a very short distance geographically—was bound to strike them very forcibly.

One of the most important problems was a shortage of trained manpower, of weapons and ammunition, and the clash between the need for troops with which to conquer a place and those who would replace them as a holding force. It was very difficult to reserve the manpower needed for advancing; it meant handing over conquered sectors to untrained troops, which involved everyone in a lot of strain.

The commander of the northern front [Moshe Carmel] said, "The truce came upon us like a dew from heaven." The units were tired. Every battalion of the northern command had lost about a quarter of its strength. Add to that number, the wounded— For instance, he said, one battalion had lost about four hundred and fifty; now it had no more than two hundred men. I have to tell the truth, that some of them—a few—deserted.

Carmel went on, "We are reaching a critical phase. Because of our weakness in manpower, we could be condemned to remain on the defensive instead of continuing our attack. We need new recruits. It will be dangerous to delay. There is an improvement in the weaponry of the enemy. We need a strategy planned in advance and not only in reaction to the moves of the enemy. It would be a disaster to remain on the defensive, and it will be impossible to take the offensive all over the country. We must concentrate our powers and decide where to take the offensive and where to remain on the defensive, where to make a division between the active forces and those tied to the defense of local settlements.

"I want to say a terrible thing. The situation is so dangerous that every man has to know that he runs a greater risk if he deserts than if he does his duty and goes into battle. I will not hold back from calling for the death penalty for deserters. It will be a drastic measure, but we cannot afford to forgo such means."

This report speaks about Jerusalem. It says the citizens were terribly weak because of malnutrition; they were living on three hundred grams of bread a day—bread and canned food. They had suffered three weeks of bombardment. "We've lost a lot of the people from Khish in Gush Etzion and Neve Yaacov. A lot of the men are reduced to a terrible mental condition. The battalions of the civilian army [Khim] go up to the age of forty-five. We have about 2,500 of these in seven small battalions, but in terms of numbers we have only four battalions. Conditions are bad. Desertion is high. We have 300 military policemen. There are more people in the service branches than there are fighters—some of these are as much as fifty-five years of age. We have 600 wounded. People take themselves off on leave and we have to bring them back by force.

"Manpower in Jerusalem is being used much more than in other parts of the country. It is very clear that the enemy is being directed by the British. In a contact after the cease-fire, British officers appeared. I heard them say that if it hadn't been for the British, the Arabs would have stopped fighting. The morale of the Arab Legion is relatively high. They are hoping to win by having a long encirclement or siege, cutting Jerusalem off from the rest of the country, which they have a good chance of doing for a long time, enough to force the city to surrender. It was estimated they have more than fifty big guns. Toward the cease-fire they were using 100-

pounders. The effect on the citizens of such a bombardment was very serious, especially on the members of the Old Yishuv."

The report went on, "There is too much talk about taking loot. There is some looting, but it is under control. But there's a big black market—even officers take part. One can see that there is a lack of faith among them in the tactical ability of the area command."

There was an impression that some of the motivation among commanders was primarily political rather than military. And coordination between Khish and the Palmach was very bad, which was serious. It was as bad as possible. And it was not one-sided. There was great weariness in the strongholds. Some of the Tel Aviv forces had begun to desert. Leave had been given, but, the report said, "Who knows if they will be back? Don't be surprised if the strongholds have to be abandoned."

Then Rabin talked about Har El's heavy losses in the Jerusalem sector—from two battalions, 617 wounded, 200 killed, another 200 unable to fight. "The first need is for manpower.

"The soldiers held on in the strongholds for about five days under heavy bombardment. In the battle for Beit Machsir, two battalions were active for three days, and after that they couldn't continue the fighting over the northern strongholds. In one day, six concentrated waves attacked one stronghold."

Avidan was in charge of supplies for the Haganah, and he said, "We are going to be strangled over the issue of oil."

And then Ben-Gurion told them that at least there would be more arms. "Within a week there will be nearly five hundred rifles for each battalion. They will get a full consignment—everything that is needed to be fully equipped. Even nineteen machine guns for each battalion." He spoke of plans to open training centers in the use of machine guns, morters, and sharpshooting for about nine hundred youngsters aged around seventeen who would be recruited in the camps. It was the development process of the coming army.

Of course, all this had to go on during the cease-fire. I dare confess that for us in the Haganah, with responsibility for the life or death of the Yishuv, we were not confined by declarations of stoppages or embargoes. We needed every opportunity to enlarge our arsenal. While the British had been around, it was impossible to bring in the arms we so badly needed. Now we had the use of airports and we could bring things in despite the embargo, and we could camouflage them to get them past the U.N. truce observers. For instance, containers camouflaged as boilers, machine tools, and road-making equipment. You can open the roller with a blowtorch and put arms inside. That king of thing. We had bought Messerschmitts in Czechoslovakia, which were dismantled, put in Dakotas, and brought here for reassembly. All this, in the event, took time, and we were very short of specialists. It was all very complicated. But it had become somewhat simpler with the declaration of partition, the recognition of our right to sovereignty by the U.N. I was able to cable all our agents to apply to sources of arms, including governments, on behalf of the state of Israel even before it was in existence. Ben-Gurion agreed. It was a big advantage.

To return to the meeting— To his credit, Ben-Gurion did not spend time trying to smooth the situation, because he was convinced that intelligent men didn't need to be buoyed up with false assurances. He described the prospects of war as very dangerous—he said the war was only just beginning. He emphasized the role of the British in the war, bearing the main responsibility for the war, pointing out that our strongest enemy was the Arab Legion, because the British were behind them.

The reason I have dwelt at length on this meeting is because the commanders—by relating what happened on their own fronts—expressed the crucial problems of transition from a volunteer army, an army in the making, to an army of the state.

Ben-Gurion's emphasis was on the necessity to improve
"discipline" before entering on the decisive next phase of the war.
Netanel Lorch, in *The Edge of the Sword,* quotes him as saying:

> "Because of lack of discipline we have lost positions;
> because of lack of discipline we have not fully exploited
> possibilities and have not gained achievements that were in
> our reach. If we had one army instead of a number of
> armies, and if we had operated according to one strategic
> plan, we should have more to show for our efforts. We
> must have a plan for victory; otherwise we will be defeated.
> If we subordinate everything to that supreme objective, we
> are likely to win."

This evaluation of the situation led to his controversial
decision—fully implemented, finally, during the second truce,
several weeks later—to disband the Palmach as a separate
organization and weld it together with the rest of the Israeli
forces. One of the most unpopular moves Ben-Gurion ever made,
its results were perhaps more effective upon the future of Israel
than he or anyone could have imagined at the time, when all that
seemed important was rationalizing the armed forces and bringing them under a unified command.

Several conflicting views on the matter may cast light on why
this seemingly reasonable move was to arouse passions that have
not entirely cooled today. Chaim Laskov was one commander
who agreed, then and now, that the dissolution of the Palmach
was necessary and even desirable:

☐   I belonged to the group which, when we returned from the
    British army, was used by Ben-Gurion. And we supported
    him, because we thought he was right. He harnessed
    everything we had in order to prosecute a war against
    regular forces.

    When I was demobilized from the British army I
    became director of military training—to retrain Haganah
    people and those from the clandestine organizations and
    weld them together. It wasn't easy. The underground armies
    wanted to stick to their own methods and of course their

own loyalties, which were not necessarily to the government. But a personality like Ben-Gurion's and the threat of war forced people to conform. Of course, I was accused of being "Ben-Gurion's man" by Palmachniks, who were somebody else's men. All this sort of nonsense— It lasted a couple of months and then it vanished, because we had the war at our throats.

My method in the officers' training course was to appeal to logic and to demonstrate. For instance, if you haven't got proper equipment, and you're faced with barbed wire, you take your rifle and you crush the wire with your body. If you are killed, the others pass over you and conduct the assault. I told them this and some Palmachnik said, "This is nonsense, what are you talking about?" So I said, "Okay, I'll show you." I took a friend of mine and we did it. This other fellow said, "My God, they mean what they say." I said, "Now, go ahead, you crush it."

On one early operation I was given a composite force, one company from each area. One was a Palmach company and they refused to take orders from me until Yigal Allon vouched for me. Later on, I took over a Palmach battalion and it went on strike. Eventually their previous commanding officer came over and said, "Look, Laskov knows the business better than I do. Play the game. You've got a war on your hands."

We spoke the same language but with different meanings. For us, when the order was to deploy, we deployed. For them, the word "deploy" was just a suggestion—if you want to do it, fine. If you don't—we'll do it tomorrow. So I had to move a battalion. They had to pass through my hands. I was told to deploy by such-and-such a time and I ordered a deployment. They didn't move. I said, "What the hell do you think is going on? This is an order! Move!" They said, "No, we're not going to move."

We're talking now about discipline. The Palmach were excellent human material but their background and experience was different. Luckily they picked it up very quickly.

By June everyone saw the light clear enough. No nonsense!
It wouldn't do. Discipline isn't doing what suits you, it
means going against the grain, same as duty, same as loyalty.
I taught them the organization of war, battle procedures,
how to assault and charge your enemy, rout him and destroy
him and take over the territory. By fighting for it. That takes
organization. Method. Administration. Discipline.

Others took a different view. Shimon Avidan, as a kibbutznik, had a strong feeling for the Palmach's ethos:

☐   Ben-Gurion wanted one thing: to close the gaps between
     underground organizations and a modern army as quickly
     as possible. But this was not an entirely good thing. It went
     against the type of people we had, against their education,
     against their deepest feelings; they couldn't accept the
     discipline and the order demanded by a regular army. I
     myself tried to learn as much as I could from the "regular
     officers," knowing we had to fight against regular armies—I
     learned such things as order of battle, organization of
     manpower, how to prepare, control things, order my mind,
     write reports. But I did not accept *all* that was connected
     with the British way, which in many respects ran counter to
     things which were vital to us.
         I never behaved as a regular army commander behaves,
     because if I had I would have lost credibility with my people.
     They would have stopped regarding me as one of them-
     selves. You cannot just give orders to men like that, who
     have been trained in that special way to look upon all their
     fellow soldiers, commanders included, as comrades; you
     have to explain, to be open in discussion, never deceive
     them; nor must there be distinctions between you and them,
     not in clothing, not in the food you get, not in living
     quarters, not in privileges. Commanders had one privilege—
     to be the first in battle. Our men had to trust us.
         When the IDF was reorganized, they tried to impose
     upon formations like ours commanders of another type,

with the style of the British army. Maybe it's a good way for Britons; but at this time, it didn't work with us.

Israel Galili:

☐   Until that time the Palmach was composed of an elite. Much higher than the average. So I remember that when I first convened the commanders and tried to elaborate with them the problems of ranks and punishments and military police, the representatives of the Palmach said, "*We* don't need all this because we have no problems." I told them, "When there is general recruitment you will get another type of human material. Then you will find you need these means in order to keep discipline." And I was right, of course. Even before general conscription came into force, the Palmach tried to recruit youngsters from poor quarters, but in the beginning the ratio was different. There were few enough of the "other sort" to be absorbed within the Palmach units. But later the proportion changed. So you had to bring in more stringent measures.

But there was, and remains, a good deal of bitterness among the rank and file. Netiva Ben Yehuda:

☐   I used to think Ben-Gurion hated the Palmach, though he relied on us. They didn't send us clothes, they didn't send us bullets, all the time there were arguments. So I had the feeling that he was favoring the Jewish Brigade, Laskov and these people, who had not actually been fighters in the British army because the British would never let them be fighters. What did Laskov do in the world war? He was commander of a company that transported water. But Ben-Gurion had been a private in America in the first world war and he was impressed by the uniforms and the rank insignia, and discipline, and big troop movements and things; that was why he encouraged people to join the British army, though he knew they wouldn't let them go through combat courses—very few did, maybe twenty. Not that it wasn't a good thing—they helped the Jews in Europe; at the end they stole guns for us and so on, so there were good points. But it emptied Israel of young men. They all went through the bullshit of the British army—sitting in Ismailia for five years, doing nothing but left-right, left-right, polishing their boots, telling jokes, buying in the NAAFI. That's all. But Ben-Gurion was waiting for the day the British would go so that he could make the people from the Jewish Brigade into the official army. And Yitzhak Sadeh knew that we couldn't rely on them, because they would bring in foreign tactics and strategies.

We were born here. The kibbutz system was suited to the mind of the *sabra*. We knew the topography in our very feet. We conquered the night. Till then the night belonged to the Arabs—a Jew was afraid to go out in the night for fear he'd get a knife in his back. And we knew, before the war already, that the night was ours.

Uri Avneri:

☐ The Israeli army came into being only in the middle of June. Until then we were called the Haganah battalions and various other names. It was a tremendous youth movement. The war brought about something like a great explosion of youthful exuberance, affecting a whole generation which had, till that very moment, been rejected. *Sabras* were considered as nobodies, good-for-nothings. The old men ran everything.

So when the war started there was an upsurge—of literature, poetry, everything. Overnight my generation came into its own. It became fashionable to be young. We were spoiled and lionized—we felt like heroes. I believe we were revolutionaries in many respects, with a whole new ideology, a new language, a new style that went with everything. It was the first self-assertion of Israeli youth.

It came to nothing. Ben-Gurion suppressed it in a

number of ways. The outward form was a debate about what
the army should be like. For years afterward there was this
catchphrase. Whenever anyone in Israel gave a lecture and
then asked for questions, some joker would stand up and
say, "Why did they disband the Palmach?" But it means a
great deal more than that.

I was in Khish at the time, so I can take an objective
view. The Khish was a field army of young people, which
was quickly mobilized at the beginning of the war. The older
people had Khim, which was a sort of home guard or
territorial army. Then there was the Palmach, which was
based on the kibbutzim; they had a left-wing ideology but
not really in a political sense. It was the ideology of equality,
of a popular or revolutionary army whose officers were not
superior to the men but only had the expertise to lead. It
didn't confer on them any special rights; on the contrary, the
officers had to do exactly the same as the men only more so,
in order to command their respect and obedience—discipline not by saluting or ranks or separate messes or
punishments but by personal example, being a better human
being and a better soldier.

There's a legend now that it was an undisciplined,
irregular kind of rabble, but I think it was the most
disciplined army I ever saw. People were consciously trying
to be as good as they could be, which meant that before
every action the commander would call the people together
and say, "We're going to do so-and-so because of such-and-
such"—explaining the whole thing, the plan and the context
of it. Of course, this made for a very special kind of
relationship within the army.

And not only between commanders and men. In every
army, in every war, the first thing that happens is that you're
taken out of your milieu and thrown in the melting pot. You
meet people you didn't even dream existed. People like us,
from north Tel Aviv, met people from south Tel Aviv: a
totally different society. Today you'd call them Moroccan
Jews, but one didn't call them that then. We were quite

happy with each other. We discovered each other. I remember it as a very happy army and a very happy period. In the beginning.

The press spokesman, who worked close to Ben-Gurion from the time of the first truce, comments (anonymously):

☐   Ben-Gurion was a good man to work with, largely because he was conscious that if he wanted to get something done, he had the power to see that it got done. But he was very open-minded. He never got irritated or upset if you came to him and said, "You know, Mr. Prime Minister, I think this is a mistake." He'd ask why you thought so, and then you'd tell him, and he'd say, "Well, there may be something in that, but nevertheless I'm going to go ahead and do what I want to." He very rarely took advice. What he did take in was information. Put it this way, he wasn't chairman of a board. He didn't come into meetings and say, "Gentlemen, let's hear your views," and get a consensus. On major issues, military or political, he would come into cabinet meetings knowing exactly what he wanted already. He'd listen to what people had to say, but by and large he would go ahead with his own view. And usually they'd go along with him.
     I remember once when he said to me, "The cabinet decides what has to be done," and I said, "Ben-Gurion, look, you know you've never been overruled on a major issue." He denied it. Of course he did on occasion get his way by threatening resignation. But what he was saying was, "I'm not threatening resignation as a way of dictating to you. I cannot, in all conscience, continue to lead this country if you don't carry out this policy."
     In Ben-Gurion's struggle to subordinate the Palmach, I was on his side. I was in the army at the time, and I reckoned you couldn't have two general headquarters. What would happen would be that Haganah headquarters would say, "We need to attack here, we want to use this Palmach brigade and one other." They would send this plan along to

Palmach headquarters with a "Please" and *their* staff officers would sit around and decide whether they would fall in with it or not. You can't have that. I mean, quite apart from the political side. He was very much concerned with statehood, and order, and unity—and especially unity in the armed forces. You couldn't have two GHQs.

One of the first things Ben-Gurion achieved in his efforts to unify the Israeli forces was the agreement, signed by the commander of the Irgun, to submit all but those soldiers still based in Jerusalem to the unified command. (The few members of the Lehi had not engaged in maverick actions for some time.) Battalions of former dissidents were now assigned to Haganah brigades. Commanders were able to concentrate on regrouping, retraining, and reequipping their seriously depleted forces.

Among the vital priorities needing reorganization was the medical services. Lionel Meltzer, a doctor living in South Africa, was personally sent for by Ben-Gurion. Here is his account of the situation he found on his arrival around this time:

☐   When I arrived in Israel there was still a remnant of British medical services there—some ambulances and personnel in Haifa. [The very last of the British left Haifa during the first truce.] I was immediately attached to the HQ of the army medical services and given the post of head of medical services.

Before the first truce, the headquarters of the medical corps was in Tel Aviv, so I went there. Actually, medical services were all but nonexistent. Up till then they had worked in the underground. I'll give an example. When I asked for the names of regional medical officers, they didn't know any—there were no lists and they didn't know even *where* the doctors were because the various kibbutzim and areas appointed their own doctors. At HQ they didn't know about them. The pay was the same for medical officers as for other personnel—they were getting about two pounds sterling a month each. If a unit had, say, 500 personnel they would get a thousand pounds, and there was no indication of whether any of it went to a medical officer.

So it took me quite a time to find out who was in the medical services at the time. I even had a board map made, pinpointed with the names of medical officers, but that was only after quite a lot of investigation.

Then we organized forward medical units between the hospitals and forward areas. Each unit had its own medical officer; we formed units of stretcher-bearers and small medical-aid posts where the wounded were brought in and then taken by transport to hospital. At that time the air force had precisely three aircraft. You know, at the moment Israel has one of the most sophisticated medical services in the world; at that time they were completely without equipment—without blankets, even. There was even some antagonism between the army and the Magen David Adom [the Jewish equivalent of the Red Cross], who *had* blankets because they had the civilian voluntary service, whereas the army had just been created and had nothing. The Magen David Adom did cooperate from time to time, but very reluctantly—they wanted to hold on to what they had.

I had to threaten them. They had a very strong organization in South Africa, and I threatened to tell people in South Africa that they were being uncooperative in the war effort. I went right to the top of their organization, and since I was right at the top in mine I was able to lean on them. During that period I went to South Africa and addressed a meeting there. I didn't tell them about the antagonism, but I did manage to get quite a lot of blankets.

My main task was organizing medical services in the field. At that time there were very few jeeps. Transport was altogether very difficult and they didn't allow any jeeps anywhere but in the forward areas; but I had a jeep in Tel Aviv where my HQ was because I visited the front every day. I had to see the various units and find out what they needed. What they needed was everything. Getting it was a question of using my influence with the army quartermasters and

others. Still, things were so bad from the point of view of
equipment that we organized special units to go into battle
with the troops, not so much in a medical capacity as to
retrieve any captured medical material from places like
Ramle, Lydda, and Beersheba, for instance, before it was
destroyed, lost, or stolen, and also to ensure a fair distribution among all units.

Despite all this we were constantly short of blankets,
ambulances, stretchers—everything. After a time we had
trained people from South Africa, England, the U.S., and
other countries, so personnel was not such a problem.

There were no military hospitals, but then, as now,
civilian hospitals received the wounded. I think there was
adequate space, although there were more wounded in '48
than in any other war. A lot of the wounds were from land
mines.

Inexperience was one cause of much of the trouble. The
youngsters used to walk into ambushes simply through
inexperience. And the medical staff were also inexperienced.
There were many unnecessary amputations. I went to
inspect a hospital and was told quite proudly that they'd
done six amputations that morning. I looked into it and
found some were unnecessary. I told the surgeons not to be
so drastic, to go steady with amputations—it was all due to
inexperience.

Netanel Lorch recalls the first contact with the enemy after
the truce came in:

☐   I claim that I am one of the authors of the armistice lines of
'49, because in Jerusalem they were the truce lines of '48. I
was the first one to meet with Abdullah El Tel [the Arab
commander of the Legion under Glubb], not because I was
important, but because I was considered expendable. There
was a little no-man's-land between us and the Arab Legion
and on the map this was marked as mined. So somebody had
figured out that if someone is to be blown up by mines, it

might as well be me. Well, thank God, the shelling had been so heavy that not a single mine was left, so nothing happened. I went across and met Abdullah El Tel and his second in command, a British officer.

We started negotiations about where the truce line would be. By that time the higher-ups had come—Shaltiel was there and we were discussing where we had been the night before, and Abdullah El Tel wanted to see the fortifications. But as I said, we had only captured certain buildings the night before; they hadn't been fortified, which meant we couldn't claim them. So somebody wisecracked that we had fortified them with our shirts, and Tel said, "Well, I'm convinced it's otherwise, but I'll take your word as an officer and a gentleman." This just overwhelmed Shaltiel. The following day, in the Jaffa Gate sector, we gave up a bit of territory—the Fast Hotel, it has been torn down now—which was really in our possession, but Shaltiel said, "All right, since you were generous yesterday, I'll be generous today, and we'll make this into no-man's-land." That's where the line was until 1967. I then went home, and my mother tells me I slept continuously for thirty-six hours.

The sorely needed arms that Ben-Gurion had promised his hard-pressed commanders at the meeting began to arrive. Shulamith Hareven:

☐   There was an incredible feeling during the first cease-fire when the first Czech rifles arrived.* They came in crates with a layer of tomatoes on top to get them past the U.N. observers. There was an airstrip down there in the valley [Jerusalem, near Neve Granot] to which our Piper Cubs brought in those crates, and it fell to me to entertain in conversation the U.N. major—I think he was Dutch or Norwegian—to keep him from checking those crates too

---

*In fact, the first shipments from Czechoslovakia arrived in April.

closely. I'm quite sure he knew what was in them, but either way he did nothing about it.

So we got the rifles out...and I will never forget the feeling I got from holding that rifle in my hands. It was incredible! The feeling that we were not passive any more, that now we can fight back! As for the tomatoes, they were eaten right away, of course. Everyone enjoyed them—we hadn't seen a tomato for months—and then everyone got diarrhea. The whole cease-fire was spent running from diarrhea! There was another delicacy at that time, a coconut sweet which everyone was eating because we'd captured the Arab factory where they were made. Those, and some cough drops! Actually, it wasn't so bad. In the Haganah we got two sandwiches a day, with sardines and things. There was a weed like spinach, and if you gave blood you got a cup of coffee, ersatz but still coffee, and *two eggs*. I would take one to my mother without telling her where I got it. And once I found some onions growing in an abandoned hotel garden.... It was the shortage of water that was terrible.

And at the same time there was a feeling that this was the transition from being second-class citizens to being first-class citizens. And that was tremendous.

The Legion made clear their intention to continue the siege in order to force the Jews of Jerusalem into surrender. But the Israelis refused to accept any inspection of supply vehicles traveling up on the new "Burma Road," and when it was put to Dov Joseph, the military governor of Jerusalem, that food supplies should be the same at the end of the truce as at the beginning, he replied, "No one is going to tell the people of this city how much they can eat after they have been starving."

In the south some soldiers had been on duty continuously for seven months, and they could not all be relieved, nor could they completely relax because the Egyptians still had to be contained. In contrast to the frenzied training programs that were going on in the north, Yehuda Amichai relates:

☐   We went to another kibbutz, Dorot; we were in a wadi there,
and I remember it turned into a sort of jamboree because
there were a lot of grapes there, and these youth-movement
kids sat eating grapes and planning for the future. Everyone
knew that in a matter of days the truce would be over. There
was a little training, not much.... By this time we'd been
reinforced by a group of young European Jews who'd been
in the camps and then been detained in Cyprus by the
British. They were a very good group. Some had seen action
in the Red Army. They were a bit older than our kids and
very eager to fight.... But for the time being we just sat
around and ate grapes and enjoyed ourselves.

The operation of bringing in these refugees, who for so long
had been prevented by the British blockade from reaching
Palestine, was carried out somewhat haphazardly by groups of
volunteers, many from America. One of them was Yochanan
Dreyfuss:

☐   In about June, we came from the States in President Roosevelt's private yacht. Not Franklin D. Roosevelt's—*Teddy*
Roosevelt's. You can imagine how old it was. It had been
completely refurbished, but that didn't prevent it from
stopping all the way across the Atlantic with all kinds of
engine trouble. The whole crew was American, and apart
from a sprinkling of professional seamen—the second mate,
I remember, was a Jew who'd been to sea during the second
world war—we were not sailors, we were just volunteers,
including about ten members of Hashomair Hatsa'ir.

When we got to Marseilles the ship was refitted and
bunks were put into the holds. Bunks—! They were wooden
shelves, five or six layers. This was where the refugees were
to sleep. The whole back deck of the ship was cleared and
outhouses were put up. This took a couple of weeks. Then
we picked up the refugees.

There were about 2,000 on that trip. On what had been

a private presidential yacht.... We picked them up in the middle of the night at a tiny, beautiful little harbor not far from Marseilles. It had cafés playing music. It was all very hush-hush because the British were still hanging about. We tied up at a breakwater. The refugees had had quite a long walk. I will never forget the sight of those people, a long, long line of them, *shlepping* up the gangplank, carrying suitcases and bags and all kinds of personal belongings; they looked so tired. It was nighttime and they kept coming, coming, coming—that was what got me.

It took about seven or eight days to cross the Mediterranean. Living in those bunks was horrible for them. No air. A terrible smell. They had to come up on deck in shifts. It was very unpleasant. In the middle we had a very bad storm; a lot of them were seasick, and one picture that sticks in my mind is of a woman, lying on deck with her baby, so terribly sick that she couldn't look after it. It was in danger of going overboard.... We took it away and took care of it till she was better. People were lying around all over the deck in a terrible state.

When we'd come across from the States the ship was empty, so the officers all had cabins, one or two to a room. When the ship was loaded with refugees, women with babies used our cabins during the day.

When we knew we were close to shore, a small warship approached us. We were very anxious—we didn't know whose it was. But we found out it was "ours," and very soon after that we had our first view of Haifa. Everyone came up on deck. It was so crowded no one could move.

We disembarked the refugees straight onto the shore. That first trip, we arrived during the first truce. Various U.N. officials supervised the disembarkation. They were supposed to check papers and so on, because there were still some regulations at that time.... Of course, it was completely meaningless. Anyway, they all got on shore. We spent that night in Haifa. There was an air-raid warning, which woke me up, but nothing came of it.

It was my first time in Israel. During the turn-around period we went with an Israeli naval officer to visit Kibbutz Ein Hashofet ten of us, the Hashomair Hatsa'ir-niks. And we traveled around a bit, to see what we could of the country. Then it was time to go back and get another load.

The ship broke down again. It was almost a disaster. The storm broke when we were in the Strait of Messina, and a very strong current pushed us toward the rocks until we finally rigged up a jury rig and got going again.

By the time we brought the next lot back, it must have been August. We went then to join Ein Hashofet; some members of our group had already been there for six months or so and had gone through the battle of Mishmar Ha'emek. Half of our group were sent to Sha'ar Hagolan. This kibbutz had been overrun by the Syrians and evacuated by the kibbutzniks, some say on orders from above; others said it was a misunderstanding. Anyway, Sha'ar Hagolan and another kibbutz, Massada, had been occupied by the Syrians for two days until they were driven back out.

What the Syrians managed to do to that kibbutz in those two days was unbelievable. It had been a beautiful place. They had destroyed every single house. Not just destroyed. The houses there were built on concrete with wooden doors and window frames and tiled roofs. They had taken the roofs apart, taken away the tiles and the wooden rafters and ripped out the door frames and window frames, and then they crapped in each room and lit fires in the middle of every floor. When we came in the Syrians had gone off, without a fight, leaving empty shells. Filthy. Unbelievable.

We spent possibly two or three months there after that, doing some repair work. In six months we couldn't have finished repairing the damage they wreaked on that place in two days.

If the Israelis were licking their wounds, so were the Arabs. They, too, had taken heavy casualties and were short of ammunition. Only the Syrians had made any inroad into territory allotted by partition to Israel, though the Jordanians had taken the Old City and the Etzion Bloc, and the Egyptians had also captured several outlying settlements. This was not, however, the swift and total victory the Arab politicians had promised their people, or what many Arabs in Israel had expected. Anwar Nusseibah:

☐　At the first truce, things were still evenly balanced. I could not believe that the Arab armies would be unable to contain the situation, that they would sue for a truce until the situation was restored. It was hard to believe. I did not know then how much better prepared the Israelis were for what was happening.

A traumatic event that illustrates the lingering disunity of the Israeli forces, despite Ben-Gurion's efforts to bring them all under one command, was the *Altalena* incident, which occurred a few days after the start of the first truce. The story is told here by Eliahu Lankin, now a Jerusalem attorney, then a member of the Irgun. He had been sent into exile in Africa by the British for terrorist activities, found his way back to Palestine in 1945, and was given the post of commander of European activities by Menachem Begin, then commander in chief of the Irgun.

☐　The story starts in November '47. The *Altalena* was a Normandy invasion vessel, which we acquired from the U.S. Navy after the world war. We bought it cheap and brought it to Europe.
　　　We were busy organizing Jewish youth all over the world, training them, and our plan was that one day there would be an internal uprising in Palestine and at the same time we would bring ships to the shore and join the rebels and expel the British from the country. The *Altalena* was originally intended as an invasion ship. Meanwhile, partition occurred, the British decided to evacuate, and the Arabs

attacked the Jewish population. I received an order from Begin to collect everything we had—weapons and people—because the Yishuv was under heavy pressure.

We undertook political negotiations with the French, who were very friendly then: the French government promised us a supply of weapons, which, as a first step, would be enough to equip an infantry division. We thought this amount of weapons might be decisive in our struggle against the Arabs; the shortage of weapons for all three Jewish armies was critical. So we concentrated all our efforts on these negotiations and postponed our plans for bringing the *Altalena* to Israel with what bits and pieces of arms we had collected in the hope of bringing in a large quantity of first-class military matériel. I still believe today that if these weapons had arrived in February, March, of '48, when there was no other supply—we only started receiving from Czechoslovakia in April—we could have taken the whole West Bank then. That would have strengthened our position in the armistice talks in '49. Jerusalem [i.e., the Old City] would not have been defeated, and they would not dare to claim now that we should give back [East] Jerusalem just because they kept it for nineteen years.

Negotiations dragged on. Those were the worst months of my life. The French kept changing governments and putting our "case" on one side. You must understand our feelings: We were youngsters, full of excitement and idealism, and we were seasoned underground fighters. Yet there we were, sitting in Paris—I would not say in comfort, but safe, while day after day we heard of Arab attacks.... We were helpless, waiting for those weapons.

We called *Altalena* "the Savior Ship," because we sincerely believed we were helping to save the Jewish people. We saw it as a great historical action. We kept pressing our representatives to hurry the French up. It was terribly frustrating; those months of nervous tension were appalling.

By the time the French approved the grant of weapons, it was already the eve of May 15th. The state was proclaimed. But till we actually obtained the weapons and sailed from Port de Bouc, it was already June 11th.

So that's how it happened that we came a little bit late. By that time the Czech weapons had started to flow. Mind you, the French *gave* us the weapons, whereas we had to pay the Czechs—in dollars!

The ship arrived ten days later, on June 20th, by which time the picture was different in Israel. There was already enough equipment for the soldiers, and as a matter of fact the interference of foreign powers was bringing the war to an end [*sic*]. The weapons aboard the *Altalena* were important, even coming so late, as an additional supply, but they were no longer at that stage decisive.

We were accused of intending to use the weapons for a *putsch*. If that were so, would we have informed them [the high command of the Haganah] a week beforehand that we were arriving? Would we have presented them with a full list of weapons carried on the ship? Would we have proceeded to Kfar Vitkin, the place designated by them?

Our rule in the Irgun always was, "Don't raise your hand against a Jew." This atmosphere of hostility was all due to Ben-Gurion's hatred. I don't minimize his greatness in our history. No doubt of it—our greatest leader in war and the first years of statehood. I wish we had such a leader now. But that doesn't change the background of his hatred. Galili and Allon didn't agree to "the season" [in which Ben-Gurion ordered the Haganah to catch dissidents and hand them over to the British] of which I was the first victim.

The discrimination against our boys was strongly felt by Begin. So that he, naïvely, demanded that his boys in Jerusalem be equipped with weapons, because of this long history of discrimination and persecution by Ben-Gurion's regime.

Until 1971, when Israel Galili published a series of articles in the Israeli newspaper *Ma'ariv,* the version people in Israel believed was that Ben-Gurion knew nothing about the *Altalena,* that when he heard about it he assumed that it was the beginning of an insurrection, and also that it would break the terms of the cease-fire.

The moment Begin heard that we had sailed from Port de Bouc, he cabled to the ship saying, "Keep away. Await instructions." He could not undertake to break the cease-fire. When I read the next instruction, that we should bring the ship in to Kfar Vitkin, I was very happy, because I assumed then that it was aboveboard, that the government must have given permission.

Dan Even [the commander of the contingent of the Alexandroni Brigade, dispatched by Ben-Gurion to intercept the unloading of the ship] didn't even come to Begin and tell him personally, as nowadays they do even to Arabs, "Listen, this is serious, you have to hand over the arms or I must open fire." If that had happened, I can tell you without the slightest doubt that the weapons would have been handed over. But instead we got this ultimatum, which technically we could not have obeyed—it gave us only ten minutes to hand the arms over.

The big boxes were piled on the sand. Each box weighed about a hundred kilos—how could we have handed it over? Only a well-organized unit could handle such an operation. There we were, standing in the open on the shore—it was daylight—with the ship a couple of hundred meters away. And suddenly, shots and explosions of trench mortars from all sides....

Afterward the captain [Munroe Fein] said that when he heard the shooting he started moving away for fear of the explosives on the ship going up. We on shore meanwhile immediately fell to the ground to take cover, and there was a brief consultation. Begin said, "I must go to Tel Aviv to consult with someone. Here they can just slaughter us!" So we decided to go on board ship, and Yaacov Meridor, the second in command, stayed on shore while we ran to the boat, rowed away, boarded the ship, and sailed to Tel Aviv, so that Begin could get in contact with one of the five ministers who were *not* members of the Labor party.

We arrived in Tel Aviv at night. Meanwhile, Meridor somehow got in touch with the commander at Kfar Vitkin and surrendered, because there was no intention on our part to fight. They said we opened fire, but if we had, I believe they would have suffered casualties. Only our boys were killed or wounded, proving the fire came only from the Haganah.

We ran the ship aground a hundred and fifty meters from the shore, and waited to send a boat ashore in the morning. The boat was fired on, and two of the boys were wounded. So the boat returned to the ship. Then we saw how they'd prepared positions on roofs and in windows, catching us in cross fire to stop us from trying to get to shore.

That situation lasted all day. Begin called to the shore with a loudspeaker: "Brothers! Jews! We don't come to fight you—get word to our representatives!" and so on. It didn't help. As soon as they had their positions ready they began to fire. I snatched rifles from the hands of our boys on the ship to stop their returning the shore fire.

Many were wounded and a few were killed. Then the heavy guns began to fire. The ship caught fire and we were ordered to abandon it. Then the explosions started— Captain Fein and myself jumped last and came to the shore. I couldn't swim so the captain pulled me.

The same night I was at my brother's flat and they came to arrest us and send us to jail.

Begin was the man who prevented civil war. He always insisted that under no circumstances should we raise our weapons against our own brothers. He educated his boys— "Our weapons are sacred to the battle against our external enemy."

Needless to say, this is not the only side to the story. David Cohen, a member of Kibbutz Beit Alpha, insists that none of the several books and accounts of the *Altalena* saga written by members of the Irgun is accurate. "If you want to see the inaccuracies," he maintains, "just compare them—not to the

Haganah version, as written by Uri Brenner, but to each other. Of all the Irgun-niks who wrote about the affair, only Begin was even in the country at the time."

As liaison officer between the Haganah and the dissident organizations, Cohen participated actively in all the early stages of the drama. The sequence of events, according to him, was as follows:

☐ On June 1st, Begin and the Haganah signed an agreement to disband the Etzel and all its formations.... Chaim Landau* and Begin signed it. It was an agreement that Etzel should cease to exist throughout the whole country "in all territory administered by the government." They claimed later that this did not include Jerusalem, which at that time was not part of the state of Israel, but of course it was administered by the government—as such, it was *not* excluded from the agreement. Members of Etzel were to join the official army, yielding up all their armaments to the forces of Zahal [IDF]. The men of the Irgun were to be recruited in battalions, and a special HQ was to be set up temporarily in order to recruit more people. All this was to make their integration into the regular army easier, after all the years of antagonism.

It later emerged that the Etzel leaders were hiding the whole inside story of the *Altalena,* which was, at that time [beginning of June] docked in Port de Bouc waiting for the consignment of arms promised by the French government. Even Begin didn't know when it was due to sail.

On June 2nd, the day after the signing of the agreement, Begin had promised to get on to his people in Europe, so that they would know about the agreement and adhere to it. But when the Etzelniks who were sitting in France waiting for the arms heard the terms of the agreement, they repudiated it. They didn't feel themselves bound by it.

Shaul Avigor was our government representative in Europe. The Etzel people there were supposed to hand over

*One of Begin's deputies.

all their contacts to Avigor on June 5th. But Avigor sent a
telegram to Zahal HQ that they refused to comply. [Eliahu]
Lankin later said that he had not received orders from his
commanders in Israel and he would not honor the agreement.

On June 5th two members of Etzel, Arieh Ben Eliazer
and a man called Germant, were sent to Israel from France
to make technical arrangements with Begin—where to send
the ship, how to unload, and so on. On the day they arrived,
they claimed that they had had no instructions from Begin to
fulfill the conditions of the agreement with the government.

On the 6th they heard that the weapons had begun to
arrive at the French port, and Begin informed me that
Germant was on his way back to France with instructions.
Begin demanded to be told (by Shmuel Katz in Paris) when
the *"Miriam"* (code name for the ship) would be reaching
Israel.

June 9th, Germant left Paris for Marseilles, where all
the Etzel European contingent had gone by that time.

Avigor sent a telegram to say, "There is nothing to
report" [meaning that the Europe-based members of Etzel
had not yet complied with the agreement]. I went to Begin
with it and said, "What's this? How can this be?" Begin said,
"It's a misunderstanding. I will inform them again." *We are
sure that he never informed them.*

June 11. The ship sailed. We and the whole world
learned it from the BBC. Nothing was said about its
containing arms—only men. Begin was very upset, because
he didn't know what was going to happen.

June 12. Telegram from Begin to Paris: "The ship can't
arrive here now. Inform immediately what you are going to
do." Katz replied the same night, "Your telegram arrived too
late. *Miriam* will contact you at the latest after eight days.
Maybe you can contact her earlier."

June 13. Begin: "I will try to contact the ship. You
should also try to stop her. She must not come too soon."

But contact was not made until five days later, on June

15 at night. On the *Altalena* the officers decided to ignore the message sent to tell the ship to go slow—it was sailing toward Israel at full speed.

On the 15th I was told to attend an urgent meeting at Etzel HQ in Tel Aviv. We suspected it was about the *Altalena*. I decided after talking to Galili to ask Levi Eshkol to be present, because he was the deputy defense minister. The meeting took place at one o'clock at night, 15th to 16th June at the Freunde Hospital in Tel Aviv. Begin, Chaim Landau, Meridor, "Gidi" Paglin,* and Ben Eliazer were all there. The atmosphere was very dramatic, very serious. From Begin's tone one could gather something extra-ordinary was in the wind. For the first time he informed us that "fighters" and "arms" were on the way, expected to arrive within a few days. Eshkol asked for details of the arms. He didn't get them, except for the information that there was "a lot of ironmongery," enough to make all the difference to the war. More details they got only a few days later, not at that meeting.

There was no mention of any condition that Etzel would specify when the ship arrived. They wanted the government to decide what to do.

This situation demanded a top-level decision. This was at the time of the first cease-fire, and it still was not clear to us how far the U.N. would enforce its terms [which forbade the importation of weapons or fighting men]. It was not that the government didn't want more arms, but the arms that did arrive at that time arrived secretly, and this would be open—the world knew about the ship and would be watching. All kinds of questions were raised. Could the ship be instructed to enter a neutral port? The government said it needed time to decide and would do so in the morning. They told Begin to delay the ship. Begin informed the meeting that he could not contact the ship and could not give them any

*The Irgun's chief hit man, the executor of such actions as the blowing up of the King David Hotel and the hanging of the British sergeants in 1946.

instruction, and that she was on her way. The meeting closed with our promise to give a definite decision the following day.

After a very short discussion, the government decided that they had no option. There was no way to communicate with the ship, so we must let it come in. Begin was very pleased.

June 16th. Begin asked me to discuss details. He asked that the Etzel should be allowed to help off-load the ship, as compensation for all their efforts. I said that the man to decide such things should be the man who had always been responsible for bringing in illegal arms ships, and that was Pinchas Vaseh. On the same day we had a meeting with Vaseh about the technical and logistical details.

June 17th. We decided that the ship should come in to Kfar Vitkin, which was near the arms depots of Zahal. We would load the arms onto trucks there. The nine hundred men on the ship would be used as porters and stevedores. The beach at Kfar Vitkin is more gravel than sand which would make it easier for the trucks to get to the shore. The loaded trucks would go straight to Netanya and from there to the arms depots.

Begin initially agreed to the plan, but the Etzel didn't seem to like this arrangement. Begin said, "My comrades want the stuff to be stored in the Etzel stores." How could this be, when Etzel was no longer formally in existence? Begin said, "It is in the nature of a symbolic participation by the Irgun." We replied that this request was beyond the authority of the army, it was a political matter, and we would have to pass it on to our superiors. The last of Begin's arguments for putting the arms into Etzel's stores was that the arrangements about Jerusalem had not yet been concluded with Galili. The meeting ended by our telling Begin that we would bring him the decision of the government as soon as possible.

June 18th. Another meeting—the same people. We told them that the decision of the government was that the arms

must come into government depots. In the course of the
discussion, Paglin shouted that he would not agree to
anything except the Irgun plan. It was out of the question
that the arms should go anywhere but into the Etzel depots
under Etzel guards. Meridor and Begin sat agape while
"Gidi" insisted. Begin asked for time to consult with his
comrades. Later I asked him what had finally been decided.
The answer was that Etzel was not prepared to change its
decision to put the arms into their depots. In principle, he
was prepared to hand the stuff over to the government forces
on the shore, but at the same time he insisted on putting it
into Etzel depots!

Later that day Begin wrote a note to Galili to say the
ship was about to arrive. Galili answered him that the arms
should be handed over on the beach to Zahal.

June 19th. There was an urgent government meeting
with Ben-Gurion, and Galili rang Begin to tell him that there
was no change in the government's decision, and that Begin
would have to bear full responsibility for the outcome of any
breach. So the Irgun knew that the government would insist
on its rights and they would have to obey. Zahal got the
order to get ready to carry out the government's decision.
Meanwhile—in connection with Jerusalem—Galili agreed
that 20 percent of the arms on the ship should go to
Jerusalem, *but not specifically for Etzel.* It was to be used
cooperatively by all forces.*

On the night of the 19th, the ship arrived at Kfar Vitkin,
but could not land, went back out to sea, and returned on the
20th. Meanwhile, the Etzel soldiers who had previously

*In *The Revolt,* Begin says that Galili agreed that 20 percent of the arms
should go to the Etzel forces, still functioning separately in Jerusalem. Galili
says, "We did not go into details about how the 20 percent was to be distributed.
There could have been a clash over the issue, but Begin never raised it when we
negotiated about the *Altalena.* Not with me, not with Eshkol, not with Cohen—
it never arose. It was a post facto interpretation. We agreed to allocate such-and-
such a percentage to Jerusalem, but went into no details. There was no
contention about it at that time."

joined Zahal under the agreement left their posts and hurried to the shore to help unload the ship. So that, on the beach at Kfar Vitkin, Etzel soldiers—some who had not joined Zahal yet, others who had deserted—were ready for action; while still more poured in, especially from nearby Netanya, Zahal prepared to respond in kind.

Interrupting the story at this point, I want to bring in the account of Alexander Zur, the Khim officer formerly stationed near Jaffa. His personal experience of the behavior of the Etzel troops at this time confirms that their first loyalty was still overwhelmingly to their "disbanded" force:

☐   After the fall of Jaffa, our headquarters moved to the police station at Beit Dagan. This was during the first cease-fire. Now, the task of our brigade was eventually to take Ramle, that was its main purpose. We were around Ramle on the west side, and the Etzel had its main force on the southwest side. So when the Haganah came to an agreement with Etzel as a result of which the *Altalena* was brought in, the Etzel force was put under the command of my brigade.

Meridor, the deputy commander of Etzel, came to us to make arrangements for his unit to come under our brigade. They were in Be'er Yacov, southwest of Ramle. They were in a terrible position regarding ammunition and food—they had nothing. So we put them on our list and we fed them and gave them arms and ammunition, and we told them to "keep the front moving"—in other words, to keep the Arabs too busy to come against us.

Incidentally, they kept telling me stories—hundreds of stories—about their "attacks" on Ramle, which never even came close to the truth. It was all bluffing. We never believed them. They were just braggarts—and this was the main Etzel force in Israel. As to how many of them there were, you could never tell. As far as rations were concerned there were hundreds. As far as operations were concerned—maybe twenty.

On the day the *Altalena* landed near Netanya, and then in Tel Aviv, we received orders to prevent "our" Etzel unit from going to Tel Aviv. These orders came from GHQ. That was in the morning, and immediately after receiving that order, we planned to block the Rishon road, the road from Beit Dagan, which was the route the Etzel would have had to take to get to Tel Aviv. By chance a convoy of Palmach soldiers came by. We stopped them. We told the soldiers to get out of the trucks and proceed wherever they were going on foot, leaving the trucks blocking the road.

An hour later, a convoy of the Etzel force from Be'er Yacov came from the direction of the Rishon Road. They started shouting at us to get the road cleared. At that time we'd already heard on the radio the whole episode of the *Altalena*. I sent a message to this convoy saying they had no business leaving the front line without orders from us. And we ordered them to go back, which they refused to do.

About fifteen minutes later, their commander, whom I knew personally—he'd served under me in the British army—asked to see me. I ordered a machine gun to be set up on the veranda of the police station, although stupidly enough I actually believed this former comrade of mine, and I went to meet him at the crossroads.

The moment I got there he threatened to shoot me like a dog if I didn't immediately order the road to be cleared. I'd left my deputy at the machine gun, and by a previously arranged hand signal I ordered him to open fire. (He had to man the gun himself because some of my soldiers didn't want to shoot at fellow Jews.) So my deputy opened fire, first into the air and then at the Etzel group. There were casualties—I think one dead and a couple wounded, I don't know exactly—and they panicked. Their commander, who was pointing a gun at my stomach, heard the shooting and I think he got the wind up.

Anyway, the Etzel men abandoned their trucks and then passed the roadblock on foot and went on to Tel Aviv. As far as I know, they arrived after the whole thing was over.

As a result of their desertion of the line, I had to thin out our force and replace them with units of our own to cover the gap around Ramle.

Shimon Avidan more tersely relates a similar experience:

☐   When, in June, the Revisionist underground armies were incorporated into the Israel Defense Forces, I got a battalion of them. They served for three weeks, and then they deserted. They left the front and moved to Tel Aviv to help to unload the *Altalena*. So my experience of them was short, and not so sweet. I am not objective about them. I don't like them.

Continuing David Cohen's narrative of the *Altalena*'s arrival:

☐   The Etzel supporters emptied an immigrant hostel in Netanya to be used as a hostel for the incoming volunteers from the ship. Zahal set up a new HQ in Camp Dora, where I sat with Galili and Dan Even, the commander of the Alexandroni Brigade. Zahal brought in more men till they had the beach encircled, recruiting more people to strengthen their force. The order was passed to Begin, who was on the beach: "The government is going to enforce its rights. The arms must be handed over." But this ultimatum, of course, demanded a *decision,* not the physical handing over of the arms.

     In order to prevent bloodshed, Dan Even requested a conference. Begin refused to comply with the ultimatum but said he was prepared to receive Even on the beach.

     By this time, some arms had already been unloaded but had not been allowed by the Zahal troops to leave the beach, though the men from the ship were leaving in buses and were being passed through.

     Sympathizers were lined up by Etzel; everything was prepared for a major confrontation. They would not let the army approach the arms piled up on the beach. There was shooting and there were injured on both sides.

Two government naval vessels were circling about out at sea. Most of the arms were by now on the shore. Only minor matériel—medical supplies, small arms, and so on— was left on the ship.* These two naval vessels gave the order that the *Altalena* was to follow them out to sea, to return next night to complete the unloading, because of the cease-fire.

Begin, their top commander, was on shore all the time in direct charge of operations, giving orders through a loudspeaker. Instead of stopping the whole thing and falling in with the government's orders, he was urging his men on— to defy the government.

Instead of following the naval vessels, the ship crept along the coast as far as Tel Aviv, avoiding the vessels which could not come in so close to shore.

Captain Fein of the *Altalena* wrote later that he had no intention of carrying out the vessels' orders. "We used all sorts of tricks to circumvent them." By then, Begin was on board the ship with him.

The original plan—when the ship had been expected much earlier—had been to beach it near a slum area on the shores of Tel Aviv where the Etzel had many supporters. Chaim Landau was based in Tel Aviv, and so were many members and adherents of Etzel. The whole thing was organized in advance—people flocked to the shore from all over the city.

I arrived at the Red House, which was Zahal HQ in Tel Aviv, at about 4 A.M. Nearby was the Café Ritz, where the U.N. truce observers sat watching the drama unfold. On the beach the Etzel supporters were milling around. From the

---

*This is in direct and vital contradiction to Begin, who, in the broadcast he made following the incident, and in his book, berated the government for depriving the struggling nation of quantities of arms, explosives, and military equipment that went down with the ship.

ship, loudspeakers harangued the crowd on shore, saying that the "treacherous government" would not allow them to unload the much-needed arms and so on. Shots rang out. The army gave the command that there was to be no disembarkation, because men on board had let down boats and were trying to come ashore. There were orders and counterorders, shooting....

I waded into the sea up to my thighs in my clothes. At a distance of not much over a hundred meters I could see Begin walking up and down the deck. I shouted through a loudspeaker: "Listen, listen! The government representative will come on board to supervise the disembarkation. Aid will be given to the wounded if needed." The reply came back: "No! No! We don't agree!" And they went on calling on the population to oppose the "traitor government," warning those on shore not to shoot at the ship because it might set off a terrible explosion like the one which had destroyed Ben Yehuda Street [in Jerusalem]. Two streets were then evacuated.

I returned to Ben-Gurion at the Red House and told him the reply I'd received from the men on board. Ben-Gurion ordered me to return to Camp Dora and see how the matter was going there.

Back at Kfar Vitkin, Meridor had been left in charge of the arms. When daylight came, fearing that a stray bullet would set off the explosives on the shore, he surrendered to Dan Even, who took charge of the matériel. He made the remaining Etzel soldiers sign on, allowing the commanders to go with their personal sidearms, according to the rules in the British army. And that ended the affair there.

When I got back to Tel Aviv, the ship was already burning—that was at 10 A.M. All I could see was a lot of smoke.... Because of Etzel's refusal to obey orders, Yigal Allon had been ordered to take over. Some people did come off the ship, including Begin. I was told to take in hand the arrangements in Tel Aviv to calm the situation, and meantime a lot of army personnel took over and quieted things down.

While all this had been going on, two religious ministers had resigned from the government in protest. They were with Ben-Gurion in the old opera house where government meetings took place. When I got back to tell Ben-Gurion all was now quiet, he turned to the ministers and said, "You see? All is well." And they backed down.

David Cohen's opinion is that Begin personally had no intention of starting a revolt. He was "drawn into it" by circumstances and by others of a more radical temperament like Paglin, but his main culpability was that he was, ultimately, in the center of the affair and in a position to stop it, to bring it to a bloodless conclusion by giving way to the government's demands, and he did not do so.

Cohen, of course, although a witness and a participant, had no control over events. One of the few surviving "prime movers" on the government side is Israel Galili. He told me how Ben-Gurion replied to his letter of that morning, giving news of Begin's refusal to give way on the arms.

☐ *"I don't know what has happened during this morning, but this time it is impossible to compromise. Either they accept orders and keep to them or there will be shooting. I am against any negotiations with them and against any agreement. The time for agreement is past and will not return. If one has power one should use it without hesitation and immediately."* The last word, "immediately," was added by Ben-Gurion in his own handwriting. The letter was signed at 12:15 [afternoon] on the day of the 21st when the boat was at Kfar Vitkin. I received it in Camp Dora.

I'd sent Ben-Gurion a message describing the situation. They had refused to obey the orders and the answer to our ultimatum was in the negative. Not after ten minutes but after some hours. But I did not order the soldiers to open fire. To tell the truth, I was looking for some arrangement which would avoid a clash. We had a mediator, Ben Ami, the mayor of Netanya; and he sent a delegation to Ben-Gurion in Tel Aviv. Ben-Gurion, ironically, called them "volunteers." And before giving the order for action I wished to be sure, because I was well aware of the responsibility upon my shoulders, and I sent a messenger to Ben-Gurion relating their refusal and telling him of the political complexities and bearing in mind the special paragraphs that Ben Ami proposed.

You have to remember one detail—very important to me: When the cabinet was in session [Yigal] Yadin was sent to Camp Dora, and he told Ben-Gurion he was not ready to go there without being accompanied by a minister. It was then that Ben-Gurion had called me and said, "You have to go with Yadin."

For my part, I am sure that some people like Paglin "overran" Begin, persuading him that the government would refrain from strong action, convincing him that the government was weak and that it was safe for Etzel to persist. And they had an alliance with their supporters and friends within the government, religious Zionists who tried to pressure Ben-Gurion, to intimidate him. Maybe these partners within the government misled Begin into believing that he could rely upon them.

At all events, from my heart I wished to avoid bloodshed, so I instructed the area commander [Dan Even] to use the services of Ben Ami and to have everything documented. Dan Even told Ben Ami that he had invited Begin to come to his headquarters to talk things over, and reminded him of the seriousness of the ultimatum. He said that Begin had refused to come, had asked Even to come to him on the beach, and that at that point the negotiations between Dan Even and Begin came to a stop.

By this time they had unloaded some of the arms and they were having a celebration. We have witnesses. When they got the ultimatum, they crumpled up the paper and didn't pay any attention to it. They were sure they were going to get the arms, and they didn't tell their own people that there would be a clash with the newly founded government. Not only the new arrivals from the boat were uninformed, but their people who had come to the shore to help .... Many were sure that *everything was occurring with the agreement of the government.* The deserters from Zahal, who had earlier been instructed that they must now recognize the authority of the government forces, were called by their former command to a "holy mission"—to help unload the boat—and many were misled into believing that the government had agreed. Those who had come on the ship were very happy—they were coming to Eretz Israel and bringing with them weapons to save their country and their people.

There were some nine hundred of them, and they went off in buses to Netanya. The Haganah opened the line to let them through. It was the weapons we wanted. We had nothing against the men and women from the ship.

When I came to the Red House in Tel Aviv I tried to persuade Ben-Gurion not to act without convening the cabinet. I said to Ben-Gurion, "Don't be hasty. I am older than you. (Though of course I was not.) I warn you to consult the government." In the end the decision to fire on the ship was a joint decision, and afterward it was up to the commanders on the spot. At some stage Yigal Allon was called to take over command; when the forces in Tel Aviv couldn't manage, Yadin suggested that the Palmach be brought in. So Allon was called and Yadin ordered him to take over.

I was appalled, very appalled to see what followed. But I was convinced that the fate of the newborn Jewish state depended on national discipline, and that we could not bear any attempt to destroy the new structure of statehood and independence. That was the real rock of contention between us and Etzel. We had hoped we might skip over it, but still, it occurred.

We were not certain that Begin was on the ship—he could have left by boat before the ship reached Tel Aviv. It was very interesting—to make such a drama a few steps from the headquarters of the U.N.—in front of the whole world, to break the U.N.'s rules. It was not just that these men were irresponsible. They hoped that the government would not dare—in front of everybody—in front of the U.N. Or maybe they hoped that the citizens of Tel Aviv would intervene on their behalf—come to their aid. A few did, but they were the minority.

It was this, above all, that determined the outcome of this traumatic confrontation between the government and the dissident forces—the fact that, when it came to it, by far the majority of the Yishuv supported Ben-Gurion and the Zionist establishment, whereas only a relative few wished to support the Revisionists to the extent of abetting a possible coup, spearheaded by extremists like Paglin.

A postscript to the affair by Netiva Ben Yehuda shows that not every member of the government forces was willing to engage in battle with the dissidents, even at this crucial moment:

□   I remember the *Altalena,* how we were ordered to go and fight the Etzel and how I said, "What for? We need civil war? I'm not going to fight the Etzel! Besides, we need the arms on the ship." And after that I was kicked out—not kicked out, just got rid of, the way they got rid of a lot of officers besides me. They just posted everybody else, but I received no orders. I was simply left out of the orders, as if I no longer existed. It was only when Yigal Allon heard, that he sent for me specially. So I went down into the desert and stayed there:

Meanwhile, political moves to extend the truce were failing. The U.N. mediator, the Swedish Count Folke Bernadotte, put forward a proposal that the two projected states should form a union, or that the Arab sector should be part of Transjordan. There were also territorial amendments, giving Jordan most of the Negev and the Jews, western Galilee. Both sides rejected this plan. Bernadotte then suggested extending the truce for another thirty days. Israel agreed; the Arabs did not. Therefore, on

Friday, July 9, at 6 A.M. the first truce ended and the war was resumed.

Phase 3:
The Ten-Day War and the Second Truce

THE SOUTH

The Egyptians had not been very scrupulous in their observance of the truce. They had blocked the Jews' route to their southern settlements and had even bombed them, violations about which the U.N. seemed unable to do a great deal. And a full twenty-four hours before the truce was scheduled to end—on the morning of July 8—the Egyptians launched their offensive against the Givati and Negev brigades.

Their main objective was finally to subdue Negba, together with neighboring strongpoints, to cut off entirely the southern Jewish settlements from their supplies and to secure their own advance toward Tel Aviv without fear of attack on their own communication lines.

The saga of Kibbutz Negba now came to its climax. Kuba Villan:

☐   When the truce ended, in July, we were attacked again. It was on the anniversary of Negba's founding, July 12, and we got a little poem that our kids had written for us, something like "Negba exists, Negba never falls." And that day I issued an order: We cannot fall, we cannot be conquered, we cannot disappoint our children. And that day, we won, because we were fighting much better.

They started at 4 A.M. Wave after wave after wave, attacking with artillery fire in order to hold us down; then tanks and some air raids to make us retreat from our positions. But the main battle started at four in the afternoon. I felt that this was going to be the decisive moment.

I went to the hospital, such as it was, and said, "Those who are able to hold a rifle, go to your positions. The situation is very dangerous. If we hold on, we have a chance of being evacuated tonight to a proper hospital. If we don't, they will probably kill us. So it is much better to go into the lines." Thus I got some people out into the lines who were already at the end of their strength.

And we held them. They could not defeat us. The wire fence was already cut in several places, and Negba was one big fire. Everything was burning. And in headquarters they heard we had fallen—how? The Egyptian commander announced it on the radio—perhaps he wanted to receive his medals one day earlier: "From the roof of the fort [Iraq Suweidan] it can be seen that the fence is breached—all of Negba is conquered!"

When Hagana HQ heard this, their hearts sank. Israel Galili, who was then chief of staff, mentioned it to his friend, Barzilai, who was a member of Negba. He was preparing himself to go to Warsaw as the first Israeli ambassador to Poland, but when he heard the report of our defeat he went at once to Herzliya where our people had been evacuated to be with our wives and children.

The first thing we repaired, when the bombardment quieted down, was the radio, and we reported that we were holding out. So Shimon Avidan asked what we needed. We said water, and try to evacuate the wounded that night. And he asked me how he could help me from a military point of view. The day before I had been quarreling with him because, on a certain hill we called Hill 105, near Negba, there'd been an Israeli position which he had withdrawn, leaving my flank exposed, and I'd asked him why he'd done it, and he'd said, "Since when does a junior officer ask questions like that from a senior one?" And now, when he asked me how he could help me, I asked him, "Since when does a senior officer want advice from a junior one?"

That night they could not help us. But the next night they reconquered Hill 105 and Hill 113, and after that the road to Negba was reopened. They brought us some water and they took out our wounded and brought medicines and so on and some fresh soldiers to replace our people. In the morning when I went to inspect the positions, I found our people sleeping and the fresh soldiers in their places. I say "fresh"— They'd been fighting too, forty-eight hours before. Nobody was fresh.

From then on, the Egyptians knew they would never take Negba. They tried to bypass it and move north through Ibdis, but the army stopped them in a big battle. They tried it through Julis, but again they were stopped. So really, Negba halted the Egyptian army until our forces had had time to organize themselves.

From my experience as a professional soldier in World War II I still find it hard to believe in our victory. The odds were so great against us. I was able to weigh the position, taking account of tanks, artillery, an air force, guns...and on the other hand, I knew what strength it gives when you know what you are fighting for. But still. The odds were five to one.

The Egyptians lost of lot of men. Over fifteen hundred fell, not all at Negba of course. Afterward they came, with the Red Cross, to take away their dead, and I went out and spoke to them. I asked one of them, "What are you doing here? Wouldn't it be much better to sit on a hot day like this at Groppi and have a nice ice cream?" Groppi was the most elegant café in Cairo. The officer said, "How do you know what Groppi is?" I told him that I'd been there several times during the world war when I was in Cairo with the British troops. So he treated me to a cigarette. I asked him, "Aren't you ashamed to offer a cigarette to your enemy?" "No," he said. "We're not enemies. We are soldiers. Everyone has to obey his orders."

The battle of Ibdis, mentioned above, was one of the decisive battles of the war. It was where the Egyptians were stopped. Shimon Avidan:

☐   The battle of Ibdis began with a patrol which I assigned to go through a couple of hills from which very heavy sniper fire was being directed at vehicles going out of Kibbutz Negba, which was very heavily embattled; and this patrol began battle with a battalion which was already in a defense formation behind our line. And this was one occasion when the Egyptians turned the tables on us: They moved at night with a battalion, and we didn't hear them and we didn't stop them—we didn't know about it. So this patrol, about thirty people, began fighting this battalion. We sent reinforcements, and by the end of the day the hills were in our hands, together with a lot of equipment, which we immediately used—even at this time I hadn't enough arms for all my people. We had, for example, trained squads of artillery men without artillery; we took them with us, and as we captured the artillery pieces we put them straight into action with our crews.

This was a very important spot for the Egyptians. You see, it was the turning point for their operational plan to break our front, because in the south there was a flat terrain with only now and then a hill. So they tried by counterattacks to recover these important places. This battle lasted for a week, and every day we changed the formation, which was in the "holding" position. Our casualties were very high, but we understood that that was one of the decisive battles of the war.

The Egyptian army tried everything to recover these areas, from which they could have taken Negba and moved on to the north. And then at last there was quiet, after these seven days of ceaseless noise. And the flag over the Egyptian headquarters at Migdal Ashkelon was lowered to half mast because they had lost about two thousand killed.

Uri Avneri recalls:

☐ We picked up a certain amount from other people's wars, other people's armies. And we got certain ideas from the Bible. Samson's foxes, for instance. Samson tied foxes together in pairs with lighted torches between their tails and let them loose in the fields of the Philistines. So my brigade formed a sort of commando unit called, at first, Negev Rats, and later renamed Samson's Foxes. It was a company-sized unit mounted on jeeps with two machine guns per jeep—we had no armor at that time. It became quite famous—we took part in the biggest battles of the war, Negba and Ibdis.

We used to attack at night. In one famous engagement, we literally overran the Egyptian command position with jeeps. . . . Later, we found out Gamal Abdul Nasser was wounded there. It was called Hill 105. Negba was completely cut off, and we literally overran them, charging through their lines with our jeeps, firing our machine guns as we went.

Following that was the battle of Ibdis, on a hill north of Negba. It was the last big Egyptian attempt to storm our positions. There's a film called *Apocalypse Now* in which there's a night battle where nobody knows who is who or who's in command or what's going on—a total muddle—chaos. Ibdis was very much like that.

We were sent in to bring ammunition in full daylight. We took our jeeps and just went blazing through under intense gunfire. When we got there, the position was almost empty because so many had been killed or wounded—only a handful still functioning.

Then—like in a film—we saw the Egyptian troops advancing in long lines, supported by some tanks, but still unable to storm the last hundred yards. We had one machine gun still firing. It was the height of the war—the closest the Egyptians came to breaking through our positions. It was where their onslaught finally stopped and the tide turned, where we became the attackers and they the defenders.

Yehuda Amichai:

☐ The Egyptians were advancing, with their armored cars and tanks and everything else they had, to a place a little east of the present city of Ashdod. And there was actually nothing to hold them back, only two brigades holding out there, the Givati and ours, the Negev Brigade, plus members of some kibbutzim; and Allon's idea was that everything that could be mustered from the Negev to help these two brigades was to be hurled against the Egyptians.

I was deeply involved in it. There were several miscalculations. We marched toward them all through one night, then encamped in a deserted British camp, and then we heard that the Egyptians had found out about us, so the attack had to be canceled. We had to go all the way back. We tried again, but this time we'd lost the element of surprise.

All I remember of this battle was the way we just burst in through the Egyptian lines and started shooting in all directions. No one knew exactly what was going on. It was a big battle and a big *balagan*—our line inside their line. We did as we were told. My company just shot wildly in all directions— It was a crazy muddle— But this battle—this battle saved Israel.

You can't even say we won, because it all ended in chaos. Dusk came, and we had to retreat, because we had no planes and no big guns. We did have a few guns—and I remember they told us, "We'll lay down an air barrage on the Egyptians," which made us very happy. It turned out that their idea of an air barrage was throwing out bundles of hand grenades on the Egyptians from one or two Piper Cubs. Just a joke, you see, but I think the idea was to bolster our morale.

Avidan has a different version:

☐ The day the Egyptians arrived at Ashdod we made every effort to stop them, which means using three airplanes— Spitfires—which had arrived a week earlier; and I got an order from high command to stop an enemy convoy of about a thousand vehicles, which was advancing bumper to bumper, being absolutely sure we had nothing with which to attack them. We sent the planes up to strafe them. The sky was full of anti-aircraft shells, and this battle ended with our losing 30 percent of our air force, which means one plane shot down and the other two were put out of action.

As for artillery, that was mainly a morale factor. There was a battery of four artillery pieces from Mexico, which had been made at the end of the last century, with wooden wheels, no sights—you just had to kick them into position. But we were very happy because they gave us some backing, firing over our heads; it was only later, we found the diary of an Egyptian artillery officer who fought at Negba, whose hobby was to note down how many of our shells exploded; so we learned that only about 30 percent did, and a number of those only burst in half!

Yehuda Amichai recalls:

☐ The retreat from Ashdod was the worst thing I've ever experienced in my life. We had to retreat through sand dunes, wading, after two nights without sleep. I was carrying a wounded friend on my back, along with a machine gun, and we had to go through an opening between two dunes; an Egyptian machine gunner was concentrating on the gap, so that every third man was killed—it was like meat going through a mincer.

Anyhow, I made it through and laid the wounded man down. He had one little hole in him; I thought he was still alive.... We set up my small machine gun to cover the retreat of the others, three of us and this unconscious man. And I'll never forget it, there was a man lying next to us, dying. He was British. You know, the Negev Brigade of the

Palmach had all sorts of strange elements. This Englishman wasn't even a Jew. And we had a group of about forty French who had been in the Maquis, led by a French nobleman, a great idealist—he was an anti-Nazi hero and he came as a volunteer, bringing all these ex-Maquis people.... Later on, half of them were killed in one battle. But anyhow, this wounded Englishman was wearing a sun helmet and had a lot of tattoos all over him. A professional soldier of some sort.... He lay there dying and I asked him what his name was, and his last word was his name. Shelley. Shelley, like the English poet. In the midst of that mess, that big retreat, men dying all around me—Shelley....

In the end we made it back to Kibbutz Nitzanim, and there they told me, "You carried a dead man all that way."

This battle, whatever sort of terrible mess it seemed at the time, was vital. We felt its importance, because they took out everything to throw at this column of Egyptians. If they'd attacked in the Negev that night, well, they'd have found it empty. But the Egyptians were completely tied to British military doctrine: Never lose the main body of troops. They were afraid to leave their lines. And also, due to our guerrilla actions of the months before, they thought the desert was filled with our troops.

THE CENTRAL FRONT

The Arab Legion was still in control of the twin towns of Lydda and Ramle, constituting a threat to the densely populated coastal plain and Tel Aviv; they also still held Latrun, which, despite the "Burma Road," was a major threat to Jerusalem.

Colonel "Mickey" Marcus, before his death, had been planning Operation Lar Lar: Lydda-Ramle-Latrun-Ramallah. But the plan was changed and so was the name, to Operation

Dani, after the leader of the thirty-five university students who were killed on their way to relieve Gush Etzion. The first stage of it was the capture of Lydda (or Lod) with its strategic airport. Yerucham Cohen, Allon's intelligence officer, recalls:

☐ Operation Dani was planned with two arms, one from Kibbutz Na'an and one from Petach Tikva. Moshe Dayan arrived at 2 P.M. and his deputy briefed him on the situation and the action that was to be taken the next morning and the objective to be captured. Dayan didn't agree with the plan and he changed it without informing his brigade commander or the operation HQ. This already caused some difficulties, because if he had followed the agreed plan, his first step would have been complete about 11 A.M. (this was July 10th) and he was immediately to continue to a point close to Lod Airport, which would be captured by tanks, and to go to Beit Naballa and from there to join the main forces in Ben Shemen.

This caused a delay of twenty-four hours. In the morning the Yiftach Brigade in Ben Shemen couldn't wait any longer for the tanks to arrive to help us with their guns. This attack took place on the morning of the 11th, and Dayan, who was supposed to return with his commando battalion to the airport and allow the tanks to go on to Ben Shemen to join up with us, arrived himself with his soldiers in their jeeps.

Allon realized the situation, but decided that the attack on Lydda should go ahead, even though the tanks were not there. Dayan was ready to push toward the center of the city, instead of the armor, hold positions there, draw fire aimed at Yiftach, and help Yiftach to penetrate deep into the city.

So Dayan's commandos stormed into the city, but he had no control of them. Instead of turning into the heart of Lydda, he turned south and found himself instead in Ramle. He suffered a lot of casualties; he had wounded and dead in the jeeps, which had leaking radiators and punctured tires and so on, so he had no choice but to return to Lydda.

Netiva Ben Yehuda, also with the Yiftach Brigade but not
this time as a fighter, takes an even more negative view of Dayan's
famous charge:

☐   The Lydda-Ramle campaign, logistically speaking, was a
     tremendous burden. I think Yigal Allon was the only one
     who knew how to operate such a thing. Every brigade was
     assigned to a certain part of the front. The main target was
     Lydda. It was decided not to encircle it completely, but to
     leave an opening, for the Arabs to run away either across the
     border or to Ramle.
          Between the twin towns there was a fort, one of the
     Teggart forts, left by the British in Arab hands. I think it was
     the Legion, I don't remember exactly, but it was unimagin-
     ably well fortified, guns, armaments, everything.
          The tank brigade reached a spot where they came under
     heavier fire than they'd expected, so, as had been arranged
     beforehand, Allon asked Yitzhak Sadeh to lend his mobile
     regiment in their jeeps (because all the rest were foot soldiers
     in those days). But it didn't come, and it didn't come, and
     suddenly we learned that it was caught in heavy cross fire at
     this fort, which by the way is now Ramle Prison. People
     were getting killed, and suddenly came the question: "Who
     is it? Who went to that spot? No one was ordered to go there,
     it's against all reason!" Because the Palmach under Allon
     never went head on at a target; they would think, where is
     the soft spot, how to approach by night, to smuggle someone
     through—to save lives, to make it feasible. Ten people
     killed, twelve—they began calling for help—the whole
     operation was stopped, and a big part of it was diverted to
     pull out those jeeps, but until they succeeded even more
     died. Eighteen altogether.
          Then we found out that this was Dayan's regiment.
     Dayan had gone against orders, without the infantry, which
     was occupied somewhere else according to the plan; he had
     passed through part of Lydda and then shot off toward the

airport. It was a typical piece of Dayan bravura. Afterward
he got a telling off for it.

Soon after the battle, those of us who were in the
forward HQ—about three kilometers from Lydda—came
into the town. There were some terrible things there. First of
all, it was the first time a large group of Arabs were collected
together in a prison camp. We'd never seen it before. People
hadn't run away as we'd wanted. Some did; but the others
were collected in this camp near Ramle.

A few of the Arabs (Legionnaires) were caught in a
garage with their armored cars. Things had gone quiet, and
all the tired Israelis were sitting around in the square in the
middle of the town; the Arabs, not hearing anything,
decided to come out of the garage to see what was going on.
They came out and suddenly found themselves surrounded,
so they began to shoot and throw hand grenades. A friend of
mine had a grenade land near him. He threw it, and lost part
of his arm. Then somebody went through the streets of
Lydda with loudspeakers and promised everybody who
would go inside a certain mosque that they would be safe,
that if they sat in there quietly with their hands on their
heads, nothing would happen to them. So hundreds of them
went in. But something did happen. You will not record
what I am going to tell you now.

Later I had to drive along the road from Lydda to
Ramle. The side of the road was strewn with the bodies of
dead Arabs and dead donkeys.

Yerucham Cohen stoutly denies any malpractice:

☐   A rebellion broke out because there were some units of the
Jordanian army trapped in the town and they tried to break
out, shooting. The townspeople, who had already surrendered, thought the Legion had launched a counterattack
and some of them started to fire on our troops from their
buildings. Our Yiftach Brigade was outnumbered by the

armed Arabs in the town, and the uprising had to be firmly suppressed.

I arrived in Lydda at 10 A.M., shortly after the suppression of the rebellion. The Arab notables came to the commander of the town to ask permission to leave for the Judean hills. I was there when they came because I spoke Arabic. And the order was given to the soldiers to allow anyone who wanted to leave to pass without any search of their belongings; they were free to take what they wanted. That was between 10:30 and noon.

Less than an hour later the move started in the direction of Ramle. Not a single shot was heard from the moment the rebellion ended till four or five in the afternoon when we went back to my HQ. People were leaving all the next day, on horseback, in cars, on donkeys.

There are two accusations that have been made regarding our behavior in those towns. One about the people leaving and one about the mosque. It's said that we deliberately killed people by blowing up a mosque. But when the rebellion broke out, it was being used as a stronghold, with rifle fire coming from it.

All our lives in the Haganah and the Palmach, we were continually impressed with the doctrine of the purity of arms. This was a way of life. And I don't remember any time in the War of Independence when our soldiers contravened this doctrine, even against soldiers, let alone civilians. I was mixed up in the Lydda-Ramle operation and I know everything about it. I know that after the rebellion was suppressed, nothing wrong was done. I can't imagine that any of my fellow soldiers would have dared do anything like what has been suggested and not be punished immediately by Yigal Allon or Yitzhak Sadeh.

The truth about what happened in Lydda is hard to come at. As with other controversial issues, everyone tells a different story. On balance, it seems likely that Yerucham Cohen's version is somewhat sanitized; he arrived after the revolt had been put down and may be justified in believing that there was no terrorization of the civilian population to make them leave. Meir Pa'il, as a historian, takes an objective view of the operation and its results, which is probably as close to accuracy as one can now get:

☐   When the Israelis encircled Lydda and Ramle, there was no
    preplanned concept as to what should be done with their
    inhabitants. There was no plan to evacuate them. It
    happened that the Israelis encircled three Arab towns at
    about the same time—the third was Nazareth. When they
    surrounded Lydda and Ramle, an Israeli battalion got in
    and occupied Lydda only temporarily, because it was a
    small battalion and the town held 30,000 people, swelled by
    refugees from Jaffa. And Ramle was not even occupied
    then. There was even a police station in Ramle still in
    Jordanian hands.

    So there was a curfew. And next day, there was a small
    Jordanian counterattack—just three armored cars, which
    entered the town and made some kind of row and shot all
    over the streets and then withdrew. But quite a few
    townspeople joined in from their windows, shooting at the
    third battalion.

    The Palmach responded very heavily. They killed
    around two hundred Arabs, mostly men, not women or
    children. And then, after this, Yigal Allon, who was
    commander in chief of this operation, recommended to the
    government that instead of holding quite a lot of our
    military to maintain law and order there, shouldn't we just
    expel them? And he got permission.

    The expulsion of these people was a harsh punishment,
    but I think it should be considered natural in a war context.
    Those kinds of things happen in war. And let it be noted that
    at the same time, in Nazareth, where there was no trouble,
    the Arabs were allowed to stay.

At all events, the tens of thousands of inhabitants who fled from these two towns swelled the numbers of refugees who crossed the border into Jordan. The Legion, which had withdrawn from the two towns in advance, was later much abused by these refugees for deserting them. Sir John Glubb excuses them on tactical grounds:

☐ We had 4,000 men and Israel approximately 60,000, which was a very good argument for not advancing much farther. Of course, the main reason was that if you've got very few men, you hold the hills. If with a tiny force you move out into the open plain, you're immediately surrounded by people with more men. I'd discussed all this with the Jordan government, and they agreed that it would be inadvisable with our tiny numbers to attempt to defend those two towns.

Mrs. Alexander Zur adds a postscript to these events from, as it were, behind the scenes:

☐ I was five months' pregnant at that time with my second child. I had trouble with the pregnancy and they had to take me to the hospital in Tel Aviv and for five or six days I didn't see my husband. Then a bomb fell just next to the hospital. I jumped out of bed, and as a result I lost the child.

I tried not to cry, but it was hard for me because my husband couldn't come to me for several days. At last he came, and he brought me a very thin piece of paper, saying, "I have a present for you. The most beautiful present you can imagine." And he unfolded the paper and showed me that it was the surrender of Ramle, written in his own handwriting and signed by the Arab leaders of that town.

He had written it out from what he remembered of the king's regulations in the British army. He told me how the Arabs had come at two o'clock one morning to Kibbutz Na'an to sign the terms of surrender. And I was so glad at the time, I remember it, even though I had lost my child.

For years we kept the paper, and finally, about fifteen years ago, a fellow came from the army museum in Haifa. He said, "I understand you've got the original of the surrender of Ramle." I showed it to him. "All right," he said, "give me the original for the museum, and I'll send you a copy." Of course, it belonged to the state, not to us privately, and so I gave it to him very carefully, and after a few days we got a photostat. And this is our most guarded treasure.

THE NORTH

The Israelis, having gained control of western Galilee at the outset of the "real" war in mid-May, had been trying since then to widen their holdings eastward, where the hill strongholds and the towns of Nazareth, Tahshika, and Zippori were in the hands of Kawukji. There had been some fighting in this area even during the first truce, because this disaffiliated Arab leader did not consider himself bound by cease-fires or truces. Fearing that he might have designs on the coastal road and other vital Jewish areas, it was decided to attack Kawukji's bases and at the same time widen the narrow coastal strip Zahal held between Haifa Bay and the Lebanese border.

Chaim Laskov was put in charge of this operation.

☐   The operations of Dekel [Palm] and Brosh [Cyprus] allowed us to test out the "gains" of our action inasfar as our entire fighting machinery was concerned. We lacked supplies, although they had started to filter in, and now we made use of certain enemy equipment. We had trained men—those who had served in the British military forces in World War II, and for once, and for the first time, we really felt that we could by ourselves pick the targets that we wanted to take.

The Seventh Brigade had fought in two assaults in the Latrun area and suffered casualties; the spark had gone out of its fighting spirit. The Seventh Brigade, the Twenty-first Infantry Battalion, plus four 65-mm. mountain guns, mule-pack type—this was the sum total of the force that had to engage the enemy: Kawukji, Lebanese mercenaries, and others in western Galilee. And this was the force that went into the Dekel operation, which was under my command.

While initially our attitude toward the whole sector was a defensive one, we conducted a number of successful small-scale operations, which helped to reinvigorate the flagging spirits of the Seventh Brigade.

These operations were also used by us for scouting purposes, to assess the type of enemies we were facing, where they were located, and what they might be thinking about us.

Information came in steadily, mainly from Druze* sources. There is a man in the village of Shefaram to whom we owe the conquest of the western Galilee. Moreover, we owe to this man so many lives that at times I feel it is beyond the capacity of people to repay a debt like that. Aided by the Druze, we took Shefaram and the nearby villages of Ibleen and Tamra. We then began to approach the area of Zippori, a village known in Talmudic times as one of the largest centers in the Galilee where, in 1187, Saladin conquered the Crusaders who sallied forth from Zippori to Tiberias.

GOC Northern Command issued instructions for the capture of Nazareth and, in coordination with the Thirteenth Infantry Battalion, we moved out. The infantry were to attack from the area of Kfar Hahoresh, on the principle that the Seventh Armored Brigade would come under its command. No one in the Seventh liked the idea, but the orders were very clear, so we moved on.

Zero hour struck, but there was no sign of the Thirteenth Battalion. We therefore attacked alone, and during this action we spotted about eight armored cars moving toward us "on the serpentine," from Nazareth-East, coming down from Nazareth to the approaches of Zippori.

---

*The Druze are tribes of Arab origin but with their own religion. Their political alignment is based on pragmatic considerations; the Druze in Israel have usually taken a pro-Jewish position.

With no anti-tank weapons at our disposal, we deployed our heavy, light, and medium machine guns and sprayed those armored cars as rapidly as we could, while the 20-mm. Hispanos Suisse guns used us as cover to fire at the armored cars.

The gunner was uncannily accurate. He conserved his ammunition and fired at the bases of the turrets and jammed them, thus putting their weapons out of action.

We then charged and gained control over all the sites that commanded the town of Nazareth. On the eastern crest of the mountain, we could see the remnants of Kawukji's soldiers running away.

We had specific instructions not to harm anyone or anything, which meant that we had to take over the town of Nazareth by stratagem. In control now of the sites, we sent across a half-track platoon, covered by 65-mm. cannons at the ready. Not a shot was fired against us, and when we reached the police station on the other side we saw that it was deserted. Then, looking out to the area of Kfar Hahoresh, we could see the advance guard of the Thirteenth Infantry Battalion coming across.

At eight o'clock we signed the terms of surrender of the town of Nazareth. We then quickly dispatched an armored-car squadron from the area of Mee'ar en route to Ilabun, at the same time capturing the villages of Araba and Sashnin.

At about that time we were informed that the cease-fire in place had been signed, and our instructions were not to move farther forward.

It was due to the cooperation and intelligence supplied by the Druze, under the leadership of Sheikh Saleh Chnefes, that these operations were achieved with very few casualties. I believe that when we took Zippori we lost two men, and when we took Nazareth we had one dead and one wounded.

Operation Dekel became the basis for the further operations that were mounted by the Seventh Brigade under Ben Dunkleman for the conquest of central and northern Galilee, up to and including the Litani River.

The capture of Nazareth was the climax of the operation in the north. Although the Carmeli Brigade failed in its attempt to encircle the Syrians in their bridgehead at Mishmar Hayarden, when Operations Dekel and Brosh ended, the whole of Lower Galilee, from Haifa Bay to the Sea of Galilee, was in Jewish hands.

Seif Addin Zu'bi, former mayor of Nazareth, gives an Arab's viewpoint on his city's fall:

□   I, as a landlord, went down among my own villages, which were in a corner of the Jewish area near the Jewish front, and I stayed there until Nazareth was captured by the Israeli army, when I came back here. While in the villages, I was between the hammer and the anvil, because I was subject to pressure from the Arab side and the Jewish side. Some members of my clan, the Zorbieh—a great clan—were killed by the Jews. The way through my villages was intersected by the Tiberias Road, which was in the hands of the Israeli army, and when my people tried to pass, they were sometimes killed. There were even casualties among those trying to reap their harvests in nearby fields. Many of the inhabitants of my villages came into Nazareth, but before the occupation they went back again.

The Israelis took Nazareth by day [July 16] and that night my wife and family came back to Nazareth. There was no fighting; Nazareth gave itself up peacefully. There was no other course; that was the proper way. The Arab Liberation Army, which had been here, fled away.

I cannot say I was glad. Many others were—I was the only one I know about who wept. My sentiments overcame me. I had never wanted war. I wept because the result was as tragic as it was. If the Liberation Army came to fight, why did they run?

Later I took it upon myself to help the refugees. When Tiberias fell, there had been many refugees, and I opened the Casanova [a huge monastery] and other places and paid out of my own pocket for food for the people. And many who had fled from Nazareth, I helped to return to their homes. Six months after the fall of Nazareth I became one of the first Arab members of Parliament, but even before that I helped thousands of refugees to return. Those in my position, leaders, who fled the country made a mistake. My people *wanted* me to become a member of the Jewish Parliament. Through influence on government circles, I was able to legitimize thousands of refugees who returned to their homes illegally after the war.

Avraham Yoffe explains another angle on the peaceful take-over of Nazareth:

☐   Nazareth was a different story. The area commander "gave" me and my battalion to a certain brigade. He told me he wanted me for a job, and he sent me with my brigade to do it. They were moving along the road from Shefaram to Nazareth, and he wanted me to secure his southern flank, which I did, and then we took Nazareth together. There wasn't much to it. I took a few strongpoints and protected the main column from any molestation.

   The first person I saw in the streets of Nazareth was one of the men who had left that town we took in Beisan. He came up to me and said, "Have you come to turn us away again?" And I said, "No. Not in Nazareth. Nazareth is a holy place, a holy town. The whole world is watching us.... You are not going to be a victim." And I assured them that they would be all right there.

The army commanders were very anxious that there should be no incidents of looting or disrespect for holy places in Nazareth, because of its importance to the Christian world. Compared with the Arabs' record for looting—they had totally sacked the Old City Jewish quarter and any other Jewish settlements they took, even for a day—the Jewish record had not been bad, but there had been lapses. Meir Amit recalls:

☐   We learned a few painful lessons—there's no school where
     you can learn such lessons in advance. At an early stage, we
     were called in to help, though it was not our area—near
     Mount Tabor; it was inhabited by semi-nomads who were
     causing a lot of troubles to the settlers, and we had to go
     there and push them out. One of my platoons—I was not
     present there—started to loot. They forgot themselves, they
     forgot everything. And then the Arabs came back and killed
     or wounded most of the Jews. Out of some thirty, twenty
     were caught in the fire. So I always used that afterward as an
     example, that looting is not only an immoral thing, it is also
     an impractical thing.

Kawukji, having failed to defend Nazareth, made his escape
with most of his forces during the night through a gap in the
Israeli lines and hid in the hilly region north of the city. When the
second truce came, the Syrian advance westward had been halted,
although they still held their bridgehead at Mishmar Hayarden.

THE JERUSALEM SECTOR

The Arab Legion, meanwhile, stubbornly defended Latrun
against yet another attack by the Israelis. Sir John Glubb:

☐   We held Latrun with 700 men. The Arab Legion was
     extremely good. Not that they had any weapons, or any
     ammunition, or anything else, but they were men of
     extremely good spirit. Good solid country people, with no
     frills about them.

Chaim Laskov:

☐   The turning points were the attacks on Ashdod, Latrun, and

Jenin, all of which ironically enough failed, but strategically we got the initiative into our hands. One can't only consider lives that were lost. Lives were lost in other places where people were better trained . . . and those who came from the camps were hardly trained. The British commander of the Arab Legion used the firepower which they had and we did not. Excellent—you could see the hand of Brigadier Lash [a British officer serving with the Arab Legion] behind every fire plan. You have to hand it to them, they were very good. But technically, though we failed, we opened a route to Jerusalem. Jerusalem was resupplied and therefore we saved the New City from the fate of the Old City.

However, north of Latrun, Israeli units, based now in the captured cities of Lydda and Ramle, pushed east and captured a number of Arab villages. Southeast of Latrun, the Har El Brigade widened the Jerusalem corridor by taking important strongpoints along its southern edge. "Boaz" was involved in this operation:

☐ During the first truce, most of the people in my battalion had been taken out of the infantry and trained to use the newly arrived weapons. I was put into a machine-gun crew and taught to use Bazers, a medium-caliber machine gun mounted on a tripod. Everyone was thrilled with these brand-new, impressive-looking things. Up till then we'd been dependent for automatic firepower on the Spandau, a light machine gun with a barrel that was liable to bend if it got too hot.

The first time we used the Bazer was at Hartuv during the Ten Days. We were taken in jeeps along low-lying ground to the base of the hills, where we unloaded and waited for complete darkness. We then learned what hard work it is carrying a Bazer, although we each carried only a part of it. We went up and then across a hill, which was partly in our hands, crawling as we neared the Arab forward entrenchments. We found a broken low wall and as quietly as possible set up our guns and a few protective stones around us.

We were to lie quietly until the first "Davidka"* missile landed—hopefully on the Arab side! We heard a faint rustle behind us as our infantry got ready. Then we cringed as the Davidka "shell" whirred erratically over our heads. Fortunately for us, this time it landed squarely on the Arab positions, with a terrifying blast that sent fragments flying in all directions. We heard their shouts, and a piece of corrugated iron sheeting landed right in front of us.

We got the signal to open up. After the months during which we had relied on rifles, sometimes antiquated, and on flimsy Stens, it was exhilarating to be on the right end of a regular machine-gun barrage.

The Davidkas and the Bazers seemed to have frightened the enemy even more than they did us; there appeared to be panic among them, and our infantry went in, running past and through our positions. One unit, made up of recent immigrants who had fought with Russian partisans, shouted incongruously: *"Zhe Stalina u Zarodina!"*—"For Stalin and the Motherland!"

A full moon was up now, lighting the contours of the surrounding hills; we sat low, near our guns, in case of the odd sniper. So it was a surprise to see three of our people walking quite upright. They were from field HQ, come to see the battle's progress. One of them was Jimmy, a familiar figure in Har El. Up to the first truce, he had been a field officer, often to be seen, in a large steel helmet, shorts, and plimsolls [sneakers], striding about battlefields encouraging his men and urging *them* to keep their heads down. During the truce he'd been promoted to planning officer; this was his first big operation and it was going well. I suppose he was so used to being in the thick of fire that he felt embarrassingly safe behind the line, as some of us did, sitting now idly by our Bazers.

---

*The so-called "Davidka" cannon earned fame in the early phases of the war before the Jews had any real artillery. It was a home-made weapon which fired, without any pretense at accuracy, a missile containing various metal bits and pieces. It made a terrific noise but did very little actual damage.

He noted with satisfaction that our infantry was going steadily forward, marked by our grenades lighting up the darkness. I heard Jimmy say, "Like fireworks—" Then he moved through the moonlight and a sniper caught him. Unbelievable— He'd led men through so many actions—on the convoys, Jerusalem, the hills around Bab el Wad—and the first time he was out of the first line of fire, he was killed by one lousy bullet.

The task of telling parents of the deaths of their sons was often done by women. Aliza Guri, the wife of Chaim Guri, was one of them:

☐   When we heard Jimmy had been killed,* I took the car of my commander with his driver and traveled north to find his parents. First I went to Kibbutz Magan Michael, where he had a brother. The brother wasn't there but a friend of the family offered to go with me to see his parents who lived in Haifa. Again we failed to find them—the father was an artist, and he was in Safed, painting. So we drove on to Safed. By the time we got there it was ten o'clock at night. The moment I walked into their house, they knew something had happened because they didn't know me but I came with someone they knew. When I came to the door they said, "Something to do with Jimmy—" And from that moment till we came to Abu Ghosh, where he was, I didn't hear one word from either of them.

They were in the back seat of the car. Not a word. Not a cry. Nothing, till we came to the place where he was.... It's a long trip from Safed to Abu Ghosh. We drove all night and at three in the morning came to the place where he was lying.

His father uncovered his son's face and they looked at it. Not a word. Not a cry. And he took out his paints and started to paint him—then, that same night, after the journey from Safed to Abu Ghosh.

---

*Notification of death is invariably a face-to-face matter in Israel, usually made by a visiting officer.

In Jerusalem itself, though the Jordanians harassed front-line Israeli positions with constant shell and machine-gun fire, they made no further effort to advance into the New City. The Jews, on the other hand, were still desperately anxious to recover the Old City, but because of operational delays the attack was postponed until the night before the second truce came into effect.

The plan involved a combined break-in through the New Gate by units of the still-separate Irgun and Lehi and through the Zion Gate by units of Khish. Netanel Lorch recalls:

☐   We were supposed to rush across from the Tannous Building to Mount Zion. They said that in a few hours they were going to open Zion Gate again, and we would have to be there to rush into the Jewish quarter. Instead of which, they didn't even give me time to go from Tannous back into the city and then to Yemin Moshe. They said there was no time, and that I should make a dash across an open field.

    Well, there was a full moon and our movement was noticed. We had a number killed and wounded, just trying to move out from Tannous to Yemin Moshe, which is now a very pleasant walk....

    I remember that when I finally counted my people I found out that there were some missing, presumably lying out in that open field. I went back with two volunteers to try to look for them. How does one look for a wounded man in the middle of the night? If I shouted, I would draw fire. If I didn't, I wouldn't find them. It was quite a decision, every time I shouted a name. In the end we were able to locate them, and carried them back to Tannous.

"Boaz":

☐   The idea was to blow a hole in the wall of the Old City and then make an attack on the Legion with Molotov cocktails. The day before, at our headquarters—I think we were based at the Shneller Orphanage at the time—we were shown these things, homemade, in bottles, and instructed how to set them off. Then when it was dark we set off, with all our kit, rifles in one hand, bottles in the other.

We had to go across some bit of no-man's-land, a sort of valley I think, clamber up a slope, and then we found ourselves in a huge cemetery. As we crawled among the graves, they started shooting at us from two directions with tracer bullets. We were dead scared because we'd been told that if we dropped these bloody bottles they'd blow us up. My sidekick actually did drop his. I suppose it couldn't have exploded because he's still around.

I think it was the Zion Gate we had to blow a hole in, although to tell the truth we'd been fighting for so many months by then that the details are blurred— Anyway, we got there, and waited a few minutes, and then some sappers came and set their charges to blow a hole for us to get in. What a cock-up—bottles against the Legion—! Anyway, we didn't have to do it in the end because after the bang, our commanders were left staring at a rather small crack in the wall, or the gate, or whatever it was, and then we heard them frantically calling HQ on their walkie-talkies to say it hadn't breached the wall and what should we do next? The explosion had been just enough to alert the Legion, who were now dropping hand grenades neatly on us from the walls. HQ said okay, you'd better come back. So the whole thing was called off, and we had to crawl back across the bloody valley, through the tracers, still clutching our bottles.

Of the main attack on the New Gate, Ezra Yachin of the Lehi gives the following account:

☐   The next day was Friday. The government had agreed to a cease-fire beginning on Saturday morning at 5:30. And our commanders told us, "Tonight you are going to liberate the Old City of Jerusalem."

We felt everything was being changed—the whole world. What had happened until that minute was like nothing, compared to it.... All our bodies were full of happiness, of joy. It was not just a matter of breaking through those stone walls or having to go through the very heavy fire which awaited us there. None of that bothered us. The Jewish people after more than two thousand years were going back to Jerusalem!

But we asked, "What about the cease-fire?" And the commander said, "Well, at that hour we will be in the midst of fighting, and you know in the narrow lanes of the Old City we won't be able to stop it, even if we tried. So it will go on, despite the cease-fire, till the Old City is liberated...."

We were told that, from ten to eleven at night, the Haganah would bombard the Old City with shells. Eleven would be zero hour.

We gathered in our groups. Everything added to the excitement. For example, the wounded actually came to bless us. They couldn't join us because they'd been wounded in other attacks. The girls cried and the men tried to console them.... And then the commander read us the order of the attack and said a few words: "Tonight is the night for which we've waited for two thousand years. Two thousand years our fathers and grandfathers prayed for this night when we go to liberate the old City of Jerusalem. *And you are the ones who are going to do it!*" When he said that— How can I explain what we felt? We knew that, throughout the ages, there were great Jews who gave their lives for their people— when they were in the hands of the Crusaders or in the hands of the Spanish Inquisition. And we felt humble because, you know, how were we better than those who gave their lives down the years for Jerusalem and the Jewish people and the Jewish religion? In what way are we more deserving than they, that we should be the ones who would have this great honor?...

And then when we came to the trucks, something else happened. In our neighborhood was an orphanage. We suddenly heard all these children, these orphans, shouting to us: "Go in peace and come back in peace. God bless you. We wish you success!"

Then we moved off. It was forbidden to sing or switch on lights for fear of attracting the attention of the enemy. Because I felt under such pressure of joy and excitement, I was afraid that my nerves would not stand it. That I might get out of control. I might go mad— That was the fear of the moment, not the enemy's fire.

When we reached the area, we split into groups of about thirty each.... Ten o'clock came. We couldn't hear if the Haganah was bombarding the Old City because the enemy was shelling the New City all the time. The shells came close. Every minute we thought the building we were in was going to collapse. We waited. Ten, eleven—and no order to start.

What was happening? Maybe it took some time for the sappers to blow the wall. We waited, and were told that Haganah had asked for a delay of one hour for technical reasons. That hour became two hours, three, and the order did not come. We were told that at any minute the sappers would blow the wall, so we had to get out of that building and approach. So we moved into an open space behind the wall of a convent. Our backs were to the wall, and we faced the city, and shells were falling on the Jewish city, one after the other. I noticed that when a red rocket fell, in that area shells would drop. So when I saw, right in front of us, a bright red light, I told my friends, "Listen, our backs are to the wall. Maybe we'd better cover our faces with our helmets." Everyone did as I'd said, and immediately a shell fell just beside me.

I didn't see it fall. It blew up and a piece of the shrapnel penetrated under my helmet, as if to tell me, "Listen, if I want to get into your head, I'll find a way."

I was bleeding. I was sure my eye was out. I stood up and tried to reach a first-aid girl who was nearby, but I felt paralyzed.... A voice asked, "Who is wounded here?" No one else answered, so I stood up and said, "I am."

The nurse couldn't see me in the dark. She asked if I could cross the street and walk fifty meters to a first-aid station. I was in a dilemma. If she helped me cross the street she would endanger her life. But I was afraid I'd fall, in which case *two* people would be in danger, to carry me. So in the end she supported me to the bank, where the first-aid station was set up for that action.

I was blind in one eye and I kept the other closed. I heard familiar voices around me. One asked, "Who is it?" He couldn't recognize me, and I didn't want to upset him, so I started singing one of our old songs, to give him hope. And then I stopped, and said: "Giora, what about the Old City?"

Before he could answer, we heard an enormous explosion and someone said: "The wall has been breached!" I wasn't sure I would survive. Maybe I'd be blind, or mad. But still it was the happiest moment of my life. I told the boys, "God bless you, I'm sorry I could not join you but you have my blessing."

When I was taken to the hospital, I thought it unlikely I would live. I felt I was facing God. I prayed, "God, I don't know if I am to die or not. If I am, I won't ask you to spare me—who am I? I am no better than those who gave their lives already. But one thing I ask of you, God, before I die, is to hear that Jerusalem has been liberated"

Then I heard nurses talking. One said, "Did you hear? The attack failed because of the cease-fire agreement."

I didn't want to believe.

After a while, our Jerusalem commander came to visit us in the hospital. He asked me, "What happened?" I told him I lost one eye, I was seriously wounded, but I said I didn't care. "Tell me what happened in the Old City!" I shouted. "It's all right, it's all right," he said. But I knew. The attack had been stopped before it had started.

It must be said that, affecting as this account is in its genuine zeal and tragic ultimate frustration, there is something typically abortive in it. After the time of the hit-and-run actions had passed and real soldiering became the order of the day, Lehi and, to an only slightly lesser extent, the Irgun became all hyperbole (in which they had always specialized) and very little actual achievement.

Despite the failure of the final attempt till 1967 to take back the Old City, the Jews managed to capture Ein Karem and Malka after heavy fighting. The only Legion gain was the capture of a house belonging to a Jew named Mandelbaum. This building became famous as the crossing point between Israel and Jordan during the years between '48 and '67.

Phase 4:
The Second Truce

The second truce began on July 18, 1948, and was open ended. It was intended by the U.N. to last until a peace settlement could be reached. But most people on the spot regarded an eventual resumption of fighting as inevitable.

Nothing was settled. The tide had turned in the Jews' favor, but none of the Arab armies had suffered an outright defeat, though the Lebanese had quietly withdrawn. The Syrians still occupied a finger of land allotted by partition to Israel; the Jordanians still threatened Jerusalem and its lifelines at Latrun and from the east. The Egyptians, though their advance had been stopped, were far from routed and held a large area of the northern Negev, making the southern Jewish settlements hard to reach.

The Negev Brigade had been on duty in the desert since the opening phases of the war—some of its soldiers had not seen their homes for eight months. The second truce was gainfully employed to mount an airlift to fetch this entire brigade back home for rest and regrouping. A special airstrip was built for the purpose at Ruhama. The budding Israeli air force with its newly arrived Czech-made planes now came into its own; heavy transport aircraft, hopping over the well-entrenched Egyptian lines, flew more than four hundred two-way trips between August and October to deliver supplies to the southern settlements and depots for the assault the Israelis expected to make when fighting was renewed, as well as to relieve the weary Negev Brigade.

They were replaced by the Yiftach, who—because southbound planes were full of war matériel—had to infiltrate the Egyptian lines on foot. The Egyptians, aware that something was going on, did their best to interfere with these operations, and throughout the truce there were spasmodic battles. The members of Yiftach, whose battle experience had all been in the north, had to adapt to the relatively cover-less conditions of the desert and suffered severely in the attacks on their scantily protected positions; but the Egyptians also lost both men and prestige, because, despite a few "near things," the strategic strongpoints remained in Israeli hands and the vital airlift continued.

Yehuda Amichai was involved in these operations:

☐   During the second truce I remember the commander of my company tried to get a little military order into this whole business. He told me, "Listen, you were in the British army—" I had reached the great rank of unpaid local temporary lance corporal "—maybe you can bring a bit of your experience into this disorder." I told him, okay, I'd try, and so he made me some kind of deputy or second in command. We tried to organize the unit but it was pretty hopeless, in a nice way.

This is probably a bit of genuine poetic license! A new order *was* now coming out of the previous *balagan*. The high command continued with the reorganization of forces, which the ten days' fighting had interrupted. The separate Palmach command was finally abolished, and ranks, insignia, pay, and other differentials came into being. Chaim Guri:

☐   The Palmach stood out for a long time against the

conventional idea of ranks and different rates of pay in the army. Everyone was equal and everyone got the same pay, whether he was an officer or not. They thought this was only right. "Those who face death together should be equal in pay too." But when Zahal became an established army, they had to have ranks. Still the Palmach said, "No, we won't have ranks, and we will keep the same rates of pay for all of us." They felt it was a grand gesture.

But when they told the new immigrants about it, they weren't at all impressed. "Oh, come on!" they said. "When you're offered money, take it! Will it really make you happy not to get more money? If we don't get higher pay, will we be happier to think that you won't get it either? Don't run away feeling good that you did us some kind of favor!" And so of course, in the end, they got ranks, they got their differential rates—a tragedy.

"Boaz" remembers making his protest:

☐   I remember a parade they held, on the tarmac of Lod Airport, when the dissolution of our Palmach into the "real army" was supposed to be complete. It was quite a grand occasion. There was a rostrum draped with flags and some bigwigs on it—I think Ben-Gurion was there—and we were supposed to demonstrate our unity by marching past *at the salute*. Salute! We'd never even learned to salute.

We arrived in buses. Our own commanders had been ordered to put on shoulder flashes showing their rank. Until then you didn't call them lieutenant or sergeant, you'd call them section leaders or company leaders, and they just had little colored stripes to show what they were. Well, they'd stuck something onto themselves, but they made sure it was upside down or in some way not according to regulations.

They'd also been told to smarten *us* up. We were ordered out of the buses. We shambled onto the parade ground, dragging our rifles. The Khish officers, dazzling us with polished buttons and new insignia, ran around us in circles, trying to make us look like their idea of proper soldiers.

When they saw how we were *shlepping* along, refusing even to march in step, they barked at us to sing something, thinking, no doubt, that we'd break into some stirring battle hymn, which might put a bit of backbone into us. Instead, as one man we burst into the most unbelievably filthy army ditty we could think of. When they realized what we were singing they raced back to us, screaming, "For God's sake STOP THAT!" I *think* we more or less wrecked the parade. We did our best, anyway.

Personnel and equipment for the newly reorganized armed forces were no longer a problem. Israel was soon to have eighty thousand men and women under arms, so that a number of young people could now be released to establish new settlements. Supplies of weapons, planes, armor, and ships were still coming in. New backup services were being established.

Meanwhile, the U.N. mediator, Count Bernadotte, who was planning to move his headquarters to Jerusalem, was working to try to turn the truce into a permanent settlement. In mid-September he brought his revised proposals before the secretary-general. They provided for Ramle and Lod to be given back to the Palestinians; the Negev was also to be part of the Arab area, with the Jews getting the whole of Galilee instead. Haifa Port and Lydda Airport were to be used by both sides, and Jerusalem was to be under U.N. supervision, with local autonomy for the Jewish and Arab populations. He also stressed the urgency of the refugee problem—there were by then 360,000 Arab and 7,000 Jewish refugees.

As the refugee problem still exists, here are some comments on it made with the benefit of hindsight.

Avital Mossinsohn, who was still a child in 1946 when the Arab town of Balad e-Sheikh near Haifa was evacuated following the killing of forty Jews in a riot at the Haifa Refineries, recalls:

☐ We saw nothing of the Haganah raid on the town, but we saw what followed it. Streams of refugees moving along the road past our kibbutz [Yagur] with their bundles and their donkeys, heading for Nazareth . . . the town and the village beyond it were cleared completely.

Next day I and two older children went to the village and got some loot. The Jews from Haifa and the kibbutz, too, went and took furniture and whatever was left. I took a pack of cards and a donkey.

The sight of the refugees is very vivid in my mind. I didn't really register the pathos of it until I was older and began to form a parallel in my mind to the films I saw of Jewish refugees in Europe, who looked so similar. It was then that compassion came, and it has stayed with me.

In 1967 I was working close to Prime Minister Eshkol. I was closely interested in his plans for relieving the situation of the refugees who had come under Israel's control. I remember him saying, "For years we've accused the Arabs of keeping the refugees in misery, as pawns. Now, with our experience of settling Jewish refugees here, we can do something for them. We'll show the world how much better we can do." I remember my bitter shock and disappointment when those plans of Eshkol's were scrapped.

Mattityahu Shmuelevitch, the apologist for Deir Yassin:

☐ There are so many lies told about these events that nobody in the world who is not an expert can ever know what really happened. If you ask, for example, what was the number of refugees who really escaped from the boundaries of Israel, some Arabs will claim that there were, at that time, two million refugees living in camps. Yet according to British statistics there were only 550,000 Arabs within the '48 borders, and 140,000 stayed. So it is impossible that any more than 400,000 left. It is still a large number; but at that time we brought some one and a half million Jews from

Arab countries, while the Arab refugees were kept in camps in inhuman conditions as a propaganda weapon against us. Since we took over in '67, you wouldn't recognize them. Three or four years ago, the Israeli government ordered new houses built for them, but they were ordered by the PLO not to leave the camps.

Yoseph Varshitz, who tried to stop Arabs from leaving Haifa:

☐ At that time, we did not think in terms of the departing Arabs leaving useful space. For one thing, most Arabs didn't live in the kind of houses Jewish people wanted. It took some time to realize that we would need them for new immigrants and demobilized soldiers. At the time it was not something that appealed to people; only later they took advantage of the situation. The first thought was that Arabs who left must be hostile, and it is true that those who did stay were, to some extent, pro-Jewish.

Anwar Nusseibah:

☐ I remember making a statement, as secretary of the National Committee, on Palestine Radio toward the end of the mandate, calling on people not to leave, to stay where they were and tend their work. So it is not true that we told people to leave. But you know how it was, especially after the Deir Yassin massacre, people were frightened, particularly about their womenfolk. You know how we look upon these things. We were afraid for what we called honor—a woman should not be molested—so one must remove her from areas where she might be molested. There were four or five other massacres that encouraged people to leave. I was involved with that because refugees came to the offices of our committee and we had to find food and shelter as well as defend ourselves against Jewish incursions.

Michael Kennet, a Jerusalem businessman who entered the war as a platoon commander:

☐   We conquered one Arab village in order to open the road from Kfar Saba to Tel Aviv. We surrounded it one night and all the population left. They left everything they had and fled to Tira. The main road passed through the village so that we were cut off for ten days. The village doesn't exist anymore; it was demolished after the war.

I have no feelings now, looking back, about what happened to those Arab villagers. Till this very day the Arabs see us as foreigners in this area—they don't want us here. So we survive physically because we have a strong army.

Anyway, most of the Arabs did not leave because they were chased out. I had many Arab friends in the village next to the kibbutz where I was born. We grew up together. They left during the war, and when I met some of them again in Nablus after '67 they told me that they'd been told to leave, for at most a fortnight, to make it possible for the Arab Legion to take action in the Jewish area.

I'm not talking of those who left because of military actions carried out by us. I myself was in charge of ensuring that Arabs of a certain village reached the border safely. And another time, when we had to open a road, ten or twelve of us went out one night and started shooting in a village, and they left.

Of course, many who still live in camps have hard feelings. The interesting thing is that the same men who, after the Six-Day War, blamed their leaders and the Arab nations who forced them to stay in refugee camps to keep their problem before the world don't repeat this today. Now they say a great wrong was done them because they were chased out of their homes.

Sief Addin Zu'bi, the former mayor of Nazareth:

☐   The English were responsible for the refugee problem. They incited the Arabs to run, telling them the Jews would kill them. The Jews went about with loudspeakers, begging the Arabs to stay. The best-known place where this occurred was, of course, Haifa, but it happened all over the country.

Netiva Ben Yehuda:

☐   Many of those who ran away as refugees were not rooted in Israel. They came here, as we came, in the last sixty or seventy years. So they can go to Egypt, to Syria—it is not such a big thing as for me to go back to Lithuania.

Meir Pa'il:

☐   What caused the exodus of Arabs from Israel? You might ask, what caused nine million Germans to leave Eastern Europe during '44, '45? What caused the French refugee problem in 1940? Or why did a million French flee Algeria when it got its independence in the sixties?

The Arab refugee problem is a direct outcome of their defeat in war.

Around one-third fled out of fear. One-third were evacuated by force, for example from Lydda and Ramle. Around one-third were encouraged by the Israelis to fly. These were not driven out, nor did they go of their own free will, but they were outmaneuvered into running. But the Arabs bear responsibility for the war. They initiated it. Their intention was to undermine the U.N. resolution. In short, they began the war, and they happened to lose. And for any nation which is defeated, one of the outcomes is the problem of refugees.

There were places where *we* were beaten, for example the Jewish quarter of the Old City. So we had to absorb our two thousand refugees there. There were women and children who had to be evacuated from Negev or Galilee settlements. One of the by-products of defeat is, inevitably, refugees.

So as a Jew, I have no remorse. I have some responsibility, as a partner in the war. But I have no sense of moral shame, except about those places where our people behaved in an inhumane manner.

The day after signing his report, Count Bernadotte was driving through the Jewish quarter of Jerusalem when his car was halted by a roadblock and he was fatally shot. Geula Cohen, now an extreme right-wing member of the Knesset, played a role in this assassination as a member of the Lehi:

☐   In the War of Independence I was in the army but not used for combat because I was married. But I was the broadcaster for the Stern group, a very extreme branch of the underground, the smallest but the strongest from many points of view. When Bernadotte was assassinated, I was called to Jerusalem, because that called for a special broadcast.

I was sent for two days in advance. I did not know they were going to execute him, but I knew he was "on our list." In my broadcast I spoke about Bernadotte and his plans, how much his concepts and policies would have hurt the Jews, especially in Jerusalem. The worst was his plan for the internationalization of the city. He was determined that this should happen, and he worked hard to get it passed by the Security Council, as indeed it was. And till now, due to this decision, tens of embassies are in Tel Aviv because the world does not recognize Jerusalem as our capital.*

The assassination could not wipe out this decision, but by it we showed the world our seriousness in wanting

---

*Those few countries who initially supported Israel's claim by siting their embassies in Jerusalem withdrew them when Mrs. Cohen's recent Jerusalem bill, declaring Jerusalem to be the eternal capital of Israel, was passed by the Knesset.

Jerusalem for our capital. Every time you fight for something instead of giving way, you strengthen yourself.

I didn't write the broadcast myself—I hardly ever did. But I always agreed with what I had to say on the radio. I can't read anything on the air that I don't agree with. My broadcast did not try to justify the execution of Bernadotte. We simply explained it. His plans would result in killing Jerusalem for our people.

It was our movement which executed Lord Moyne as well.* And not only him. Many others who were not only obstacles between us and our homeland but were trying to encourage another enemy [the Arabs as well as the British] against us. So it was not even a matter of executions. It was a war. They killed us and we gave them an answer. Though I didn't know we were going to kill Bernadotte, as a member of the underground I endorsed this policy. And my view now is no different.

The government press spokesman, who worked very close to Ben-Gurion at the time, recalls:

☐   At that time I looked on Begin as somebody on the opposite side of the political fence. I thought he was a bad man because, once we had a state and an army, he should have conformed. Right up until July, or so, there were still Etzel units in Jerusalem—separatist units which did not function as part of the armed forces. The same applied to Lehi.

After the Bernadotte murder, Ben-Gurion decided to rout them out. That was one of the decisions that he made, which the army was rather reluctant to carry out. But Ben-Gurion insisted. There were these dissident units operating in Jerusalem, and he felt it had gone too far.

So he called in his General Staff and said, "I want these

*Lord Moyne, a British diplomat stationed in Cairo, was assassinated together with his chauffeur in 1944 by two members of Lehi. This action effectively killed Winston Churchill's support for Zionism.

people to give up their arms. And if they won't, I want you to force them to surrender." The General Staff said, "Well, we can't do that with the people we have got in Jerusalem now. If you want us to do that, we'll have to send for reinforcements rather quickly." And Ben-Gurion said, "What's the nearest place where you've got troops?" They pointed to a map and said, "A few miles northwest of the city." Ben-Gurion said, "Okay, do it." They said, "But if the Jordanians get wind of the fact that we've thinned out the lines, they may march through—so we're against taking troops from there." Ben-Gurion thought about this, and then he said, "I want you to do it anyway."

That proved to be an absolutely right decision.

I remember they were having to complete their move from this spot at about two o'clock in the morning and then surround the Lehi camp just outside Jerusalem at first light. I was not with the unit then, but up at headquarters, and after midnight I was with Ben-Gurion and I said, "What about getting some sleep?" and he said, "I won't get to sleep until I get word that those men have moved out." I don't say he didn't trust them, but he wanted to be sure that they really were on the move to take this action in the morning.

He said, "We have an army in Israel now. How can one tolerate a separatist unit? We have just got to liquidate it." I remember at about 2:30 we got a signal that the men had moved out and were on their way to Jerusalem. They surrounded the camp. Fortunately there was no bloodshed; the dissidents were told to hand over their arms, which they did, and shortly after that they were absorbed into the Israeli Defense Forces.

Netanel Lorch had a hand in this absorption.

☐   After Bernadotte was assassinated, the Etzel, which continued its independent existence in Jerusalem as late as September '48, was finally wound up. They had one platoon up on Mount Zion and the idea was tactfully to recall these people and incorporate them into Zahal. I called them in and explained to them that we were there to carry out orders. In order to sweeten the pill for them, I had rounded up all the chocolates I could find in the NAAFI* and I said that whoever handed me a rifle would get a bar of chocolate, which, even after the siege, was quite something.

So they all did it, and got their chocolate, and then I found out that I had nobody to replace them. So I had to say, "Listen, there's been a mistake. Won't you stay on?" And the commander said, "We have no authority any longer, we've been disbanded. But if you ask us to, we're willing to stand as volunteers until you've got someone to relieve us." Which I thought was a very nice gesture.

Geula Cohen:

☐ When Ben-Gurion broke up the Lehi after the Bernadotte affair, we were mad against him; though it's true we asked no one's permission before acting, we felt he should have realized we did as we did for the sake of Jerusalem, and when he punished us for it—we thought it would hurt our cause in the world.

Of course, if you ask me now, I realize that no prime minister can allow a dissident group to dictate policy to him. But at that time things were not so stable, everything was in its beginnings.... Jerusalem was not part of Israel then, it was outside its sovereignty. It was only in Jerusalem that we broke the law. We did what we thought was best, and I don't regret it now. If, since the Six-Day War, Jerusalem, the whole of Jerusalem is our capital, it was due to that assassination. I am sure about it.

And that action, and my broadcast, was the swan song of the Lehi.

A number of the rounded-up members of Lehi (though not

---

*Forces' canteen—British army slang.

Mrs. Cohen) were imprisoned briefly; after a number of embarrassing incidents, however, it was thought politic to release them. After that, the dissidents genuinely became amalgamated with the regular forces.

But great harm had been done to Israel's image and support for the country waned. Bernadotte's proposals gained, rather than lost, impact because of his murder, and it appeared that many governments might espouse the idea of allocating the Negev, in particular, to the Arabs. So when the Egyptians broke the terms of the truce by persistently refusing to allow Israeli supply trucks through to her desert settlements, Israel seized the chance to renew the war.

Part 3
The Desert Campaigns

☐ By the time the third phase of the war started, we were more organized, and we got more and more arms while we were fighting. The fighting itself took a more conventional form, with trained brigades and all that—the Negev Brigade, the Yiftach and the Givati, among others.

The battle against the Egyptians was really the most intense part of the war, more than any other because the Egyptian army was the largest, the best trained, covering the largest area—the whole Negev, plus areas on the way to Ashdod—the Ashkelon area—all the way to southern Jerusalem. They were altogether better organized and better at defense than other Arab forces. The Syrians were much smaller, though also not badly organized. The Iraqis didn't really leave much of a mark. A small army but very efficient was the Arab Legion. If we could have beaten *them*, we could have taken Hebron and Bethlehem—but there was political pressure as well to leave them be.

This is Ephraim Shorer's summing-up of the forces still facing the Jews when the second truce ended or rather was breached for the last time—it had never been very strictly observed, though it lasted officially from July 18 until October 15.

The Israelis had completely reorganized and refurbished

287

their forces during the uneasy intervening months and, after the inevitable tug-of-war within the leadership, had at last agreed on priorities: The fundamental objective must be the Negev. Even Ben-Gurion, with his obsession about Jerusalem, was compelled at last to recognize that breaking the Egyptian blockade in the south was crucial.

Phase 1:
Operation Yoav*

Yerucham Cohen:

☐   When Yigal Allon was appointed commander of the southern front, he immediately grabbed Yitzhak Rabin and me to work with him. I remember what he said: "I know Ben-Gurion didn't want me appointed, but we have to liberate the Negev. It has been besieged already for four or five months; the situation of the kibbutzim from the point of view of supplies and so on is very poor; the Palmach Negev Brigade is there, but they are few in number for the vast area they have to defend."

   And from the moment we arrived in Gedera, Yigal started pressing the government to be allowed to liberate the desert. He did his old trick. He got together leaders of all the kibbutzim in the area and said, "Look, I can do it, but I'm a soldier. *You* put pressure on the politicians." They went to Ben-Gurion. He came down to visit us and look at the situation, and, as we later learned, he went back to the cabinet and said, "Allon says if we give him *this,* he can do

---

*Also known as Operation Ten Plagues, after the legendary plagues visited by God upon the Egyptians to force the pharaoh to let Moses lead the children of Israel to freedom.

that; if we give him this *plus*, he can do that *plus*." In the end
we managed to bring the fresh forces we needed to the Negev
by air, by night only, because the Egyptians had quite a good
air force.

We insisted that according to the Security Council's
resolutions we were allowed to bring supplies to our settlements through the Egyptian lines. But this the Egyptians
refused. So on October 14th, being well prepared, we sent a
convoy, with the knowledge of the U.N. truce observers, and
the Egyptians opened fire on it. That same evening we took
all steps to enable the convoy to go through. We attacked at
several points which would enable us, in at least one place, to
penetrate the cut-off Negev by pushing the Egyptians away.

The Israelis, by now, had the Egyptians' measure. Despite
disillusion with the corruption in Cairo, and a shortage—though
by no means a total absence—of success in the field, their morale
was not broken. Nine battalions, plus volunteers, backed with
heavy artillery and armaments including tanks, held three strong
lines: one along the coastal strip they had conquered from Rafa to
Ashdod, the second from Rafa through Auja to Beersheba,
Hebron, and Bethlehem just south of Jerusalem, and the third
connecting the ends of the other two, effectively cutting off the
Negev from the north. Their troops were well dug in to fixed
positions all along these lines, and their main strength lay in
defending them very effectively.

It had been clear to the Israelis for some months that in order
to break through and scatter the Egyptian lines they must muster
the largest force of the war so far. The danger of this was obvious.
If other Arab armies cared to come to Egypt's support, they could
take advantage of the thinned lines in other sectors.

Despite the elaborate preparations in the south, the main
push was to come from the north. Shimon Avidan:

☐   The plan was to penetrate the very good, deep defenses of
the Egyptians and open up the highway, which would make
it possible to send strong enough forces to conquer the

central point of the northern Negev, Beersheba, to hold all the coastal roads, and in this way, in fact, to change the balance, which at that time favored Egypt because they held the most important highways and water points, the vital things for any modern war.

With the coming of stronger forces to the south, together with a commander like Allon, we could begin to plan how to destroy all the Egyptian forces. My plan was to infiltrate the Egyptian line and put them in a position where, if they didn't want to be surrounded, they would have to attack. We'd developed a technique for holding the hills and strongpoints between the Egyptian lines, hindering their free movement, and waiting for them to attack. It is much easier, and much cheaper in lives, to repulse an attack than to initiate one.

But Allon decided to act on a different principle. He wanted to make a push through, as fast as possible, into the heart of the Negev, and he believed that with the forces at hand he could do it.

We had some very good information about the dispositions of the enemy. We had to fight our way through some nine very narrow, well-fortified strongpoints defended by four battalions—one Saudi, the others Egyptian—in all, nearly 5,000 men. This defense line was organized to a depth of twelve kilometers, so we planned how to roll them up. My brigade at this time consisted of five battalions instead of the usual three, and all "battle-proofed"—experienced fighters. We'd had enough time to train our people and had in our hands an exact plan of the enemy's organization.

The beginning of the operation was not our job but that of Yitzhak Sadeh and our only armored brigade. He tried to fight through in one place called Iraq el Manshieh and suffered very badly. This happened also to another brigade which made a frontal attack.

Yehuda Amichai experienced this failure at firsthand:

☐   There was a very unlucky assault—our first tank assault. We had two tanks, I think they were Cromwells, anyway World War II tanks, manned by two British deserters. We had no experience of course in tank warfare; we all thought, well it's like in the movies—you see a tank and you run after it— It ended very sadly, a lot of us got killed. We didn't realize you had to synchronize these things. It's very difficult, tanks and infantry— We had some little French tanks, tiny little tanks for two men, and the night before this battle the battalion commander sent me over to take messages to the "tankists" who were in Kibbutz Gat. Most of them were Russian Jews; they didn't know one word of Hebrew, so I had an interpreter, and I told him what our camp commander had told me, that we needed their cooperation. So the Russian major came in and started cursing me in Russian—"You bloody infantry!" So I came back and told my commander that I just got cursed out for my pains.

Shimon Avidan:

☐   Then it was our turn. We attacked at night. We had learned by experience how to fight the Egyptians; also, our soldiers had the feeling that here was the beginning of the end, and so it was important how they conducted themselves . . . . So we attacked, and soon one-half of a hill was in our hands and one-half in the hands of the Egyptians. Two of the commanders were wounded; one, an American marine who had volunteered, was blinded. But this group fought on and was isolated all through the day—only at night could we come to their help. The same night we advanced, and in four days we had fought our way through the Egyptians' lines and, still fighting, over the last position. A convoy of the Israeli army moved through the battlefield in the direction of Beersheba.

    This battle brought about the surrounding of two Egyptian brigades at a place called Faluja. Among them were the same officers who later created the Free Officers'

Movement in Egypt and brought about the downfall of
Farouk—Nasser, and a lot of his comrades.

Yerucham Cohen:

☐   We knew that the U.N. Security Council was meeting and
would press for a new cease-fire, and at the last moment—
realizing that as long as the Arabs were sitting in Beersheba
in the heart of the Negev they still had the advantage—we
decided, instead of taking the Gaza Strip, to take Beersheba
and cut the road the Egyptians held from the south to
Hebron and southern Jerusalem, where they had forces.
        That operation was successful. At the end of seven
days' fighting, the road to the Negev was open, the Egyptians evacuated the coastal strip between Migdal Ashkelon
and the northern region of Gaza. The so-called Faluja
Pocket was created: The best Egyptian brigade of about
thirty-five hundred soldiers was surrounded in a pocket in
the middle of the Negev, and the Egyptian forces in the
southern part of the Judean desert (Hebron and Bethlehem)
were completely cut off from their main forces in Rafa,
Gaza, and El Arish. That was the end of the first phase of the
war in the south.

The taking of Beersheba is described by Yehuda Amichai:

☐   Troops to conquer Beersheba were all lined up where Beersheba University is today, north of the town. Again, after
marching through the night. And, again, one big hell of a
mess, nobody knew what was happening. Anyway, it was
very successful, but at the time I had the feeling that there
were no plans at all. Oh, I'm sure now that there was a plan,
but I remember in the night when shelling started and everything went topsy-turvy . . . and suddenly a man appeared, in
very long shorts like they wear in the British army, and in a
heavy German accent he asked me, "Excuse me please, vere
iss brigade headkvarters?" I could hardly believe it—men

were dying all around and all hell was breaking loose and he was so polite, like in a drawing room in Vienna.

The press spokesman:

☐ The press learned to accept that the Arabs weren't telling the truth. By and large they tended not to. One example was when we captured Beersheba in October. I was down there when we captured it, and I raced back to Tel Aviv to tell the press. Cairo Radio was putting out a story that they'd cleared the south and that they still held Beersheba. I told the reporters, "Follow me. I've ordered a whole squad of taxis to take you to see for yourselves." So down they drove in convoy to Beersheba, where they saw that we were there and were able to file their stories datelined "Beersheba."

The fort of Iraq Suweidan, outside Negba, had, until November, resisted all efforts to capture it. It had become "The Monster on the Hill." Meir Pa'il:

☐ I was the deputy commander of the Seventh Palmach Battalion with which I fought some very harsh battles, some successful, some unsuccessful. For example, I attacked Iraq Suweidan twice, and twice we failed. We lost quite a lot of people, because it was arranged to be defended against our methods—night attacks, and so on; our usual raiding techniques were not sufficient. I took part in the last attack, commanded by Yitzhak Sadeh, which was a regular daytime attack, using tanks and artillery and half-tracks—it was magnificent to see it, and we conquered it.

The Monster on the Hill provided the last link in the chain now surrounding the Egyptian force in Faluja. They were trapped; yet if they fought on, they could still cause casualties and delays to the Israelis. Allon decided to try to shorten the campaign by means of a bold stroke of diplomacy.

Yerucham Cohen retells one of the most astonishing personal accounts of the war:

☐   On the 11th November, after the eighth attempt, the fortress
     of Iraq Suweidan was finally captured. Yigal Allon realized
     that if he could meet the commander of the Egyptian bri-
     gades surrounded in the Faluja Pocket, he might be able to
     convince him to accept his proposal to avoid bloodshed by
     retreating, with all his men and their personal arms, but not
     heavy armaments, across the Egyptian border.
          So he asked me if I knew anyone who would agree to
     approach the Egyptian lines surrounding the pocket and to
     organize a meeting between the two commanders. So I said,
     "All right, I'll think about it," and I went out of the room and
     came back without taking my hand off the door handle. I
     said, "I have one." He said, "Who?" I said, "Me." He said,
     "No." I said, "Why?" He said, "I am not going to risk losing
     any further opportunities to eat in your mother's kitchen."
     My mother was a very good cook in the Yemenite tradition.
     So I said, "Yigal, I don't know any other man. You've sent
     me many times across the border. All right, I'm a bit afraid,
     but I'll do it. In any case, if you think it's dangerous, I
     wouldn't like to send anybody else to do it instead of me."
          So I went to a place to the east of the pocket, near Iraq
     el Manshieh. I had an armored car with me, with loudspeak-
     ers, calling in English and Arabic across the eight hundred
     meters or so—that was the range of their antitank guns—
     "Hello, hello! An Israeli officer would like to meet an Egyp-
     tian officer." That went on for about twenty minutes, and
     then, on the road that led from Hebron to Faluja, I saw three
     figures standing. So there was no use going on shouting—
     they had heard me.
          I left everything, took off my gun and gave it to the
     driver and said, "Stay here. I'll walk." I knew that the area
     was a jungle of mines and we had no map, because most of
     the people who'd laid the mines had been killed. On the
     other hand I knew that the asphalt road was the target of all

the rifles and machine guns and mortars; but I decided it was safer to walk on the asphalt road than risk the mines.

And I walked and walked, and I could see all the Israeli soldiers standing around like trees, looking at this crazy man walking, because they had had instructions: From six in the morning no one opens fire toward the pocket. When I was about ten meters from the men, I noticed that one was a major and the other two, captains.

I had never saluted in my life, but I was a captain at the time, and I thought, well, you've seen a lot of movies, you can do it. And I actually banged my forehead with my hand, through not knowing exactly how. And I said, "Gentlemen, I am Captain Cohen. How do you do?" There was a hesitation, and then they shook my hand. And the one in the middle, who was the major, said, "I'm Gamal Abdul Nasser."

And there we stood for about a minute, and there was what we called a "spanish donkey"—two crosses of wood with a lot of barbed wire— and they decided to open that and come to my side. I introduced myself as the representative of the commander of the southern front and explained that I had come on a mission to ask their commander to meet ours. And he said, "I suppose that means you will ask for our surrender." And I said, "No, just a normal meeting between two commanders, in which each side will try to explain to the other his military position."

So after that Nasser sent one of the officers to Faluja, and meanwhile we sat—it was winter, there was already some fresh grass—and we talked for about six hours till the answer came: "Come tomorrow morning. We have to take instructions from Egypt."

When I left, I was driving my jeep, and I saw a battalion of jeeps rushing toward me, with Yigal Allon in the first one. He shouted, "What happened?" I said, "Nothing." He said, "What do you mean, nothing? I am coming to rescue you! I am going to attack the pocket!" I said, "If you want to attack it, go ahead, but I am here."

The next morning I went back. The answer was yes. So I said: It's not nice for generals to meet in the open. I suggest you meet either in Bet Jubrin or Beersheba." Nasser said, "No, I'm sorry, I can't allow you to go there." "What do you mean, you can't allow?" "I can't let you enter Bet Jubrin or Beersheba." I said, "But we have occupied these places for nearly three weeks already!" He said, "No, I hear on Egyptian Radio that we are still holding Beersheba and Bet Jubrin." I explained that I had taken a group of fifty world journalists to Beersheba and told them, "Gentlemen, this is Beersheba, and all the soldiers you see here are Egyptian— except us." I said, "Come on, don't you see you're being lied to?" But he wouldn't give way.

So I said, "Well, have you captured Kibbutz Gat?" He said, "No," "Well, will you come to Kibbutz Gat?" He said, "If you invite us, we'll come." "So at three o'clock I'll meet you here and take you." "Good." I went back to Kibbutz Gat and I told them, "I want one room." Most of the kibbutz had been destroyed, but we found one place where we could hold the meeting. I told them to prepare some cookies and orange juice and so on, and I phoned Allon.

"Yigal, I want you to be here at three o'clock." He said, "Where?" I said, "At Kibbutz Gat." He said, "Why?" I said, "Because I've fixed it. The Egyptians have agreed to come to the kibbutz." He said, "Are they crazy?" "No, no, don't worry. They're coming."

So then I went and fetched the Sudanese commander, Colonel Sayid Taha Bey, [together with Nasser and other Egyptian officers] and I brought him to Allon and introduced them. Allon welcomed his guests in Arabic, but the Egyptian commander said he would prefer to speak English. Neither Allon nor the other Israeli officers spoke English at that time so I acted as interpreter. This was the conversation:

ALLON: Allow me, Colonel, to extend to you my compliments on your soldiers' courage. They fought very bravely at Iraq Suweidan.

TAHA: Thank you, sir. I must say that the tenacity of your forces astonished me and put me in a very difficult position.

ALLON: Is it not tragic for the two sides, who actually have no reason to fight, to set upon each other mercilessly?

TAHA: A real tragedy, but that is the way of the world. Fate is fate, and there is no avoiding it.

ALLON: I hope that you have noted that this war was imposed on us by force. It is being fought here in our country, not in Egypt. It is clear that we are winning, and it would be better to put an end to the fighting.

TAHA: Perhaps, but I, as an officer, can only carry out my government's orders.

ALLON: It would be worth your while to realize that you are fighting a war without any hope of winning, and that all your efforts will be in vain. In your country the British army is in control. *We* have just gotten rid of them.

TAHA: You have astonished us with your success in ousting the British. It will not be long before we throw them out.

ALLON: But how will you get rid of them if your whole army is stuck here, after a great defeat? Do you not feel it would be best for you to go home to Egypt and look after your own problems, instead of getting involved in troubles in a land which is not your own?

TAHA: As long as my government orders me to fight here, I will do so. When I am told to make peace, I will do so. When I am told to go back to Egypt and fight the British, I will do it with pleasure and as ordered.

ALLON: I have a high regard for your obedience, Colonel, that is the way of a soldier. I also must obey my government's orders without question. All the same, it seems to me that you should inform your commander, or prove to him, that there is no hope for your army in this war. I do not try to hide my thoughts, my problems, and my worries, or my demands for the right to fight, from my government. But this does not mean that I am defying the law of the land. Only through such frankness can there be an alliance between statesmanship and military strategy.

TAHA: There is no doubt that the position on the front and in Egypt is clear to my government, and I am sure that they will do everything that is necessary.

ALLON: This was surely your belief when you invaded Palestine, and see how wrong your leaders were. If not for the intervention of the United Nations, the Egyptian army would have been completely crushed by now, including your brave and courageous brigade. You must understand, Colonel, that the situation at the front has been settled. Your brigade is now besieged on all sides and has no hope of breaking out. It is my duty to avail myself of any opportunity to destroy your formation. What purpose would be served by your desperate stand? The fate of the second half of the pocket will not differ from that of the first.

Taha was silent for a moment, then replied: "Yes sir, I see. But as long as I have soldiers and ammunition there is no reason why I should stop fighting."

Allon realized that he was confronting an obstinate fighter. Nevertheless, he resorted to diplomacy again.

ALLON: I greatly admire your courage, Colonel, but do you not agree that the lives of men are precious and that there is no logic in sacrificing your men in fighting a nation that does not consider itself your enemy, and which has only good intentions toward you? I am not advising you to surrender dishonorably but with full respect and military honors, with the possibility of an immediate return home. Think about it. Let us save the blood of our soldiers and cease fighting. I cannot cease fighting as long as foreign armies are on our soil. But you do not fight on your soil. Try to understand that I am right.

Nasser and the other Egyptian officers present at the meeting watched Colonel Taha anxiously, wondering why he was hesitating to reply.

Finally Taha, staring directly at Allon, said in a quiet voice charged with suppressed emotion: "Sir, there is no doubt that your position is much better than mine. The planning of your operation and the performance of your soldiers have been admirable. You have broken through our strongest lines, and you have put to shame the Egyptian army, which has never before tasted defeat. I do not flatter myself by thinking that I can possibly change the existing situation to our advantage. But there is one thing that I can save—the honor of the Egyptian army. And that is why I shall fight until the last bullet and the last soldier, unless I receive different orders from my government.

ALLON: As a soldier, I can understand your sentiments well, but you must know that under extraordinary circumstances a local commander must take responsibility for decisions, as Paulus did at Stalingrad. Believe me, Colonel, your government would have little reason to criticize a soldier of your caliber. Consider your men and your country and lay down your arms.

TAHA: No, sir. I have no alternative but to continue fighting. It is clear that I must preserve the honor of the Egyptian army.

ALLON: May I ask you to give your government and your commanders a description of the real situation and to request their consent to my proposals?

TAHA: I will send a full report of our talk to them.

As the tension eased, Allon invited his guests to help themselves to refreshments. Suddenly Major Gamal Abdul Nasser turned to Colonel Taha Bey and said, "May I ask the Israeli commander a question?"

ALLON: Please ask, and I am sure that if your question does not deal with military secrets, you will receive an answer.

NASSER (with a smile): Is the emblem on your lapel, showing two sheaves of wheat and a sword, that of the Palmach?

ALLON: Yes. I see that you are a good intelligence officer.

NASSER: Now I understand our difficulties. We have been fighting the Palmach.

After an hour and a half, the meeting ended, and Allon and his officers accompanied the Egyptians to their jeeps. As Taha climbed into his jeep, Allon said: "I am pleased to meet you, Colonel. If you should wish to see me again, you can always send me a message. May we meet in better times." Taha: "May we meet in peacetime."

I then escorted the Egyptian officers back to Faluja, and as I said good-bye to Colonel Taha I inquired: "Sir, may I ask why you took such a chance in coming to meet us? Were you not afraid of a trap?" Taha smiled and said: "Major Abdul Nasser told me about you and I was convinced that he trusted you completely. So I did not hesitate to go. And now we see that he was not mistaken."

One last word on Operation Yoav from Shimon Avidan:

☐   Later, we gave the hills names of men who had fallen in the battles. One hill, which was called before Hill 130, we called "Arnon." Arnon was a scout, born in Germany, the son of a doctor who practiced in Tel Aviv. He was at the head of the formation which began the battle, and he was wounded going through the barbed wire. He called his friends to step on him and so get over. They wanted to take him back, but he told them that now was not the time. They should go and fight and pick him up on the way back. But when they returned to him, he was already dead.

A truce—the third—was now officially in force, although actions continued on several fronts. In the north, Kawukji continued spasmodic attacks. He captured a number of strategic strongpoints and cut the road from Kibbutz Menara to Nebi Yusha in hill country near the Lebanese border. Moshe Carmel, still commanding the northern front, with the assistance of the new Israeli air force, counterattacked from his base in Safed. All was not plain sailing, as Yehuda Bauer tells:

☐   I participated in a very inglorious retreat of the Ninth Bri-

gade from what is now Ma'alot against Kawukji and his
irregulars. As a historian, I might say that Kawukji was
absolutely no use as a military man. He was an Iraqi ex-
officer who thought he knew something about military
affairs. He positioned his troops in the worst possible way.
He didn't really control the road from Nahariya to Tah-
sheikha [now Ma'alot]. He put his major fortifications in the
right places, but he didn't really fortify them. His main
position was opposite Kibbutz Yechiam, with its old Crusader fortress. Now that was all very romantic, but from a
military point of view it's quite useless. He wanted to kill the
Jews from his position overlooking the settlement. The
members of the Kibbutz simply went behind the walls of the
fortress, where they were absolutely safe. The walls are three
or four feet thick and no conventional weapons can pierce
them.

Carmel didn't know what the Ninth Brigade was like.
Absolutely untrained. Not that the Arabs were any better—
they were no soldiers at all, they ran at the first opportunity.
But at least there was someone who knew what he wanted
from them. *Our* unit was just chaotic.

To begin with, morale was pretty low, because they
were new immigrants from Bulgaria and other places and
they had no idea what was happening. They knew they were
fighting for the independence of Israel, but nobody spoke
Bulgarian, you see. To use an English expression, they were
cheesed-off, because no one could talk to them. A few
understood some snippets of Hebrew, but in general, though
they were very willing, it was the Tower of Babel all over
again.

They were shoved up a hill—just pushed up—and then
they didn't know where to turn, because they couldn't
understand the commands. After the enemy opened up with
machine guns, no one could communicate with our men or
tell them what to do. I remember thinking what a great
shame it was, because we were far superior to the enemy in
that particular sector. All they had was three or four

machine guns.... Of course, we had no proper equipment
either, no proper weapons, just a mixture—Bren guns,
German Spandaus, Mausers, submachine guns, Canadian
rifles—just about everything. The unit had been thrown
together without prior contact, and the Israeli officers
couldn't make sense out of it.

The attack was aborted before it was fairly under way.
The Arabs were shooting as we retreated, but absolutely no
harm came to us because it was pitch dark and they couldn't
see us. When we got the order to retreat, we slowly walked
down the hill—they were up on the crest, and we were in a
"dead" area. A few bullets whizzed around our ears at the
bottom. The trucks which had brought us were there waiting, and the commander ambled down.... We weren't
under any pressure. No one was chasing us—the last thing
the Arabs wanted was to endanger themselves. Of course,
that was not always the case. Occasionally they managed to
stir themselves up into a fanatic fighting frenzy; then they'd
rush madly into the fray without any attention to personal
safety whatsoever.

After our failure, Kawukji was quite hopeful, but Carmel sent a second brigade in, commanded by Dan Even, an
experienced South African, who just cut through Kawukji's
troops and conquered Sasa. After that, Kawukji withdrew
and didn't reappear. That was his last operation.

In his postscript to this story, Yehuda Bauer draws attention
to an extraordinary aspect of that war, the fact that people were
maintaining absolutely normal lives a few hundred yards, or a few
miles, behind the lines.

☐   After that withdrawal there was a reorganization, and our
officers thought that the best thing would be to let the
soldiers roam about and recover their nerve. I went to the
commander and said, "Can I have the day off, because
nobody is doing anything today anyway?" And he said, fine.
So I took my kit and my rifle, and got a lift, and after

three-quarters of an hour I was in my parents' home in Haifa
where they were having afternoon tea with biscuits and
cakes. I had just come from this bloody engagement. It was
terribly peculiar. All I wanted was a bath. I remember I felt
very superior to all these little middle-aged ladies and gentlemen sitting around eating and drinking. I thought they
should have been up and doing, somehow. My mother
regarded me as a hero, which, considering the circumstances, was rather ironic.

Netanel Lorch had experienced something of the same feeling, coming to Tel Aviv from Jerusalem:

☐   I thought I was coming to a different city which had not
known what war is. They had yogurt, they had milk, they
had fresh tomatoes and they had showers. Although we slept
on the roof of a hotel, if felt like paradise—to have a night
which was absolutely quiet and in the morning to have a
shower and a good breakfast—that was quite an experience.... We had a marvelous time, feeling just like young
boys again.

With the whole of Galilee in Israeli hands, and the Arab
Legion virtually isolated and neutralized at Latrun by the end of
October, there were no actions and no more truce violations in the
north and central areas during November and December, but the
southern front was not so quiet. There was deadlock of a sort
around Faluja: The Israelis refused to release the trapped Egyptian force until Egypt agreed to hold peace talks, and the Egyptians continued a militant policy of harassing Jewish settlements,
sabotaging communications, and interfering with water supplies.
Uri Avneri recalls:

☐   I got my wound on the last day that my brigade was on the
southern front. I wasn't on the jeeps any more. It was after I
became a section leader. I'd been given a choice between
leading Poles and Moroccans. I chose the Moroccans. I

always liked them more—I was intrigued by them. But I couldn't talk to them—none of them knew Hebrew. We communicated in sign language. What an experience! But I tried to put into practice the kind of officership I had learned from the Palmach, which had already been "absorbed" into the army by then.

My men, a section of fifteen, had all come from North Africa and been put straight into the army. They had no pullovers, nor any warm clothes—only summer uniforms. The army couldn't cope with so many. But I was a veteran, which means being very good at stealing things from army stores. I got pullovers for some of them, but then I didn't wear my own winter uniform because my men didn't all have sweaters.

Another time when we were traveling in open trucks in the rain, I didn't sit in the cabin as a section leader was supposed to but stayed in the open back with them. That was my idea of how to be a leader. And it paid off for me, when I was wounded.

That was sheer carelessness on my part. We were investigating the Faluja Pocket (where Kiryat Gat is today) and there was a forward position, totally exposed, to which a section would be sent at night. They'd stay there during the day, and the next night a relief would be sent. Every night I'd go and have a scout around there.

One day the new company commander—who was a fool—decided for some reason to relieve in the middle of the day, and sent me with my section. An old-timer like me, who had come through so many engagements unscathed, to do what I did—! But somehow we were in a different kind of mood. We were tired, apathetic— So in broad daylight I went up that hill, leaving my people below, and stood at the top, totally exposed to the Egyptian positions. I called the other section leader and he showed me the situation, and while we were standing there, of course they opened up machine-gun fire and I was wounded in the stomach.

I lay there, right out in the open. The other fellow was

not wounded. He ran back to my people, and they came up and took me out, though it must have looked like suicide. Those Moroccans probably wouldn't have done it for someone they didn't like.

Phase 2:
Operation Horev*

The high command then decided to launch Operation Horev, with the aim of driving the Egyptians out of the country altogether.

Yerucham Cohen recalls:

☐ That operation took place near the end of December, after we had realized that the Egyptians were making movements from the Gaza Strip toward the east, after first capturing hills and putting mines on the roads we were using. In addition, we had information that they were intending to attack Beersheba, so we got permission to throw them all out of Israeli territory.

The "information" was gleaned in part from the interrogation of prisoners. This was the task of the intelligence team of which Shmuel Toledano, who had been so moved on entering Jaffa, was a member.

☐ I was put in charge of interrogating prisoners of war, mainly Egyptians. Again, I was facing tragedy, because every prisoner was part of the tragedy of war—part of a family, a human being in a horrible situation. Perhaps other men faced this tragedy in a more cruel way, in battle. But for

*"Horev" is a poetic name for the Sinai Desert.

them it was a matter of fighting for a short period. It was different for me. We had hundreds of prisoners, and as I had to interrogate all of them, I spent many months meeting these people and learning about their lives while I tried to gain information.

There are two methods of doing this: the tough one, which I didn't use, and the other, which is to try and associate with the prisoner to gain his confidence. That takes longer, and you get more involved with the man. For a year that was my job, after every battle. Either the prisoners would be brought to a rear base, where I had to find out general information about the war, or, if they were caught while the battle was actually going on, one had to obtain information of immediate importance.

I remember a case— It's hard to believe. Until today I find it hard to realize I was part of it. Before the war started we had taken some people from Jaffa—Arab civilians. We tried to interrogate them, and one of them was— I think I came to the wrong conclusion then. I thought he was one of their fighters. And it was according to my recommendation— At that time, there was no argument, you could decide in a minute to kill somebody. It affected me very much. I was young then, we were at war . . . yet I was one of those who recommended that he be executed. Until today, thirty-two years later, I still remember the face of that man, and I can't get over it.

Later on I moved toward exactly the opposite position, and I think I took part in saving more than one man. At the beginning, you know, there was no army, nothing. It wasn't the same sort of war as we make now. Now you have rules, you have officers. In '48 everyone could do what he decided to do, and in many cases I saw to it that none of the prisoners I was responsible for was touched. There were many incidents where some of the soldiers felt, "Who needs this one? Why let him live?" And I saw to it that he remained alive. I was just a lieutenant then, but as we say, "That was when a lieutenant was a lieutenant—when a pound was a pound—"

Someone else who had contact with Egyptian prisoners was
Netiva Ben Yehuda. It will be recalled that, after her traumatic
experiences earlier in the war and her refusal to fight the Irgun at
the time of the *Altalena,* she had been reassigned to her old
brigade, the Yiftach, by the personal intervention of Yigal Allon,
but no longer as a combatant.

☐   The first job I did when I joined the high command in
    Gedera was to put flares around the captives, which would
    go off if someone escaped. It was a very easy job—at the
    worst, if something goes wrong you can lose an eye—and I
    couldn't do it, my hands shook so much.

    There was a special officers' camp for the Egyptian
    prisoners. You can't imagine what a difference there was
    between the Egyptian officers and the men! The officers
    treated their men like dirt; they wouldn't associate with
    them. One Egyptian officer called to me in English, "You
    have been a sapper, eh?" And I said, "How do you know?" "I
    am also a demolition officer." So I said, "You should keep a
    better eye on your subordinates." He asked me what I
    meant. "In Beit Daras, we had to clear a minefield, and four
    or five officers, including one religious one who wouldn't
    work on Saturdays, divided up the field between us and kept
    a distance so that if one got blown up, we wouldn't all get
    hurt. After taking two or three antitank mines out of the
    sand we discovered that your soldiers hadn't primed them.
    So the officers were running around digging out the mines
    with their feet, but I thought, there might be one honest
    Egyptian private and I went on dismantling them carefully."

    I became friends with this officer. He gave me a button
    off his uniform, which I still have, and I gave him cigarettes.

Yerucham Cohen describes the famous ruse that resulted in
the rout of the Egyptians in Auja:

☐   We used an old Roman road that was covered with sand
    dunes, leading from Beersheba up to a point on the Egyptian

border very close to Auja el-Khafir, which we captured. And then, with the idea of forcing them to withdraw from the Gaza Strip, we followed the retreating Egyptian forces to Abu Ageila and from there across the desert to El Arish on the coast. We intended to capture El Arish and then go back to the Israeli-Egyptian border.

On 29th December we reached the airport of El Arish and actually cut off the whole Egyptian army—all of it: There was nothing left of it in Egypt! There was a huge group in the Gaza Strip and another in Faluja.

"Boaz", battle-worn but still in active service, took part in Operation Horev with the Har El Brigade:

☐   We were attached to the Golani Brigade, which were infan-
     try, to lend support with our Bazer machine guns. By that
     time equipment was much better, but not exactly up to GI
     standards. We were issued with winter uniforms, all second-
     hand leftovers from World War II—we looked as if we'd
     been to a vast army jumble sale and emerged wearing our
     motley purchases, satisfied customers unused to such rela-
     tive luxuries. What if buttons were missing and nothing
     fitted properly? We even had greatcoats. Mine was so big
     and heavy that even loaded with equipment and carrying
     boxes of ammo and so on, it was still the most cumbersome
     burden I had to bear. But winter nights in the desert were
     bitterly cold and we were glad of any sort of warmth, includ-
     ing what passed for sleeping bags.

     Beersheba, recently captured, had become an Israeli
     garrison town. Several brigades, armored columns, and
     even some tanks of our very own were massed in preparation
     for the final push to dislodge the Egyptian forces. When
     possible we strolled the streets to admire the new weapons
     and sometimes there'd be a joyful meeting with old friends,
     either from previous battlefronts or from the vague past of
     shared classrooms or ghetto streets. And there was the
     boyish figure of the commander in charge of all this, Yigal

Allon, hurrying purposefully and cheerfully along the road
followed by his aides carrying papers. He looked as if he
might trip over his own greatcoat, which almost reached his
boots, so who was I to complain about mine?

Hardly any of the rest of us lower ranks knew what the
plan was. It was a secret and depended on surprise. We
moved from Beersheba at night, arriving at the most south-
erly Israeli settlement—at that time, Chalutza. We rested,
ate, reorganized, and traveled endlessly along rough trails,
leaving behind Israeli territory and eventually all vestiges of
roads. We found ourselves in the cold of early dawn, bogged
down in sand.

Everyone got out to push and lay mesh under the
spinning wheels, and with the help of a couple of Caterpillar
tractors we finally made it to another bit of trail and so on to
Auja el-Khafir, which was our first objective.

The surprise was total. How could they expect Israelis
to appear at this camp in the middle of the desert on the
borders of Egypt? We hadn't even come along the main
road. Egyptians were standing in line for their chow or
hanging about half-dressed when our armored column,
including the dreaded *Shualei Shimshon* [Samson's Foxes],
suddenly appeared just outside the camp.

They ran in panic from our line of fire, scattering up
the hills, which were soon strewn with their dead. So despite
the difficult journey and our late arrival, our first encounter
was encouraging.

For the next few hours—or days, I can't remember—
we were busy mopping up in and around Auja, driving the
enemy back relatively easily. I remember one lull, when we
were resting, and someone shouted, *"Hineh Hazaken!"*—
"Here comes the Old Man!" meaning Yitzhak Sadeh, the
already legendary founder of the Palmach and more recently
the commander of the Eighth Armored Brigade. We rushed
toward the approaching armored cars and there in the
command jeep sat that unmistakable figure, like a bald,
bespectacled Santa Claus—rotund, ruddy, with his white

spade beard—waving cheerfully at us while we shouted our approval. Some of us ran alongside his jeep as he drove on to some further action.

With the capture of Auja and its environs, the main road, which led from Egypt through Auja northeast to Gaza and northwest to Beersheba, was in our hands. Next we had to cut off the main body of Egyptians concentrated between Rafa and Gaza.

We were traveling in convoy toward Rafa when I saw my first enemy airplane of the war zooming toward us with clattering machine guns. We jumped off the trucks, scattering in all directions. I can never forget trying to push my body into the sand and seeing the plane's shadow growing, while my exposed back tingled in anticipation of the bullets.

But even that wasn't worse than the sand. It got into every orifice, into the food—and it clogged our weapons. There was one incident when two small convoys traveling in a sandstorm noticed each other simultaneously only when they were almost nose to nose. Both commanders jumped out of their vehicles, walked toward each other—and suddenly realized that they were enemies. They turned, rushed back to their columns, and turned about sharply.

Another time we were trudging through what seemed like a wall of sand. The wind was howling so that we could hear nothing else, and the heavy equipment we were carrying seemed to drag us down into the soft sand. We were painfully trying to reach the enemy strongholds near Rafa, almost doubled up in an attempt to keep the sand out of our faces.

Suddenly a great roar broke through the sound of the wind, directly overhead. We looked up, cowering, to see the huge shape of a British Spitfire above our heads. The pilot must have been as shocked as we were to see the ground and people immediately below. The plane made a sharp U-turn and whooshed up out of sight.

We trudged on. The storm died down a bit. We saw men coming toward us and recognized them as our people—

but some of them had bits of their clothing missing. It seemed that they had been holding a hill nearby and this same bloody sandstorm had enveloped them They had lain down, covering themselves and their weapons in an attempt to keep the sand out. Suddenly an Egyptian armored column loomed through the whirling sand right in front of them.

When the CO shouted "Fire!" hardly a gun worked— all were jammed with sand; the machine guns couldn't even be shifted. The Egyptians used flame throwers, which seemed to set the hill on fire, and our people fled from the hopeless situation, tearing burning clothes off themselves and each other. Many of the enemy guns were also sand-clogged, so there were only a few wounded, who were dragged along in the retreat.

The sandstorms were sometimes used as a smoke screen by our armored columns, and we were able to watch them once, from a ringside seat. My unit had stormed the hills—or rather, sand dunes—along a broad plain, on the other side of which the Egyptians had strongly entrenched themselves with heavy artillery ready to defend Rafa. There was some excitement on our side now, all having gone according to plan. The Israeli army had pinned down a large section of Egyptians in the Gaza Strip, and we were poised to pounce on the southwest side of it. We heard rumors that Yigal Allon was determined to take it despite orders from Ben-Gurion to stop. Ben-Gurion was under political pressure, from Britain especially; the British had sent reconnaissance planes to frighten us and ease the Egyptian dilemma, and five of them were shot down, one by a young girl firing a Bazer mounted on a tripod. She had recently arrived from England, and before that had been a refugee from Germany. I believe she was killed soon afterward.*

Anyway, there we were, digging into the sand on this

---

*There is some doubt about this. Lorch insists that these planes were all shot down in dogfights with Israeli aircraft.

hill facing Rafa and preparing our machine guns for action
when a storm started up again—not so strongly this time,
but we could see that the jeeps and half-tracks that had been
hidden between the sand dunes just below and to the side of
our position were inching into the plain toward the enemy
positions.

When the sandstorm eased sufficiently for them to see,
and be seen by the enemy, the drivers accelerated and the
gunners whipped the covers off the machine guns. We
stopped everything to watch the scene going on below. It
was an impressive sight—jeeps and half-tracks whizzing
around at full speed with their guns blazing. After only a few
minutes they were out of the line of fire, with one half-track
burning. We opened up with our guns to cover them. It must
have terrified the Egyptians; after that, every time there was
a sandstorm they expected another attack and pounded us
with mortar and cannon.

The last day of the campaign came. It's a cliché to say
that the nearer you are to the front, the less you see or know
of the broad picture. We knew nothing—all seemed as usual.
Shells were falling on either side, but most of it was heavy
artillery trying to hit each other, so we kept our heads down
and ate what passed for our breakfast crouched in our
dugouts—sardines and sand, with dry biscuits and some
stale, tepid water. We had to keep digging sand out of our
trenches as the wind filled them up.

Any information we did have came from the field
telephone. It was rumored there would soon be a cease-fire.
Mixed feelings: "Thank God! Alive! Out of this awful sand.
. . . . But here we are, ready to take the Strip—what about
that?"

Then, just as the information got to us that there would
actually be a cease-fire in two or three hours, the Egyptians
started to throw everything they had at us. I suppose they
thought we might try to take advantage of the last few hours
and were determined to hold us off. I hadn't been under such
a pounding before. They seemed to be concentrating on our

section. Perhaps because I knew there were only a couple of hours to go before the cease-fire, I felt suddenly exposed. After all I'd been through it seemed such a shame to get hit now. And how could they miss? They seemed determined to blast our entire hill out of existence.

I had the idea they could see me, and suddenly I couldn't sit still any longer. I jumped out of my slit trench and ran to a lower-lying spot. A pair of eyes stared at me from under a huge steel helmet. It was one of our boys recently arrived from Poland, and he shouted in Yiddish *"Kimts arein!"*—"Come on in!" I jumped into his dugout. He was apparently glad to have company, but that was small comfort to me when he dug his fingernails into my ankle every time a shell whistled over and wailed "OY OY!" as we lay there top-to-tail like sardines. He was kind enough to tell me repeatedly, "You can lie on top of me! I don't mind!"

After a bit someone came crawling across the sand to ask for help with something—I can't remember what—and I was glad enough to jump out and get busy.

The bombardment lasted full force for over two hours and then stopped abruptly several minutes after the appointed time of the cease-fire. We wandered about in a daze to see what had happened. Amazingly, only one dugout, with its two occupants, had been hit. There were also some wounded, but the soft sand had absorbed the shock of impact, so that few of the hundreds of shells had actually done any harm. But when I found the trench that I had evacuated, I had to dig to quite a depth to get my greatcoat out. If not for that moment of intuition, or terror, I might have been under there with it.

The "broad picture" is sketched in by others. Yerucham Cohen recalls:

☐   At this time the American ambassador here—he was actually called a minister, James Macdonald—met Ben-Gurion and gave him an ultimatum from the Americans, under pressure from the British, to retreat immediately from all Egyptian territory, otherwise the British would "take steps."

Ephraim Shorer:

☐ I'm not alone in suspecting that, while we were allowed to conquer areas originally assigned to the Jewish state in the '47 partition plan, as soon as we started to push a little farther—either toward the mountainous area, which we now call the West Bank, or toward the south, across the international border—immediately we were warned off. Mainly by Britain at the time. And sometimes it went beyond a warning, as when those British aircraft buzzed the battle area. It was a threat of military action, and it prevented our achieving all that we could have done.

A historian's view from Meir Pa'il:

☐ I took part with the Negev Brigade in the last operation, Horev, when we conquered Abu Ageila and threatened El Arish, and we almost occupied Gaza but were stopped by the Israeli government.

   As a historian I know now that there was no actual ultimatum as such, issued by America on behalf of the British, for us to get out of Sinai. They put pressure on us, but Emmanuel Shinwell, who was the British minister of defense, has denied there was an ultimatum. I think Ben-Gurion took the British pressure too seriously. It think he made a mistake.

   I am a "peacenik" now, and I think we should evacuate the territories for peace; but I think in those days we'd have done better to stay in Sinai for another week to encircle the Gaza Strip and force the Egyptians to an armistice while their troops in the Strip were cut off. Then we could have demanded as a condition of the armistice that they take their troops out of the Faluja Pocket and also out of Gaza.

   I think that our government in those days was not bold

enough to carry the war a little bit further, relying on the Israeli forces, which were more efficient than Ben-Gurion had anticipated. I think he wasn't smart and bold enough to use the international political backing we had at that time— even the Soviets, because of their political interests, were even more wholehearted than the Americans. That way, we could have made better terms with Egypt.

I can understand Ben-Gurion's concept, not to drive out the Jordanians. I was against it then, but looking back from a historian's viewpoint, I think it was wise. But the best scheme would have been, first, to drive the Egyptians out of Israel altogether [including the Gaza Strip] so that we could have faced the Jordanians and said, "Okay. First of all, convince the Iraqis to go home. Second, you have to choose between two possibilities: Either we'll drive you to the east side of the Jordan River, the way we drove out the Egyptians, or, if you want to stay—fine. We'll let you stay on the West Bank and keep the eastern part of Jerusalem. We'll even let you have an outlet to the Mediterranean through Gaza. *But* let's make a political peace, sign an agreement, and that's it."

But to do this we'd have had to drive the Egyptians out and hold the Gaza Strip as a bargaining card. I think Ben-Gurion had this concept of finding some modus vivendi with Jordan; but by the end of the war he was a little bit tired and not so bold as some journalists and historians would like to paint him.

A sidelight on these and other campaigns was the entertaining of the troops. This was undertaken even in the most remote areas and during much of the most intense fighting by a number of groups. One of the best known was Chaim Heffer's "Chizbatron,"* which produced the definitive songs of that and subsequent wars. Heffer recalls:

Chizbat is a "tall tale" in Arabic; *teatron* is Hebrew for theater.

☐ I formed the first entertainment group around January, February '48. From then on we traveled about like the minstrels of old, from front to front, about ten of us, and sometimes those we sang to were hardly more in number than we were.

When the Negev was under siege, for example, we flew over the Egyptian lines and then traveled about from strongpoint to strongpoint; in some spots we would do our show for just one squad of men. We would take our instruments—a guitar, an accordion—and do our performance, and suddenly you would see that squad's mood change. Maybe they had been stuck in that one spot for two or three weeks, and our coming to entertain them would make them feel they were important. Conditions might be terrible. The Negev is a bad place for flies. Some of the boys might open their mouths to sing and swallow a dozen flies! It was very hard, but they liked us so much that sometimes they would want to see the performance again and again.

Our show lasted about one and a half hours. We sang our own special songs, we did skits . . . . Sometimes we had to make it shorter because we couldn't all go. When we could "set up" properly we had scenery of a kind, but often when we had to be smuggled through the lines maybe I would only take two or three of our performers with me, and just sing for half an hour, twenty minutes . . . . Soldiers had to guide us through the lines. They always guarded us very strongly. That was nice. But they knew we weren't the sort of troupe which wants to perform safely at base—we wanted to go to the front line, to the battlefronts. That was one of my conditions—I told Yigal Allon—we demanded to go, even to take part in some battles.

For example, we went with one of the regiments south of Beersheba and toward the Egyptian front. That time I only took my two star performers, a boy and a girl, and my accordionist. We traveled by half-track. And that time we were armed—I should say, we armed ourselves, because we took spoils—rifles of the Egyptians that we found, two of them, which meant two guns among four of us, which was quite a firepower in those days!

And later in the battle, when we were in the half-tracks, we chased an Egyptian regiment. We had a fight with them and did some shooting. There were other army troupes, by the way, but we were *their* troupe, which went to the front, and that's why the soldiers trusted us.

At Hannukah we were in Egypt already. It was very cold, really cold. And our command car got stuck. There were maybe twenty boys sitting there. We sat down in the desert, singing Hannukah songs to an accordion, and they took used mortar shells, put gasoline in them, and lit them .... That was a very tough road, in a wadi, where command cars and tanks had to pass through. From time to time you could see a bunch of them stopping and joining us for a song or two and then going on.... We always used those little pauses in the war; when we were very close to the front, we used to sing in the dark.

The feeling of closeness to the soldiers gave us inspiration for a lot of our songs. They were written at the time and for the time, as in the days of the troubadors. The words told about what happened yesterday. They were—*immediate.* And they were not all lighthearted. I sang songs which made soldiers cry, and afterward they would come to me and say, "Listen, it was a moving performance." It was *this* they were waiting for.

Because if you are at the front and friends of yours are killed, you don't want to put it some place at the back of your mind. You want to talk about it, about the guy. It's important. It's a catharsis. Israel is a big tribe, and we know each other. I always had a feeling that these soldiers are my family. So I couldn't cover it up. I couldn't say, "Well, somebody died, so let's forget it and sing, la, la, la—" No. You make the dead boy a hero if he was one, and you sing about it, and you remember him.

Operation Horev effectively ended the war (though there

was one last campaign to come). Yigal Yadin describes the
Rhodes armistice talks in which he played a major role:

☐   It all began at the end of December '48, after a series of
     victories in what turned out to be the last campaign of the
     War of Independence against the Egyptians. The British
     tried to come back again through the back door by sending
     some force to Akaba to threaten us; but the Egyptians saw
     that despite all these pressures by Britain, and to some
     extent the United States, which helped them a little, but not
     enough, they were in desperate straits from the military
     point of view. We were still in the Sinai; we had smashed a
     large part of the Egyptian army; but an order from Ben-
     Gurion forced us to withdraw from Sinai. America and
     Britain obliged him to give that order. But we were still on
     the international border between Sinai and Palestine and in
     some places a little bit inside Sinai.
          Then came the request from the U.N. for armistice
     talks. The Egyptians for the first time actually agreed,
     because there was another very important factor, which
     played a vital role later on, and that was that there was one
     Egyptian brigade still trapped at Faluja (including Abdul
     Nasser) and they wanted very much to retrieve that brigade.
          By the end of December or early January '49 we
     received word that the Egyptians had agreed to armistice
     talks if some conditions were met, which were more face-
     saving than practical. And we were told that Dr. Ralph
     Bunche would be sent to conduct negotiations, assisted by
     Brigadier Riley.
          The Egyptians wanted to give these talks, as far as they
     could, a military character; they didn't want it to have a
     political flavor in case it should be interpreted as something
     more than an armistice.
          We, on the other hand, wanted the exact opposite. The
     word *armistice,* in the parlance of those times, based on the
     world wars, was generally accepted as meaning a prelimi-
     nary to peace talks.

So it was decided to put at the head of our mission Dr. Walter Eytan who was the director general of the Foreign Office. I, who was Israel's top-ranking officer except for Yaacov Dori, who was ill, would head the military mission, but Walter Eytan was at the head. The Egyptians, for their part, sent a large and "respectable" team—a military one— led by Seif El Dinn, a very distinguished officer, half Sudanese, and they added a gentleman who was King Farouk's brother-in-law, Colonel Sherin, obviously as a sort of watchdog, who was very much disliked by the other Egyptian officers.

We finally arrived in Rhodes around the 7th or 8th of January. It was a very strange meeting. Of course we were met by Dr. Bunche and Colonel Riley. All three delegations— the other was from the U.N.—were staying at the Hotel de Roses. At first, the Egyptians would pass us in the corridors without so much as a nod, let alone sitting together; but slowly but surely we began to greet each other, and after that they realized that they had been involved in a rather childish game—each side going to Dr. Bunche and saying, "Tell *them* so-and-so"—so at last we sat down together and began to make progress.

There were two auxiliary negotiators, both registered as "tourists," staying at the hotel, who played important roles. The Egyptian, a high-up member of their Foreign Office, was Abdul Mun-Al—I think that was not his whole name; and ours was Eliahu Sassoon, an Orientalist, an old hand in our intelligence with special emphasis on dealing with the Arab countries; quite a lot of behind-the-scenes talks took place between these two gentlemen, and whatever was agreed with this Abdul Mun-Al was subsequently agreed with their military group.

The Egyptian leaders hadn't told their people the truth about the military situation, and they had a very tricky problem. For example, we had taken Beersheba, which had been in Egyptian hands before the last battles; but the Egyptian people never knew that their army had lost this town.

Now, in addition to all the rest of what we wanted from the Egyptians, they were afraid that, when the terms of the armistice were made public, they would be accused of giving us Beersheba and its surroundings as part of the armistice. The second problem was that they wanted the release of the brigade in Faluja as a precondition of the armistice talks. Of course we refused that outright; we knew we had a trump card—basically they only came to Rhodes in order to retrieve that brigade.

I'll tell you two incidents concerning each of these two very serious problems. First about the Beersheba business. We were having an official meeting between us and the Egyptians, with the U.N. and Bunche, and everyone, and they came to us with a demand that we should *give them back* Beersheba. It was only later that they admitted what was behind the demand—their problem with their people; at that time they simply said that we had infringed the truce and taken Beersheba and that it must come back to them. I was rather furious—I can lose my temper sometimes; it was a round table, I was sitting next to this Muhammad Seif El Dinn, and I said to him, "Look here, you will get the sun first; you will get the stars first—before you will get Beersheba!" And as I was talking, the pencil slipped out of my hand, bounced on the table, and flew right into the face of the Egyptian.

There was a terrible lull. Of course I apologized, but the thing was beyond repair—can you imagine? But there was a very nice Egyptian colonel, good-hearted with a strong sense of humor, Rahmani, his name was—and after this silence, which seemed to last for years, he asked permission from the chairman to speak, and he said, "General Yadin, I've listened very carefully, and I heard you say that you would give us the sun first, you'd give us the stars first— I wonder, why didn't you mention the moon—?" That immediately broke the heavy atmosphere, everybody laughed, and we passed on to other things. Beersheba was not mentioned from that moment on.

The second incident was very typical of the negotiations, and that concerned the Faluja Brigade. At one time that was the last remaining obstacle; we had agreed to most points, but they insisted that the brigade should be released at the end of the talks. They realized they would have to face the Egyptian people with all sorts of bad news, but at least they wanted to be able to tell them that the brigade was out. Ben-Gurion recalled me to Tel Aviv for a day, and when I got back to Rhodes I learned that Walter Eytan had agreed in my absence to release the brigade.

I said to him, not in so many words: "Are you crazy? If we agree to give them back the brigade, we might as well pack up and go home—they won't agree to talk to us any more." He said, "But I promised them." So I got on to Mr. Ben-Gurion and said I thought this was a most foolish thing, and he backed me, so we went to Dr. Bunche and said, "Yes, I understand that Dr. Eytan agreed, but that was a misunderstanding, and we shall not release the brigade before we sign the armistice agreements. Then they can be released simultaneously." Dr. Bunche, black as he was, turned white, and said: "Do you know what you are doing? The Egyptians are going to pack and go home tonight." I said: "I'll make a bet with you. They won't pack, because then they know that they won't get the brigade at all, and that is the most important thing to them at this moment." He said the responsibility was on me.

Later he came back and said, "Well, the Egyptians are very generous and they have decided to stay after all." Looking back, I don't say that the talks could not have concluded successfully if we had released the brigade early, but it would certainly have prolonged the whole thing and might have endangered the outcome.

The national sport in Rhodes is cycling. During the days and weeks when talks were deadlocked we used to bicycle to all sorts of beauty spots, being absolutely unemployed! But at last came the day of the signing of the agreement. Dr. Bunche made a great fuss of the occasion; after all, it was no less a triumph for him than for the negotiating teams. He had special porcelain plates made commemorating the event and so on; and it was decided that after the signing, there would be a ball. We wanted to provide at least half the provisions for the party, but Muhammad Seif El Dinn, in typical Oriental fashion, said, over his dead body; *they* would like to be the hosts. They would send a plane to Groppi's in Cairo—"And you know about Groppi's! We shall bring back all the goods on earth!" So we agreed to this, and off went the plane, returning with turkeys, wine, you name it. And after a very successful party in the evening, we all sat together as if there were no war. On my staff was Yitzhak Rabin, then a colonel, with the Southern Command, whom I had brought with me, and he sat with this Rahmani, and I with Seif El Dinn, and we were all saying things like: "You were a fool! Why didn't you attack us from *here?* If you'd done that, we would have been completely annihilated...." And everything was okay; Seif El Dinn came to me and said, "I only hope that by signing this agreement we are paving the way to peace. On behalf of our army I can tell you that we will do all we can to promote peace." That was the atmosphere. And I confess that we all thought, that evening, that we had signed the final-document-but-one in the peace process, particularly since the preamble to the armistice agreement with Egypt became the standard form of all the armistices we signed with the other Arab countries: "The aim of this armistice is to bring peace" and so on and so forth. Even the Camp David agreement didn't have so many mentions of peace as there were in ours.

That is what I remember of the first armistice. But I must add one more thing that had a serious development later. The Egyptians were the first to sign the armistice, but there was a problem about the southern Negev vis-à-vis the Jordanians, because in Eilat all the borders—Jordan, Israel, and Egypt—nearly meet. Egypt wanted a considerable part of Israel, near the Egyptian border, to be demilitarized as part of the armistice agreement. We said, "We could do that with you because you have signed the armistice, but we have another enemy just there—the Jordanians."

So the Egyptians—I think knowingly—agreed to our making a straight line from Beersheba to Eilat. The west side, facing Egypt, was to be demilitarized, but not the other side. I think they understood that we were preparing ourselves to occupy Eilat, which was not yet in our hands.

The conquest of Eilat was one of the most ticklish operations of the war for the Israelis. It had to be bloodless, because the armistice talks between Israel and Jordan were already in progress in Rhodes; Israel had its eye not only on Abdullah as a future peace partner but on world opinion. However, the southern Negev with its Red Sea outlet at Eilat was not only very important to them—they felt entitled to it, because the original partition plan had allocated the region to Israel.

There were no Jewish troops in the southern Negev, only a few Legionnaires, and for this reason the British were claiming that the area should be considered "Jordanian-occupied territory." Israel's obvious move had to be to occupy it herself as conspicuously, but unbellicosely, as possible, hoping that Abdullah would cede the Negev as a quid pro quo for the West Bank. The world might then be expected to accept the fait accompli. On this (correct) premise, the aptly named Operation Fact was launched.

Meir Amit takes up the Eilat story:

☐ The climax of my career as a battalion commander was the conquest of Eilat. In early March we started preparations on what we called Operation Fact—going down to Akaba. Most of our people didn't know where we were going, though I did and so did a few other officers. The main problem was administration, because for us to venture to a depth of a hundred and twenty miles was an enormous challenge, with all the logistical problems—fuel, ammunition, food, and water; that was my main concern, not the fighting so much. We were experienced in fighting and I was not worried about that side of it.

The interesting thing was that for the first time I fell foul of political restrictions and constraints. Before we started to move in our "concentration area," from which we would start south, the chief of operations came to me and I had to sign—to *sign*—! He told me that I was not allowed to cross the international border. Now the route from the northern corner, where we started, down to Eilat ran parallel to the border, maybe twenty or thirty meters from it, and this officer said, "You are not allowed to go alongside the border." I had to sign that I had received this order.

And it was very strange, because after we went down about thirty kilometers we met some Jordanians. Naturally what you do in such a situation is to try to flank them, to bypass, but we couldn't, because on one side there were mountains and on the other was the border, and so we stopped. That was toward the end of the first day, and during the night I used all kinds of tricks, roaring around with half-tracks and so on, to scare them, and it worked, because by morning they had fled.

The journey down was nerve-racking. We were suspicious of everything! I remember we came to a wadi and we saw a cloud of dust in the distance, a few miles away, and we were sure it was some enemy forces flanking us. We had to stop, take up positions and so on—till we realized it was just a bit of a whirlwind! We were supposed to defend ourselves, not to attack if we could help it. The armistice talks were going on in Rhodes and we didn't want to get involved in any battles if it could be avoided. We got to Eilat in the late afternoon of the second day. Of course there had been a race between my battalion and another, of the Palmach. They came down from the Egyptian side, and they didn't pay any attention to the orders—they crossed the border when they felt like it—and got to Eilat about three hours before we did.

We arrived with the mass of armor and so on. There

was a feeling of having crossed a great distance—you must realize that at that time a march of one hundred and twenty miles across the desert was like two thousand miles would be to an army today.

The most thrilling feeling was when we got to Eilat, the "promised land," so to speak. The sun was setting, it was just dusk, and the granite mountains shone a burning red next to the deep blue sea .... There was nothing else there except a few huts. It was something virgin, something basic, almost primal. I named my daughter Eilat for that moment I experienced that evening.... We had the feeling that we had achieved perhaps the climax of the war, and I remember that the day we got there was, according to the Jewish calendar, the anniversary of the battle of Tel Hai when Trumpeldor was killed in 1920. We sent a telegram—which I composed—saying that the Negev and Golani brigades presented Eilat as a gift to the state of Israel. That telegram is famous, and it bears the stamp of my battalion.

Chaim Heffer, with his Chizbatron troupe, made the journey on the heels of the advance guard.

☐ I took a Russian melody— And on the day we liberated Eilat, I went down there in a command car, and on the way I wrote a song. When we got to Eilat, the song was ready. "A little bit south ... go a little bit south to Beersheba, and you feel the wind of the desert. And the regiment went down to the Arava.... A little bit south, you come to El Raumel ... But it's still far away from Eilat...." It went on like this, you know, mentioning place-names, speaking about the situation of the regiment, the tiredness, the thirst, and in the end it came with a burst: "And here is the beach of Eilat!"

Yigal Yadin:

☐ So we proceeded to conquer Eilat, meeting only one or two Jordanian companies commanded by British officers. And the Egyptians did not even protest. That paved the way to talks with Jordan, which also took place in Rhodes.

I did not take part directly in these. The main participants were Moshe Dayan, who was commander of Jerusalem at the time, and the chief of staff of Jordan. They came to a complete deadlock in Rhodes; there were very delicate problems—Jerusalem, the West Bank area, and so forth.

At that time, through our intelligence, which had intercepted messages, we were informed that the Iraqis were about to withdraw. They were holding the whole central front, from Ramallah just north of Jerusalem up to the valley of Jezreel and Jenin, while the Jordanians were north of Jerusalem and on the route to Eilat. The Iraqis had suffered heavy losses in the war; they informed the Jordanians they were going home, that they didn't want to sign an armistice (and in fact, they still haven't).*

When we heard that, we mobilized forces and demonstrated rather plainly that if the Iraqis were going we would enter that area, because we had never recognized the right of Abdullah to the West Bank.

When Abdullah heard the news and was informed that we knew about it too, he faced a terrible dilemma: either to be stubborn and refuse to give in at Rhodes or to give way to us, because he knew that potentially we had the capacity to conquer that whole area. So he gave us signals that he would like to have talks in Jordan, parallel to the talks going on in Rhodes.

It was decided that Walter Eytan and myself would go to the king's summer palace somewhere between the River Jordan and Amman. His commander of Jerusalem, Abdullah El Tel, who was supposedly his most loyal aide, though afterward he turned out to be quite a traitor toward the king, was supposed to take us every night through the Mandel-

*There is, of course, a topical reference here. The fact that the Iraqis are still officially in a state of war with Israel was one of the official justifications for the Israeli air raid on the Baghdad nuclear station in June 1981.

baum Gate on the border to the palace. We were to dress in mufti as United Nations observers, and his car had to reach the palace in Shuni at 7:30.

Every fifty meters for about two kilometers, from St. George's Cathedral down the Street of the Prophets, were roadblocks, and Jordanian soldiers would stop us, but our escort would say, "I am Abdullah Bey."* They saluted and let us go on, until, on that first occasion, we reached Jericho.

In the main center were thousands of Palestinians with guns, shouting. They stopped the car and asked, "Who are you?" "Abdullah Bey." "And who are these people?" "They are U.N. observers." They said, "We don't believe you! We want to check!" And Tel shouted to his driver, "Step on it!" He nearly crushed several of them but we got away.

We came to Abdullah's palace. It was very interesting—simple, but with lots of leopard and lion skins and so on. The king asked about the trip. When we told him about the incident, he was furious, and said to Tel: "How dare you do this to my guests! Do you know what would have happened if any harm had come to them? From now on, when you come here, my royal guard will go with you up to the border. I don't want to take any risks!"

First there were some preliminaries. The king brought all his cabinet, including the prime minister, and we spoke through an interpreter, though I spoke Arabic with the king. He began by making a long speech—about half an hour—talking, apparently to us, but actually he was speaking indirectly to the cabinet because it seems that his move was not popular with them.

He said he could be objective about the war. It was forced on him by the other Arab countries and kings. The British had betrayed him and sent him "shells filled with straw instead of gunpowder" (and all sorts of strange stories) and that's why his army was beaten. That, he said, was the way things were.

*"Bey" is an Arab title given to a leader.

"Unlike some of my cabinet," he said, "I am a true Arab, a Bedu, while some of *these* are from the cities. I still remember a Bedouin proverb my father told me. If you are running from your enemy on a horse which is loaded with all your possessions and you see that the distance between you and your pursuers is becoming shorter, you must decide, either to keep all your goods and be caught, or to throw packages away to let the horse run faster. I invited you gentlemen because, to tell you frankly, I have decided to throw away packages."

Then he turned to his prime minister, who wore a *tarboosh,* and said, "Now you tell our friends the whole of what I told you."

The prime minister stood up, coughed a little, and said, "Your Majesty, I would like you to release me. I am sick in my stomach."

The king looked at him for a few seconds and then said, *"Etla!"* which normally one says to a dog—"Scram!" Then he said very graciously, "Now we will adjourn for dinner."

We went to another room, full of lavish presents he had received from kings and notables, where dinner was laid out—a royal dinner, I must say. I sat on his left. I spoke Arabic well, and after some small talk he said, "My passion is pre-Islamic poetry." And then something providential happened.

At the university I had studied three subjects—archeology, Hebrew literature, and Arabic literature. For this last, we had a teacher we hated because he forced us to study a group of poems which were very difficult and we had to learn at least one by heart. And now, as the king spoke, I remembered it, and recited that one poem I had learned, about a mother lamenting the death of her son in battle. He stared at me in amazement and then embraced me. "What!— you know that one? That is my most beloved poem of all!" And that helped to break the ground.

I should mention that before I went I had told Ben-Gurion; "I won't be able to consult you on every point, so

I've prepared three lines on the map. The red line is the maximum boundary line; the green one is the minimum, and the blue in the middle!" The term *the Green Line* is still used and no one asks "Why the *green* line?"—it's not because we have more green plants there! But that green line was the last alternative. And Ben-Gurion gave me a free hand, more or less, not to go beyond the green line but between it and the blue.

Abdullah wanted to bring Glubb Pasha in on his behalf, but we objected, because later on it would be possible for them to say, "We didn't sign this—it was the British. We are not responsible." So instead he brought Crocker, Glubb's chief of staff, as an adviser on borders.

We began by trying the red line, but of course they said "No." Their minister of defense was in Lebanon at the time, and I said to the king, "I don't think we'll make progress without your minister of defense." So he sent Abdullah El Tel to go and get him. And we *didn't* make much progress, though the king came in every half hour, dressed in night attire, to ask what was happening. His ministers would say, "Don't worry, go to sleep, we shall achieve something eventually."

In fact, we didn't, and it was decided that we'd have to return another night. The king had given us, or rather, the State, a gift of a silver sword, and we knew we would have to bring a present in return. So on our next trip we brought with us the usual thing—a silver-bound Bible. Before the talks began I said to the king: "First I would like to return our respects. We have something which is dear to you and to us."

He opened it, and the first thing he saw on the inner binding was a map of Israel from the time of Solomon, which shows the borders extending from Iraq to Egypt! When I saw that, I thought I would faint. He looked at me and said, "What is this?" I said, "Your Majesty, it's a pity you can't read Hebrew. If you could, you would be as delighted as we. It's the Holy Land in the time of Suleiman,

who is our common ancestor, yours and ours." He kept
looking at me and I saw a twinkle in his eye, and then he said,
"Okay. Okay." But it was a very embarrassing moment.

The minister of defense arrived and we made some
progress. Eventually the king was ready to give us back the
Wadi Ara, which today is the link between the north and the
coast, then occupied by the Iraqis, and the small Triangle,
which faced Tel Aviv and which we thought was too near us.
I was sitting with the minister and Crocker and they were
marking a line very near to my green line. So I said to the
minister of defense, "Look, you are drawing a border by
which villages will be on your side and their land on our
side." The minister said: "The Arab world doesn't know
where lands are, they know *names*. We have to show them
that the villages are in our part. Whether the land will be in
your part doesn't matter a damn to us." That's why a lot of
villages remained on the other side of the border and the
land on Israel's side. It has been the cause of a lot of trouble
to the present day, because the villagers were cut off from
their land just so that the Jordanians would not have "given
a name" to us.

When it was all agreed, on the last evening, we insisted
that the agreement be typed in English as well as Arabic, so
they sent to Amman to bring an English typewriter. Meanwhile, the king's adjutant, a captain who had graduated at
the British staff college in Haifa, said: "You know, the king
has sacrificed quite a lot, in fact his own reputation perhaps;
but there is a small gesture you could make. Tomorrow is his
birthday, and he would very much like you to give him—in
exchange for what he gave you—a village in the south called
Bet Jubrin. It's famous in Arab history as the site of a great
victory of Salah-al-Din over the Crusaders. If you gave him
that he would be very happy."

I said, "Are you crazy? I came here to take back what
does not belong to you, and I have already given way by not
insisting that all the West Bank should be ours. I can't give

anything—I'm not a king! You must understand." "Oh, all right," he said.

The king kept looking in, and at about three in the morning we told him that we had reached agreement. I was a lot younger then, and he was already an old man, but he embraced me in front of everyone and said, "Ya Yadin, Ya Yadin, give me Bet Jubrin!" It was the most embarrassing moment of my life. A king, a wise and respected king, in front of all those people, asking me like a beggar. I said, in Arabic, "You are a king. Who am I but a dog? I cannot give you anything. If I do, I'll be thrown out. I wish I could." He said, "I understand. I thought perhaps you could."

Then we all signed the agreement.

The next day we all went back to Rhodes where they had been arguing for days over a certain hill. Dr. Bunche was amazed at our agreement and map. That was the preliminary to the actual peace talks in which I did not participate. Later on, the king was murdered, and I think the whole course of history could have been different if he had been saved.

Then came armistice talks with Lebanon, then the Syrians who were the most stubborn of all, as today. The talks dragged on for months and months, with our side headed by Mordechai Maklef, afterward my successor as chief of staff.

Eventually it was signed, with a lot of demilitarized areas in the north, which remained for many years a cause of friction. Sir John Glubb adds a postscript to these negotiations:

☐ I think this was one of the great mistakes the Israelis made. After the fighting, Abdullah was prepared to talk. He confided this to me, just talking you know, and I remember his saying, "Now this is going against the Arab world, I shall be terribly unpopular." He must have said to the Jews, "If I'm going to talk business with you, you'll have to give me something, so that I can show the Arab world and say,

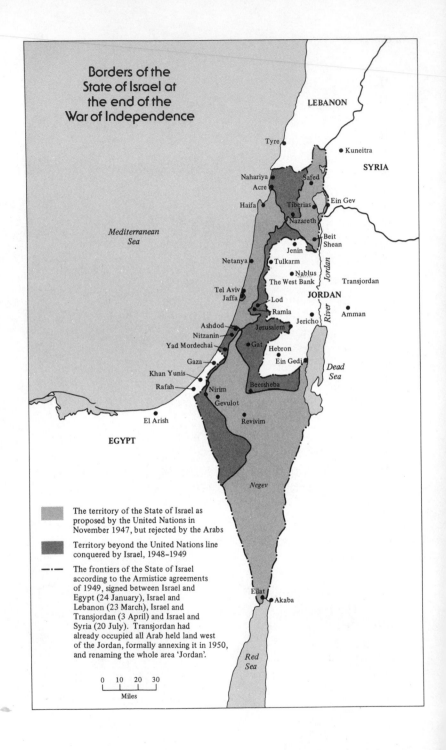

Borders of the
State of Israel at
the end of the
War of Independence

LEBANON

SYRIA

● Kuneitra

Mediterranean Sea

Tyre ●

Nahariya ●
Acre ●
Haifa ●

Safed ●

Tiberias ●
Nazareth ●

● Ein Gev

Netanya ●

Jenin ●

● Beit Shean

Tel Aviv ●
Jaffa ●

Tulkarm ●

● Nablus
The West Bank

Jordan River

Transjordan

JORDAN

Ashdod ●
Nitzanin ●
Yad Mordechai ●

Lod ●
Ramla ●

Jerusalem ●

Jericho ●

River

● Amman

Gat ●

Hebron ●

Gaza ●
Khan Yunis ●
Rafah ●

Nirim ●
Gevulot ●

Ein Gedi ●

Dead Sea

Beersheba ●

El Arish ●

Revivim ●

EGYPT

Negev

The territory of the State of Israel as proposed by the United Nations in November 1947, but rejected by the Arabs

Territory beyond the United Nations line conquered by Israel, 1948–1949

—·— The frontiers of the State of Israel according to the Armistice agreements of 1949, signed between Israel and Egypt (24 January), Israel and Lebanon (23 March), Israel and Transjordan (3 April) and Israel and Syria (20 July). Transjordan had already occupied all Arab held land west of the Jordan, formally annexing it in 1950, and renaming the whole area 'Jordan'.

Eilat ●
● Akaba

Red Sea

0   10   20   30
Miles

'Look, it's far better to negotiate—I've recovered this and this, you see!'"

But the Israelis said, "No concessions. Take it or leave it." But then, I don't think the Israelis wanted a settlement really. At the end of the war, the Jordanians were holding in Latrun, and up north in Kalkilia and Tulkarem, and also we'd nipped around and got Hebron and so on, and the Israeli army was not prepared to accept that. They didn't want it to settle down; they wanted to keep the whole situation open until some suitable international situation arose which would enable them to attack. Meanwhile, they'd build up more and more money and weapons and so on. So that even if Abdullah had made a treaty with them, I think Israel would have found some opportunity break it, because the Israeli army was not satisfied with that boundary.

In the Six-Day War, of course, Nasser handed them everything on a plate. I got the sack, mind you, for saying to Hussein, "For heaven's sake, don't ever fight Israel again!" And when I said that, the king got up and said, "I shall never surrender an inch of my territory, and if you advise me to . . . ." A month later, I was sacked. Of course, he was a very young boy. What did you or I know at nineteen? I don't want to speak against him. Nasser had done everything he possibly could to betray Hussein, but still Hussein had a generous emotional response. He said, "I can't allow these fellow Muslims to be wiped off the face of the earth." Silly, from the point of view of strategy— I did warn him.

But, of course, after '48 the Jordan army was rather cock-a-hoop. Everybody else had been driven off the field, but we had held our ground and even captured a few bits, though nothing from the area of the Jewish state. But they hadn't quite realized—and this was what I was trying to bang into Hussein—that the Israelis had unlimited money, compared to Jordan. Their military budget was, I think, twelve times ours, and you can't go on like this for years and years and keep on equal terms. Of course Hussein made a mistake, coming in on the side of Nasser. But I can't help feeling that in any case, sooner or later, the Jews would have made a pretext to get the Jordanians out of Palestine.

Would they? Well, it is an academic question now, and assuredly no Israeli leader, past or present, could be found who would admit retrospectively to such an intention. The fact remains that the armistice agreements did not lead to peace. The armistice lines gave rise to infiltration, which led to sabotage and terrorism, which provoked counter-terror raids by Israeli commandos, which in turn exacerbated the border situation until it exploded, first in the 1956 Sinai campaign and then the 1967 June war.

Though, of course, this, too, is an oversimplification. Many Israelis deny that the armistice lines, which in some cases excluded villagers from their land, were anything more than an irritant to a situation that carried the seeds of its own violent readjustment sooner or later.

Part 4
Reflections

Arabs and Jews

The attitudes of Jews and Arabs toward each other—their deepest feelings, prejudices, and responses—are obviously of the greatest relevance, not only to that first war but to all that has followed it. Several of those interviewed brought out such feelings, subjective and objective, personal and political and military.

Avraham Yoffe, who was born in the northern part of the country and grew up surrounded by Arabs, is currently at the center of a controversy concerning the so-called Green Patrols, for which, as head of the Nature Reserve Authority, he is responsible. The Green Patrols, whose job is to prevent the Bedouin of the northern Negev from allowing their herds to stray onto Jewish land, have been accused of bullying and worse; but Yoffe is unrepentant. His views on Arabs are interesting. He mentioned in the interview with me that from his childhood he had had "a bad feeling" about Arabs, having always heard that they were cruel, that they robbed and killed the Jews, and so on. Yet according to his own account, his treatment of them during the War of Independence was pragmatic but fair and even friendly. His acknowledgment of his negative early conditioning toward Arabs, taken

337

together with his war record and his present attitude, is just one of many examples of the complexity of relations and personal feelings.

Yoram Kaniuk, the writer, who is regarded by many as a "dove," had some of the harshest things to say about his enemies of '48:

☐   Whoever I killed, I feel bad about it. But what could I do? And then, I saw a lot of very terrible things. The heads of my friends on sticks, friends who'd been tortured to death. In the battle of Nebi Samwil, they took bodies and cut off the heads and stuck them up on sticks—you know, over the tops of hills, so we could see the heads of our dead friends.

It was a very cruel war in '48, not much "protocol," or rules, or that sort of thing. I am a liberal in many ways, but one has to be honest about one thing: The Arabs are very cruel fighters. You could see it in Lebanon, during the civil war there, and in Iran. In Tel Zatar, in Lebanon, hundreds of mutilated bodies were found, penises in the mouth, eyes plucked out, things like that. When they get into a frenzy, they are much more cruel than we are.

In our case, cruelty is an exception to the rule. I have seen, not cruelty on our part, but unjustified killing; but it was always opposed by the majority. I've seen hatred of Arabs by Jews, but I've never seen it turn into lynching or mutilating. I don't think we ever did anything in cold blood.

Netiva Ben Yehuda, who has a very clear eye for breaches of the "rules of war" on both sides, witnessed many examples of savagery on the battlefield:

☐   It was a terrible shock for me, the first time I saw what some Arabs will do to a dead enemy. But after the first time I was never shocked, any more than by mutilation by a mine or a gun—after death, it doesn't matter. It's the Orthodox, who are even against postmortems, who of course react strongly to it.

It's not an easy thing to do, to mutilate. Not all the Arabs do it; we used to say it was only certain tribes, in certain areas, who ever did. They have to be taught to do it; it is done as a prolongation of the fight, to hurt us. They have a kind of ritual—the same way always. It's part of a culture. It does them good, satisfies their feelings—continues the war.

But is this the one thing we can say that "only the Arabs do it"? I can think of much worse! "Only the Arabs" send up bombs in airplanes to kill all sorts of people on board. And take Kaddafi now—all the Libyans who leave must be killed! "Only Arabs do it!" And there are people here, now, who are looking for flaws in their genes. They point out that they were pirates, that they were slave traders. Maybe. So what? Do you know how many crimes Jews committed when they came from Egypt to Israel three thousand years ago?

Cruelty, mutilation—this is not a point in which we should claim superiority. I don't feel superior to anyone in the world. It is quite a mistake to argue that the Arabs, on the whole, are more savage and barbarous than the Jews. Maybe in '48 there were more cruel Arabs than Jews—so what? Maybe in '43 there were more cruel Germans than Jews, and *maybe* in 1980 there are more cruel Jews than Germans. Maybe at a given time, in a given situation, any people can be cruel. And if the reasons for wars were removed, the cruelty would stop.

Remember when there was all the discussion with Sadat about peace, one of the provisions of the peace treaty was that we should allow the Egyptians to build monuments for their dead on our land. Moshe Shamir [a well-known novelist, once a left-winger and now an extreme right-wing member of the Knesset] lost control in the Knesset. "You are a traitor!" he shouted at Begin. "You agreed to give those murderers a piece of our holy ground to build their stinking monument to their stinking soldiers?" I saw it—a direct broadcast from the Knesset. And I felt I wanted to kill him. Uri Avneri shouted at him, "You ask soldiers who were in the battle if they agree! Soldiers on the battlefield will agree to give a place for a monument to any soldiers in the world!"

The dead are the same, ours and theirs. It is just a dead human being. If you want *not* to think so, you have to convince yourself. The natural way of thinking is, it is the same for us as for them: The leaders quarrel and the soldiers pay the price.

An illustration of cruelty of a different kind is given by Yousuf Yaacub, an Arab villager from the north of Israel who now lives with his family in Haifa. I am presenting his story at length at this point because it covers the whole period of the war and beyond and gives a different slant to the picture of Arab-Jewish relations.

☐   In November '47 I was in my village of Kfar Baram on the Lebanese border. It was a small place, about fifteen hundred people. Olives, corn, figs, and tobacco were our crops. I was eighteen at the time.

When we learned that an Israeli state was going to be established, we were quite glad. We were Maronite Christians, so we were a minority among the Muslims of the north. We were always under pressure. We had a lot in common with the Jews of Safed: They were a minority, like us, and we used to meet as brothers.

As soon as partition was declared, all the trouble started, with Muslim Arabs attacking the Jews. Our village played no part—we stayed neutral. But we witnessed parts of the struggle.

An inter-Arab force from Syria, under Kawukji, came to the northern area and encamped near us. Some of Kawukji's soldiers came and asked the village leaders to recruit young men to take defensive action against the Jews, who, they told us, had come to conquer the country. All the young men ran away and hid in the hills because they didn't want to serve under Kawukji.

Then he wanted to take our village by force and use it as a base. We went to the Ministry of Defense in Lebanon, which was administered by Christians then, and told them Kawukji was imposing his will on us and we needed help. But what we were really waiting for in our village was the coming of the Jews. We thought of them as saviors who would help us in this bad situation.

Most of our neighbors had run away up north to Lebanon and other Arab countries; only we of Kfar Baram and another village, called Ikrit, stayed. We had confidence in the Jews and felt sure we would be quite safe.

When the Israeli army came, we were good hosts to them. We opened our doors and we fed them. At first they treated us well, and good relations continued. Then, after fifteen days, an officer came and told us, "You must evacuate your village in forty-eight hours." We supposed there was some security reason, though he didn't explain, and so we left and went to Me'esh, a village in southern Lebanon.

We stayed in this village for over two weeks. The war was over; the armistice talks were going on in Rhodes. Then a message arrived from the Israeli side which said: "You made a mistake. We didn't ask you to cross the border, but to stay on this side."

So we came back and were given houses in an Arab village in Israel called Gush Khalav, or Jish. The village consisted of two sectors, Muslim and Christian. The Muslims had all run away to Arab countries, and we were put into their houses, which were such that donkeys would be ashamed to live in them. The Christians did not have much contact with us because we lived at a little distance, and anyway they looked down on us because we were refugees.

We were told it was only for the time being, until the Israeli soldiers passed by, and then, we were told, we could go back to our village. They never told us why they needed it.

All our possessions had been left behind in Me'esh. The Israelis had said, "Leave everything there, and when you are permitted to go back to your village you can return to Me'esh and collect them." So we had almost nothing.

For five months our village stood empty—it was not

being used by the Jews. We were always in contact with the military supervisor and there was even a court case. Ben-Gurion was prime minister and he sent us a letter saying that the government never thought of snatching our lands from us. President Chaim Weizmann sent a letter to our bishop in Lebanon saying that we must get our lands back. We still have copies of these letters.

The decision of the high court was that we must go back to our land. And after that decision was taken—which was not until Christmas 1956—the Israeli army came with tanks and airplanes to our village and destroyed it.

Gush Khalav stands on one hill and Baram on another, only two kilometers away. When they bombed our village, we watched it. Women started wailing and crying.... Soon afterward the kibbutz which is called Baram after our village was founded near there, and now those kibbutzniks farm our land.

For thirty years we have been promised we would go back. We have never given up hope. We regard those kib-butzniks as our brothers. They farm part of our land, but we deserve part of it, too. Many parties have supported us. We feel that 90 percent of the educated, intelligent Jews do too. In the son of Ze'ev Jabotinsky we had a champion—he fought our cause in the Knesset. But then he died. And it always seems to be another group which controls things.

In all the wars since the first, our villagers have been loyal to the State of Israel. There has never been a spy or a terrorist among us. Some of our people have joined the border police and even the army.

Before becoming prime minister, Begin promised that we should go back, but he has done no more than Golda Meir did. Her excuse was always "military reasons, security reasons," because our village is right near the border. But now that Israel has influence on the other side, in Lebanon, it has become clear that it has nothing to do with security. Now we are asking ourselves, why is this one village closed in our faces? Why?

Of course, the problem of the status of Israeli Arabs, and the delicate question of the justice of such situation as Yousef Yaacub describes, cannot be divorced from the whole ongoing balance of hostility between Arab and Jew in the region. Meir Pa'il, who witnessed the Deir Yassin massacre, tries to view the dilemma objectively:

☐ Palestinian nationalism is not the result of the refugee problem. Even if there had been no refugees, nothing would be changed in terms of peace. There would still not be any. Palestinian nationalism was viable in the early twenties too, without any refugees. The mufti was elected and happened to be the most fanatical and radical leader of the Palestinian cause, many many years before any refugees existed.

Every national movement must be mature enough to take responsibility for its behavior, including us, now. That is my belief. We happened to occupy the West Bank and the Gaza Strip in the Six-Day War. Because of our victories in that war, we became custodians of many Palestinians. We are pregnant now with the Palestinian problem, from 1967. So we must behave like a pregnant human being. We occupied those territories, those people are living under our sovereignty—we can't just, as it were, register the effects of morning sickness and ignore the real problem. We must find a solution to it, by evacuating the territories and enabling the Palestinians, for God's sake, to establish some kind of national independence side by side with us and to find an outlet for themselves.

By the same token, I think the Palestinian leadership must understand and take responsibility for their behavior in 1948. They cannot say, "We are wretched, and because we are wretched that makes our cause right." I say: "In 1948 you were on the wrong side, morally and militarily. You lost the war; you must be grown up now and take responsibility for that. You should say, "Okay, we have rights to come back to Jaffa and Haifa and Lydda and Ramle and Ashkelon, but we won't, because we lost them in the War of Indepen-

dence." Then the Jews should say, "We have our rights to
Nablus and East Jerusalem and Hebron and Bethlehem and
Jenin and the Jordan valley, but we are ready to concede, to
pull out, to let them establish their right to self-determination
there." And that's it.

On a more subjective level, those who are not public figures
but private individuals believe that it is possible for Arabs and
Jews to coexist on some better basis than at present. Rika Meidav, who fought in the Old City and organized the children there,
has tried it:

☐   I was in Jerusalem before the war.... I came there in '46
    from the Belgian Congo and I was there with the English
    before the mandate ended. I saw that Jews and Arabs can
    live together. The main problems are nothing to do with
    Arabs and Jews—they are outside problems more than any-
    thing else. If the outside powers would live and let live—
    allow the Arab and Jewish peoples in Israel to try to find
    themselves—they could do it. I see how much we are all
    Semites. We are not Europeans. We could understand each
    other if only we were left alone.

Rivca Weingarten, the *mukhtar*'s daughter, is at great
pains to stress how good relations were in the Old City in her
father's time and illustrates the residue of goodwill with a story of
her return after the Israelis recaptured her quarter in June 1967:

☐   My father, as head of the Jewish community, had organized
    a few institutions in the Jewish quarter to help residents. For
    instance, there was a clinic which gave free medical aid to
    every resident of the quarter, which of course included
    Christians, Muslims, and Armenians.
        When we came into the Old City after the Six-Day War,
    I saw an old Arab coming toward me. He kissed my hands
    and cried, "It's the daughter of the *mukhtar*! But for her
    father, I wouldn't be alive today!" What did he mean? I will
    tell you.

When the siege started, the non-Jewish residents had the same difficulties leaving the Old City as we did: No convoys were reaching the quarter and we had to make the best of everything we had. When bread was distributed to the Jews, my father took it upon himself to declare that every person who was here would get the same portion of bread or milk or whatever we had. And when a bomb fell on our house and we moved farther into the quarter, my father took this Muslim and his family and an Armenian family who were also our neighbors with us, and we all lived together until the surrender.

When I returned in '67 I saw that nothing had changed since '48—the same destruction, the same rubble and stench and dirt—it was terrible. And when I came to our house, where we had lived for five generations, I found that part of it still existed, and I decided immediately that I would move back into it and use part of it as a museum, which would be a reminder of the life of the Jewish community in the past.

There are Arabs too who remember times when there was not the segregation and hostility that exists today. Anwar Nusseibah:

☐ We had business and social relationships with Jews. We were sharing the same country! In times of crisis we would stop meeting, to save embarrassment, but during normal times we would drift back together, talk . . . . Some of them I liked very much, and I don't think they disliked me. One never thought—at least, I never did—this is a Jew. I should wish to fight or kill him. Such an idea was crazy.

We saw no reason why we shouldn't live side by side together in the same country. But an *Arab* country. That was how we viewed it. But the Jews didn't want that. They wanted a Jewish state, in which the Arabs would have no part to play at all. In their Declaration of Independence they said something else, but to what extent they were able to fulfill those intentions is something that can be judged only in the light of what they did afterward.

The situation is complex, but I don't think that ignoring the Palestinian situation, suppressing their hopes and disregarding their rights by force of arms is going to bring justice and peace. I am still hopeful that, by means of understanding and reconciliation, not by war, a formula will be found whereby our two peoples can live side by side in peace.

Ephraim Shorer has an insight into the Arabs' profound humiliation at their defeat:

☐   In the past the Arabs were one of the greatest powers in history, culturally and otherwise. But they lost it. This is not the time or place to try to analyze why the Muslim and Arab world lost out to the West in every field, economic, philosophical, and cultural; but despite all that, they still saw themselves as great warriors.

And they looked upon the Jews as underdogs, people who didn't carry arms and were therefore not real men. For the Arabs, the one with the big mustache who carried a gun—he's a man. They had that image of themselves. To be beaten by the Jews of all people was therefore a great blow.

In our optimism, we thought that this was the war to end wars in this area, that after it we would find peace. We didn't believe the Arab world would never forgive us for existing, for trying to find a little corner for ourselves. We were attacked as "foreign invaders".... We were naïve not to realize how ferociously they hated us.

Chaim Guri, poet and film director, who loves Jerusalem not least because Jews and Arabs share it, makes this philosophical point:

☐   All the flags and all the wars and all the great slogans— everything becomes very tiny and insignificant compared to the tragedy of a mother losing her son. It doesn't really matter that Sisera is an enemy; it doesn't change a bit the burden that his mother has to carry.

Logic says, This is the enemy, and one must fight. We are justified in our fight, in our wars; we have a right. That first war was a war of survival, not of conquest. But there's the other side, which is always pushed away because it's not nice to think about, but it is always somewhere in the background and it never lets me rest. The problem of the "other side" is the human problem.

I was born in Tel Aviv, near Jaffa—an Arab town then. It is part of my childhood memories. We lived together, between the historical and political dimensions, and that other—the human dimension—of one person confronting another. And it keeps repeating itself. It was like this when I was a child in Jaffa when we lived with the Arabs. Now I live in Jerusalem, it's the same: We know the people here, and we love the sounds and smells and tastes of things in the Old City. I have Arab friends and, really, there is a kind of comradeship, a closeness of tastes, despite the conflict that always exists between us.

There are those in Israel who hate everything to do with the Arabs. They haven't the slightest idea of what people like us see to like in the Arabs. But for many who live here in Jerusalem and are in everyday contact with them, there are many things we love in their way of life. It's an Oriental way, after all, and we are Orientals, too. When we go outside Jerusalem into the hills, we feel at home, because the view is meaningful to us. And this must be a link between us and them.

The Role of Women

The active participation of women in the fighting forces in the War of Independence was greater than in any subsequent Arab-Israeli war, and yet it was not so great as many outside Israel still seem to believe. Such actual fighting as women did was largely confined to the prewar phase, and even then there was no parity in numbers of fighters, still less of officers, with men. Later, as the armed forces were reshaped along more conventional lines, they were phased out of the front-line troops for a variety of reasons including those that follow.

Their auxiliary roles as nurses, drivers, radio operators, and—no less important—as comrades made a vital contribution to the total war effort and to the morale of the male soldiers. Shimon Avidan, the southern front commander, could not over-praise their influence:

☐　Twenty percent of our formation were girls. In the beginning they participated in the fighting. But Arab soldiers were less gentlemanly than Glubb Pasha, so we decided to take them out of the front-line positions and use them only in the services. We saw what the Arabs did to the boys. It was enough. We didn't want any wounded girl—or any girl—to fall into their hands. That was the only reason.

But what I learned was, first of all, that a girl was able to endure more than a boy, to suffer without being a crybaby. And their influence within the formation was so total that I think they often had the key to victory in their hands simply because they were there. And they brought to the men such gentling things as some flowers, a clean shirt, a nice word. They looked upon themselves as equal comrades in the "family." Their influence was very strong.

The man I have called "Boaz," who fought throughout the war with the Har El Brigade after being selected for army service by his kibbutz, had a profound empathy for the girls he encountered in and around the battlefields:

☐　Some of the girls went into battle with the boys, but chiefly as field nurses, a job just as dangerous as any. It must have been horrifying for them to have to treat those awful wounds on the young bodies of their friends. Those who had to stay behind, doing other chores around the camp, would come rushing along whenever the boys returned from battle, to see who was safe and who had not come back. This agonizing apprehension, night after night, must have had a searing effect on girls scarcely out of childhood.

Gabriel Cohen, the historian, does not believe women fought because they wanted to or were suited to it.

☐ The women took great risks. My wife, for instance, took part in defending the convoys in Galilee. But you know, I don't think the girls were eager, let's say, to take part in battles in the field. I can show you letters and articles by girls who were rather disorientated at this period—girls of the Palmach—because on the one hand they felt they should participate in every aspect of the war; they also knew they ought not to go into battle, but some of them were frustrated because they thought they were not sharing in what the boys did.

Netiva Ben Yehuda, the demolitions officer who did fight in many engagements and proved herself as brave and tough as any man, sees the problem from many angles and has recently published a novel, *Between Calendars,* about her experiences:

☐ "Suffragism" was written on the flag of our political movement, Achdut Ha'avodah; socialism went together with the idea of equality for women. And those from our youth movement who were heading for kibbutz life were in favor of equal rights, and equal duties, for women.

But then in the middle of the war, people started to enlist who were not trained in the youth movement—people from urban and suburban backgrounds, *bourgeoisie* who had no mental preparation—and they didn't like to have a woman commander.

When the war started there were around twenty women officers, three or four captains and the rest lieutenants or sergeants. Even at that time I, as a woman officer, had to prove myself more than a male. This burden was terrible. Of course, every new officer has to prove himself, to get control of the men; it's not enough that you've been given the assignment—you have to gain their respect. The men succeeded in doing this very easily compared with us. We had a very hard job proving ourselves.

Every one of us had a few tricks up her sleeve. For instance, I was an athlete. I was very strong. I used to throw the hand grenades farther than any untrained man could—I was due to go to the Olympics that year in London as a shot-putter, and believe me Israel never came nearer to getting a gold medal!—that was before the Russians participated. But still, because it was not the custom, and because of the usual sneers about women, when I got my own platoon I had a very hard time.

But you know, there's another reason why a woman should not be in battle. She has all kinds of calculations which are not purely military. For instance, if I happened to say, "Are you sure this is the right thing?" the officer would turn on me. "Are you *khosheshet?* [doubtful]"—insinuating that I asked the question because I was frightened. Maybe my doubts are right, but if I hear *khosheshet* I'll climb Mount Everest with a heart attack and I'll manage. I saw women do it—I've done it.

Another aspect of women fighting is what the Arabs think about it. If the leaders didn't spur them on enough, there's no reason to incite them more! You have to reduce their power to fight, not increase it, and if they see a woman, you can't imagine what they do! They go mad to capture her.

I never made a distinction between myself as a woman soldier and men soldiers; but a distinction was made by others who thought of me as a woman. I myself never thought that modern women have to be kept out of things as if they were old or children. A woman is part of the hatred and she is part of the game of the war—why shouldn't she be killed? And if she were wounded—if she were to lose her ability to give birth—that is not so bad as it is for man to lose his potency by a wound. There is no comparison.

One woman, "Hava," now an author and a teacher of English at a seminary, had precisely the opposite experience to Netiva Ben Yehuda's. She had recently married in her native country and immigrated to Israel, where she was "parked" by her husband in a fairly safe location while he went off to fight. Though several men I spoke to declared that this was a war in which every citizen participated, "Hava's" story indicates that this was not so, and that some of those who were "left out" resented it:

☐   I can't believe today that I lived through that war with such a degree of nonparticipation. Today I am completely involved, constantly aware of what is going on in the country—my whole existence is based on this awareness. But in those days I was only aware of myself—my marriage, my pregnancy, the new language; having my baby; becoming a teacher—in general, adjusting to my immigration. I was completely absorbed in this tiny little individual life. Because of this, my war story is a nonstory. The storms raging just outside the windows of my life were wisps of wind.

My husband was away most of the time. He was a trained pilot. To this day I don't know exactly what he was doing, but I gathered later that he was a hero. When he came home, he was morose and never told me a thing. I only half knew he was in on the beginnings of the Israel air force. After the British left, he was one of their first pilots and must have taken part in many actions about which he told me nothing. To men friends he would talk incessantly, but he never involved me or shared anything with me.

If you didn't have an actual part to play, you remained an outsider. Looking back, this gives me a sense of unreality. I was so taken up with my feminine concerns—our little house in the mountains, the first in its neighborhood, where I was so lonely. I moved to Ramat Gan to be nearer my husband, who was stationed at Lydda. My sole preoccupation at one stage was finding things to eat. My baby was unhealthily fat; I spent most of my time trying to scrounge food for her, while I lived on macaroni, the only thing that was off the ration and cheap enough to buy. I didn't even have coupons, because we'd moved.

My husband never tried to find out how I coped. I was too proud to complain or ask his help. It's odd how blind he was to my needs. We shared a house with a Polish woman. I used to watch her, incredulously. She was a marvelous cook and a marvelous coper. She must have seen I had nothing, but she didn't offer to help. Her children were thriving.

I remember we had one air raid. That meant lying under the bed, on top of the baby, because the only shelter was too far away. There were some bangs, but I wasn't frightened. I think I was too low in vitality to feel much of anything.

Looking back, I think that if I'd had a better relationship with my husband he would have enabled me to participate more, even if only indirectly. For a young woman who has no direct involvement in the war, it's only through a meaningful relationship with a participating man that she can become committed and involved. I feel, in a way, that I was cheated of an important experience through this failure to become involved. I missed something I should have had.

For the young girls who were participating, it was a strange time, by no means devoid of excitement, pleasure, and romance. Talila Ben Zakai, now a newspaper columnist, remembers it as a time for love as well as battles:

☐   We were cut off from our normal environment. We were not at school or at work or at home—we were thrown together. There was danger. There was excitement. It was like being on another planet, it was so different—something vibrated there. And it led to a lot of lovemaking.

First of all, there were fewer girls than men. The girls were following their boyfriends. Jerusalem was so small and cut off. The girls would run to the boys, to be with them, to stay with them, even while the war was at its height. There were no camps. We stayed in old houses in Sheikh Jerach or flats in Yemin Moshe. The atmosphere was tremendously emotional. We didn't want to miss any of it—it was so exciting. It was even fun. We were "high"—maybe because we had to keep ourselves high to defy death, to defy hunger . . . the very air seemed to make us drunk.

I don't remember being scared except when I was at home. Sometimes I would leave Yemin Moshe and go home to Rehavia, and then, when I heard the shells whistling over, I'd get scared. So I'd pick up my things and run back to the others. With them I had a feeling of confidence, of togetherness, the feeling that something was being done.

I don't remember the war as a time of fear or horror. Sorrow, yes—deep sorrow when people we knew died. Not that we realized yet what death was. You'd hear someone had been killed but you couldn't realize it, there was no time to realize that that person had really disappeared forever. I don't say it was a beautiful time that we want back again, but there was an atmosphere of people living together. We had parties and singing—we would sit all night through, making coffee, talking, singing . . . and making love.

Yehuda Amichai, the poet, also found time for love:

☐   I wasn't a poet at that time. I felt a lot of things, but it didn't come to my mind to write; all the poems about battles and things were only written later. But I would say that at least 50 percent of what I have written had its roots in that war. It triggered off my writing. The first two main events of my life were the war and love. Strange as it sounds— In America they have the slogan "Make love not war" and in the Book of Ecclesiastes you have the part about "A time for war and a time for peace, a time for love and a time for hate"; but you can't divide them. Sometimes you have to do everything at once . . . .

I had my first love together with my first war, so I would say these two antitheses of my life made me write. And thank heavens I have had more loves than wars.

Rationale and Realpolitik

Reflections on how the war was conducted and on the conditions that dictated underlying attitudes, which emerged almost incidentally in a number of interviews, provide illuminating sidelights on the war.

Malca Tarragan, who watched with such an objective eye the slow, creeping defeat that started in the streets of the Old City, had some questions to ask afterward:

☐   The Government of Israel had a program at the beginning of the war to hold on to every part where Jews were living. But Jerusalem is a holy place of all religions. The four foreign governments most closely concerned—Britian, France, Russia, and America—said to the Jews: "Don't worry about Jerusalem. It is to be an open city. Between us, we will take care of it."

How do I know? After the war we met all the officers who had been concerned with Jerusalem, and we asked Yigal Yadin, "Why were there so many mistakes made in the Old City?" And he told us: "Ben-Gurion didn't put a very high priority on defending it. It was a holy place and was to be an open city. The foreign governments would make a peace...." In other words, Ben-Gurion said that the problem of the Old City would be decided later. It was more important to him to get hold of the Negev, where there was space for settlements.* The emphasis in that war was on the

*This is the precise opposite of what is usually believed—that Ben-Gurion had to be persuaded to put the Negev before Jerusalem on his list of priorities.

whole country and not on the Old City; that was why there was no order between the forces in the army—everyone did his own thing here. There was no cooperation because B.-G. thought it was not necessary to take the Old City back. Not then. It could wait. It's true we got it back twenty years later, but even then, in the Six-Day War, we had no plan to take the Old City—we only got it because Hussein made a mistake and opened a front with us.

Dan Bitan, the director of the Department for Gifted Children, who is also a student of his country's history (he is currently studying comparisons of the present situation between Jews and Arabs and the situation in Ireland), has come to a somewhat similar conclusion about the realpolitik underlying the war strategy; he also comments on the special nature of that war:

☐   Wars in Israel have always held a kind of excitement. But the War of Independence was more of a people's war than the others, because it was the only war in which most of the country and most of the people were involved, and from this point of view it was a unique national experience. Even as a child I can say that I participated.

   In some ways it's a good thing for the citizens of a country to be involved in a war, though I must qualify that, since, of course, where they are involved they are also liable to be killed. But people ought to understand the price of victory or of any national goal which has to be fought for. Policies of peace and war can only be judged by the people of a nation if they know what war is, what is involved in it; for that, they must have seen it for themselves.

   Of course, the War of Independence was not like the European wars or even like our later wars, because it was essentially a war of small units. Then, too, it was conducted by "half-soldiers" or "nonsoldiers"—a group of middle-aged Yecces [German-born Israelis] defending the Old City or marching on Katamon—a most unmilitary war! From certain points of view, it hardly looks like a war at all. Though I still have a sense that it was the most important moment in

Jewish history, by a paradox it was in practice a very small business.

And it was not so simple, either. Now I've studied it, I've learned that things which looked simple for years, which created their own legends, were in reality much more complex. The true history of that war is not yet written. In ten or fifteen years, we shall know more. There are questions that have not been answered. What we do know is that each Arab country had more than one objective.

We Jews believed, and are still taught, that we faced five Arab armies, single-mindedly bent on exterminating us, but each of those armies was intent also on outdoing one or more of the others. In a sense, Egypt was opposing Jordan, and Jordan, Syria, and so on. Why didn't the Arab Legion, or other Arab forces, make a more determined effort to capture Jerusalem? Maybe they couldn't. Maybe it's true that Glubb was deluded about the number and strength of our defenders and didn't want to risk his soldiers in Jerusalem's streets, as he said.* But at one point the Egyptians were somewhere near Beit Shemesh, the Jordanians were sitting in Latrun, and there was a corridor left empty between them. Why? Why didn't they join forces? Was there some collusion?

One of the legends is that we prepared ourselves for war, but we didn't. Our leaders made some kind of promise to the Americans, that if the local Arabs attacked us, we could very quickly manage to beat them. But again, we didn't—up till March we were in a very bad situation, which was why the U.S. began to reconsider the feasibility of partition.

When did people begin to prepare Jerusalem for siege? In '47 when B.-G. knew a war was on the way, why didn't he do more to prepare for it? Maybe the real reason was that B.-G. knew that Jerusalem was not in any real danger.

Supposing he made a deal like this with Abdullah: The Israelis wouldn't try to recapture the Old City in July if

*He did not say this to me.

Abdullah and the Legion wouldn't try too hard to get the New City.

B.-G.'s place in history is assured, but there are questions. Nonreligious people might think he was quite justified if he *was* in collusion with Abdullah, with whom he was anxious to make peace when things settled down. But, of course, religious Jews would think it unspeakable to give up the Western Wall and the Jewish quarter on any account. I'm not suggesting, of course, that every effort wasn't made at the time the Old City was lost to hang on to it.

In any case, it was the last war in which a citizen army went out almost consciously to destroy the stereotype of the Jew without muscles, the Jew unfit to bear arms. We were raised on a new stereotype, that of the tough, heroic, undefeatable Jew. But this, too, is a sort of myth, one which may suffer if historians one day prove that it was not, in that very special war, a case of "the few against the many"—that we were superior in manpower—or that politically it was much more complicated than a lot of us realize.

And we shouldn't forget that one myth can breed another. We are now in a situation when part of this country believes that we can continue to stand against the whole world, but I think that the David-and-Goliath myth is somehow supporting this belief, so it's important to get matters straight.

In connection with Dan Bitan's ideas about the desire of the Jews to prove something to themselves about themselves, Netiva Ben Yehuda confirms:

☐   In the early days there was always the fear that maybe the Jews couldn't protect themselves. It was in all the protocols of the second aliya. There was a whole—you might say, a negative—myth about it. Could Jews start a new country? Could Jews cultivate the land, conquer the fields, the mountains—nature—sport? Jews were haunted for two thousand years by Bible legends, like the one in the Book of

Ezra where the Jews were coming from Iraq. They couldn't
protect themselves, so they had to buy mercenaries from
other nations—but they didn't have enough money. They
went back to the Jews who were left behind and said, "You
don't want to come with us, all right; give us money so we
can buy protection from other nations."

So now we had a land, a language, famous Jews all over
the world, so what was the problem? The problem was,
could Jews be *physical* enough? And those early Jews found
out they *could* stand in the sun and burn their noses and get
calluses and blisters. They used to show them off: "Look, I
have calluses—I'm a Jew, and I have calluses!" At that time
a friend of my mother's lived with the Arabs for *seven years*
to learn how to be a shepherd. Imagine, what an inferiority
complex! What is there to learn for seven years?

The war of '48 was fought in a way to prove that we
could fight. In the troubles of '36, '39, the Arabs used to stick
knives in our backs, to chase us and kill us. And in Europe
the Germans had "herded us like sheep to the slaughter." We
were going to show that it did not have to be like that.

But we soon found out that we were not fighting the
Germans! I remember an argument once. People like me
told the high command: "Listen, they're not Nazi storm
troopers, they're Arabs! Maybe we have to change our
concepts. They don't fight as we thought they would, and we
must take that into account—maybe it's enough to give
them one *sbeng* [blow] and they'll run." They wouldn't listen
to us. Maybe it was important to them to think they were
fighting someone very strong. I personally got the feeling I
was fighting children.

The gap in the classes among the Arabs was enormous
in those days, you know. One Arab might be an *effendi* who
owned half the Jezreel Valley and the rest were like serfs.
Serfs—real serfs that get beaten—can't be soldiers.

Now it is entirely different. A friend of mine who came
back after the '73 war told me what a shock he got, interrogating prisoners. Practically every one of those Egyptians

was a university graduate!—spoke English, spoke French, knew mathematics.... It was clear that Nasser, and Sadat after him, knew the importance of improving their manpower, so they sent everyone possible to the university. And if they could send, as privates, to the front line such intellectuals, then they are getting just like us. And, of course, a man who can think and understand what he is doing will fight better.

But still, in the last war, pilots said that when they met Egyptians in air battles, eye to eye, the Israelis were still stronger. They had more will. Because, after all, what will an Egyptian gain if he conquers Israel? Not half of what we will lose!

Many soldiers who were interviewed commented on the relative strengths and weaknesses of the Jewish and Arab forces. The army press spokesman, now a well-known writer on history and archeology:

□   That war, more than any since, was decided by the caliber of the fighters and their motivation. Israel was outgunned and outnumbered when she was attacked by regular armies with proper, standardized equipment, including armor, tanks, and artillery. But in any battle you have a critical moment when, perhaps, if you can hold out for another hour, you can win. If the enemy had known how weak we were in—oh, a score of places along the frontiers—they'd have driven us into the sea. We had our defeats; but on the whole, we won, and what enabled us to do it was the quality of the man and the motive that drove him.

Professor Gabriel Cohen, the historian with theories about British strategy, makes an interesting comment on the man behind the myth of toughness:

□   I remember a conversation I had with a friend of mine in the war. I met him in June, on the outskirts of Lydda, during the attack on that town. I hadn't met him throughout the seven or eight months of the war till then.

This man was already preparing himself to be a professional soldier. Later he rose to the rank of general—very tough, politically and militarily. We only had five minutes to talk and we only dealt with one topic. He said: "Gabi, you know I'm happy that although I've fought, to this day I can't be sure I really killed anyone. Because it so happened that I've never fought face to face, always from a distance. Maybe I killed, but I never saw myself kill."

I remember this because that was my feeling too, and still is, even today. I went through many, many battles, but I couldn't remember seeing that my bullet killed a man. Of course, it's a small comfort, but to hear that from a friend whom I knew to be, shall we say, not a hesitant soldier—I would say on the hawkish side and by no means a lenient man—yet, in 1948 that was his feeling. I was not surprised to feel this way myself—on the contrary, I thought I was too soft. But to discover that he felt the same way— Of course you may say, what sort of justification are you looking for, what sort of self-righteousness? What's the difference if you saw yourself killing or not? But men as well as women have these kinds of inhibitions.

People didn't usually speak about it; they were shy. Nobody wanted to appear soft. Once you did, you might not be selected to take part in the most dangerous operations, and the ethos was, of course, to try to take part in them. In the Palmach, those who were sensitive tried to hide it from the others.

Uzi Narkiss, who has suffered a certain amount of criticism for his action in withdrawing his men from the Old City after opening, briefly, the way from the Zion Gate in May:

☐   Ever since that time people have been looking for scapegoats. After thirty-two years I am much wiser, I have more patience, and I'm prepared to discuss what could or should have been done. But personally I regard what we did achieve as a miracle.

We took Romema—the entrance to Jerusalem—and the villages of Ein Karem and Malchia. The Arab quarters of Katamon and Talbieh in the heart of the city. Baka. And Mount Zion. All these Arab sectors we conquered, not to speak of Kastel and Colonia and all the Arab villages on the way to Tel Aviv. We also stood against the best and strongest Arab army, the Legion, and held them.

If there is any blame for such failures as there were, it must fall on our weakness. We were very weak. First, there was a weakness in command. There were four armies in Jerusalem. Even the Palmach, which was part of the Haganah, didn't accept *orders* from them, only requests, which they considered if they would obey. We of the Palmach were always assigned the most dangerous and difficult operations, including those in Jerusalem, where so much blood was spilled that we called it "the Arena of the Butchers." We were the best-organized force of the Haganah, and we did not want to lose any of our independence or our autonomous status.

There were other weaknesses: shortage of arms, a critical shortage of food and water. And there was apathy among the civilians. I will never forget how they stood in line at water points or outside clinics while shells fell around them, scarcely moving.... That was the effect of the long siege. There was also our terrible weariness.

In a way, the Zion Gate operation was a symbol of the whole situation in Jerusalem then. Nevertheless, out of all the operations I participated in—including the victorious ones—I regard our achievements in Jerusalem as the most important. As Ben-Gurion said, "Jerusalem can survive without Israel, but Israel can't survive without Jerusalem." Whoever fought there, contributed something to his people.

Yitzhak Rabin, speaking from the viewpoint of both a soldier and a politican, compares the war with others that followed:

☐   No doubt that anyone who participated in the War of Independence cannot forget it. First, it was the longest, the bloodiest, and the most cruel war that we have ever fought. The number of people who were killed in battle, plus the number of civilians lost, are about 50 percent of all those who have lost their lives in the struggle for the defense of Israel, until today. If you bear in mind that we were a little more than 600,000 in the Jewish community, that means that 1 percent of the total population lost their lives in the fighting.

Second, it was the war which, at least in its first phase— I would say throughout most of it—had no clear line dividing soldiers and civilians, who were either engaged in fighting or caught between the fighting forces. Therefore, it was an entirely different war from any which came later on.

Above all, it was the war that brought about the independence of the Jewish state. I don't believe that one can repeat the feelings of those who fought. They had a sense that they were carrying out an almost messianic mission. We knew that the United Nations partition resolution that recognized the right of the Jewish people to have a state in Eretz Israel would be just a piece of paper if we could not successfully defeat, first, the local Arab forces and later on the armed forces of the Arab countries.

No later war had the clear marking of being the first— the war that brought about our national revival. This cannot be repeated, this sense of responsibility that was carried in the hearts and minds of the people who fought them. They felt that they carried upon themselves the hopes of generations of Jews.

For the local population, Anwar Nusseibah describes the plight and condition of the Arabs of Israel and also comments on the Jews' archenemy, the mufti of Jerusalem:

☐   We were caught at a time of total unpreparedness. It was our mistake, and our immaturity, that we were in that state when our opponents were so well prepared. Here on the local level, our leadership had been expelled—or at least were outside the country: the mufti, Nashashibi,* and others— they were the ones we looked to for political leadership, and they were gone. Younger people had to take over, in a situation of complete unreadiness, and fight a war at the same time.

Though I was a civil servant and not a military man or a politician, I had a great deal of respect and admiration for the mufti. He was a man who had his own foibles and weaknesses, but he was a man of conviction; he believed in what he did. He believed that what was happening was wrong—unfair—unjust, and that it was only right for the Palestinians to defend their national rights and to fight for self-determination in the country to which they belonged, to which they had an assoication that went back as far as anybody else's, perhaps even longer—to which they felt a very deep attachment.

Of course, the mufti was a very simple man, a very dedicated man. The Israelis blame him for going over to the Nazis and so on, but he was chased from pillar to post by the British. He had to run away from Palestine in 1947, pursued by the British. After he was chased away from Lebanon and Iraq, he had nowhere to go . . . . He wanted to remain free to work for his people, outside his country. Why he went to Germany I don't know. I don't believe that he participated in any of what they call vindictive measures against the Jews.

I knew him very well. He was motivated by love of country and people. Maybe he was a one-track-minded sort of person, maybe self-centered—you know, all who work on that level are like that. But he was not motivated by hatred of the Jews. On the contrary, I don't believe there is any hatred in the Arab heart for the Jews. We Muslims, you know—our religion is rooted in Judaism, in Christianity; we don't have that kind of hatred. The religious wars which took place in

*One of the most important Arab families in east Jerusalem.

Europe are something alien to us. The mufti disliked the
Zionist philosophy very much, he disliked seeing his people
displaced, but it wasn't so much hatred for the others as
wishing to protect his own people that motivated him.

If you will carefully analyze the incidents of violence
that were caused by the Arabs, these were incidents in the
context of a war situation, rather than those springing from
personal hatred. They may appear to be personally motivated, but it was more because they were less able efficiently
to plan large-scale operations. Most of these events were
motivated by the need to assert what you believe to be your
right, to fight for your home and your survival.

Anwar Nusseibah's apologia for the mufti is one that most
Jews would surely contest on the basis of the record. To hear him
called "a simple man" is a challenge to belief: Rather, his actions
indicate a subtle and complex personality. To imply that he made
common cause with Hitler not out of hatred against Jews but
because he had nowhere to go other than Germany to escape the
persecutions of the British is, to say the least, ingenuous.

With the best will in the world to be fair to the Arabs, it is
also hard to avoid cynicism at the claim that it is not part of the
Muslim ethic to indulge in hatred or in religious wars.

On the other hand, it is quite easy to sympathize with the
Arab view of the mufti as a national hero. On that basis, his
actions do not call for any apology: As he was the enemy of the
Jews, he was the would-be savior of the Palestinians. All Anwar
Nusseibah's arguments, when read between the lines, reflect the
ongoing dilemma of an Arab notable living in Israel today, who
must temper his speech and measure every public utterance,
walking a tightrope of diplomacy over the twin chasms of
treachery to his own people and sedition against the ruling power.
Such men, although appearing to live a normal family and business life in Israel, do no such thing, in the terms of men who are
free of constraints. Every move and word is watched, not least by
his own side. These built-in restrictions would have driven a lesser
man than Anwar Nusseibah into leaving his home or at least

shutting his doors against the likes of me. The fact that he walks his tightrope on request, with no outward display of nervousness, should ensure that his statements are not dismissed without careful scrutiny, however questionable some of them may appear.

Yehuda Bauer, the professor who stopped a fellow officer from turning Arabs out of their village during the war, compares tactics:

☐ The regular Arab armies we faced were terribly careful. They had to have overwhelming superiority over us, otherwise they would not budge. When they did, they moved in tremendous force, and with our very light and mobile tactics we usually just danced circles around them; it might happen that they would launch a huge attack on a place where we had already cleared out.... There was no point in sitting there to be bombarded.

There were exceptions. There were so many Arab contingents and each one was different. For instance, there were the Sudanese in the south, who were magnificent fighters, absolutely fanatical. They knew they were supposed to kill Jews, and they were very willing to do it! They were terrific in hand-to-hand fighting, so the idea was not to get too close to them. So we dodged, and often the blows of the Egyptian army went into empty space.

We were so inferior in everything except, shall I say, soldierly intelligence. Compared with that of the Arabs, our equipment was ridiculous, and we were fighting certain parts of the war with absolutely untrained people. That's one thing.

The other thing was the enormous inventiveness of the ordinary soldier. We had a very large number of "generals." Nobody told them what to do; they had to think for themselves and do the right thing. If you are alone with a squad of ten men, and your commander gets killed, you have to carry on fighting for the position or maybe counterattack.... The Jewish penchant for decision by committee doesn't work then! Somebody would say, "You've got to lead." There

would be a quick consultation, perhaps, and after that the
man would go into action and usually in the right way. There
were many such cases, because of our idea at the time that
the commander leads his men into battle, so he was often the
first to get hit.

Shimon Avidan, now living tranquilly in his kibbutz in the
Carmel hills, was praised to me before I met him by Netiva Ben
Yehuda, who was once posted to his headquarters in Sarafand,
which she found "so smooth and quiet.... *We* were always shouting and arguing, despite all the shining brass and white-painted
stones everywhere. With Avidan's lot, there were just lists on the
walls and everything in order—and they fought better for it."
Avidan reflects:

☐   In history there are many examples of small nations defeat-
     ing large ones, but in modern times it is much more difficult.
     Today you can, with the help of modern weapons, destroy
     every living thing for many miles, so justice or theories are
     not so important—they are not enough. But two things
     made it possible to fight this sort of war and be victorious.
         The first was that feeling that we were the last hope of
     the Jewish people. Other nations may lose a war, and within
     a generation, being settled on their own soil, they will build
     their lives again. But for us to be defeated means the end of
     the dream. And the second reason which made it possible to
     fight in this way was what happeneed to us in Europe.
     Again, the feeling that, if not we, there was no one to help the
     Jews who were left to build a new life. That is not to say that
     every soldier, every morning, thought of these things; but as
     background motivation, they were very important.
         There is no "nice" war. Maybe for generals somewhere—
     but for the ordinary soldier, it is kill or be killed, and the
     commander is educating his soldiers in one thing: to kill
     better. You are awakening all the animal instincts which are
     normally a little bit dormant, and if you wake them success-
     fully, your side can be victorious. But here is the important

thing about the War of Independence: We never lost our moral point. We educated our people not only to be good soldiers, but also to remain human beings—a very hard thing during a war, even a just war. Men turn into animals, as we are learning today—every day.

The Aftermath

Israel has fought three major wars since the first: the Sinai Campaign in 1956, the Six-Day War in 1967, and the Yom Kippur War in 1973. It has, in addition, survived innumerable skirmishes and crises, military and political, as well as the undeclared, but devastating, War of Attrition following the Six-Day War.

Aside from these struggles, and in part because of them, the country has undergone radical changes, both within and in relation to the rest of the world. A number of those interviewed, reflecting on the Israel of 1947–49 and the Israel of 1980, commented on various aspects of these changes and of the intervening wars.

It will have been noted that a few of the people interviewed for this book asked to remain anonymous. In all these cases, anonymity was requested not because they were reluctant to attach their names to their comments but for reasons of modesty. The following interview, however, was given anonymously, I think, by reason of its pessimism. I quote it nevertheless because it represents a genuine voice among those who speak, or refrain from speaking, in Israel today.

☐ The Palmachniks I meet year by year in the cemetery for our fallen in Kiryat Anavim—you can tell them from afar, and not just by their white shirts. They have a different look. Most of them have preserved some inner quality of uprightness in themselves, something others in the country have allowed to slide. So many who fought in that war with such

high hopes and ideals have changed; they've become mate-
rialists, hawks—there's nothing left of the inner strength
they had. And it shows in their faces and their bodies—the
one, coarsened and hardened; the other, flabby and soft.

Having ideals when you're young is easy. Hanging on to
them, fighting for them when you're getting older, preserv-
ing the old values in the face of what we go through here day
by day—that's the real triumph, the true, quiet heroism.

To the ceremony at the cemetery, the government
always sends a representative. It gets harder and harder to
find someone who will not turn the stomachs of the old-
guard Palmachniks. They can no longer find an innocent
man.

In that first war, you knew you were part of something
sound. The whole business was clean and necessary, there
were no moral ambiguities. Since then, so much has
changed. You can tell by the songs. The songs from the wars
were so different. In the '48 war we didn't taunt our enemies
with "Nasser Waits for Rabin" or sing about Jerusalem's
"empty market-places" as if we were blind to the people we
conquered. Our battle songs had an honesty and a freedom
from hatred, a sort of compassion for the whole situation—
But then, being a socialist wasn't a label in those days, it was
a way of life.

I believe the *Altalena* was the most disgusting episode
of the whole era. We were so short of weapons! Yet we knew
that if the Irgun got those guns, sooner or later they would
be turned on us. There'd have been a revolution. Begin's
people were determined to get power. Well, now they've got
it and look at us—divided against ourselves and the butt of
the whole world, which, in 1948 and for long afterward,
supported us. And we deserved it then. The oil war is only
part of the reason we have lost it now. How could it be
otherwise, when there are friends of mine whom I can no
longer look in the face or talk to because we no longer think
or feel alike about anything that matters.

The poet Yehuda Amichai also takes a sober view of developments since 1948, but, with a new young family, has turned sadness into a philosophy:

☐ Looking at Israel now, comparing it to what we were, it would be easy to say: "Look what they've done to my country!" But I don't believe in saying that. Look at the Communists in Russia at the time of the Revolution; look at Britain after World War II—so hopeful, believing they were bringing in a new future for mankind— Yct poverty remains, the class war goes on, and in Russia even from the beginning, the Bolsheviks were completely corrupt. So I don't think one should lapse into cynicism or say this very banal and tiresome thing, "We fought for a good country and look what's come of it."

So—we weren't as good as we thought we were. But our people should see that ideals decline with time—they always do. The country is not as bad as it seems now, although Begin is turning us back into a ghetto. When one looks around at the rest of the world and its leaders—Khomeini, a religious maniac, Hussein, who butchered thousands of Palestinians, and so many others—one is tempted to say that at our worst we are better than most of them. But that is not the point.

The point is that we must hold ourselves upright, we must struggle against all this evil. What do we need with the West Bank? It drains us, morally and financially, and for what? Give it back to the Arabs, not for their sake but for ours, let them settle what to do with it, who will rule it—let them kill each other over it, which they will very happily do.

I don't have any great ideals any more, but that doesn't mean I've lost hope. My only ideal now is that to have ideals is better than not to have them. The lesser evil is the only ideal—the best course can only be the less evil course.

Avital Mossinsohn, who was a child at the time of the war

and now describes himself very ruefully as "51 percent dove—the other 49 percent is all hawk," draws a distinction between those whose memories stretch back to mandatory times and those who were too young:

☐   One of my younger brothers, two years my junior, was killed in the Six-Day War. It was around that time that I realized something—that people of my exact age are the last to know what independence really meant to the Jewish people. My surviving brother belongs to the first "generation," which began to try to make Israel like America. He takes independence for granted. I am farther from him, the gap is bigger—though the age difference is only five years—than between me and my father, who is twenty years older than me, because he and I can remember the mandate and events leading up to statehood. Both my brothers were too young. They and all their contemporaries and juniors were deprived of the comparison, the before-and-after which makes it possible for me to value what that war won for us, whatever it cost.

Pinchas Blumenthal, who believed in the "personal approach" to the enemy, reflects on the special inner integrity of the time for him:

☐   As I went through that war I was quite conscious of one thing, and I remember telling my wife: "This I hope will be the only war in which I have to take part though I'm afraid there will be other wars. But *I shall never be as happy as I am now.*"
      Though I was perfectly certain we would lose! The odds were against us. I was among the officers who knew how bad things were; until today I don't understand how we won with the weapons we had, how we came through . . . . But I was happy! One had a moral attitude. It was a war of defense. I felt absolutely no moral compunction. If we had not fought, we would have been massacred.

Even today, a rifle, to me, is an instrument of murder. I have no nostalgia for anything like shooting or fighting. But there is nostalgia for this: that for once one was not a divided personality. I could not stand on one side, leaving my people alone on the other. *Now* it seems possible that if there were better politics it need never come to the point of war. At that time it seemed quite obvious that one couldn't help but fight.

The United Nations had given us our state—it was formally our right. And the Arabs attacked, and they were pretty cruel, and it seemed clear that if we didn't stand up for ourselves they'd slaughter everybody. Although I am desperately aware of how bad things are in this country now, from every point of view, including morally, Israel remains our only hope.

It is very cheap and easy to be a Jew outside Israel, to be a rabbi in London or New York and tell us we have to be nice to minorities, that we have to show charity to the old and poor—it is an interesting subject of conversation, from there. Here, charity means more on our income tax, and kindness to minorities, in the case of the Arabs, might cost me my life.

Meir Zeira, a kibbutz teacher from Hungary:

☐   When I arrived in Israel, aged twenty-three, alone— my whole family gone—my main, my deepest feeling was that wherever I went, *here,* I was not defenseless. I had a gun, I could fight, and not be anybody's helpless victim.

I saw so many victims of war, without arms, unable to resist. In '48 we fought every day. Every day. Even during the cease-fire I could still carry on with my reconnoitering. In the end, it scarcely mattered if I died or somebody else died, so long as there was somebody left to go forward.

Nobody questioned orders at that time. They did whatever they were told, almost automatically, and the worst punishment was *not* to go into action. I remember one evening we were told to cross a river. I was doing intelligence

work at that time—crossing the border to look around,
maybe take some prisoners. So our group swam across.
When we started I was near my friend Eli, but when I got to
the other side and looked around for him, he wasn't there. I
heard some splashing and went back; there was Eli, thresh-
ing about, half drowned.

I helped him ashore and said, "What happened to you?"
"I can't swim," he said. I asked him why he hadn't told
someone. He didn't seem to have thought of it. When you
got an order, you just obeyed it.

I don't think Eli was trying to be a hero or play some
great role in history. He just knew, like all of us, that he had
no choice. We were fighting for our lives. The questions I'd
ask myself in the concentration camp about what human life
means didn't occur to me now. I knew one thing: Whether
you fight or whether you run, you can still die. The difference was whether you died in hope or in despair. The whole
meaning of life for me was hope—something I didn't lose
even in the camp, because somehow I always believed it
would end, that it was worth hanging on.

"Boaz" went back to his kibbutz after the war and lived there
for twenty-two years. But he observed the effects of the war on
others who belonged to his movement:

☐   Our commander at the beginning seemed to us a most
     remarkable leader. He was an experienced Palmach officer,
     older than some of the others—all of twenty-seven, twenty-
     eight—and he really endeared himself to us. He was more
     like a friendly instructor than an officer, training us while we
     actually fought, telling us, right in the thick of battle, how to
     hold a rifle properly, how to keep out of sight and so on. He
     seemed to have a personal interest in all of us, especially the
     new recruits.

     It makes you think how these old-timers must have felt,
     getting all these young boys who had no idea and having to
     make soldiers out of them. A lot of our people fell *because*

they had no idea—they used to chase about with their friends as if they were on an outing. Many of them had known each other from childhood. Most of my group were homogeneous bunches of kids, girls and boys who'd grown up together in kibbutzim or been together in town-based branches of Hashomair Hatsa'ir.

And they had to watch each other drop. By the time the first cease-fire came, we in Har El had lost more than any other brigade: all these youth groups had been decimated; they'd lost friends and comrades. All the excitement, ebullience, and enthusiasm had turned, for many of the survivors, into a sort of cynical fatalism.

And it had its effect later, obviously. Their leading lights had led in battle too, and often had been the first to fall, and groups from the towns who should have settled on kibbutzim and carried on the ideology of the youth movements— that marvelous thing we all started with—despaired and gave it all up, simply through shock and loss and loneliness.

On the other hand, many still retained the strength and determination to carry on their lives as they had intended, and the feelings of closeness and comradeship that were generated by the war even enabled some new immigrants, who had none of the ideological background, to join groups of youth-movement people and start up their own kibbutzim.

Menachem Roussak, who witnessed the surrender of the Old City from the bell tower, reflects:

☐ Until the War of Independence we might *say* we were a people like all others; but in the twentieth century the tangibility of a people is a state. Perhaps if the visions of the Prophet Isaiah come about it won't be so, but meanwhile every people has a state, an army and so forth, and we acquired all this in the War of Independence.

Whatever problems we have had with the rest of the world since, at least they must all take into account that we have a state and a territory. So it was a historical step that I participated in. We had to have a base. Now we have one, and with it comes all the troubles that other people have, plus the special troubles of the Jews. We were a people not used to physical work.... And we have the Jews of the Diaspora to worry about. But it is better than being as we were.

Sir John Glubb, the Israelis' old foe, now in his eighties, ruminates on the results of the war:

☐   That was the war which had the greatest effect on the subsequent history of the Middle East. It's the key to the disappearance of the British influence in that area, which she largely forfeited owing to the problem of Israel, because she originated that problem with the Balfour Declaration.

I'm too old to be bitter, or "anti," or "pro," but I do feel for the large number of Palestinians who have been completely driven from their homes, often in the clothes they stood up in. Subsequently, whole villages were bulldozed into the ground, ploughed over, planted with trees, so that there's no trace of where their inhabitants were. And judging by the news, something of the kind is still going on. Arab land is still being seized by the Israeli government and implanted with Jewish colonies.

If one looks at it from the point of view of international law—which nobody seems to do—it's laid down that if there's a war and one side occupies the other's territory, it's classified as occupied enemy territory, and the victor is not allowed to make any fundamental change. Until a peace is negotiated, you're not supposed to change the other fellow's country.

There were only two countries really involved in that war against Israel—Egypt and Jordan. And now Egypt has negotiated a peace treaty, but only on condition that Israel gives autonomy to the Arabs of the occupied areas. But meanwhile the Jews are still annexing more and more Arab land. There's no sign of autonomy at all. This makes people say, well, this is merely a racket. The Israelis simply wanted to get the Egyptians off their backs so that they could annex a bit of Lebanon, drive out the remaining Arabs from Palestine, and clean up generally. Far from intending to give autonomy to the Arabs, the treaty with Egypt has enabled them to seize more and more of those Arab areas, meanwhile bashing Lebanon the whole time.

I do have the deepest sympathy with the Palestinians, though not with what they're doing now. I am opposed to terrorism and assassination and so on—this is no way to carry on public affairs. They should place the whole thing before the United Nations, the world at large.... But you see they're all ignorant peasants. That's why it's all very well to blame them, but.... Well, European colonialism in Africa is denounced by everyone as unfair. If you're a one hundred percent up-to-date Western nation, of course it's unfair to set yourself up against the Congo, or Bonga-Bonga, or Timbuktu, where the wretched people don't know how to behave and haven't got a clue.... And that was so in Palestine. They were very simple village people, who were played upon by all the lawyers and politicians, such as the mufti. I didn't admire the man, though I suppose you have to sympathize in a way—his was the leading family in Jerusalem before the first world war.

You know, I don't feel I'm hated in Israel. I sometimes get letters from Israelis on various subjects. But the farther you get from the place, the more fanatical the Jews seem to get. By golly, if you go to New York—! My books on Arab history were all published by a Jewish firm there—very friendly. But two years ago I published a book about World War I, which you'd think was sufficiently removed from the Arab-Israeli conflict. My literary agent sent this over to get a publisher and it was returned with a letter saying, "You don't think any publisher in New York would publish a book, on any subject whatever, by Glubb Pasha!"

"Beni" Meitiv, then a member of Kibbutz Nirim who now

works among the Arabs of the Gaza Strip, reflects on the demographic problems of Israel:

☐ For all my life till then I had been sure that all Jews would want to come to Israel, that only this Englishman or that Arab stood in the way, but that as soon as they stepped aside, the Jews would come in—all of them, immediately. I had to learn the hard way that this was not so.

I learned it by meeting them and talking to them in Europe, hiding my feelings—only after 1953, when I first went abroad. In the first years after the war, so many newcomers did arrive that I thought it was happening as I'd expected. I thought, those who need a refuge more will come first, of course, but the rest will follow soon. I watched the children come with Youth Aliya*—the first lot from Europe—and then from North Africa—I was convinced this was what Israel was about, the ingathering of exiles. Living in the kibbutz, I suppose, sheltered me from the truth, or perhaps it was lack of education— We worked so many years for an ideal, to make Israel "a light unto the nations." And now when I see—not just that many do not come but that many leave—it hurts me. I think that is the word. It is a feeling of pity. It hurts me.

Uri Avneri, who, as a politician and a journalist, has also campaigned against narrow ethnic definitions of race or religion within Israel, lays emphasis as much on changes that did *not* come about after the war as on those that did:

☐ I try not to idealize the war. I very rarely go to these old veterans' reunions and so on. Once a year on Independence Day there are memorial meetings at the military cemeteries, and this year for the first time they offered me Negba. So I couldn't refuse. I went, and for the first time in my life I

*Youth Aliya: an organization to aid, settle and, where necessary, rehabilitate displaced or deprived Jewish children in special villages.

spoke on behalf of the Israeli government . . . . I couldn't even make a joke about it because it was a solemn occasion.

This experience—this war—was the climax of our youth. I think we are all deeply attached to those times. The war was, in its way, a cultural revolution. And it failed.

The new state was taken over not by our generation but by the one before us—the Ben-Gurion generation. It should have been taken over by men like Yigal Allon, who was the embodiment of certain feelings, certain ideals—a certain style. I would even go so far as to say that they embodied the beginnings of a real Israeli culture. Something totally new. It could have been the beginning of a different people—a different Israel. But it was frustrated after the war—stifled.

The question of "why" is one which some of us are still debating. I would say it was partly because of the attrition of the war, which was much too big for us to absorb. There is an analogy to the British in the first world war. A whole generation was wiped out in Flanders in a few weeks—I mean a whole generation of leaders of a culture. And that happened to us, too.

And what were left of us were inadequate. Because our "elite" was brought up in the shadow of the old-timers who were much stronger than we, and somehow we could never reach the point of rebellion against the generation above us. We never became really independent; we were tricked by Ben-Gurion and these old party hacks who took us over again after the war as if nothing had happened. The whole intermezzo was just an episode, nothing more; it left nothing but a few books, poems—relics.

If people have nostalgia, it is for the loss of their own sense of worth—for the time when they felt motivated to do something and really did it. There was a sense of direction, but this is usual in wartime. It was more than that. It was a possibility of something which might have been but which came to nothing.

Certainly one reason these possibilities were submerged was the catastrophic dimensions of the new immigration.

Six hundred thousand people absorbed two million—the original few could not possibly put their imprint on the newcomers after the attrition of the war itself. This wave of immigrants coming in '49, '50, '51 changed the whole picture of the country. . . . There is just so much you can absorb without changing the whole texture.

The State of Israel which grew out of the war was definitely totally different from what we wanted or imagined it would be at the beginning. Perhaps after every war you have a kind of disillusionment— If you look at the literature of the first world war, *All Quiet on the Western Front,* and then the follow-up books, *Way Back* and *Three Comrades,* you get the same feeling of terrible disappointment after the war of those coming back. The front-line soldier, returning full of expectations, finds he is looked on as a fool who was away fighting while all the important things happened behind the lines. It happens in all wars. But if your state is new and small, it is worse.

A lot of our war was spent in talk. One hour's fighting, and maybe a day or a week of waiting. And while men waited, they sat around and talked. The talk of that war was of great hopes, of what the State of Israel would be like. And when they came home, full of memories of the fine ideas they'd exchanged with their comrades around the campfires, they found that the state already existed—created by somebody else. The new society had been formed by those who stayed behind. And the spirit of it was totally alien.

That was the beginning—the beginning of class differences, which had never been there before; the beginning of the gap between so-called Oriental and Occidental Jews; the race of the old-timers to get their hands on the spoils of war, including the immense property of half a million Arabs who fled. It was booty, taken not by the front-line soldiers who had not had time but by those who least deserved it.

People who remember the war remember a time when everything was much nicer, more beautiful and so on. But they also remember the terrible letdown immediately afterward. They were tired. It had been a long war for most of them. They wanted quickly to found a family, start a career, take something of what was left of the spoils....

Of course, you can't blame the old leadership. No elite ever relinquished power willingly. The trouble was, people like Allon were such nice boys. Nice—and always number two. Dayan as well—always on the verge of being number one but couldn't make it. They grew up as nice boys among other nice boys who sacrificed themselves for this land which never came into their hands.

Dayan had never been anything but somebody else's man. First Ben-Gurion's, then Golda's, and Begin's—a news media invention. The one who did reach number one, Rabin, was inadequate for it. Ezer Weizman, now he has to stand up and fight against Begin, is hopeless—he can't, he's the wrong type of person. Being a leader means being able to stand up and say to hell with everybody, let's fight. Some people simply can't do it.

There was one person who could have been the great figure in postwar Israel: Yitzhak Sadeh. The founder of the Palmach, a commander, a great personality with personal charisma—he had an almost pedagogic influence. But he died early. And now we are left with empty shells.

Shulamith Hareven, the "medic," notes an interesting shift in personal loyalties:

☐   When I evaluate it all now, that war seems to me to have been wholly necessary and valid. In a way it was a continuation of Hitler's war. We had the feeling of "last stand." And I had a feeling of privilege, too, from two sources. One was that it fell to our generation to change Jewish history. And the other was that there was no draft. Everything was voluntary. It was not that we were such a heroic generation. Take my class at school, for example. Lots did no fighting at all. Some ran away abroad, and others took no part in active service. But those who did—"we band of brothers"—we felt immensely privileged.

Yet I am not so much in touch now with the people who

fought with me then. My closest friends now are kids between twenty-five and thirty who are with me in the Peace Now movement. Israel has been through such a lot since those days. I feel now I have more in common with those who are working for peace than with those who fought with me in the war.

There is one more thing that I think is important about the War of Independence. It's the feeling that there was no one in the whole world to help us if we didn't fend for ourselves. You know there was a sentence written by a journalist here after the Entebbe rescue. He wrote: "We waited for them in Auschwitz too. But they couldn't come."

Finally, Ephraim Shorer, the artillery officer who fought in all Israel's wars and lost his only son in one of them, sums up for himself and, no doubt, for many others:

☐   It was a very long war. No other war of ours lasted anything like that long. Casualties were very heavy—over six thousand dead and nearly twenty-five thousand wounded. The fact that our medical facilities were not as good as they are now meant that very many people died of wounds and many remain invalids even today.

Yet people talk about the war as somethng beautiful— "the beautiful War of Independence." We were young. We were optimistic. We didn't realize the dangers. We believed that this was—I don't know—a resurrection, that after it there was going to be a Jewish state, and that everything, forever after, was going to be different and better.

Some people who knew the odds didn't believe that we would win. But most of us never doubted it for a moment, even we professionals who knew it was going to be tough. And it was! Nearly every family lost somebody. I lost my brother, my only brother, in that war. I myself was injured. But I lost him.

You know, it was the best who died—the young, the vigorous, the courageous. They were there when the mines and the shells and the bullets were exploding. We survivors were just the lucky ones. We had our lives given to us as a present.

The war ended and we found ourselves in a little, ruined country: economy completely wrecked, because this was a war of eighteen months, not of six or twenty-one days— eighteen months in which everybody was at war, both men and women; everything rationed, agriculture and industry at a standstill, even orange groves left to die because there was no one to work them. And yet, we celebrated the victory.

And we opened our gates to huge numbers of immigrants, coming to this place where you ate egg powder because there were no eggs, milk powder because there was no milk, fish fillets that we couldn't look at—and it was an Israel of hope and great joy. In a very short time—a few years—one million immigrants came from North Africa and Iraq and Yemen, plus all the refugees from Europe, and somehow we found that we could absorb them, and manage. Today we have over three and a half million people, with everything—a fine industrial complex, a powerful army— and yet the spirit is so low.

Maybe we'll have to fight again. One hopes not—in view of what's happened recently with Egypt. Perhaps that will spread to other Arab countries. Unfortunately, Europe doesn't help us. They give hope to the Arabs that they need not make peace. But if we have to fight, we'll fight.

I don't believe we'll have all-out war with the Arab world or that there will be a nuclear war in this region. Egypt is out of the fighting for the foreseeable future for its own reasons, and without Egypt, the Arab world—despite the power the Iraqis have gained—has not the slightest hope of winning a war. They won't start a war they have no hope of winning. They are not that crazy. It would mean destruction for us but more terrible destruction for them.

I don't know how it is for the younger generation, who look back on that war as a historical event; but we who carried it on our shoulders from the very beginning cannot but regard it as a magnificent war. Despite the fact that friends and family were lost, not to speak of many battles; despite the feelings men had that they were not soldiers yet, that they didn't always know what they were doing; despite occasional despair— Looking back one can only say this was the greatest event in modern Jewish history.

And it was not for nothing. Nor were our subsequent sacrifices in vain. We are here to stay.

List of Participants

Aloni, Shulamith. b. Israel. Politician, teacher, journalist, author (*The Citizen and His Country, Rights of the Child in Israel, The Arrangement, Woman as a Human Being*). Organized Movement for the Rights of Citizens, 1973. MK, Labor, 1969; Citizens Rights, 1977–81. Chairwoman, Israel Consumers Committee.

Amichai, Yehuda. b. 1924, Germany; immigrated to Palestine 1935. Jewish Brigade, British army, World War II. Author (six books of poetry, two novels, short stories); teacher (poetry and Hebrew literature at Greenberg Teachers College, Jerusalem).

Amit, Meir. b. 1921, Israel. Major general (reserve) IDF. Deputy commander and commander, Golani Brigade. Minister of transport; chief of military intelligence, Israeli Secret Service; MK, Labor, 1977–81.

Avneri, Uri. b. 1923, Germany. Journalist, editor of *Hoalam Hazeh*; author of five books including *Israel Without Zionism*. MK, ninth and previous Knessets. Co-founder of Israeli-Palestinian Peace Movement.

Bauer, Yehuda (Ph.D.). b. 1926, Prague. Secondary school headmaster; director, Institute of Contemporary Jewry, Hebrew University; member, Scientific Consultative Committee of Yad Vashem. Director, holocaust studies, Hebrew University. Author of seven books and many articles in academic publications.

Baum, Shlomo. b. 1928, Israel. Reared in *moshav*; joined Haganah at 16; farmer till 1953. Commando, Company 101, special commando

385

raids against Jordan. Reg. army paratrooper, wounded three times. Construction worker. Reg. army officer, 1967. Director, Strategical Research Unit, Jerusalem.

Benvinisti, Meron. b. 1934, Jerusalem. Doctoral candidate Harvard University. Author of four books, two on Jerusalem. Historian of Crusader period. First administrator of Old City after Six-Day War. Deputy mayor, Jerusalem, until 1979. Candidate for the Knesset, Civil Rights List.

Ben Yehuda, Netiva. b. 1928, Tel Aviv. Joined Palmach 1946. Studied art at Bezalel and in London; studied philosophy and philosophy of language. Published (with Dahn Ben Amotz) *Dictionary of Colloquial Hebrew*. Studied public relations and communications in U.S. Public relations, Israeli government. Author (*Between Calendars*, 1981).

Bitan, Dan. b. 1937, Jerusalem. Studied history and philosophy Hebrew University. Director, Department of Gifted Children, Jerusalem.

Blumenthal, Pinchas, Dr. b. 1912, Berlin; immigrated to Palestine 1935. Teacher and educator. Inspector of English, Teaching Ministry of Education. First director, Pre-academic Training for Culturally Deprived. Director, Educational Television in Israel, 1968, and Center for Humanistic Judaism.

Cohen, David. b. 1902, Russia; immigrated to Palestine 1935; veteran Zionist family. Full-time in Haganah from 1938. Member, Kibbutz Beit Alpha. Missions abroad for kibbutz movement. Developed agriculture for kibbutz. Still active despite three heart attacks; employed in packaging for export.

Cohen, Gabriel (Prof.) b. 1928, Jerusalem. Joined Haganah 1942, Palmach 1946. Twice wounded. Member, Kibbutz Palmachim. Director, historical research, IDF. Two years at Oxford University. Professor of medieval and modern history of Palestine, Tel Aviv University, 1962– . MK, 1965–69.

Cohen, Geula. b. 1925, Journalist, author (*Women of Violence*). MK, Techiya. Introduced Jerusalem bill in the Knesset 1980.

Cohen, Yerucham. b. 1916, Tel Aviv. Joined Haganah 1932. Intelligence officer; worked behind lines in Syria, Lebanon. Established Arab Unit in Palmach. Helped organize Jewish self-defense units throughout Middle East after World War II. Student, Mid-East studies and political science. Journalist, diplomat. Director, Special Division Programs, Tel Aviv University.

Diskin, Israel. b. 1901, Jerusalem. Lawyer and historian. Publications include *German Reparations* (in German). Submitted memorandum on Palestine to Anglo-American Enquiry Committee and to U.N., 1946. Translations into Hebrew. Secretary, military governor of Jerusalem, 1948.

Dreyfuss, Yochanan. b. 1925, Munich. Zionist youth movement from age 10 in Vienna. Immigrated to U.S. 1939. U.S. army, in Germany, participated in capture of Munich and liberation of Dachau. Immigrated to Israel 1948; member, Kibbutz Sasa. Proprietor, jewelery firm, Jerusalem.

Edelstein, Yaacov. b. 1928, Poland. Writer, journalist, rabbi, poet. Survivor of Kfar Etzion massacre; five of his six books are on this subject. Shapira Prize, 1970. Jerusalem Municipality Prize for *History of Jerusalem*, 1975. Columnist on religious daily *Hatsofeh*. Working on study of pupils of the Gaon (Holy man) of Vilna.

Galili, Israel. b. 1911, Russia. Immigrated to Palestine 1914. General organizer of Working Youth, 1925. Founding member Kibbutz Na'an. Underground munitions; Haganah, 1920s. Commander, Haganah, 1947. Member, first Knesset. Twice U.N. delegate. Minister without portfolio, 1965–74. MK till 1977. Chairman, Committee for Policy of Labor Party prior to 1981 elections.

Glubb, Sir John Bagot. b. 1897. KCB, CMG, DCO, OBE. British army, Royal Engineers, 1914–18, wounded three times; awarded MC. Served in Mid-East 1920–32. Chief, General Staff, Arab Legion, Transjordan, 1939–56. Author of nineteen books (*Story of the Arab Legion, A Soldier with the Arabs, The Middle East Crisis, Short History of the Arab Peoples, Life and Times of Mohammed, A Purpose for Living*). Lives in retirement in Sussex, England.

Guri, Aliza. b. Poland. Immigrated to Palestine at age 4. Entered Palmach from school. Welfare worker, elementary-school teacher. Three daughters.

Guri, Chaim. b. 1923, Tel Aviv. Member, Kibbutz Beit Alpha. Founding member Palmach 1941. Journalist, broadcaster, poet, documentary film maker (*The Eighty-first Blow*, 1973, and *The Last Sea*, 1980).

Hareven, Shulamith. b. Warsaw. Author, essayist (seven books; one novel, short stories, children's books). Translator of classics into Hebrew. Only woman member of Academy of Hebrew Language. Prime Minister's Prize for creative writing. War correspondent. Recently chosen to represent Israel in international anthology of women's short stories. Active in Peace Now movement.

Heffer, Chaim. b. 1925, Poland. Writer, journalist, lyricist, playwright. Active in illegal immigration after World War II. Founded entertainment troupe Chizbatron.

Herzog, Chaim. b. 1918, Belfast. KBE, LL.B. U.N. representative, 1975–78. Chief of staff, Southern Command, 1957–59. Director, Military Intelligence, 1948–50. First military governor of West Bank after Six-Day War. Military and political broadcaster. Journalist and author of five books about Israel. Directs legal firm, Tel Aviv.

Inbar, Ben Zion. b. 1914, Tel Aviv. Joined Haganah at 17. Reg. army, 1939–50, lieutenant colonel. Worked in national building firm, Koor. Retired; works part-time in industrial management.

Kaniuk, Yoram. b. 1930, Tel Aviv. Painter, journalist, lecturer, author (*The Acrophile, Adam Resurrected, Rocking Horse*), widely translated. Active in Civil Rights List, candidate for tenth Knesset.

Kennett, Michael. b. 1923, Germany; immigrated to Palestine 1924. Graduated Mikve Israel school. British army, 1941–45. Farmed *moshav* till 1967. Diplomatic service, Africa. Director, Jerusalem Housing Authority.

Kollek, Teddy. b. 1911, Vienna. Founding member Kibbutz Ein Gev. Various missions abroad, 1930s and 1940s. Chairman, Joint American-Israeli Nuclear Water Desalination Project; chairman, Israel Museum. Author of two books. Mayor, Jerusalem, 1967–

Lankin, Eliahu. b. 1914, Russia. Reared and educated in China. LL.B. Lecturer in Russian language. Member first Knesset. Governor, Hebrew University. Chairman, Bar Association of Israel. Member, Committee of Research into Organized Crime in Israel. Ambassador to South Africa, 1981.

Laskov, Chaim. b. 1919, Russia. Studied Oxford University. Former chief of staff, 1958–61. Member, Enquiry Committee into Yom Kippur War. Founder, Israel Defense Forces Officers School, 1948. GOC,

Southern Command, 1957. Director general, Israel Ports Authority, 1961–70. IDF ombudsman.

Lorch, Netanel. b. Israel. Reg. army officer till 1955. Director, military history. Diplomatic service till 1972. Published books on War of Independence (*The Edge of the Sword, One Long War*), and on Israeli diplomacy, and studies on parliaments and audio-visual media. Secretary general, Knesset till 1981.

Meidav, Rika. b. 1925, Belgian Congo. Immigrated to Palestine 1946. Studied sociology, psychology, Zionist problems. Taught French. Teaches girls' arts and crafts seminar.

Meitiv, Ben Zion. Founding member, Kibbutz Nirim. Author of short stories on Bedouin themes. Military and civil administrator. Works among Arabs of Gaza Strip.

Meltzer, Lionel. b. 1917, Johannesburg, South Africa. Commanding officer, two field ambulance units, Africa and Europe, World War II. Senior district medical officer, Johannesburg, prewar and 1945–48. Second in command, Israeli Army Medical Services. Returned to South Africa 1954. Private practice as anesthetist.

Mossinsohn, Avital. b. 1937, Israel. Reared in kibbutz. Television producer, impresario, government spokesman. Director Jerusalem Theater, 1973–80. Inaugurated and directed Jerusalem Spring Festival five years. Director, Klal Enterprises; active in Civil Rights List.

Narkiss, Uzi. b. 1925, Jerusalem. Battalion commander, 1947–49. Director, Operation Division, GHG, 1956. Diplomatic service, France. General and commander of troops that liberated Jerusalem 1967. Director general, Department of Immigration and Absorption, Jewish Agency.

Nusseibah, Anwar. b. Jerusalem. Lawyer. Former Jordanian defense minister. Now chairman of board of directors, E. Jerusalem Electric Co.

Ornan, Uzi. b. Poland. Immigrated to Palestine as a child. Joined Lehi; arrested by British; spent war in detention in Africa. Now dean, Department of Linguistics, Hebrew University.

Pa'il, Meir. b. 1926, Jerusalem. Colonel (reserves), IDF. MK, Sheli. Published articles on history of Haganah. Lecturer in history, Hebrew University.

Peled, El'ad. b. 1927, Jerusalem. Ph.D., Columbia University. Major general (reserves), IDF. Director general, Ministry of Education and Culture, 1970–76. Visiting senior lecturer, Ben Gurion University. Vice mayor, Jerusalem.

Rabin, Yitzhak. b. 1922, Jerusalem. Reg. officer IDF from British mandate times; chief of operations, 1959; chief of staff, 1964; rank of general. Ambassador to U.S., 1968. Prime minister of Israel, 1974–77. Recently published autobiography.

Salmon, Elon. b. 1937, Tel Aviv. Studied history, Hebrew University. Journalist, *Jerusalem Post*, Israel Broadcasting. Chief de Bureau to Teddy Kollek. Ministry of Tourism, Denmark. Author of three novels. Editor, *Jewish Observer*, London.

Shaltiel, Mrs. Judith. b. 1921, Berlin; immigrated to Palestine 1935. Montessori teacher. Specialized in teaching delinquent and handicapped children. Organized institution for retarded children. Married David Shaltiel, 1939. Accompanied him on diplomatic missions while studying physical psychology. Psychologist, Ministry of Health and in private practice.

Shorer, Ephraim. b. 1920, Russia. Officer, British army (Indian Division). First commander of artillery, IDF. Active with Aliya Bet in Europe after World War II. Manager, El Al Airlines, Stockholm.

Soroka, Yitzhak. b. 1927, Ein Harod. Joined Haganah at 15. Civil engineer. Dean, civil engineering, Technion Univeristy.

Tarragan, Malca. b. 1922, seventh-generation Jerusalem family. Studied biochemistry and Talmud. Worked with youth and deprived in slums. Secretary, biology section, *Encyclopaedia Judaica*. Teaches Judaism, Public University.

Toledano, Shmuel. b. 1921, Tiberias, seventh-generation Israeli. Joined Etzel 1945; Haganah 1946 as intelligence officer. Secret Service, tracing Nazi war criminals in Latin America, 1952–56. Adviser on Arab affairs to government, 1966–77. MK, chairman, State Control Committee, 1977. Till 1981, MK, Labor.

Toubi, Tewfik. b. 1922, Haifa. Deputy general secretary, Communist party in Israel. Journalist. MK. President, Committee for World Peace; president, Israel Peace Committee.

Vashits, Joseph. b. Berlin. Arrived in Palestine 1936. Journalist on left-wing weekly and later became specialist in Arab affairs. Editor. Author of *The Arabs in Palestine* (1947); liaison officer between Jewish military and Arabs remaining in Haifa after War of Independence. Director of Centre for Arab Studies, Givat Haviva, 1963–78.

Villan, Kuba. b. 1917, Lódź, Poland. Joined Hashomair Hatsair at 12. Immigrated to Palestine 1935; joined Kibbutz Ein Shemer. Farmer, builder, dock worker. Founding member Kibbutz Negba. British army, World War II. Former president, Israel Football Association. Executive committee, Histadrut. Operates kibbutz computer.

Villan, Rachel. b. 1913, Poland. Immigrated to Palestine 1932; joined Kibbutz Ein Shemer. Construction worker. Founding member Kibbutz Neba. Worked with dairy herd thirty years. Computer bookkeeper.

Weingarten, Rivca. b. 1923, fifth-generation Jerusalem family. Government service; director, Accounts and Collection Department, Ministry of Finance. Since 1970, director of Museum of the Old Yishuv in old family home in Old City of Jerusalem.

Wissman, Leo. b. 1906, Germany; immigrated to Palestine 1932. Master carpenter Grade 1, Israel's foremost cabinetmaker until retirement.

Yachin, Ezra. b. 1928, Jaffa. Joined Lehi at 15. Proprietor, Ezri Gallery, Jerusalem. Published autobiography in Hebrew.

Yadin, Yigal (Ph.D.). b. Archaeologist. Professor of archaeology, Hebrew University. Chief of staff, 1949–52 (lieutenant general). Director, Massada Archaeological Expedition. Author of many books on archaeology and of papers on Dead Sea Scrolls. Winner of Israel Prize and Rothschild Humanities Prize. Deputy prime minister and leader of Democratic party.

Yoffex, Avraham. b. 1913, Israel. Served under Orde Wingate. Commander, Northern Command. Led march to Sharm el Sheikh, 1956. Commander, Officers Training School. Commander, Southern Command and Sinai Front in Six-Day War. MK, Likud, and chairman, Nature Reserve Authority.

Zeira, Meir. b. 1925, Hungary; immigrated to Israel 1946. Concentration camp survivor. Founding member, Kibbutz Yasur. Teacher and educator, photographer, master baker. Married with five children.

Zu'bi, Seif Addin. Clan elder and landowner in Nazareth. Member of founding conference of the State of Israel. First Arab member of the Knesset. Vice speaker, Knesset. Mayor, Nazareth for ten years. Chairman, Arab bloc in the Knesset.

Zur, Alexander. Joined Haganah at 15. Jewish Brigade, British army, six years. LL. B. Foreign Service (three years in Africa, two in Panama) Legal adviser to Hebrew University. Retired.

Index